797,885 Books

are available to read at

Forgotten Books

www.ForgottenBooks.com

Forgotten Books' App
Available for mobile, tablet & eReader

ISBN 978-0-282-39427-1
PIBN 10129269

1 MONTH OF FREE READING

at

www.ForgottenBooks.com

By purchasing this book you are eligible for one month membership to ForgottenBooks.com, giving you unlimited access to our entire collection of over 700,000 titles via our web site and mobile apps.

To claim your free month visit:
www.forgottenbooks.com/free129269

* Offer is valid for 45 days from date of purchase. Terms and conditions apply.

English
Français
Deutsche
Italiano
Español
Português

www.forgottenbooks.com

Mythology Photography **Fiction**
Fishing Christianity **Art** Cooking
Essays Buddhism Freemasonry
Medicine **Biology** Music **Ancient Egypt** Evolution Carpentry Physics
Dance Geology **Mathematics** Fitness
Shakespeare **Folklore** Yoga Marketing
Confidence Immortality Biographies
Poetry **Psychology** Witchcraft
Electronics Chemistry History **Law**
Accounting **Philosophy** Anthropology
Alchemy Drama Quantum Mechanics
Atheism Sexual Health **Ancient History**
Entrepreneurship Languages Sport
Paleontology Needlework Islam
Metaphysics Investment Archaeology
Parenting Statistics Criminology
Motivational

WILD LIFE IN EAST ANGLIA

BY

WILLIAM A. DUTT

WITH SIXTEEN ILLUSTRATIONS IN COLOUR BY F. SOUTHGATE, R.B.A.

METHUEN & CO.
36 ESSEX STREET W.C.
LONDON

First Published in 1906

TO
MY MOTHER

PREFATORY NOTE

FOR permission to reproduce certain passages in Chapters IX, XIII, XV, and XX, I am indebted to the kindness of the Editor of *Country Life*; and I am under a like obligation to the Editors of the *Globe* and *Chambers's Journal* in respect of some of the matter contained in Chapters X and XI.

I must also acknowledge my great indebtedness to several works dealing entirely or in part with the Natural History of East Anglia. A list of these is given at the end of this book.

W. A. D.

LOWESTOFT.

CONTENTS

CHAP.		PAGE
I.	Past and Present	1
II.	Lost Breeding Birds	31
III.	Wild Life in Breckland	57
IV.	Wild Life in Breckland—*Continued*	75
V.	The Reed Pheasant	96
VI.	The Norfolk Gulleries	108
VII.	Denes, Dunes, and Meal Marshes	118
VIII.	Denes, Dunes, and Meal Marshes—*Continued*	137
IX.	Smelts and Smelt-Netting	151
X.	The Edible Frog	165
XI.	An Upland Rover	174
XII.	The Old Fen	194
XIII.	The Water-Bailiff	221
XIV.	Some Celebrated Trees	230
XV.	Swan-Upping	251
XVI.	Some Old Methods of Wild-Fowling	263
XVII.	Some Heaths and Common-Lands	276
XVIII.	Some Old Acts, Rights, and Customs	294
XIX.	With Crabbe at Aldeburgh	307
XX.	A Night with an Eel-catcher	321
XXI.	Suffolk Cliffs and Shore Broads	337
Appendices:		
I.	East Anglian Bird Names	355
II.	East Anglian Names for Wild Flowers	359
III.	Bibliography	361
Index		363

LIST OF ILLUSTRATIONS

	PAGE
Wild-Fowling with a Stalking Sledge . . .	*Frontispiece*
Common Bitterns	40
Rabbiting in Breckland	66
Stone Curlew	72
Black-Headed Gulls following the Plough . .	110
The Ringed Plover's Ruse	128
By the Sea Bank at Flight-time—"A Bit too High"	136
Pink-Footed Geese	146
Smelt-Netting in a Mill Pool	162
An Upland Rover	178
In the Old Fen—Heron and Starlings . .	216
Setting the Bow-Net	224
Plate of Swan-Marks	252
Swan-Upping	258
Plover-Netting	268
Wild-Goose Shooting	298
Autumn Immigrants—Hooded Crows and Snow Buntings .	346

WILD LIFE IN EAST ANGLIA

CHAPTER I

PAST AND PRESENT

AMONG the English counties, Norfolk and Suffolk take first rank as naturalists' counties, their physical characteristics being such that they can offer an unusually varied, and in some respects unique, field for the observation of wild life. If there were any vantage-point from which a bird's-eye view could be obtained, their surface, notwithstanding its general flatness, would present a considerably varied aspect. The modern aspect—that is to say, the cultivated portion—would naturally be most in evidence; but in the west, and less noticeably in the north and north-east, we should get glimpses of the primitive, represented by extensive tracts of sandy warren and heathland. In the east, in a triangular tract having its angles, roughly speaking, at Cromer, Lowestoft, and Norwich, we should see, not only what is perhaps the most recently formed land of any extent in England, but what may be said to be land in making. For there, by processes largely natural but partly artificial, a remarkable change has been brought about and is even now proceeding; within a measure of time which, as geological periods are reckoned, is infinitesimally small, land has taken the place of water; but against this the sea has made considerable inroads upon the land. In neither county is there any large tract of woodland; but nearly everywhere there are large or small plantations, which relieve the monotony of the arable and unreclaimed lands. Along the coast are many miles of cliffs, sandhills, salt-marshes, sandy beaches, and shingle banks. In counties subject to such conditions and possessing such physical characteristics, it is not surprising to find a rich variety of wild life.

Even without making an extended inquiry into the geological history of East Anglia, it is not difficult, thanks to the combined efforts of geologists and paleontologists, to form some idea, not only of how this part of England became possessed of its existing mammalian, reptilian, and amphibian fauna, but also of the character and origin of much of the animal life which inhabited Eastern England in very remote periods.

That Great Britain was formerly connected by land with the Continent of Europe is sufficiently attested by the shallowness of the North Sea and the similarity of the geological formations, the flora, and the extinct and existing mammalian faunas met with on both sides of the North Sea. Mr. R. Lydekker remarks that "to unite the whole of the British Islands to the Continent would require an elevation of one hundred fathoms at the most; and that these islands formerly stood at a much higher elevation than is at present the case, we have abundant evidence." After mentioning, in support of this assertion, the occurrence of submerged forests in the neighbourhoods of Torquay and Falmouth, he draws attention to the existence on the East Coast of Norfolk and Suffolk of that remarkable series of deposits, attributable to the base of the Pleistocene or the upper part of the Pliocene period, and generally known by what Mr. F. W. Harmer describes as the "somewhat misleading name" of the Forest Bed. The breadth and length of the Forest Bed area must have been considerable, and it is generally agreed that at the time of the deposit of the beds—in a period antedating the Glacial epoch—Great Britain and the Continent were united, and their mammalian faunas were practically identical.

What a wonderful fauna it was the fossils found in the Forest Bed reveal, notwithstanding that "these fossils do not occur in complete skeletons, preserved on the site of an ancient forest, as was formerly supposed, but are the drifted and fragmentary remains of animals which were surprised and carried away in time of flood by a river, probably the Rhine, flowing from the south, being afterwards, on their way to the sea, stranded and buried in its flood gravel, or in the muddy sediment of its estuary."[1] Among the Carnivores were a terrible sabre-toothed tiger (probably *Machærodus cultridens*), a beast as large as the lion; the cave hyæna, representing, it is now believed, a large race of the existing South African species (*Hyæna crocuta*); the gigantic cave bear (*Ursus spelæus*); a smaller bear, considered by some paleontologists to have been identical with the American grizzly, but which Mr. Lydekker is inclined to believe is represented by the brown bear; the wolf, the fox, the otter, the marten, and the Arctic glutton, the occurrence of the last-named being, as the before-mentioned authority remarks, "somewhat remarkable, as showing that even at this early epoch, northern types were capable of existing in England before we have any evidence of the incoming of strongly-marked Glacial conditions." Of marine forms we find a walrus, which is regarded as being distinct from the living species, and the bearded seal.

Among the Ungulates were some existing species, as well as some remarkable animals now extinct. The presence of such creatures as the hippopotamus, the

[1] F. W. Harmer in *Norfolk*, 1900.

wild boar, and the horse side by side with the musk ox, the glutton, and the walrus is, as Mr. Lydekker remarks, a puzzle calculated "almost (to) break the heart of the paleontologist." Remains of the bison, a large sheep (*Ovis savini*) allied to the Central Asian *Ovis argali*, the extinct Steno's horse, and the Etruscan rhinoceros also occur in the forest bed. Contemporary with these animals there existed in this country not only the roe deer and the red deer, but *Cervus savini* and *Cervus sedgwicki*, the last-named being a huge creature, hardly exceeded in size by the extinct Irish elk, and possessing antlers of remarkably complex structure. An elk (*Alces latifrons*) and *Bos primigenius* have also been identified. The mammoth apparently had not come into existence at this time; but two gigantic pachyderms, the straight-tusked elephant (*Elephas antiquus*) and the southern elephant (*Elephas meridionalis*), existed in considerable numbers. Among the smaller mammals were some species still included in the East Anglian fauna: these were the squirrel, wood mouse, bank vole, mole, and common and pygmy shrews. The beaver, continental field vole, and Siberian vole have also been recognised, as well as the extinct giant beaver (*Trogontherium cuvieri*), a vole intermediate between the field vole and the water vole, and the insectivorous Russian desman. The few cetacean remains are, according to Mr Lydekker, all referable to existing forms, and "indicate the same mixture of southern and northern forms as characterises the land fauna." Bird bones have been found in the Forest Bed; but owing to their fragmentary condition little can be deduced from them. The reptiles are represented by the common snake and the viper; amphibians by the common frog, the edible frog(?), the toad, and the crested newt; and fishes, by about a score of marine and fresh-water species.

Striking as is the list of the mammals found in the Forest Bed, it does not contain all the species which, it may reasonably be supposed, inhabited or strayed across East Anglia in remote prehistoric periods. The mammoth, though its remains have not been identified in the Forest Bed, is known to have existed here before and after the Glacial epoch, and with it the lion, the leopard, the lynx, and a sabre-toothed tiger differing from the one already mentioned. During the Pleistocene period, the Arctic fox was as much at home in England as it now is in Iceland, and the Cape hunting dog (*Lycaon pictus*), the "wilde honde" of the South African Dutch, appears to have been contemporary with it. Three species of rhinoceros were included in the British fauna, the most remarkable being the woolly rhinoceros (*R. antiquitatis*), an animal whose frozen carcase has been found in the Siberian tundras, and which was distinguished from the megarhine (*R. megarhinus*), not only by possessing a thick woolly coat, but by the structure of its molar teeth. Contemporary with these monsters were the auroch, the saiga antelope, the reindeer (an antler of which was found in Bilney Moor, in Norfolk), and the huge Irish deer or elk. These are only a few of the animals which formerly inhabited East Anglia. To them may be added the many wonderful creatures of which remains have been found in the crag beds, such as the mastodon, giant panda, and the tapir.

How it came about that the wonderful pre-Glacial fauna eventually disappeared from Great Britain is still a matter of controversy. Most geologists and paleontologists are disposed to believe that it disappeared during the Great Ice Age, when the Arctic conditions prevailing in this country were probably sufficient to account for it; but Dr. A. R. Wallace, who deals with this subject in his *Island Life*, is indisposed to accept this as the sole explanation. There is good evidence, he writes, that the whole area of Great Britain "has been submerged to a depth of nearly two thousand feet, at which time only what are now the highest mountains would remain as groups of rocky islets. This submersion must have destroyed the greater part of the life of our country; and as it certainly occurred during the latter part of the Glacial epoch, the subsequent elevation and union with the Continent cannot have been of very long duration, and this fact must have had an important bearing on the character of the existing fauna and flora of Britain. We know that just before and during the Glacial period we possessed a fauna almost, or quite, identical with that of adjacent parts of the Continent, and equally rich in species. The submergence destroyed this fauna, and the permanent change of climate appears to have led to the extinction or migration of many species in the adjacent continental areas, where they were succeeded by the assemblage of animals now occupying Central Europe. When England became continental, these entered our country; but sufficient time does not seem to have elapsed for the migration to have been completed before subsidence again occurred, cutting off the further influx of purely terrestrial animals, and leaving us without the number of species which our favourable climate and varied surface entitle us to." Another theory is, that in the southern part of England a portion of the original fauna survived the Glacial period, and that the submergence was not so considerable as Dr. Wallace suggests. If this view be accepted, it is easy to understand how Great Britain became re-inhabited by the surviving species, of which our existing mammals would be the descendants.

The existing mammalian fauna of East Anglia, we may take it, is practically identical with that which inhabited Eastern England at the time of the final separation of Great Britain from the Continent. Three species, probably four—the black rat, the brown rat, the rabbit, and, perhaps, the squirrel—have been introduced during the historical period; four species—

the brown bear, the wolf, the wild boar, and the beaver, which are known to have inhabited Britain during the historic period—are extinct as British animals; and at least five species—the wild cat, the marten, the red deer, the roe deer, and the wild ox—no longer exist in Norfolk and Suffolk, excepting such deer as have been introduced into parks. Apart from these animals, the only difference between our mammalian fauna to-day and that which existed here at the time of the final insulation of Britain, is in the number of the representatives of the various species. Documentary evidence exists that the brown bear survived in England as late as the eighth century, and it is said that in the reign of Edward the Confessor the "town" of Norwich had to supply yearly a bear for royal sport. That the wild ox—which is included among the species still existing in Britain, on the assumption that it is represented by the wild cattle preserved on two or three English estates—survived in East Anglia until a comparatively recent date, is indicated by the discovery of fossil remains of *Bos primigenius* in the peaty beds of the East Norfolk valleys. Remains of the red and roe deer have been found in similar situations.

Interesting as are its mammals, it is chiefly on account of its bird life that East Anglia claims the attention of naturalists, especially those who devote themselves particularly to ornithology. Owing to its situation and physical characteristics, it possesses long lists of resident and regularly, occasionally, and accidentally occurring species. Although it has no large woods, it possesses, as I have said, a considerable number of large and small plantations, and in these most of the British woodland birds are to be found, while they are also widely famous for their game birds. In the western district known as Breckland,—a district consisting chiefly of wide expanses of heathland and warren, where roads are few and villages far apart,—the indigenous race of great bustards made its last stand against the destroyer, and the stone curlew or Norfolk plover still maintains its existence as a breeding species. On the undrained meres of that district, gadwall, shoveler, pochard, tufted and other ducks breed whenever there is water enough in the meres. In the neighbourhood of Sandringham there are other fairly extensive tracts of heathland, and in that neighbourhood a considerable number of sheld-ducks nest, generally in the rabbit burrows. Along a considerable portion of the North Norfolk coast, for a few miles eastward and several miles westward of Wells, are what are known as the "meals" or "meil marshes." These meals, which have been called the "moorlands of the sea," are level tracts of partly reclaimed land; they produce a peculiar flora, including the sea heath and four kinds of sea lavender; and they are especially interesting to ornithologists on account of their being an alighting-place of great numbers of migrants. A few miles eastward of the Wells meals are the Salthouse marshes, across which the sea, after breaking through the sandhills, has swept on more than one occasion, to the dismay of the inhabitants of Salthouse and Cley. Here also the autumnal migrants are much in evidence, and many rare birds, to be mentioned in a later chapter, have been obtained. Bordering the meals and marshes of this part of the coast are shingle banks and sandhills. Here it is that many common and a few lesser terns breed; also, perhaps, a pair or two of oyster-catchers. In winter a large number of pink-footed geese frequent the Holkham meals and the sandbanks off the coast.

The Broads district, as most people are by this time aware, consists chiefly of flat marshlands bordering the rivers Yare, Bure, and Waveney, and their tributaries. At no very distant period considerable portions of the valleys of these rivers were impassable swamps, and evidence exists which goes a long way towards proving that even at a time subsequent to the Roman occupation of East Anglia they were in a more or less estuarine condition, the sea entering them by way of a wide opening extending from Caister to Gorleston. The natural processes resulting in the retreat of the sea from these valleys, and rendering it possible for the inhabitants of the bordering uplands to drain extensive tracts of swamp and transform them into marshes and pastures, were, I believe, first described by R. C. Taylor, who in a treatise *On the Geology of East Norfolk*, published in 1827, writes: "The set of the great tidal current of the German Ocean is from the north-west, along the eastern shores of this island. It consequently happens that wherever any portion of the land projects beyond the general line of the coast, and consists of any material which yields to the action of those tides, such exposed points have, from the earliest recorded periods, been gradually reduced and rounded off, and the débris has been uniformly deposited southward, either forming shoals in the sea, or elevating low tracts of land upon its borders. Thus the detritus of the chalk strata at Flamborough Head and the diluvial cliffs of Holderness have contributed, in the slow progress of years, to increase the alluvial districts near the Humber. In their progress southward, the tides next meet with an extensive obstruction in the projecting county of Norfolk. About twenty miles of its coast has been subjected, from time immemorial, to the abrasive action of ocean currents. The ancient villages of Shipden, Wimpwell, and Eccles have disappeared; several manors and large portions of neighbouring parishes have, piece by piece, been swallowed up by the encroaching waves; and their site, some fathoms deep, now forms a part of the bed of the German Ocean. . . . In their progress the tidal currents possess sufficient strength and velocity to preserve a deep channel, locally called Roads, parallel with the shore; but they deposit, both on the sea and land sides of this passage, the alluvial matter with which the waters are charged. . . . There is reason, then, to believe that the removal of one part of the Norfolk coast has led to the consolidation of another; and has tended to silt up and raise the beds of the estuaries to such a degree as almost to exclude the ingress of the tide. . . . Everything denotes that their beds were gradually heightened by a deposition of a marine sediment. In this there is nothing remarkable; the operation is daily going on on the Lincolnshire coast, where instances are related of the precipitation of a stratum of mud an inch thick in a single day. The industry of man enables him to avail himself of this tendency;—the operations of nature are assisted by art, and large tracts of the richest land have been artificially produced from the earthy materials brought by the waters of the ocean." That the theories advanced by Taylor as to the cause of the retreat of the sea from the valleys of East Norfolk and East Suffolk are acceptable to geologists, is indicated by their adoption by Sir Charles Lyell in his *Principles of Geology*.

Such a district as came into existence when the sea was practically excluded from the valleys naturally attracted swamp and marsh-loving birds, such as the bittern, spoonbill, avocet, ruff, godwit, heron, redshank, and snipe. On the quiet waters of the Broads, the acreage of which was far greater then than it is to-day, ducks, grebes, and coots abounded; the rail skulked in the fringing reed jungles and watery wildernesses of sedge and rush; while among the reeds and in the sallow and alder carrs thousand of marsh-haunting warblers sang all the summer through. In winter, when the musical call-note of the bearded titmouse was heard in every reed bed, innumerable flocks of wild-fowl from the North took the places of the summer visitors which had gone South; and at all seasons buzzards, harriers, and kestrels hovered over swamp and marsh, or beat along the borders of the carrs. At the beginning of the last century there were colonies of black terns, common terns, and avocets in the Broads district; in the seventeenth century spoonbills nested at Claxton and Reedham; and until a few years ago the ruff nested every year in the neighbourhood of Hickling Broad. Even now, notwithstanding that persecution and changed conditions have driven several species from their old-time breeding haunts, Broadland is to the ornithologist one of the most fascinating districts in England. Such being the case, what must it have been when man had done little or nothing to mar its primitive wildness, could scarcely find foothold amid its trackless morasses, and might easily be "lantern-led" into danger by the Will-o'-th'-Wisps which flickered over its misty fens?

Although there is an old document in existence informing us that spoonbills bred in Norfolk so long ago as the year 1300, and some entries in the accounts of the Norwich City Chamberlain for the first half of the sixteenth century prove that cranes bred at Hickling at that time, we have little detailed information concerning the wild life of East Anglia which is of earlier date than that contained in certain notes on the natural history of Norfolk, made by Sir Thomas Browne during the latter half of the seventeenth century. At the commencement of them the writer remarks that "beside the ordinary birds which keep constantly in the country, many are discoverable, both in winter and summer, which are of a migrant nature, and exchange their seats according to the season; those which come in the spring coming for the most part from the southward, those which come in the autumn or winter, from the northward. So that they are observed to come in great flocks with a north-east wind and to depart with a south-west; nor to come only in flocks of one kind, but teals, woodcocks, fieldfares, thrushes, and small birds to come and light together, for the most part some hawks and birds of prey attending them." These remarks indicate, as Mr. Southwell has said, that "Browne had a fairly correct idea with regard to the migratory movements of the birds of the Norfolk coast." White-tailed or "fen" eagles appear to have been not uncommon visitors to East Anglia in those days; ospreys were frequently met with about the fens and Broads; cranes were often seen in hard winters; wild swans occurred in "no small numbers"; and storks were occasionally seen in the fens and on the marshes between Norwich and Yarmouth. In addition to the spoonbills, there were cormorants breeding at Reedham; herons and heronries abounded; bitterns were common; bustards "not infrequent in the champaign and fieldie part" of Norfolk; ruffs were found "in good number" on the marshes between Norwich and Yarmouth, but were more plentiful in the Marshland district near Lynn; and avocets, though not mentioned as breeding in the Broads district, are referred to as "not infrequent" in Marshland. Crows were far more common then than now, and ravens were present "in good plenty" about Norwich. Among the rarer birds which came under the notice of Sir Thomas Browne were the waxwing, roller, hoopoe (which seems to have occurred pretty frequently), great northern diver, great skua, and pelican.

The bird life of a district where bitterns and ruffs were reckoned as common birds must have been wonderfully abundant and varied; but even in the seventeenth century thousands of acres of fen had been reclaimed. Forty years after the death of Sir Thomas Browne—at a time when, in all probability, some of the drainage windmills still in existence had been built—Daniel Defoe, on visiting Norfolk, observed that the Yare flowed through a "long tract of the richest meadows, and the largest, take them all together, that are anywhere in England"; and that on this "vast tract" were fed "a prodigious number of cattle." "Some have told me," writes Defoe, "and I believe with good judgement, that there are above forty thousand . . . Scots cattle fed in this county every year, and most of them in the said marshes between Norwich, Beccles, and Yarmouth." The work of reclamation which had brought about this change must have affected considerably the local bird life; but until the beginning of the nineteenth century there appears to have been no very marked decrease in the numbers of the birds which regularly bred in or habitually frequented the Broads district, though the spoonbill had become extinct as a breeding species. Since then ornithologists and sportsmen have had a different tale to tell. "Since I first began to sport, about 1816," writes the Rev. R. Lubbock, in a note made in 1847 and quoted in Mr. Southwell's edition of the *Fauna of Norfolk*, "a marvellous alteration has taken place in Norfolk, particularly in the marshy parts. When first I remember our fens, they were full of terns, ruffs, and redlegs, and yet the old fenmen declared there was not a tenth part of what they remembered when boys. Now, these very parts which were the best, have yielded to the steam engine, and are totally drained—the marshes below Buckenham, which being taken care of were a stronghold for species when other resorts failed, are now as dry as a bowling-green, and oats are grown where seven or eight years back one hundred and twenty-three snipes were killed in one day by the same gun. The Claxton marshes, which formerly were almost too wet, are now as dry as Arabia." On eighteenth century maps, Broads are marked the very sites of which are now uncertain; they have vanished completely, and cattle now graze where the bittern boomed and the wild duck reared her brood. Other Broads, such as Sutton and Surlingham, are so "grown up" with aquatic vegetation as to be unnavigable except where there are certain narrow channels.

Breydon, the shrunken waters of which now represent

the vast estuary of former days, has for a long time been famous for its bird life, and has probably produced more rare birds—some of them for the first time in England—than any sheet of water of like size in Great Britain. Writing in 1834 of the wild life of the Yarmouth neighbourhood, the Messrs. Paget remark that "it would be difficult to imagine a spot more suitable to their habits than Breydon affords, consisting as it does of a sheet of water some miles in extent, with shallow borders, or flats (as they are called), and surrounded, almost as far as the eye can reach, by marshes. The water leaving its banks quite bare for a considerable extent at every ebbing of the tide, exposes an abundance of the small crustaceous animals and other food most congenial to the duck tribe. Even in the severest winters it is seldom so completely frozen over as not still to afford, in the small fish with which it abounds and the crabs and insects about its banks, a sufficiency of provision for the fowl; and it is in such seasons that the greatest numbers are secured. Almost benumbed with cold, they flock together, and while they sit crowded up in a compact mass, to prevent the warmth of their bodies escaping, the gunner may, in his flat-bottomed boat, approach within a comparatively short distance of them by means of channels made in the flats, and with a single discharge of his gun, which moves on a swivel in the midships of his boat, effect a most extraordinary slaughter."

Such immense flocks of fowl as were seen on Breydon sixty or seventy years ago, when, to quote the old gunners, "the flats were often white with fowl," are seldom seen there now, though, as Mr. Patterson makes clear in his recently published works on East Norfolk wild life, the avi-fauna of the estuary is even now of considerable variety and interest. The old race of professional punt-gunners, too, is practically extinct; for the few men who still use the heavy swivel guns do so only in the intervals of other employment.

To help to convey some idea of the numbers in which wild-fowl, especially of the duck tribe, visited East Anglia during some winters, no records are more useful than those of the "takes" made in some of the decoys. At the beginning of the last century about thirty decoys were regularly worked in different parts of the county of Norfolk alone. Most of these have vanished or fallen into disuse, and unfortunately in very few instances have lists of the captured fowl been preserved. Lubbock, however, succeeded in obtaining a few interesting and valuable figures, and of late years these have been slightly supplemented. In the second year of the existence of a decoy at East Somerton, a Lincolnshire decoyman, whose services had been engaged by the owner, took 1100 teal in seven successive days. At Wretham, the average yearly take for nine years was about 800 fowl, and at Westwick, where a decoy was established about seventy years ago, the average take was at first from 1000 to 1500 in a season, but during the seventeen years previous to 1879 it was about 400. As to the species of fowl captured, very little information is obtainable, for the decoy-owners seldom kept any account of the respective numbers of mallard, teal, and wigeon. But at Fritton, in Suffolk, care has been taken of late years to preserve detailed records, and these show that about twice as many teal are taken as there are wigeon, and twenty times as many mallard as there are teal. In the winter of 1879–80, which was a good one for the decoys, 2218 ducks, 123 teal, and 70 wigeon were captured at Fritton, 1613 of these being secured in the month of December. In the Harwich decoy, where the water was only an acre in extent, 16,800 fowl were taken in one season. In the Orwell Park decoy, 27,991 fowl, of which 5711 were wigeon, were captured during a period of eighteen years. In the Fen districts enormous "takes" were recorded. One Lincolnshire decoy took 48,644 fowl between 1833 and 1868; in one season the Wainfleet decoys, ten in number, sent 31,200 ducks to London alone. To these figures a few may be added, which go to show that, apart from the decoy "takes," immense numbers of birds of various species have fallen to the wild-fowlers. Messrs. Paget record that in the winter of 1829 one Yarmouth game-dealer received in one day from the local gunners "no less than 400 wildfowl of different kinds, 500 snipe, and 150 golden plovers." Stevenson, too, publishes a list of the fowl received by one dealer between December 14th and 28th, 1878. It contains the following items: "447 full snipe, 206 green and golden plovers, 41 water-hens, 17 water rails, 43 coots, 133 stints, 35 teal, 147 golden-eyes (chiefly tufted ducks) and other fowl, and 421 ducks and mallard (220 from a decoy), the total being 1600 birds.

From these figures it is possible not only to gain some idea of the abundance of bird life in the Broads district in former years, but to understand how it is that the district still has great attractions for the bird-lover and wild-fowler. The losses in respect to breeding species are lamentable, and, it is to be feared, irretrievable; but in Broadland we have a tract of country offering exceptional attractions to certain kinds of birds, and now that the rarer species are well protected, it is not likely to suffer any further serious loss so long as its characteristic physical features are preserved. Indeed, there is good reason for hoping that some breeding species of ducks may increase their numbers, just as the great crested grebes have done; also, that that rare and beautiful little reed bird, the bearded titmouse—which, so far as Great Britain is concerned, is now confined to Broadland as a breeding species—will be able to maintain its existence there. This is a glimpse of the bright side of the picture—on which, however, a shadow is cast when we think of the vanished bitterns, spoonbills, avocets, godwits, ruffs, and black terns.

The study of bird migration is so complex and offers so many difficult problems, that few naturalists care to speak on the subject with any degree of confidence. The fact, too, that most of the information concerning the movements of our British birds is buried in the various reports of the Migration Committee of the British Association, makes them practically inaccessible to a great number of field naturalists. That bird migration is not simply a matter of movement northward in spring and summer and southward in autumn and winter is, of course, fully recognised; but how complicated are the movements of some species is not easily realised. In proof of this, it is only necessary to refer to a statement of Mr. Eagle Clarke to the Migration Committee in 1901, dealing with the " histories of the various migrations performed annually within the British area by the skylark and the swallow." In regard to the skylark, he writes: " The various migrations of the species may be conveniently separated and arranged as follows, beginning with the autumnal movements; and when it is considered that several of these movements are often simultaneously in progress, some idea of their complexity and the extreme difficulty of their interpretation may be realised:

" 1. Autumn Emigration of Summer Visitors, with their offspring—*i.e.*, home - breeding and home - bred birds.

" 2. Autumn Immigration of Winter Visitors from Central Europe.

" 3. Autumn Immigration of Winter Visitors from Northern Europe.

" 4. Autumn Passage from Central to Southern Europe along the British coast.

" 5. Autumn Passage from Northern to Southern Europe along the British coast.

" 6. Winter Emigration from, and Partial Migration within, the British Islands.

"7. Spring Immigration of Summer Visitants, and return of Winter Emigrants.

"8. Spring Emigration to Central Europe from the British Isles.

"9. Spring Emigration to Northern Europe from the British Isles.

"10. Spring Passage from Southern to Central and Northern Europe along the British coast."

In addition to these movements, there are others between Great Britain and Ireland, and between Great Britain and the Hebrides and Northern Islands.

The skylark, it may be said, is an exceptional species, seeing that there is no more migratory bird; but in the cases of other species, such as the song thrush, chaffinch, common bunting, and meadow pipit, movements almost equally complex to those of the skylark might, in all probability, be discovered to take place in the course of the year. In the cases of these birds the obtaining of a food supply cannot be said solely to account for their emigrations and immigrations; for when the summer birds move southward, other birds of the same species from the North take their place and are able to maintain their existence.

In East Anglia several migratory movements are noticeable in the course of the year, and they may be said to be in general agreement with those of the skylark, as indicated by Mr. Eagle Clarke. Commencing, as he does, in the autumn, we have—(1) An Autumn Emigration of Summer Visitants, such as swallows and warblers; (2) an Autumn Immigration of Winter Visitants, such as the skylark and thrushes from Central Europe; (3) an Autumn Immigration of Winter Visitants, such as the snow and Lapland buntings from Northern Europe; (4) an Autumn Passage along our coast of Migrants from Central to Southern Europe and Africa, in the course of which barred warblers have been met with; (5) an Autumn Passage along our coast of Migrants from

Northern to Southern Europe and Africa, in the course of which bluethroats, terns, and several kinds of waders are met with, chiefly in the neighbourhood of Cley and Blakeney and on Breydon; (6) an Autumn and Winter Emigration southward of home-bred birds, such as the song thrush and blackbird; (7) a Winter Immigration of Northern species, such as ducks, pochards, swans, and geese; (8) a Spring Immigration of Summer Visitants; (9) a Spring Emigration of Autumn and Winter Immigrants; and (10) a Spring Passage of birds from Africa and Southern Europe to Central and Northern Europe along our coast. Mr. J. H. Gurney remarks that "it may be said, without any exaggeration, that every species of bird in Norfolk is migratory except pheasants and partridges and tame swans, which are parasites of man, and perhaps I may add sparrows and green woodpeckers."

Without even a glance at a map, it is easy for anyone acquainted with the geography of Europe to understand that East Anglia occupies a position affording exceptional facilities for the observation of birds during the periods of migration. Especially favourable is its situation for watching their movements in the autumn, when vast hosts of birds from Central and Northern Europe arrive here and pass along the coast. "This vast array," writes Mr. Gurney, "is heralded by the arrivals, in September, of redstarts, wheatears, pied flycatchers, little stints, pigmy curlews, common sandpipers, dunlins, etc.; but when October sets in, the greatest rush takes place. There is no more remarkable sight than the movement of birds which then presents itself to a discerning observer, especially when he remembers that for every bird he sees, two others at least come in the night. Buzzards, and other birds of prey, soar aloft in circles, while the eye which knows her flight will catch the distant falcon, or, more frequently, the kestrel. Short-eared owls, at other times solitary, are discovered in flocks of fifteen or twenty; and the gamekeeper, going his morning rounds, finds that long before he was up there had been an early arrival of jays and sparrow-hawks and other noisy thieves. . . . Grey crows, jackdaws, and rooks dot the air for days together. Flocks of snow buntings and various kinds of finches appear in the fields nearest the cliffs. Bramblings, twites, and siskins are heard of at our bird-catchers. Skylarks come over literally in clouds, and mingled with them are regiments of starlings, flying onward with steady purpose. The popular woodcock, tired with his long flight from Norway, halts to rest on the first land he comes to, which is generally sandhills and marram-grass, after his nocturnal journey. The northern thrushes appear, and I have often been perfectly amazed at the numbers of common thrushes in our turnip-fields; but when November draws to a close, the main rush is over, though a few flocks come dropping in afterwards."

From this interesting description of the great autumnal movement as seen in East Anglia, it might be assumed that the general trend of the movement is from east to west rather than from north to south; but, as Mr. Gurney says, the general trend of autumn migration is southward. This southward movement, however, is subject to deviations, chiefly owing to the configuration of the land, but occasionally to the direction of the winds or the strength of the gales. In the case of East Anglia, there can be little doubt that the large influx of birds of certain species during the autumn is due to the birds, in the course of their general southward movement, catching sight of the projecting coast of Norfolk and Suffolk, and changing the direction of their flight for a time in order to rest themselves and obtain food. Some species, however, prefer to follow, more or less closely, the trend of the coast when they migrate northward or southward, and this accounts for the regularity with which certain birds, breeding in the north of England, in Scotland, and on islands and in countries farther north, appear on our coast in spring and autumn. As Mr. A. H. Evans remarks, "It may be considered proved that the trend of a coast . . . has a very appreciable effect on the direction taken by migratory birds"; but, as he goes on to say, neither this fact, nor other causes of deviation which are known to affect the movements of migratory birds, help to explain the "tendency of many birds of Eastern Europe and part of Siberia to travel westward towards the close of summer or in autumn." That there is such a movement is, of course, well known, and nowhere is it more noticeable than along the East Anglian coast; but to account for it is difficult, in view of the fact that an overland movement southward would seem far more likely to result in the birds obtaining a food supply during the winter months. The theory has been advanced that in crossing the North Sea in a westerly direction these birds are crossing the ancient submerged land surface over which their ancestors were accustomed to fly at the time when there was a land-link between England and the Continent.

Mr. A. H. Patterson, who during many years' residence in Great Yarmouth has been a careful observer of the wild life of that neighbourhood, has noticed, among other phenomena connected with its bird life, "the extreme uncertainty of migratory movements in large bodies. In some years certain rare species have appeared in unusual numbers, as in the cases of the shorelark, Lapland bunting, little auk, buzzards, skuas, and others; on the other hand, years may elapse without such records. These fluctuations undoubtedly depend upon, or are affected by, atmospheric conditions; a sharp winter, with continuous occurrences of heavy gales from the north, north-east, or south-east, will drive in many species, more particularly during the periods of migration. . . . South-west winds are more favourable to the migratorial birds passing along our shores, whilst that from the opposite quarter, or from a westerly direction, will favour the Dutch coastline, to the detriment of our own. With light north-west winds and moonlight nights, during October and November, the woodcock are anxiously looked for. Westerly winds have been responsible for the visits of a few American wanderers."

On Breydon, in spring and autumn, the muster of passing migrants is often very numerous. In spring, the flats are sometimes visited by numbers of whimbrel, turnstones, knots, and godwits; wigeon are seen in large flocks; also grey plovers, dunlins, ringed plovers, black terns, and curlews. In autumn, several of these species again put in an appearance, and when severe weather sets in, geese, swans, and various kinds of ducks are looked for by the Breydon gunners. On the North Norfolk coast the spring movements are not so noticeable as they are on Breydon; but during the autumn migrations no better vantage-point for observing the birds could be desired. In proof of this, I quote from the *Transactions of the Norfolk and Norwich Naturalists Society* some notes contributed by Messrs. G. E. & F. D. Power, and made between September 7th and 26th, 1885:

"*Sept. 7th.*—Wind E. early, afterwards S. In the 'Scrub' at or near sandhills, willow-wrens (sixty or more), several whinchats, five redstarts, great whitethroats, wheat-ears, and black-headed bunting. . . . Nineteen geese seen in flock. Several little stints.

"*Sept. 8th.*—Wind N.W., fresh. Increase in number of pied wagtails; and swallows passing west in early morning. In the 'Scrub' warblers very few. . . .

"*Sept. 9th.*—Wind N.W., half-gale. Large migration of swallows early, and also through the day. . . .

"*Sept. 10th.*—Wind N.W., strong. A good many common sandpipers noticed, and seven little stints together. . . .

"*Sept. 11th.*—Wind N.E., very stiff, with rain. N.W. wind in afternoon. First scoter, first gannet, and two skuas seen. A good many terns observed. . . .

"*Sept. 12th.*—Half-gale W.S.W., and rain. Many

godwits, one looking very red, and several skuas observed. Common terns, twenty or more, and the last three lesser. A few waders working west along the beach; shot reeve, and several others seen. . . .

"*Sept.* 13*th.*—Half-gale S.W. Many peewits appeared.

"*Sept.* 15*th.*—Wind S.W., stiff. Fine red-throated diver, with full red throat, obtained. Swallows travelling W.S.W. all the morning. . . . From Morston Creek we shot two godwit flying together — one proving black-tailed, the other bar. . . . Several whimbrel seen.

"*Sept.* 16*th.*—Wind S.W., stiff. Great numbers of pied wagtails, and many meadow pipits, larks, and linnets, all arrived since yesterday. . . .

"*Sept.* 18*th.*—Wind E., light. Very fine. . . . More golden plovers than any day yet. . . . Green sandpiper seen. . . .

"*Sept.* 19*th.*—Wind S.W., and driving rain; fresher wind and fine afternoon. A few flocks of dunlin passed west. Some fresh and tame godwits in the harbour. . . .

"*Sept.* 20*th.*—Wind S.W. to W.N.W. A good many hirundines passing.

"*Sept.* 21*st.*—Wind W.N.W. Swallows and martins and five sand martins hawking under shelter of sea wall. First (two) rock pipits seen. . . . Several gannets observed.

"*Sept.* 22*nd.*—Wind W.S.W. and stiff all day. More godwits arrived, and a party of grey plover. Peregrine seen. Many large gulls working west over the sea, and three yellowish-looking ones observed. . . . A large flock of knot in the harbour. . . . The eider seen again.

"*Sept.* 23*rd.*—Wind W.N.W., fair, wet at night. Apparent arrival of hawks. Peregrine, merlin, sparrow-hawk, and kestrel all observed. . . . Several fresh parties of tame godwits. Several rock pipits. . . . Shearwater seen. . . .

"*Sept.* 25*th.*—Wind N.W., thunderstorm and heavy hail showers. Some skuas seen. Fresh godwits and grey plovers observed. Also some tame sanderlings on the beach. . . .

"*Sept.* 26*th.*—Gale from N.N.W. A good many wild duck and several wigeon and teal seen. Many larks coming in from N.N.E. . . . Swallows travelling S.W. in considerable numbers. First snow bunting heard."

It is worthy of remark that the Messrs. Power refer to the visit to Cley, which was the occasion of these notes being taken, as being "a very blank expedition," of which the chief points were the occurrence of black-tailed godwits and the abundance of godwits generally. Waders generally were scarcer than usual, with the exception, perhaps, of little stints.

. . . . . .

That the list of East Anglian marine and fresh-water fishes should be a fairly long one is not surprising, when we consider that Norfolk and Suffolk have nearly 150 miles of coastline, and are drained by several important rivers, including those of the Broads district. In 1884 the late Dr. J. Lowe stated, that of the total number of fishes recorded for Great Britain, nearly one-half were contained in the Norfolk list he published in that year. Since then a considerable number of marine species new to East Anglia have been identified.

So long ago as the beginning of the fifteenth century, the fresh-water fisheries of England were so important as to call for the passing of special Acts of Parliament to regulate them, and we find that at that time the corporations of Norwich, Yarmouth, and other towns possessed jurisdiction, granted by charter, over certain inland waters. In these regulations, in reports of disputes arising from their infringement, and in other ancient documents, we find mention made of eels, perch, roach, salmon, ruffe, trout, pike, smelt, loach, bullhead, gudgeon, and minnow as being fishes well known to inhabit the

East Anglian Broads and rivers; while in the *L'Estrange Household Book* there are notes concerning a few common marine species. Little or no information of any value is, however, met with in any earlier documents than the notes made by Sir Thomas Browne, whose list of Norfolk fishes is the earliest of which we have any knowledge.

"It may seem," writes Sir Thomas, "no easy matter to give any considerable account of fishes and animals of the sea, wherein 'tis said that there are things creeping innumerable, both small and great beasts, because they live in an element wherein they are not so easily discoverable; notwithstanding, probable it is that after this long navigation search of the ocean, bays, creeks, estuaries, and rivers, that there is scarce any fish but hath been seen by some man, for the large and breathing sort thereof do sometimes discover themselves above water, and the other are in such numbers that some at one time or other they are discovered or taken." He then, after referring to the common seal, and three or four cetaceans which had been met with on the coast, mentions about eighty local fishes. The rivers and Broads, he tells us, and we can very well believe it, abounded in pike, bream, tench, roach, rudd, carp, dace, ruffe, and perch. Concerning the last-named species, he remarks that "such as are in Breydon on this side of Yarmouth, in the mixed water, make a dish very dainty, and I think scarce to be bettered in England." Salmon appear to have always been of rare occurrence in most of the East Anglian rivers, though they were not uncommon in the Ouse in the seventeenth century. With the bleak and chub as Norfolk fishes Browne was unacquainted, having never met with them in any of our rivers; but he was aware of the existence here of the trout, burbot, gudgeon, miller's thumb, loach, "stanticle," lampern, and sea lampern.

His list of marine species commences with the sawfish, taken at Lynn, this being, so far as Mr. Southwell is aware, the only record of the occurrence of this southern species in British waters. Browne takes care to make it clear that he had not confounded this fish with the swordfish, which he had known to be entangled in the nets of the Yarmouth herring-fishers, in whose catches he had also identified several kinds of dogfish and the porbeagle. Indeed, he seems to have been very well acquainted, not only with a considerable number of the commoner species of sea fishes met with by the fishermen, but also with several far less commonly caught, and two or three which are exceedingly rare. He mentions the sunfish (*Orthagoriscus mola*), the skipper (*Scombresox saurus*), the sea woodcock (*Centriscus scolopax*), the sting ray (*Trygon pastinaca*), the angler, and possibly the tunny and the bonito. Still, seeing that he omits to mention some common species with which he must have been familiar, his notes, though interesting and valuable, seem to have been jotted down for some other purpose than that of compiling a complete list of the fishes known to inhabit the Norfolk waters.

After the death of Sir Thomas Browne, nearly a century and a half seems to have elapsed before any naturalist systematically devoted attention to the Norfolk fishes. The subject was then taken up by the Pagets, who in 1834 published a list of local fishes in their *Sketch of the Natural History of Yarmouth*. Their list contains eighty-one species, only two of which Mr. Patterson has felt compelled to omit from his more recently issued list for that district. Among the rarities identified by the Pagets were the gilthead, anchovy, worm pipefish, hippocampus, hammerhead, and basking shark. In Yarrell's *British Fishes* we find notes on a few rare species taken off the Yarmouth coast, and in Lubbock's *Fauna of Norfolk* there is some interesting information in respect to fresh-water species. In the *Transactions of the Norfolk and Norwich Naturalists' Society* for 1872–1873, the late Dr. J. Lowe published a list of Norfolk fishes, to which supplementary lists have appeared. Of late years several fresh species have been recognised, chiefly by Mr. A. H. Patterson, of Great Yarmouth. To this indefatigable naturalist is due the credit for adding to the Norfolk list the following species: American rose perch, streaked gurnard, boar-fish, two-spotted goby, white goby, gattorugine, power cod, pollack, four-bearded rockling, Müller's topnot, long rough dab, craig fluke, pearlsides, starry ray, and cuckoo ray.

Turning to the fresh-water fisheries, it may be remarked at the outset that the fact that in old charters jurisdiction over the rivers is granted, goes a long way towards proving not only that the inland waters were well stocked with fish, but that they furnished the inhabitants of East Anglia with a very considerable portion of their food supply. At a very early date there were men who gained a livelihood by netting fish in the rivers; and in times when sea fish were not often obtainable, save by persons dwelling on or near the coast, there must have been a large demand for pike, perch, tench, and eels, and even for roach and bream. That eel-catching and smelt-netting are ancient industries in East Anglia will be proved in later chapters in this book.

Some interesting information concerning the ancient customs and regulations in respect to the fresh-water fisheries is contained in a paper written by Mr. T. Southwell, and printed in the *Transactions of the Norfolk and Norwich Naturalists' Society*, the writer commenting on the fact "that our more remote ancestors were wiser in their generation than our immediate predecessors, and that they attached considerable value to the supply of fresh-water fish, and took infinite pains to ensure their due preservation, and to enforce judicious regulations with regard to their capture." That our "immediate predecessors" did not trouble themselves to enforce the old regulations, and permitted the most destructive methods of fish-capture to be practised without restriction, no one can deny. Up to the time of the publication of the *Fauna of Norfolk*, however, little harm seems to have been done; for, in reference to the Broadland waters, Lubbock remarks that "many a London disciple of Walton, accustomed to the Lea or Putney Bridge, would here fancy himself in Elysium. Bream, roach, and rudd, in crowds and of large size, would be ready to receive his attentions. Coarse fish are not here to be estimated by the pound or the brace, but by the stone weight and bushel measure. From five to ten stone of bream and roach are often taken by two or three anglers." Perch, he admits, though still abundant in many places, were far from being so general as they used to be; but he attributes this to the disturbance of the water by steam drainage rather than to the raids made by the river poachers. Indeed, he even goes so far as to advocate the introduction of such fishes as *Silurus glanis* and *Lucioperca sandra*, by means of which the numbers of the coarse fish—with which he says many of the Norfolk waters "are literally overstocked"—might be kept down.

Twelve years later, anglers and other persons acquainted with the rivers and Broads had a different tale to tell. The angler's catches, they said, were slowly but surely decreasing in weight, and this was due to the poachers, who by means of large draw-nets were in the habit of taking waggon-loads and wherry-loads of fish during the spawning season. The Norwich and Norfolk Angler's Society was founded, and steps were taken to put a stop to the destructive methods of the poachers, so far as they were practised in the Broads adjoining the Yare. But the law, it was discovered, could give the Society little assistance, and all the good that was done was effected by bribing the fishermen to abstain from netting while the fish were spawning. East Anglians generally were apathetic in the matter; and not until nearly twenty years had elapsed since the founding of the Society did the outcry of the anglers grow so loud as to move the Government to instruct the late Frank Buckland to make inquiry into and report upon the state of the Norfolk fresh-water fisheries.

Mr. Buckland did his work thoroughly. He questioned Broad owners, anglers, fish-merchants, and net-makers, and when his report was published it proved to be an interesting one. It appeared from the evidence he had collected, "that not only the Broads, but the navigable rivers connected with them, were extensively netted, and the fish sent to inland towns and sold for as low as a shilling a stone, or used as manure. . . . The interests of the Broads were often divided amongst small proprietors, who would give permission to the 'Yarmouth pirates' to fish, and as they were usually drawn in the nights by nets, tons and tons of fish were sent into the Midland districts during the spawning or any other season. . . . There was no close season on the Broads, but they were fished whenever it was considered likely that a market could be found for the fish; the meshes of the nets were small, and all fish were taken." As a result of his inquiries and a careful consideration of the whole subject, he came to the conclusion that "the time has now arrived when it is imperatively advisable that the fresh-water fisheries of Norfolk and Suffolk should be scientifically cultivated. The willingness to take this matter in hand is widely spread among all classes of society dwelling in the neighbourhood of the above-named rivers and the Broads. From personal observation," he adds, "I am enabled to state that the rivers and Broads are admirably adapted for the breeding and fattening of such indigenous fish as belong to the species of carps, breams, perches, and so forth. The temperature of the water in the spring and summer is such as to be favourable to the breeding of these fish; fish of this kind do not, like the salmon, require gravel beds and running water; they, on the contrary, naturally deposit, or rather suspend, their spawn on the water-weeds and other aquatic plants. The borders of the

Broads are, for the most part, margined with dense jungles of reeds, while at the same time the bottom is planted with forests of sub-aqueous vegetation; so that there are many hundreds of miles of spawning ground available for the fish which live in these waters." Mr. Buckland then, in his report, recommended that the golden tench, speigel carp, great lake trout, brook trout, and pike-perch (previously recommended by Lubbock) should be introduced into the Broads and rivers. No attempt, so far as I am aware, has been made to introduce the pike-perch and speigel carp into the Broadland waters; but some golden tench, lake trout, and American brook trout have been liberated in one or two rivers with unsatisfactory results.

That Mr. Buckland did not exaggerate the destruction wrought by the draw-netters everyone who has discussed the subject with the fishermen and marshmen of the Broads district can testify. I have met with old poachers, who, thirty or more years ago, often netted a ton of bream and roach in a single night; and at that time it was no rare thing for a wherry to land between two and three tons of freshwater fish at Yarmouth as the result of two or three nights' netting. By means of "liggers" or trimmers and snares, too, large numbers of pike were taken; during the winter and early spring scores of rush-buoyed trimmers might often be counted on a single Broad. That these wholesale methods of fish-capture must be put a stop to had been strenuously urged for a long time by a few anglers; and in 1877, not long after the publication of Mr. Buckland's report, the passing of the Norfolk and Suffolk Fisheries Act made it illegal for nets having a mesh of less than three inches from knot to knot when wet to be used. Subsequently draw-netting for coarse fish was totally abolished; and at the present time cast-nets, eel-setts, bow-netts, and nets for the taking of smelts are the only kinds permitted to be used.

CHAPTER II

LOST BREEDING BIRDS

BIRD-FAVOURED as are the Eastern counties to-day, with their gulleries, tern colonies, large heronries, Breckland stone curlews, and Broadland bearded titmice, one can scarcely realise what a wealth of avine wild life East Anglia possessed in the days when a large area of its fens was unreclaimed, its marshes were undrained, and its heaths had known only slight attempts at cultivation. Monkish chroniclers occasionally give us glimpses of the old abundant bird life, as when Robert of Swaffham tells us that he very often saw the Ely fowlers bring in "not less than a thousand birds from one single piece of water"; and in later times Defoe helps us a little when he writes of a decoy near Ely where three thousand couple of fowl a week were generally taken, while from the decoys about Peterborough fowl were sent up to London twice a week by waggon-loads, the waggons being drawn by ten or twelve horses apiece, "they were laden so heavy." Laborious searching among old chamberlains' rolls, too, has made it clear that certain birds now unknown, or of rare occurrence, in the Eastern counties, were formerly easily obtainable when distinguished guests were entertained, or there was occasion for festivity among mayors and burgesses. But when one rambles across the Breckland warrens, one can hardly conceive that even so recently as the earlier half of the last century there was always a good chance of seeing there a "drove" of indigenous great bustards; when one crosses the fens, Kingsley's famous word-pictures of their wild life seem as though they can never have truthfully described it; and when one cruises on the Broads one tries with slight success to imagine what the Broads and marshes were like when they were the breeding-places of the avocet, the bittern, the black-tailed godwit, and the black tern.

The claim of the pelican to be included among East Anglia's lost breeding birds is, perhaps, a doubtful one; but if it could be established, this bird would probably prove to be the earliest of the lost birds to cease to breed here. Sir Thomas Browne, in his notes on the birds of Norfolk, writes: "An Onocrotalus or Pelican shot upon Horsey Fen, 1663, May 22nd, which, stuffed and cleansed, I yet retain. It was three yards and a half between the extremities of the wings, the chowle and beak answering the usual description, the extremities of the wings for a span deep brown, the rest of the body white. A fowl which none could remember upon this coast. About the same time I heard one of the king's pelicans was lost at St. James'; perhaps this might be the same." Mr. Southwell thinks that Sir Thomas Browne has suggested the true explanation of the appearance of a pelican in Horsey Fen. At the same time he points out that *Pelicanus onocrotalus* " is believed to stray occasionally into the northern parts of Germany and France, so that the occurrence of that species on the East Coast of Britain, where, even at the present it would find a state of things in every way suited to its requirements (guns excepted), would not be very extraordinary." In support of this, it may be mentioned that a few years ago some pelicans are believed to have visited Jutland. That a species of pelican at one time inhabited the Fens has been proved by the discovery there, on more than one occasion, of bones of a species supposed to be *Pelicanus crispus*, one of the bones being that of a young bird likely to have been bred in the district. In a paper read before the Norfolk and Norwich Naturalists' Society, Mr. S. F. Harmer described these bones, and concluded his remarks by saying that "the evidence thus afforded of the occurrence of three individuals goes far in support of the view that the pelican was really native to this part of England." Bones of the pelican have also been found among the remains of the Glastonbury lake-dwellings.

Stronger evidence exists of the common crane having bred in the Eastern counties. Bones of the crane have been found in the peaty deposits of the Cambridgeshire fens; also at King's Lynn; and there is a record that in 1212 King John, whilst hawking at Ashwell, in Cambridgeshire, killed seven cranes; while in the following year he killed nine on one occasion in Lincolnshire. In the Hunstanton Hall Household and Privy Purse Accounts there are five entries between 1519 and 1533 referring to cranes, one having reference to a bird killed with a crossbow, and another to "a Cranne kyllyd wt the Gun." This last entry is of especial interest, for, as Mr. T. Southwell says in a paper "On the Breeding of the Crane in East Anglia,"[1] "Hitherto the wild birds and beasts had only the hawk, the snare, and the crossbow to contend against, but a new era had dawned with the introduction of the gun, and although the evil arising from its use arose at first more from the noisy disturbance caused by its unwonted explosions than from its deadly effects, still . . . it is probable that from hence dates the more rapid extinction of the crane in Britain, notwithstanding an attempt about this time to afford it protection by partial legislation, a fact which, in itself, points to the imminence of the danger." In the Chamberlain's Accounts of the City of Norwich, Mr. Southwell has discovered several entries

[1] *Trans. Norf. and Nor. Nat. Soc.*, vol. vii. p. 160 *et seq.*

respecting cranes, the most valuable being one made under the date 1542–3, and the sub-heading of "The morrow after Corpus Xti' day," which fell in that year on the day corresponding with our June 4th. The entry is:

"Itm. pd to Notyngham of Hyklyng
    for a yong Pyper Crane . . Vs.
and to caryage to Norwich . . iiijd.
to Edmond Wolcey for an other
    Crane . . . . . Vs.
                               Xs. iiijd."

The mention of the "yong Pyper Crane," remarks Mr. Southwell, leaves no room for doubt that in the year 1543 the crane bred at Hickling in Norfolk. At that time this bird was a favourite dish, and thirty years before, instructions for "displaying" it were printed in the *Boke of Kervynge*, and read as follows: "Take a crane and unfold his legges and cut off his wynges by the joyntes, then take up his wynges and his legges and sauce him with poudres of ginger, mustarde, vynegre, and salte."

There is mention of the crane, too, in a licence, granted to George Eden in August 1554, "To appoynte at his wyll and pleasure any one of his servauntes to shote in a crosbowe or handgone att all manner of dere, heron, shullard (spoonbill), wildswane, mallard, tele, crane, bustard, and all other land fowle or water fowle whatsoever, and also to use, carrye, occupie, and kepe his said crosbowe or handgone for the purpose aforesaide within the counties of Suffolk and Cambridge, and the lymyttes of the same." According to Mr. Howard Saunders, there is evidence that the crane bred in the fens and swamps of the Eastern counties until the year 1590. In Sir Thomas Browne's time (1605–1682) it had undoubtedly become extinct as a breeding species, for his reference to it is as follows: "Cranes are often seen here in hard winters, especially about the champain and fieldie part. It seems they have been more plentifull, for in a bill of fare when the maior (of Norwich) entertained the Duke of Norfolk I meet with cranes in a dish."

Whether the goshawk ever bred in the Eastern counties is uncertain; but there is a passage in one of the Paston Letters which, in the opinion of Professor Newton, is suggestive of its having done so. Writing from Norwich on September 21st, 1472, to his elder brother, John Paston says: "I axe no more gods of yow for all the servyse that I shall do yow whyll the world standyth, but a gosshawke, if eny of my Lord Chamberleyns men or yours goo to Kaleys, or if eny be to get in London; that is a mewyd hawk, for she may make yow sporte when ye com into Inglond a doseyn yer hens, and to call upon yow owrly, nyghtly, dayly, dyner, soper, for thys hawk." If the hawk were not forthcoming, he added, "I shall wax fatt for default of labor, and ded for default of company by my trowthe." In response to this request, a hawk appears to have been sent some time in November; but, alas! on receiving it the enthusiastic falconer was greatly disappointed, for on the 24th of that month he wrote to the sender of the bird thanking him for his "labore and trowbyll," but adding, "so God help me, as fer forthe as the most conyng estragers (falconers) that ever I spak with can imagyn, she shall never serve but to lay eggs, for she is bothe a mwer de hays, and also she hath ben so brooseid with cariage of fewle that she is as good as lame in bothe hyr leggys, as every man may se at iee. Wherfor all syche folk as have seen hyr avyse me to cast hyr in to some wood, wher as I wyll have hyr to eyer (lay eggs); but I wyll do ther in as ye wyll, whedyr ye wyll I send hyr yow ayen, or cast hyr in Thorp wood and a tarsell with hyr, for I weit wher on is." Professor Newton remarks that it is hardly conceivable that the writer of this letter would express so confident a hope of his goshawk nesting "unless he had some experience of a similar case, or of the goshawk breeding in Thorp wood."

That that handsome bird the spoonbill bred in Norfolk and Suffolk is unquestionable. Sir Thomas Browne, who refers to it as the "shouelard, wch build upon the topps of high trees," tells us that it nested in a heronry at Claxton, a parish on the south side of the Yare valley, and also at Reedham, where there is still a large heronry. The spoonbills came there in March, he says, and were shot by fowlers, "not for their meat, but the handsomenesse of the same." From the wording of his note it would seem that they had ceased to breed at Claxton and Reedham at the time of his writing, but still bred at Trimley, in Suffolk, a parish on the left bank of the Orwell. Mr. Harting has shown that there were colonies of spoonbills near Goodwood and at Fulham. There is every probability that in earlier times this bird bred in other parts of the Eastern counties and the Fen district. Apparently the earliest reference to it is to be found in the Patent Rolls of Edward I., where, as Professor Newton has pointed out,[1] there is, under the date March 22nd, 1300, a passage dealing with the appointment of William Haward, William de Hanyngfeld, and William de Sutton to inquire into the behaviour of certain evil doers who had entered the park and free warrens of Hugh Bardolf at Whinbergh, Wormegay, Westbrigg, Runcton, Stow Bardolph, Fincham, Cantley, Strumpshaw, Caister by Yarmouth, and Scratby, and, in addition to chasing the wild animals in the park, and the hares and rabbits in the warrens, harried the "eyries" of sparrow-hawks, herons, spoonbills, and bitterns in Hugh Bardolf's several woods at Whinbergh, Cantley, and Wormegay. Evidence of the presence of spoonbills in the neighbourhood of King's Lynn in August 1520, is found in an entry in one of the

[1] *Trans. Norf. and Nor. Nat. Soc.*, vol. vi. p. 158 *et seq.*

Lynn Assembly Books, where it is stated that Cardinal Wolsey arrived in the town on a certain day, and was presented with, among other things, "three shovelerdes."

The spoonbill is still an annual visitor to the Eastern counties, being most commonly met with on Breydon Water, the estuary of the Yare, a spot not far removed from its old-time nesting-places at Reedham, Claxton, and Cantley. In recent years, possibly in consequence of the draining of the Dutch fens and marshes, it has come to us in increasing numbers. On April 24th, 1894, thirteen spoonbills were seen by the Rev. M. C. H. Bird at Hickling. Writing in the *Zoologist* for March 1897, Mr. J. H. Gurney, while regretting the repeated destruction of spoonbills, said that it must be conceded that "the Breydon Wild Birds' Protection Society has more than justified its existence, as shown by the number of spoonbills (besides some avocets) which have visited this tidal Broad and escaped since the appointment of our paid watcher nine years ago. In May, June, and July, 1888, thirteen spoonbills (including six in one flock on June 3rd) came to Breydon. In the spring of 1889 our watcher saw three, and in 1891 two on June 14th and one on the 20th, which remained about, and was seen at intervals until July 31st. In 1893 there were thirteen on the Broad on April 28th, and eleven more in May and June. In 1894 the watcher saw sixteen on May 13th; and in 1895 a flock of twelve on May 5th, which remained until the 13th. Thus in ten springs and summers (for they seldom come after August) eighty-four spoonbills have visited this one Norfolk Broad, which has long been known—since 1851—to have far more attractions for this species than the mud-flats at Blakeney." In 1896 spoonbills again visited Breydon, Hickling, and Blakeney. On May 8th, 1898, six or seven were seen on Breydon; on May 10th, 1899, six more; and on June 4th, 1900, twelve came to the same place, and some were seen at intervals until the 27th. Several were seen in 1901, when, on June 15th, Mr. A. H. Patterson saw five pass over his head in single file: they were frequenting the Burgh marshes alternately with the Breydon flats. Only two appear to have been seen in 1902; but in 1903 one was seen on May 7th, six on May 22nd, and one as late as July 22nd. In May 1904, Mr. Patterson saw seven in one flock on Breydon.

In the Broads district, the avocet, black-tailed godwit, black tern, bittern, and some other birds to which reference will be made, all became extinct during the last century. The avocet has been lost to us as a breeding species since about the year 1824; but the precise date of its last nesting in East Anglia is now impossible to determine. Lubbock, writing in 1845, states, on the authority of an old Broadsman, that it bred regularly during the early years of the nineteenth century near the Seven Mile House on the river Bure; and Stevenson mentions Winterton and the adjoining Norfolk parish of Horsey as having been its haunts during the breeding season; also Salthouse, on the North Norfolk coast. At Horsey it bred as late as 1819, and probably a year or two later; but on the Salthouse marshes, where it used to be so numerous that the villagers collected the eggs to make puddings and pancakes of them, it lingered until some time between the years 1822 and 1825, its extermination, it is said, being brought about by the demand for its feathers, which were used in the dressing of artificial flies. In Suffolk there was a colony of avocets near Orford Lighthouse at the beginning of the last century, and Dr. N. F. Hele, whose list of birds for the neighbourhood of Aldeburgh was published in 1870, was informed by an old gunner that he could recollect the bird, which he called the "awl-bird," breeding in the Mere-lands at Thorpe. Sir Thomas Browne refers to this species as follows: "Auoseta, calld shoohing-horne, a tall black & white bird with a bill semicircularly reclining or bowed upward so that it is not easie to conceiue how it can feed, answerable unto the Auoseta Italorum in Aldrovandus, a summer marsh bird & not unfrequent in Marshland." Elsewhere he speaks of it as "a shooing-horn or Barker, from the figure of the bill & barking note, a long-made bird of white & blakish colour, finne footed, a marsh bird & not rare some times of the yeare in marshland."

Black terns are often seen during the spring and autumn migrations; but nearly fifty years have elapsed since the last British nest was found near Sutton Broad by a marshman, who shot both of the birds. Formerly the black tern nested in great numbers in the Broadland marshes and the Fens. At Horsey and Winterton it inhabited the same marshes as the avocets; and it also bred at Upton, near Acle on the Bure, where, according to Lubbock, "the nests were placed upon the dry eminences in a very swampy part of the marshes amongst low alders. And in those days," he adds, "they were spread during summer over a large extent of marsh. The fens, miles from Upton, were enlivened by blue dars, as they were always called." From Hockwold and Feltwell Fens, where there were considerable colonies of black terns, they disappeared some time before they ceased to breed in the Broads district; but after the great Fen flood of 1852–53, of which Professor Newton has printed some interesting recollections, three pairs of black terns nested in Feltwell Fen, where their nests and eggs were found by Mr. E. C. Newcome. The Rev. Churchill Babington, in his *Birds of Suffolk*, says: "It is probable that this bird bred at the beginning of this century in the fen district about Brandon and Mildenhall, as it did at Feltwell." He mentions, but not of his own knowledge, that a pair bred at Oulton in 1875.

Of the black-tailed godwit, Lubbock, writing in 1845, says that "this bird is now almost extinct in this part of Norfolk (the Broads district); it used to breed at Buckenham, Thyrne, Horsey, and one or two other places." In a footnote to Sir Thomas Browne's *Notes on the Natural History of Norfolk*, Mr. Southwell states that it virtually ceased to nest in the county sometime between the years 1829 and 1835, "but perhaps an instance or two may have occurred rather later." The last Norfolk nest appears to have been found at Horsey, where this godwit kept company with the avocets and black terns. Babington states that it bred in East Suffolk, and Stevenson thought that Whelp Moor, near Lakenheath, probably derived its name from this species, which was formerly known as the "yarwhelp." It also bred in Cambridgeshire, Yorkshire, and Lincolnshire. This bird used to be taken in nets by means of stuffed decoys, and as a table bird was considered one of "peculiar delicacy." Browne's note is: "Godwyts, taken chiefly in Marshland, though other parts not without them, accounted the dayntiest dish in England & I think for the bignesse of the biggest price."

Some idea of the number of bitterns to be found in the Eastern counties in the days when they bred there, may be formed from Lubbock's assertion that in the course of his shooting excursions he killed eleven bitterns "without searching particularly for them"; while elsewhere he states that an old keeper at Downham informed him that he had known a fen shooting party to kill from twenty to thirty bitterns in a morning. Sir Thomas Browne speaks of the bittern as being a common bird, and esteemed a better dish than the heron. In the Hockwold and Feltwell fens this beautiful bird appears to have been numerous, for in 1853 Professor Newton was informed by a Feltwell thatcher, whose father and grandfather had been gamekeepers, that bitterns used

COMMON BITTERNS

to be extremely plentiful, and were sold for a shilling each. " His grandfather used to have one roasted every Sunday for dinner, and they would lie in the sedge (which was in places five or six feet high) until they were nearly trodden upon." The exact year in which the bittern ceased to breed in England is uncertain. The last eggs were taken at Upton, in Norfolk, on March 30th, 1868; but there is a possibility that a pair of bitterns succeeded in breeding in the neighbourhood of Sutton Broad in the spring of 1886, for the once familiar booming was heard there frequently during that season, and on August 10th of the same year a young bird, " with down still adhering to some of its feathers," was sent from Ludham—a parish near Sutton—to a Norwich birdstuffer. In Suffolk the bittern bred regularly in the western fens, and there is a record of thirteen having been shot and one taken by a dog within ten miles of Orford in January 1848.

Very little doubt exists that the little bittern has bred in the East Anglian marshes and fens, even in recent years, though the evidence of its having done so is not absolutely conclusive. Lubbock believed that it sometimes bred in the Broads district, and he adds: " If the nest of the preceding species (the bittern) is hardly ever discovered, what must be the difficulty of verifying that of this minute species, with which concealment is easy in a tenfold degree." In a footnote appended to these remarks, Mr. Southwell says that Mr. Rising, of Horsey, assured him that "about the year 1822-23 a nest of little bitterns was found at Catfield, close to the parsonage. Mr. Rising saw the eggs in the possession of the Rev. J. Layton."

In the days when the fens were still deserving of the name, Savi's warbler was a regular summer visitor to the Eastern counties; but since the year 1856, when an example of this bird was shot at Surlingham, in the Yare valley, it has not been met with in England.

Although it was probably not uncommon in the Fen districts, it was not identified as a British species until about 1819. A bird was then obtained at Limpenhoe by the Rev. J. Brown, who, in an account subsequently sent to Stevenson, wrote: "Its singular note had been observed at Limpenhoe by Sir Wm. Hooker, myself, and another ornithological friend; ... but for a considerable time not a sight of the bird could be obtained. We called it the *reel* bird, on account of the resemblance of its monotonous note to the continuous whirr of the reel at that time used by the hand-spinners of wool. At length it was discovered uttering its peculiar song (if so it may be called) from the top of an alder bush that grew in the midst of a large patch of sedge, into which it fell like a stone as soon as it was approached. After, however, much patience and caution, it again reascended the alder and was shot." It was sent to Temminck, the famous ornithologist, who was in London at the time, and he, after comparing it with specimens in his own collection, returned it, with the opinion that it was "a variety of the reed wren." Subsequently he seems to have identified it with Cetti's warbler; but specific distinction was given to it in 1824 by Savi, who named it *Sylvia luscinioides*. As a British breeding species it appears to have been confined to the counties of Cambridgeshire, Huntingdonshire, and Norfolk; but in the last-named county it seems to have been a rare bird, for only six records of its occurrence there are considered to be absolutely reliable. No reliable record exists of its occurrence in Suffolk. An English nest of Savi's warbler, preserved in the Natural History Museum at South Kensington, is composed of dead rushes and flags compactly interwoven and lined with twisted reed blades. Nests found in Cambridgeshire were entirely composed of the leaves of the tall reed meadow grass (*Glyceria aquatica*).

I have included Savi's warbler among our lost

breeding birds, and it is, I fear, only too well entitled to a place among them; but it must be mentioned that Mr. J. H. Gurney, writing in the *Zoologist* for March 1899, remarks that "it may well be that Savi's warbler, a bird which leaves its shelter very reluctantly, flying only a short distance, and, dipping down again, to be immediately hidden, is still an annual visitant in very small numbers." Fenmen used to call this bird the "red craking reed-wren." Like the reed warbler and the bearded titmouse, it frequented large reed beds, and was seldom seen or heard except during fine calm weather.

The three harriers, marsh, hen, and Montagu's, were formerly common birds in the East Anglian marshes, where the first-named, Lubbock says, might have been termed the "Norfolk hawk," so generally was it dispersed among the Broads. "Almost every pool of any extent had its pair of these birds; they consumed the day in beating round and round the reeds which skirted the water; this was done for hours incessantly. All the birds wounded by the sportsman fell to the share of the Moor Buzzard. He was, as it were, the *genius loci*, the sovereign of the waste." The hen harrier, which, according to Professor Newton, used to nest abundantly in the fens below Brandon, is now a very rare bird in its old haunts, and as it is several years since there was a reliable record of a nest having been found, it must, it is to be feared, be numbered among our lost breeding birds. Of the marsh and Montagu's harriers, this, fortunately, can hardly as yet be said; for, in spite of constant persecution, a pair or two occasionally nest in the Eastern counties, though it is very rarely that they succeed in rearing their young. In Mr. Richard Kearton's *Our Rarer British Breeding Birds*, there is a good reproduction of an excellent photograph of a marsh harrier's nest found in the Broads district in 1899; also one of a Montagu's harrier's nest discovered and photographed in the same locality at the same time.

That so handsome a bird as the ruff should have survived as a breeding species so late as 1889, and perhaps 1897, is somewhat surprising, seeing that it was comparatively recently in demand as a table bird, and since bird-collecting became a mania it has experienced persistent persecution. At one time nets were used to capture it, and Colonel Montagu ascertained that ruffs were being so taken as recently as the first quarter of the nineteenth century. Ruff-catching at that time was the occasional occupation of a few men living in isolated places on the verge of the fens, and their method of taking the birds is described as follows: The fowler, we are told, as soon as he had discovered a ruff's "hill"—as the slightly elevated ground was called on which the male birds, in the breeding season, carried on their sparring—repaired to the spot before daybreak, and set up on the "hill" a kind of net known as a single clap-net, which was about seventeen feet long and six wide, and was supported by poles in such a way that, by means of a rope and pulley, it could be pulled over directly the birds were beneath it. Stuffed decoy birds were used to attract the ruffs, which usually came in a flock to their "hill" at dawn; sometimes these decoys were so contrived as to give a little jump into the air when a string was pulled, thus imitating the live birds, which have a way of leaping from the ground when they desire to attract approaching stragglers of their species. With the aid of his net and decoys a fowler could take every ruff in a fen in the course of a season. After they were captured they were fattened for about a fortnight on boiled wheat and bread and milk, mixed with hempseed and, sometimes, sugar. The fen fowlers received ten shillings a dozen for the birds; but the fatteners who bought them usually obtained two guineas a dozen for them, and never less than thirty shillings. Lubbock, whose account of the habits of the ruff is one of the best to be read anywhere, tells us that on one occasion forty-four birds were netted together in Lincolnshire, and altogether six dozen in a morning; and he himself once saw a flock of seventy or eighty in a marsh near Burgh Castle, at the north end of Breydon. This was at the end of the nesting season. In a table printed in the *Zoologist*, giving an approximate estimate of the decrease of certain species in the Broads district, Mr. J. H. Gurney reckons that in 1858 there were about fourteen ruffs' nests, in 1868 about five nests, in 1878 about two nests, in 1888 one nest, and in 1898 no nest. At the same time he wrote: " It is now several years since the reeve has bred in Norfolk, in fact not since 1889, when walking over 'Rush-hills' (at Hickling) I found the nest, and was near treading on the four eggs. The last appearance, or rather re-appearance, of these birds in any quantity was in 1893, when for some reason there was an unprecedented passage of waders of all sorts through Norfolk. On May 24th of that year my correspondent, the Rev. M. C. Bird, observed more than twenty ruffs and reeves at their old home, some of the males with fine frills, a sight neither he nor any other naturalist is likely to see again." Mr. Bird's account of this interesting sight, to be found in his chapter on " Bird Life " in my book, *The Norfolk Broads*, is as follows: " It was a bright May morning, the wind was right, and as we neared Swimcoots wall our worthy quanter, glasses in hand, spied a party of ruffs and reeves come and alight inside the marsh. Promptly lying down at the bottom of the boat, we let her drift towards land, and ere she grounded, some ten yards from the shore, first a reeve, then a ruff, and then another ruff, came over the narrow foot and grassy slope, until we had counted eight different and distinctive plumages of the almost adult males. For nearly half an hour we watched them, until, for some unaccountable reason, they took wing, and fled rapidly away to the right of us, over to the hovers in the Warbush. Whilst we held them in view on Swimcoots we saw no serious fighting. Now and again two males would play the game-cock; but more often than not they would set at and challenge one another without even attempting to spar, and when a feint was made it ended there, and if an actual blow was struck it never told, and the striker was the first to move away and commence feeding again. In fact, they were difficult to watch, for they were incessantly on the move. Some of the ruffs, none very white or yellow in the frill, were in very nearly full feather; but we saw no attention paid to the three reeves accompanying them." Against Mr. Gurney's date (1889) for the last Norfolk nest of the ruff, we have a note in Mr. Harting's *Handbook of British Birds*, that a nest was reported in 1897 near Hoveton Broad.

Sir Thomas Browne's note about this bird is rather longer than his bird-notes usually are. "Ruffes," he writes, "a marsh bird of the greatest varietie of colours, euery one therein somewhat varying from other. The female is called a reeve without any ruffe about the neck, lesser than the other and hardly to bee got. They are almost all cocks, & putt together fight and destroy each other and prepare themselues to fight like cocks, though they seem to haue no other offensive part butt the bill. They loose theire ruffes about the autumne or beginning of winter, as wee haue obserued keeping them in a garden from May till the next spring. They most abound in Marshland, butt are also in good number in the marshes between Norwich and Yarmouth."

In *A Booke of Cookery and Housekeeping*, 1707, written by Katherine Windham, and still preserved in manuscript at Felbrigge Hall, in Norfolk, Mr. Gurney met with the following recipe for "mewing" ruffs and reeves: "Put ym in a boarded Rome; feed ym with wheat boyled as for furmety, when it is cold breake it into yr troughs; give ym either bear or water to drinke; keep ye place very clean, & let ym have wheat straw to creep under; make ye meat once in 2 dayes, or it will be sower; some times give ym raw wheat; put stones in yr troughs, yt ye may not dable in ye water; let ym have gravell by ym to keep ye rome clean. All sea fowle (!) must have stones in yr troughs yt they may not get in to wash."

Sir Thomas Browne's notes on the fauna of Norfolk are far too few and brief; but we are grateful to him for the glimpses he affords us of the old-time bird life. For instance, he remarks: "Aldrovandus takes particular notice of the great number of kites about London & about the Thames. Wee are not without them heare, though not in such numbers." And elsewhere, in dealing with the coots that were found " in very great flocks upon the broad waters," he tells us that "upon the appearance of a Kite or Buzzard I have seen them vnite from all parts of the shoare in strange numbers, when, if the Kite stoopes neare them, they will fling up (and) spred such a flash of water up with there wings that they will endanger the Kite & so keepe him of agayne & agayne in open opposition; and in handsome prouision they make about their nest agaynst the same bird of praye by bending and twining the rushes and reeds so about them that they cannot stoope at their yong ones or the damme while she setteth." For many years the kite has been one of our rarest bird visitors, and more than sixty years have elapsed since it bred in Norfolk, though it nested in Lincolnshire as recently as 1870. At one time kites were undoubtedly fairly numerous, for kite-hawking was a popular pastime, and was revived by the eccentric George, Earl of Orford. In the neighbourhood of Eriswell, in Suffolk, where rabbits abounded, the kite was apparently a resident, and Professor Newton remembers having heard several old men recall the excellent flights this bird afforded, " and especially one flight which, beginning on Eriswell or the adjoining part of Elveden, ended in Lord Bristol's park at Ickworth, near Bury St. Edmunds—a distance in a straight line of some ten or twelve miles."

Professor Newton contributes to the edition of Lubbock's *Fauna of Norfolk*, published in 1879, some interesting notes on hawking in Norfolk, and quotes the following passage from Colonel Thornton's *Sporting Tour through the Northern Parts of England*:

"The southern gentlemen, particularly those in the vicinity of the metropolis, never see game of any kind without expressing, instantaneously, their inclination for a *roast*; nor is this peculiarity confined to them; for every alderman expresses, on such occasions, the same emotion. I remember a singular instance, that cannot but be recollected likewise by those members of the Falconers' Club who were present, and there was a large field. A Mr. A——, attended by a little hump-backed servant with a large portmanteau, joined our party, ranging for kite near Elden (Elveden) Gap. At length one was seen in the air, and I ordered the owl to be flown. He came, as we wished, at a proper distance. The day was fine, and the hawks, particularly *Javelin* and *Icelanderkin*, in the highest order; and with them *Crocus*, a famous flight falcon. Never was there a finer day, keener company, or, for six miles, a finer flight. When he was taken, in an ecstasy I asked Mr. A—— how he liked kite-hawking? He replied, with a sort of hesitation that expressed but small pleasure, 'Why, pretty well,' We then tried for *hare*, with a famous hawk called *Sans Quartier*. After ranging a little, we found one, and in about two miles, killed it. Mr. A——, coming up again slowly, unwilling or unable to leave his portmanteau, I repeated my former question; and though the flight of a hare, is fine, yet being no way equal to that of a kite, was surprised to see his countenance brighten up, and to hear him express himself with uncommon pleasure. 'Ay, *that*,' he said, 'was a nobler kind of hawking; the hare would be of use—a good *roast*—the kite of none.' Desirous to gratify his wishes, and to get quit, on such easy terms, of the trouble the servants would have to carry an old jack hare, in the month of May, I begged his acceptance of it, to which he very readily assented; and his servant was ordered to add this trophy on the top of the enormous portmanteau. I leave every sportsman to guess the observations that were made by a set of lively young men on the occasion."

Lord Orford, who resided at Houghton Hall, the magnificent house built by his uncle, Sir Robert Walpole, was one of the founders of a Falconers' Club, of which he was for a time "Manager" of the hawks. In an old newspaper the following advertisement appears, and is reprinted by Mr. Gurney in the *Transactions of the Norfolk and Norwich Naturalists' Society*:

"HAWKING

"EARL OF ORFORD, MANAGER OF THIS YEAR

"The gentlemen of the Falconers' Society are hereby acquainted, that the hawks will be in England in the first week in March, and will begin kite and crow hawking immediately on the arrival. The quarters are fixed at Bourn Bridge, Cambridgeshire, forty-eight miles from London, until the first April meeting, when they will go to Barton Mills and Brandon till the 31st of May, when the season will finish.

"The hawks to be out every Saturday, Monday, and Wednesday in each week at ten o'clock, provided the weather is favourable.

"Subscribers are desired to pay their subscriptions, for this season, on or before the 20th of March, to Messrs. Coutts and Co., Bankers in the Strand, London.

"*N.B.*—The cage consists of thirty-two flight falcons, thirteen German hawks, and seven Iceland falcons."

Notwithstanding its depredations on the warrens, the kite is a bird which renders good service to the farmer by preying upon several of the small mammals so destructive to crops, and although it is included among the gamekeeper's detested "hawks," it well deserves protection.

The same may be said of the common buzzard, which also was a not uncommon bird in East Anglia, breeding in various places. Lubbock mentions the woods of the adjoining Norfolk parishes of Hethel and Ashwellthorpe as having been among its breeding-places, while in Suffolk it often nested in the woods around Bury St. Edmunds, in the neighbourhood of Beccles, and near the great warrens in the north-west part of the county. In Norfolk it has not been known to nest for over half a century; but writing about 1866, Stevenson said that a single bird had for fourteen or fifteen years been observed to return regularly to Costessey Park, near Norwich, where, no doubt, buzzards had previously bred. In Suffolk it appears to have lingered later as a breeding species, for there is a record of a nest at Felsham in August 1874, when a keeper killed one of the old birds and threw it to the foxes. In the following year another nest was built at the same place; but it is doubtful whether the birds succeeded in hatching off their eggs, for we are told that the female was wounded on the nest.

The peregrine falcon, though it still breeds on the rocky parts of the coast in several English counties, has long ceased to do so in the Eastern counties, though Hunt, in his *British Ornithology*, writing in 1815, states that "a nest of the Gentil Falcon has from time immemorial been found on Hunstanton cliffs." There seems to be some doubt as to the latest date of the peregrine breeding at this spot, for Mr. Harting mentions the year 1818, while the Rev. G. Munford, who was a resident in the neighbourhood and a careful student of its fauna, states that the young birds were taken from the cliff and "trained to falconry by Mr. Downes, of Gunton, in Suffolk; till at length, worn out by their constant persecution, they forsook the place in 1821." Mr. J. Dawson Downes, who was an enthusiastic falconer, died at Lowestoft in 1829. He used to practise his favourite sport in the neighbourhood of his Suffolk home, and in his latter days, when age and infirmity prevented his doing so, he amused himself by watching a tame shrike catch flies in the room where he sat. We have it on the authority of Lubbock, that during Mr. Downes residence at Gunton, a pair of peregrines used to breed regularly in the steeple of the adjoining coast village of Corton. There, as at Hunstanton, the nestlings were taken and trained to the chase, "the clerk having a regular retaining fee for their preservation."

It might be thought that in a part of England where descendants of the Norse settlers of pre-Norman times are still to be found, Odin's sacred bird would have been afforded some measure of protection, for Mr. Bosworth Smith asserts that "in nearly all the regions in which the cult of Odin once held supreme sway, and where it may well be that some lingerings of the vanished cult still survives," the raven still holds its own. Far from such being the case here, there is scarcely any bird of rarer occurrence in the Eastern counties than the raven. There are records of its having bred in some parts of Suffolk; but not since about 1864, when a pair which had bred for several years at Icklingham or Elveden were destroyed. In Norfolk, according to Mr. Gurney, the last nests were found at Shadwell, Ickburgh, Beechamwell, and Melton. In the early part of the last century the raven was generally, if sparingly, distributed over Norfolk and Suffolk; but during the ensuing half century it seems, owing to its persecution by gamekeepers, to have rapidly decreased in numbers, so that at the time when Lubbock published his *Fauna* he was compelled to write that "it is seldom found breeding here: when it does so, its nest is sure to be plundered." If there be any truth in the assertion made by Mr. Bosworth Smith that sometimes a sort of "truce of God" seems to be established between the raven and its nearest neighbours, some of the Norfolk ravens deserve to be left undisturbed; for Professor Newton has stated that a pair of these birds which nested in the county "carefully abstained from molesting the sheep and lambs which abounded within their sight, and lived almost entirely upon the moles, whose burrows were farther away." Indeed, if a story told by Morris be true, the raven's hunting skill might occasionally be turned to good account; for we read that the landlord of a Cambridgeshire inn was in possession of a bird of this species which frequently went hunting with a dog that had been bred up with him. "On their arrival at a cover, the dog entered and drove the hares and rabbits from the thickets, whilst the raven, posted on the outside of the cover, seized every one that came in his way, when the dog immediately hastened to his assistance, and by their joint efforts nothing escaped. On various occasions the raven has proved of more use than a ferret, and has been known to enter a barn with several dogs, and enjoy the sport of rat-hunting." In the seventeenth century ravens were, according to Sir Thomas Browne, "in good plentie about the citty" of Norwich.

To the worthy and learned author of *Religio Medici* we are indebted for our knowledge that in the seventeenth century there was a colony of cormorants in the valley of the Yare, for he speaks of "cormorants building at Reedham upon trees, from whence King Charles the First was wont to bee supplyed." Until about 1826 there was also a colony in the woods around Fritton Lake in Suffolk—a colony that was in existence as early, at least, as 1775, when, according to Berkenhout, "a vast number of these birds, even to some thousands," roosted every night upon the trees on which they built their nests. At Fritton there was also a heronry, and it is said that the cormorants used to take possession of the old nests of the herons, as they do in Ireland to the present day. Since the Fritton colony was abandoned there does not appear to have been a single instance of the cormorant breeding in Norfolk or Suffolk. In the days of their abundance at Reedham and Fritton, they were undoubtedly attracted to those places by their nearness to Breydon, the estuary of the Yare. Even now they are met with more frequently on Breydon than elsewhere in the two easternmost counties.

The list of our lost breeding birds is unfortunately a rather long one; but we have nearly reached the end of it, and, having mentioned that the grey lag goose used to breed in Lincolnshire, Cambridgeshire, and, probably, West Norfolk, and that Baillon's crake probably nested in the Broads district in comparatively recent years—as it certainly did in Cambridgeshire in 1858—there only remains one bird to be dealt with, that magnificent bird, the great bustard.

The last of the indigenous race of British bustards was killed in the parish of Lexham, near Swaffham, in the year 1838; so Norfolk, while it has the credit of having preserved this bird until a later date than any other county, has the discredit of being the scene of the extinction of the native race. For centuries the bustards had been slowly but surely decreasing in numbers, chiefly in consequence of the enclosure and cultivation of many of the wide stretches of heathland which were the favourite haunts of the "droves." Even in the days when the crossbow was the chief weapon of the fowler, bustard-shooting seems to have been a popular pastime, and for a long time after guns were invented the bustard provided sport in many English counties and the lowland districts of Scotland; but until most of the great commonlands were enclosed or planted with trees for game cover or the sheltering of sheepfolds, we do not hear that any diminution in the number of native bustards attracted attention. But at the beginning of the last century it was only on Salisbury Plain, some of the Yorkshire wolds, and the warrens and heathlands of East Anglia, that a few diminishing droves were to be found. And about that time gunners seem to have realised that the bustard was becoming rare, for it was then that the persecution began which did not cease so long as a single native bustard was left alive. Had it not been for that persecution, it is highly probable that the native race would not even now be extinct, for the birds, especially in East Anglia, were beginning to adapt themselves to the changed conditions, and, while preferring the heaths and warrens, were frequently to be found in the fields at all times of the year.

From a note on the *Birds of Suffolk*, it appears that during the latter part of the eighteenth century and the early part of the nineteenth, the East Anglian bustards had three principal headquarters, at each of which a drove resided, but not so constantly that the birds of the different droves never intermingled. These headquarters were—(1) The country around Swaffham in Norfolk, and entirely included in that county, Westacre being the spot especially frequented; (2) the neighbourhood of Thetford, stretching from Brettenham and Snarehill in Norfolk across the county border to Elveden, Barnham, North Stow, Cavenham, Icklingham, and probably still farther towards Mildenhall in Suffolk; and (3) the tract around Newmarket, partly in Cambridgeshire, partly in Suffolk, and separated by a slight interval from the preceding. Concerning the Icklingham drove, Mr. C. Gwilt, writing to the *Standard* a few years ago, said: " I often heard my late father allude to the bustards having been seen there, and particularly to the last occasion of his seeing them. This was in the spring of 1827, when, as he was one day riding across Wether Hill Heath, . . . he observed a flock of thirteen bustards among the heather. . . . The birds were not at all shy, for my father was able to ride within thirty or forty yards of the flock, some of the birds being occupied in ' dressing ' their feathers as he quietly passed them." The immediate cause of the disappearance of this drove was, according to Mr. Gwilt, the "detestably unsportsman-like doings of some fellow from London," who shot some of the birds and trapped others. By 1832 the last of the drove had disappeared. Some idea of the treatment received by the bustards on the heathlands around Thetford may be formed from the statement of Lubbock, that during the latter years of the eighteenth century a Wretham keeper named Turner used to kill many bustards in the snow by keeping a look-out for their tracks, and then feeding the birds for a day or two with cabbages. "He next constructed a battery of three large duck guns, bearing on the spot where the food lay, and, coming before daylight, secreted himself in a hole dug some hundred and fifty yards from the guns. By means of a long string to the triggers, he used to effect a general discharge on the first favourable opportunity, and in this way he once obtained seven bustards at a shot." One would have had little sympathy with the inventor of this diabolical contrivance if, when he pulled the string, one—or all three—of the guns had acted like the revolving swivel guns that were formerly used for the prevention or detection of poaching!

In the Norwich Castle Museum there is a very fine case of seven great bustards, all of which were killed in Norfolk or Suffolk, and are believed to have belonged to the indigenous race. The largest bird, a male weighing twenty-four pounds, was found dead on a warren not far from Swaffham some time between the years 1815 and 1818. Another was caught in a rabbit-trap in the same neighbourhood, and a third was captured and kept alive until it met with an accident that made it a mercy to kill it. Among the birds in this case is the Lexham specimen—the last of the British bustards. Since the extirpation of the native race, solitary examples of this magnificent bird have occurred in East Anglia as stragglers from the southern countries of Europe. In January and February 1876, a male bird frequented a tract of fenland not far from Brandon for about a month, and an unsuccessful attempt to induce it to remain there was made by liberating a hen bustard supplied by the late Lord Ilford. More recently—in 1900—an attempt was made to re-introduce the species—an experiment which resulted, I am sorry to say, in almost complete failure. Sixteen birds, imported from Spain, were set at liberty on the wild heathlands of Breckland; but after the lapse of about two years only two birds remained alive, the rest having been killed in various ways, but chiefly by gunners, who, notwithstanding a widely circulated appeal for their protection, failed to spare them. The two survivors, a pair, had a nest at the end of May 1902, and the female sat for nearly five weeks on two infertile eggs; in June of the following year they made another nest, in which three eggs were laid; but these also were unincubated, the female deserting the nest after sitting for about a month.

In connection with the great bustard, it is worthy of remark that, as Mr. Southwell has pointed out, Sir Thomas Browne was very near discovering the presence of the gular pouch in the adult male of this bird. Writing to his son, he said: "Yesterday I had a cock bustard sent me from beyond Thetford. I never did see such a vast thick neck: the crop was pulled out, but as (a) turkey hath an odde large substance without, so hath this within the inside of the skinne, and the strongest and largest neckbone of any bird in England. This I tell you, that if you meet with one, you may further observe it."

CHAPTER III

WILD LIFE IN BRECKLAND

THE name of Breckland has been given of late years to a considerable portion of the country immediately surrounding the ancient town of Thetford, a border town situated partly in Norfolk and partly in Suffolk, at the junction of the river Thet with the Little Ouse. The district—which is a portion of the great chalk ridge crossing West Norfolk—consists chiefly of sandy and gravelly heathland, but it takes its name from what are known as the "brecks," by which term are recognised those tracts of heath which at some time have been broken up by the plough, but have been allowed to revert to a state of primitive wildness and barrenness. At the present time the district might almost be described as one vast game preserve, and it is partly owing to pheasants being reared here on a large scale that during the last fifty years Breckland has undergone a considerable change in aspect. In the earlier half of the last century it was a treeless waste, on which the indigenous race of great bustards had their last stronghold. For mile after mile along either side of the Little Ouse there extended wide heathlands which had known few changes, apart from those that the seasons bring, since the days when they were trodden by the men of the Later Stone Age. Tracks of green or golden bracken were interspersed with stretches of dark or purple ling; where rabbits abounded the hill or valley slopes were as sandy as the dunes. Good roads across these desert lands were few, while the fact of their being hedgeless made them wearisome to travel when the rays of the summer sun beat down upon them, and often dangerous when they were heaped with drifted snow. For man there seemed to be no place upon these barrens; yet almost everywhere there were traces of his having dwelt upon them. But these were relics of a remote past—grouped and isolated barrows, mysterious banks intersecting ancient highways, abandoned trackways, and innumerable tools and weapons of flint strewn about the sites of vanished settlements. Over the whole waste there was no shelter from winter storm or summer heat; on the lonesome meres the wild-fowl rested undisturbed for days together; and often one might ramble all day along the footpaths and trackways without seeing a single human being. And all day and all night long the wild whistle of the stone curlew was the fitting voice of this primeval solitude.

To-day there is a marked change in the general aspect of Breckland, and although the district still has extensive tracts of primitive wilderness, the outlook from its breezy heights is in few places so wide and impressive as it was of yore. Here and there, from the summit of some barrow-crowned hill, one gets a view across upland and valley which is far wider than East Anglia is generally supposed to afford, and which for charm and variety can well bear comparison with some more famous vistas; but as a rule the outlook is confined to closer limits by some of the many fir belts which have been planted during the last fifty years. The "bleak unwooded scene" and the "slopes of burning sand" which Robert Bloomfield knew when he dwelt in a quiet village on the Breckland border, have in many places been transformed into well-wooded districts, and although the area of heath and breck is probably larger now than it was in the early part of the nineteenth century, it is so broken up by woods and belts as to have lost its striking aspect of austere sterility. Yet the district is still the wildest and least populated in East Anglia, and to those who know it well it has a strange and abiding fascination. Hardly anywhere else in Eastern England can one enjoy such complete isolation from the busy world or soothing relaxation of the strain of city life, as on these wide stretches of fern and heather; nowhere is the storm-song of the pines more melodious than on the high Breckland ridges; nowhere is the air more bracing and life-giving; and nowhere are the wild-life voices so expressive of the spirit of the primeval. The district is too isolate and primitive ever to become popular with any great number of pleasure-seekers; indeed, access to it is so jealously guarded by the game-preservers, that it is practically a forbidden land to the public at large; but a few lovers of solitude and untrodden ways have come under the spell of its enchantment, and they are well content to continue under the influence of that spell.

To those familiar with Breckland there are byways known by which much of the district can be explored and made to "yield up its sweets," without the adventurer running the risk of being warned off or discomfited by vigilant wearers of velveteen. One of these byways is the ancient Drove or Drove Road, a trackway with slight resemblance in a public way, but one that from time immemorial has been a public road, and in prehistoric times was probably one of the principal highways of this part of the country. This trackway, which is a branch of that more important ancient road, the Peddars' Way, connects the latter where it crosses Roudham Heath with the Fen border at Hockwold, intersecting in its course between these two points the earthwork known as the Devil's Dyke, the main roads from Brandon and Thetford to Stoke Ferry and Watton, and some of the most characteristic heaths, brecks, and warrens of Breckland. To find this trackway the stranger to the district can hardly do better than travel by rail to Brandon, and continue his journey by the Mundford Road. Here, a short distance from the station, he will see on his left the dry bed of what was probably one of the Breckland meres, beyond it a ruined windmill, picturesque in its surroundings and its decay, and on his right some of the series of curious irregular depressions in the surface of the heathland, believed to be artificial, and which may be traces of early quarrying for flint. But nothing of very striking interest presents itself until nearly a mile of the road has been travelled, when a fine round barrow surmounted by an aspen is seen a little way to the left of the road. This barrow closely adjoins the Drove, which here intersects the highway, coming in from the left as a metalled road, but continuing its way across the heathland on the right as a very rough trackway, distinguishable here by a double line of deep wheel-ruts in the sandy soil, farther on by its low bordering banks, and in places by an opening, locally known as a "gap," between two plantations. By following this trackway eastward for a few miles, a stranger can acquaint himself with most of the striking features of Breckland scenery, and, provided he has plenty of time at his disposal, he will probably have some opportunities for making the acquaintance of the, in some respects, peculiar wild life of the district.[1]

At the commencement of this portion of the Drove the way leads across a tract of grassy wasteland, uneven in surface, with mysterious artificial banks and pit-like depressions of unknown origin; but after passing two

[1] In "A List of the Vertebrate Animals found in the Neighbourhood of Thetford" (*Transactions of the Norfolk and Norwich Naturalists' Society*, vol. vi. p. 300 *et seq.*), Mr. W. G. Clarke includes 184 species of birds, four of which must be classed as semi-domesticated. He divides these species into 53 common, 43 rather rare, 29 rare, and 59 accidental, among the last-named being included those birds which are now practically extinct; and he adds that the large proportion of 102 species are known to breed in the district comprised in a six-mile radius from Thetford. Mr. Clarke informs me that the present number of recorded species is 192, of which 106 have been known to breed in the district.

cottages the rough road is bordered on either side by flint-strewn brecks, which may or may not be under cultivation, the pursuit of agriculture in this neighbourhood being an intermittent occupation, to a large extent ruled by the demands of the pheasants, for whose benefit the land is sometimes sown with buckwheat. On the right these brecks slope gently down into the pleasant valley of the Little Ouse, which here flows sluggishly through quaint old wheel-raised stanches and between strips of water-meadow; on the left the land rises slightly to a fairly level plateau, and the brecks are divided by plantations of oak, larch, and fir. For about a mile, the road, which takes a course as straight as an arrow's flight, now climbs the western slope of Bromehill, a partly wooded hill, from the summit of which there is a wide view across the level of the Fens as far as the distant fane of Ely, the lofty tower and octagon of which are clearly visible above the elevated ground of the historic Fen isle. And here, on the heaths of Weeting, if the monkish chroniclers speak truly, the traveller is on historic ground; for they tell us that it was here the Norman Conqueror's army encamped whilst it was trying to gain access to the sturdy Saxons' last stronghold on the Isle of Ely, and here that the dauntless Hereward, disguised as a travelling potter, visited the camp and discovered the plans of his enemies. Even in those days the Drove was probably many centuries old, and as one treads it to-day it is impossible not to picture to oneself some of the strange scenes that may have been witnessed along it in days long gone by.

It originated, some antiquaries believe, as a prehistoric trackway, and if such be the case, men of the rude Iberian race may have used it when they came for or carried away the flint excavated from the neighbouring Neolithic flint quarries known as Grimes Graves. From end to end of it relics of those early inhabitants of England may be found in the shape of Later Stone

Age flint flakes and implements; similar relics have been found in countless numbers strewn over the surface of the adjoining heaths and brecks; and not very many years ago, when two of the Breckland meres were drained, traces of lake dwellings, evidently of Neolithic date, were brought to light. By these primitive ancestors of ours may have been heaped up some of the numerous barrows which are dotted about the Breckland heaths and hills, for although the round barrows are generally assigned to the Bronze Age, traces of metal have been rare indeed in those that have been opened in Breckland. Men of the Bronze Age may also have known this ancient road, for bronze celts and palstaves have been found not far from the road, and, in the opinion of students of prehistoric archæology, many of the delicately shaped flint arrowheads for which the district is famous were made by Goidelic or Brythonic hands.

The precise duration of the periods of occupation of these lands by prehistoric races cannot be determined; but by the arrival of the Romans and the dawn of English history we are brought on to surer ground, and it can hardly be doubted that if, as is generally agreed, Peddars' Way is a Roman road—following the course, no doubt, of a prehistoric trackway—the Drove, which is identical with it in character, was often travelled by the Roman conquerors of the Iceni. Those, for a while, were stirring times; but with the colonisation of the country came a time of peace, which lasted until the Romans abandoned this outpost of their empire, and left it open to the attacks of the Norse marauders. Then there were fierce battles fought on the heaths of Breckland—near Thetford, where the martyr king Edmund was defeated, and, later, when Ulfketyl, commanding the forces of East Anglia, was put to flight on Ringmere Heath by the Danes under the famous Thorkill. "Hringmara Heath," the battlefield, which, as the saga says, was a "bed of death" when "Haarfager's heir dealt slaughter there," we shall see when we have travelled a few miles farther along the road. Meanwhile, it may be borne in mind, as an added interest to our ramble, that we are following in the footsteps of some of those sturdy Fen folk, who, when the approach of the Danes was announced, hastened by this road to the aid of their East Anglian neighbours. This way, too, they retreated when the Saxon army was overpowered, and it may be that it was the leader of some attack upon them who was buried on the slope of a Santon hill, where a skeleton interred with an iron sword and two Scandinavian brooches was discovered some years ago.

Of these stirring associations of the Drove we may remind ourselves as we climb the tawny side of Bromehill, though they are hard to connect with the desert wastelands by which we are surrounded. But after ascending the sandy slope leading into the Weeting woods, the ringing laugh of the green woodpecker or the flushing of a nightjar at some spot where the undergrowth of bracken hides the fallen fir-cones strewn about the woodland floor, may well distract us from our musings. For in the daytime the cry of the woodpecker is continually repeated in the Breckland plantations and fir belts; and should you linger here until the dusk of a summer night, you may often hear at least half-a-dozen nightjars churring around you. There is, indeed, no more haunting night-voice of the fir-woods and brown barrens than that of the night-hawk—as it is called in Breckland—and at any time, as you wander beneath the dusky pines, you may chance to disturb one of these beautifully mottled birds, which often lay their two curiously-shaped eggs on a patch of level ground, without even selecting a natural depression to contain them. By a stroke of greater good fortune you may also meet with here a rarer Breckland bird in the crossbill or "robin-hawk," which now seems to be a regular winter visitor, and generally stays to breed near Brandon and at Santon Downham and Rushford, attracted, no doubt, by the changed aspect of the district since belts of firs have been so extensively planted. Mr. F. Norgate, who examined two nests near Brandon in 1885, noticed a remarkable difference between them. One, taken by a boy from the top of an oak, was large, very thick, and warm, chiefly composed of hemp-like fibre, which was probably the inner bark of lime-twigs, and most likely stolen from a squirrel's drey; the other, taken from the top of a Scots pine, was much like that of a greenfinch, and made chiefly of dry twigs and moss. During some winters crossbills have been numerous in the neighbourhoods of Santon Downham and Rushford, where their tameness, while feeding in the fir-woods, has made them so conspicuous that one could easily understand how it was that, when they were first observed in England—about three hundred years ago—it was written of them: "The thing most to be noted was that it seemed they came out of some country not inhabited, for that they at the first would abide shooting at them, either with pellet, bow, or other engine, and not remove till they were stricken down." Restless as the long-tailed tit, they are more like parrots in their way of climbing along the underside of the branches, and all the time they keep up a low chattering.[1]

[1] About eight years ago local naturalists were much puzzled by frequent reports of great black woodpeckers having been seen in the woods and plantations of Breckland. A few ornithologists considered that the birds seen might be genuine immigrants; but others thought it most unlikely that great black woodpeckers would wander from their Scandinavian or German haunts. The mystery remained unsolved until 1904, when the following note by Mr. T. Southwell appeared in the *Transactions of the Norfolk and Norwich Naturalists' Society*, vol. vii. page 737: "With reference to the repeated reports of the appearance of this species in England, most of which may at once be dismissed as 'unproven,' it may be as well to put on record a circumstance which has recently come to light. Mr. W. H. Tuck informed me that in the year 1897, seven or eight of these birds were brought from Sweden, where they had been taken from the nest by a friend of his, and, after being kept in an aviary near Brandon for some time, were allowed to regain their liberty. This fact is given from his personal knowledge, but he was not

Beyond the belt of Weeting woodland there are some spacious brecks belonging to one of the Breckland rabbit farms. The fact of furrows and ridges being traceable across many of these flint-strewn tracts proves that in the past man has done his best to cultivate the dry sandy soil; but the difficulties he had to contend against were too great, and for years many of these lands have been allowed to lie fallow, abandoned to the rabbit, the stone curlew, the stockdove, and the wheatear, and covered with an alien growth of dusty-looking Canadian fleabane. Formerly, when the district was a treeless waste, the sandstorms of Breckland almost equalled in density those of an African desert; and even now, when a strong wind is blowing, the sand of some of the slopes is blown and drifted about like that of the seashore dunes. In the seventeenth century these "travelling sands" were one of the "sights" of the neighbourhood. Evelyn, while the guest of Lord Arlington at Euston, was taken by his host to see them, and he tells us that they were about ten miles wide, and in "rolling from place to place" overwhelmed whole estates. A story is told by the late Joshua Trimmer of a land-owner in this part of the country, who, on being asked in which county, Norfolk or Suffolk, his property was situated, replied: "Sometimes in the one, sometimes in the other: it blows backwards and forwards!" Since 1668 the Suffolk parish of Downham has been known as Santon or Sandy Downham, owing to a great sandstorm which in that year buried several houses there, and for a time choked up the Little Ouse.

allowed to mention the circumstance until a period of three years had expired, and it will doubtless account for the examples reported by the Rev. E. T. Daubeney as seen at Ixworth, Euston Park, and Brandon in 1897, and possibly also for those said by Mr. Digby Pigott to have been seen in Sheringham Park in 1903. That this sedentary species should ever, of its own accord, desert its native forests and migrate hither is so exceedingly improbable, that ornithologists were fully justified in rejecting any but fullest evidence of the occurrence."

For these troubles the rabbits were, no doubt, in part responsible. The sand thrown up from thousands of burrows soon covered the scanty vegetation of the warrens, and, there being in those days no fir belts to break the force of the wind, the sand soon began to drift or "travel"; but in later years the rabbits themselves became, as they are to-day, the chief obstacle to the successful growing of corn, no field without a fence of wire-netting being free from their ravage. Now, on account of the greater part of Breckland being a game preserve, the rabbits are to some extent kept down; but even now they are probably more numerous here than in any other part of the country, and among the more interesting places in Breckland are those farms which, owing to their being hired by men whose work is chiefly rabbitting, are known as rabbit farms. To the rabbit farmer, agriculture is a minor consideration; to the agriculturist, rabbits, in any considerable number, are at the present time a pest. But this does not appear to have always been the case. Reyce, writing in 1618, says: "Of the harmless conies, which do delight to make their abode here ... their great increase, with rich profit for all good housekeepers, hath made every one of any reckoning to prepare fit harbour for them, with great welcome and entertainment, from whence it proceeds that there are so many warrens here in every place, which do furnish the next markets, and are carried to London with no little reckoning, from whence it is that there is none who deem their houses well seated, who have not to the same belonging a commonwealth of conies; neither can he be deemed a good housekeeper that hath not plenty of these at all times to furnish his table."[1]

A few years ago, when they were so abundant as to render it practicable, rabbits were caught on some of the warrens in a wholesale way by means of "tipes." These

[1] *The Breviary of Suffolk*, by Robert Reyce (1618).

RABBITING IN BRECKLAND

tipes, traces of which can still be seen here and there on Thetford and Santon Downham warrens, were almost circular pitfalls eight or nine feet deep, lined with chalk and flint. Covering the pit was a carefully balanced iron door, which turned on a swivel, and on which food was placed. The weight of a rabbit was sufficient to cause this door to "tipe" or turn in such a way that the rabbit fell into the pit, after which the door returned automatically to its original position, and was ready for another victim. In this way as many as 2000 rabbits were sometimes caught in a single night on Thetford Warren alone, most of which were sent to the London market. At that time a great number of "silver-grey" rabbits, introduced into the district about 1836, existed on that particular warren. These were valuable chiefly on account of their skins, which sold for 18s. 6d. a dozen. Eventually the importation of cheap dyed skins so reduced the demand for silver-greys, that the local race of these rabbits became neglected, with the result that in the course of a few years the variety had practically died out. When the warren swarmed with them, the men, who during the trapping season collected every morning the victims of the tipes or tip-traps, occupied an ancient Warren House, which the traveller sees on his left as he journeys across the warren from Thetford to Brandon. There the rabbits were skinned, and there, until recently, were preserved some of the curious old wooden platters which served the men for plates and dishes; also some huge lanterns used by the warreners when they visited the tipes during the night.

At the present time, during the rabbitting season, ferrets, dogs, and nets are used in taking the rabbits, this method being preferred to shooting or trapping with spring-traps, in consequence of the captured rabbits being practically uninjured. A space containing several burrows is enclosed by means of a net; muzzled or "cooped" ferrets are turned into the burrows; and when the rabbits bolt from their holes and try to escape, they run against the net and are killed by the dogs.

In connection with rabbits and trapping, a curious incident may be mentioned, which was first related in the *Magazine of Natural History* about seventy-five years ago. One of the Thetford warreners was abroad one day in October, when he noticed a fine peregrine falcon pursuing a stockdove over an open part of the warren. In order to evade her pursuer, the dove darted down a rabbit burrow; but so close was the falcon that both it and the dove were caught in a large rabbit trap set at the entrance to the hole. The falcon was probably one that had escaped from Didlington Hall, where Colonel Wilson, at that time the chief supporter of hawking in England, kept a number of falcons. The jesses were still on the captive, and were not much worn. In regard to the stockdove — a bird that nests in considerable numbers on the warrens — the Rev. W. Whitear, on the authority of Mr. J. Scales, mentions the interesting fact that when the warreners found the young of this bird in an old rabbit burrow, they fixed sticks across the mouth of the hole in such a way as to prevent their escape, but at the same time permit of the old birds feeding them. When they were in good condition, they were taken out, killed and eaten.

That the abundance of rabbits in Breckland has had, and continues to have, both a destructive and reconstructive effect on the local flora, has been shown by Mr. A. Wallis. Grass, gorse, and ling are destroyed by their being eaten, proof of this being easily obtainable in districts where rabbits abound, but where there are areas enclosed against them with wire netting. Within such areas the sand sedge is rapidly ousted by the grass; but in the open the sand sedge, for which the rabbits have no liking, flourishes amazingly, at the expense of the grass. Burrowing on a large scale produces at first what are practically deserts. "The rabbits," writes Mr. Wallis,[1] "bore into a gently sloping hillside, the soil falls down, a slight escarpment is made, and they bore again. This process, continually repeated, gives rise to considerable extents of loose sand, bounded on the upper side by a miniature cliff full of burrows, on the lower side merging almost imperceptibly into the hillside. The action of the wind upon the loose sand is such as by purely mechanical means to prohibit the growth of any vegetable life, but where stones offer any protection against the moving grains, *Cladonia* (lichen) will often be found. This may either cover in time the whole bare area, or give way to *Festuca ovina* (sheep's fescue-grass), which in turn gives way to Carex (sedge). Towards the lower edge the *Cladonia* increases considerably, with here and there a tuft of *Festuca ovina* and the straight lines of Carex shoots, until the normal growth of the undisturbed hillside is reached."

One class of plants found growing on these dry sandy warrens seem, as Mr. Wallis points out, to depend for their very existence upon the sandheaps at the entrance of the rabbit burrows. At first, of course, these heaps are bare; but should the burrow be deserted or little used, a number of annuals soon appear on them. Among these Mr. Wallis has noticed the hemlock stork's-bill, wall and vernal speedwells, early and changing forget-me-nots, the field cudweed, and the early hair grass; but this is a list he believes could probably be greatly extended, and, as it stands, it is too small to generalise from. He makes note of the fact that the two forget-me-nots "are peculiarly fitted for animal distribution." Later on, these annuals are succeeded by perennials, differing, however, from those found growing on the surrounding soil, the wall pepper and the field chickweed (*Cerastium avense*) being especially noticeable. "These seem to hold their ground well,

[1] *Handbook to the Natural History of Cambridgeshire*, pp. 226-228.

particularly if the ground is loose and very dry, as is the case upon the hillocks which are so often chosen by the rabbits for their holes." Annuals, Mr. Wallis adds, are rare plants, and what are called corn-field annuals exceedingly rare on the sandy wastes of Breckland. "These depend for their very existence upon the constant and regular disturbance of the soil. Originally such plants, in those portions of the world where they had not invaded the cultivated land of primitive man, must have led a precarious existence upon landslips, bare and crumbling river banks, but principally upon the earths of burrowing animals. It is on the rabbit earths, and on these alone, that, in the wilder portions, annuals can exist. We see to-day the rabbit performing, in this quiet corner of England, his ancient role of agriculturist."

But it is time we continued our journey along the Drove, which, after descending Bromehill, enters the heathland parish of Santon, the church of which, one of the smallest in England, stands some distance to the right of the road, near the bank of the river and a square moat which formerly surrounded Santon House. Then the road enters upon the Croxton heathlands, lying chiefly to the north of the village; but apart from the fine views occasionally afforded of the vast stretches of heather, fern, and woodland, and chance encounters with some of the characteristic wild life of the district, there is nothing calling for special attention until we reach the first of the meres on Wretham Heath. On any day between early spring and late autumn, however, it will be remarkable if we arrive at this point without seeing one or more of the Breckland stone curlews, or at least hearing their wild whistle sound with startling clearness across the wide heaths and brecks.

As a breeding bird, the stone curlew or Norfolk plover is more numerous in Breckland than anywhere else in the British Isles. From February until, it may be, as late as November, its shrill weird whistle is constantly heard here, especially in the twilight of a summer night, when solitary birds, or two or three together, are continually flighting from the heaths and brecks to the marshes; and in the daytime, as you ramble over the wide expanses of sun-scorched turf and browning bracken, you may often see them taking flight before you, flying low over the ground and screaming harshly as they fly. At times there may be several of them crouching within easy eye-range amid the moss and lichen of a heath, or running stiffly over the sand of a warren; but your eye needs a special training before it can detect a single bird, so closely does the tawny plumage assimilate with the russet hues of these eastern moorlands. An old gunner, who had accounted for several stone curlews in the days when they were unprotected, once said to me: "They're about as hard to get as any bird I know; for they keep to the open in the daytime, and see you before you guess they're anywhere about. They fly swift and low when you put them up, with their legs stretched out behind them like a harnsee's (heron's), and when they don't rise they run like hares along the ground. The best time to get them is at dusk, when they leave the heaths and go to feed in the marshes. If you lay in wait for them under a hedge, you can hear them a-curlewing as they come over. They make a rare row when they are feeding; half a dozen of them make more noise than a big flock of peewits, and often they keep on screeching all night long. Sometimes you might almost think they were a lot of boys whistling. We used to call them night-hawks when I was a boy. You don't hear so much of them during the day, and if you want to see them then you must be very careful how you draw near them. Sometimes they crouch down among the brakes (bracken) or near a rabbit burrow, and if they'd let you, you might walk over them without seeing them, so much are they the colour of the sand and leaves. I have heard of men catching old birds alive when they were lying down like that, but I've never seen it done, though I've known young ones to be picked up off the ground even after they were able to fly. The old birds run with their heads held down, so that you soon lose sight of them if there be many brakes or bushes about." Mr. W. G. Clarke, who has had many opportunities of observing the stone curlew in its Breckland haunts, states that for a time after its arrival in spring it appears to frequent the uplands both by night and by day, probably finding sufficient food there for its requirements; but when the sun has scorched the heathland vegetation it obtains most of its food at night in low-lying meadows. The stone curlews' nocturnal flighting to the alluvium, he adds, "is generally, as is the case with wild-fowl, on the same routes. Should one of these flighting-lines happen to pass over a lonely farmhouse, the dwellers therein, far from considering it a cause for congratulation, characterise it as a nuisance—and not without reason."

Insects, worms, and field mice constitute the greater portion of the diet of the stone curlew; but there seems to be no doubt that in a curlew community there is sometimes a ne'er-do-well who takes to poaching. This fact was first brought under my notice by a Breckland keeper, who told me that on one occasion he captured a young but fully grown stone curlew, which soon after its capture disgorged two tiny partridges and the wing of a young pheasant. My friend Mr. W. G. Clarke was with me when I heard this bad account of one of our favourite birds, and, not wishing to condemn it on the evidence of one man, he made inquiries in the neighbourhood with a view to having the charge established or denied. As a result, he received from the Rev. R. B. Caton—a careful observer of birds, and one who knows Breckland intimately — the following notes: "With regard to the stone curlew eating young partridges, I

STONE CURLEW

think it possible, but not very probable. Newton, in his *Dictionary of Birds*, says: 'Its food consists of snails, coleopterous insects, and earthworms; but larger prey, as a mouse or a frog, is not rejected.' Butler's *British Birds* states its food to be chiefly insects, also slugs, snails, and worms. It has been known to eat field mice and lizards, and Mr. Newton ascertained from Norfolk warreners that, when caught in a rabbit-trap, it occasionally ejects a frog. No mention here of young birds; but a small partridge is not unlike a mouse, and might be mistaken for one and swallowed." A day or two afterwards Mr. Caton wrote: "I was at Elveden on Monday, and Mr. Elliot told me that the keepers assure him some stone curlews do attack broods of pheasants and partridges, but that this is not general; only certain vicious individuals, when they do take to it, are as bad as a hawk, and are shot. Otherwise they are not interfered with. On the other hand, I heard to-day from T. G. Hill, who was keeper at Barnham for several years—a very active man and a keen observer. He says: 'As to my observation of stone curlews, I have seen nothing that would lead me to believe they would attack pheasants or partridges. You remember Tom Lusher, the warrener from Barnham. He assisted me through the egging season for thirty years. I am quite sure that had he seen anything he would have mentioned it, as he was rather given to make much of losses from any cause.' You will see from the above that there is a diversity of opinion, and I should be disposed to think that it occurs occasionally, but is by no means common." A note made by Stevenson in August 1881, suggests that young chickens may now and again be numbered among the victims of a vicious stone curlew. He writes: "On the 2nd of this month, Mr. Callow, of Northrepps, heard a screaming noise in his stackyard, which he found to proceed from a bird of this species (the stone curlew), which a hen, in fear for her chickens, was severely buffeting. The bird, scared and exhausted, allowed Mr. Callow to capture it."

Sir Thomas Browne, who refers to the stone curlew as a "handsome tall bird, remarkably eyed, and with a bill not above two inches long," and a note resembling that of the green plover, also states, in a letter to Dr. Christopher Merrett, that he kept these birds in cages; while Lubbock mentions that in 1847 a stone curlew which had been slightly wounded was turned loose in Lady Flowers' garden at Eccles Hall, where its mate used to come every evening off Eccles Heath and spend the night with it. At the beginning of August the bird managed to escape; but in the third week in September, Lubbock, whilst out shooting, found it and ran it down. He returned it to the garden, and its mate, which was with it at the time of its re-capture, at once resumed its habit of visiting it every night. The same authority mentions that the stone curlew sometimes nests very late in the year. On September 26th, 1851, he put up an old bird in the parish of Harling, and found her nest with eggs warm. He saw the eggs in a similar state on the 3rd October, after which someone removed them.

Mr. Edmund Selous, one of the latest writers on the bird life of Breckland, says [1] that the stone curlew often feeds close beside the green plovers, and also with the mistle thrushes, with which it often fights. It is, he remarks, a fighter, and "the rush of this bird along the ground, with neck outstretched, legs bent, and crouching gait—a sort of stealthy speed—is a formidable affair. . . . But what a difference when the rival male stone curlews advance against each other to the attack! Then the carriage is upright—grotesquely so, almost,—and the tail fanned out like a scallop-shell."

[1] In *Bird Life Glimpses*, 1905.

CHAPTER IV

WILD LIFE IN BRECKLAND—*Continued*

JUST before the Devil's Punch Bowl, the first of the Wretham meres, is reached, the Drove skirts a lonely farmstead, and is bordered on one side for a short distance by a high hedge and crab-apple trees. The mere, which is the smallest in Breckland, is situated close to the south side of the road. It is a deep bowl-shaped pit, with a solitary cottage standing near its southern edge, and it is surrounded by pines. Apart from its shape, which suggests that of a Roman amphitheatre, there is nothing very remarkable about it, and too often, considering it from a picturesque point of view, there is not a drop of water in it. At other times the water rises to a height of several feet, and then there sometimes appears in the air above it a circle of mist, locally known as the Devil's nightcap. Far more beautiful than this mere is Fowlmere, situated opposite the Devil's Punch Bowl on the other side of the Drove. This is the largest of the heathland meres, and when it is filled with water there is no more delightful spot in Breckland for a noontide siesta than the slope of the steepish bank on its eastern side, crowned with a group of rugged old Scots firs. For at times this mere is a very fair-sized sheet of water, frequented by an abundance of waterfowl, which may be watched disporting themselves between its swampy eastern margin and the dense growth of alder, willow, larch, and fir bordering its western shore. Its complete isolation from the more frequented highways and byways of the district adds something to its charm; perfect peace seems to have a permanent abode beside it, intensified by the dreamland music of the breeze among the pines, the silent play of sun-gleam and shadow on the still water, and the brooding hush of the surrounding heathlands.

The fact of seven species of duck—the mallard, gadwall, teal, shoveler, garganey, pochard, and tufted duck — breeding on the Breckland meres is in itself enough to give the district exceptional interest for the ornithologist. Mallard and teal, although not so plentiful now as they have been, are still fairly numerous on the meres and along the neighbouring part of the Little Ouse valley. Of the gadwall and tufted duck, a correspondent quoted in the *Transactions of the Norfolk and Norwich Naturalists' Society* writes: " I have been much struck, the last few years, with the large number of tufted ducks and gadwall we now find on the river above Brandon. Ten years ago (this was written in 1899) tufted ducks were not common, and gadwalls unknown; three years ago we killed our first pair, now they breed there every year, and we have seen hundreds in one day." These remarks chiefly apply to that part of Breckland lying between Thetford and Brandon. In respect to the gadwall in West Norfolk generally, Sir Ralph Payne-Gallwey states that its abundance here " is the result of a pair of these birds caught in the South Acre Decoy that were pinioned and turned down on the lake at Narford, where they bred freely and attracted many others, which also remained to nest on this lake. The number of gadwall which frequent one private water alone in this county is computed at from fourteen to fifteen hundred birds. They originated, as described, some years ago, and have spread all over West Norfolk, wherever they could find shelter and were allowed to breed freely, and are now as frequently seen on the wing as any other species. They are purely wild in Norfolk, and this shows how one of the most beautiful and rare of our migratory ducks may be acclimatised in suitable localities." According to Mr. L. H. de Visme Shaw,[1] it is calculated that upwards of a thousand pairs of gadwall now breed annually in South-west Norfolk.

The number of breeding shovelers has also been largely increased of late years, and since the middle of the last century, when the fact of its breeding in Breckland was first definitely established, the pochard has probably nested every year on one or more of the meres. Perhaps the rarest of the Breckland ducks is the garganey, which fifteen years ago was believed to be increasing its numbers in Norfolk, but which of late years has shown a falling-off in the number of nests. All seven of the ducks mentioned have been known to breed on the Wretham meres within the last few years, notwithstanding that the water-level of these meres has been subject to remarkable fluctuations, and in some years all of them have been quite dry. "In the stillness of the summer night," writes Mr. W. G. Clarke,[2] "the music of the meres is weird and strange to unaccustomed ears. The low, contented quacking of the mallard and gadwall, the *knack* of the garganey, the *kree-ah* of the black-headed gull, the low whistle of the pochard, the *crek-rek-rek* of the moorhen, the *currugh-currugh* of the tufted duck as he shifts his quarters, the clear, ringing, oft-repeated *koo* of the coot, the *whit-whit* of the dabchick, and the harsh *kek* of the loon, added to the wailing and whistling of the heathland birds, the lapping of the waters, and the soughing in the pine trees,—who could not wish for such nights again?"

Wild swans frequently visit the Breckland meres. In the spring of 1905 there were several on Fowlmere, and at August-end of the same year there were two there which may have stayed through the summer. At

[1] *Wild-Fowl* (Fur, Feather, and Fin Series), p. 10.
[2] *Zoologist*, April 1898.

the same time Mr. W. G. Clarke and I saw over sixty coots, twenty mallard, sixteen little grebes, and a flock of garganey on the mere, around the margin of which a pair of waders, apparently sandpipers, were flitting. For an hour or more we watched the birds paddling about or diving beneath the open water, our attention being chiefly occupied by the little grebes, of which there seemed to be three or four family parties. The parent birds are said to teach their young to dive by diving with them under their wings; but the young birds we saw had either not yet received this training or were averse to benefiting by it. At any rate, the old birds were continually diving in search of food for their offspring, whose movements, when it was brought to the surface, were very amusing. An old bird would suddenly disappear, leaving one or more of its little brown young ones swimming quietly along the margin of a straggling growth of rushes in the centre of the mere. Ten or fifteen seconds would elapse, and the old bird would reappear, holding in its bill some succulent morsel, for which the youngsters would compete in a short quick race. But they were evidently never sure where the old bird would come to the surface after diving, for sometimes, when he (or she) re-appeared behind them they would go swimming along unconscious of his (or her) emergence. Whether, on these occasions, the old bird called them we were unable to ascertain, owing to the distance they kept from the shore; but at length one of the youngsters would catch sight of it, and would scurry towards it in a most comical fashion. Generally the young one would take the tit-bit from the parent's bill, but sometimes the morsel would be dropped in front of the expectant chick. During the whole of the hour we spent watching this pretty performance the old birds seldom allowed themselves a minute's breathing time above water.

On the same day that we watched the dabchicks on

Fowlmere, Langmere, about a mile eastward on the same side of the Drove, was quite dry. This mere is oval in shape, and in the midst of it there is an island on which grow about a dozen Scots firs. It is situated in a wilder spot than Fowlmere; there are open wastes around it—wide wastes where in autumn the purple of the heather is toned down to a lovely lavender hue by a haze of tawny bents. In prehistoric times, it may be, the island in Langmere provided a safe retreat for some of the dwellers on the far-spreading barrens of Breckland, and it is probable there were pile-dwellings on the mere. At any rate, we have it on good authority that in 1851, when the Wretham West Mere was drained, the remains of such dwellings were discovered in its oozy bed. These consisted of a circular bank of hard white earth, close to the inner circumference of which was a well-like hole about six feet deeper than the bottom of the mere. A circle of alder stakes surrounded the hole, and outside the circle were traces of a flint and marl wall. The remains of a rude ladder were also met with, and in and around the hole were bones of the Celtic ox (*Bos longifrons*) and antlers of the red deer, many of which had been sawn from the skulls and broken, probably in order to extract the marrow. No trace of metal accompanied these relics of the prehistoric inhabitants of Breckland; but there was with them an abundance of those artificially shaped flint discs known to antiquaries as "sling-stones," pointing to the pile-dwelling being of Neolithic date. Five years later, when Wretham Great Mere was drained, a number of oaken posts, "shaped and pointed by human art," were found driven into the bed of the mere.

Of late years the water has rarely risen to such a height in Langmere as to surround the fir-crowned hillock in its midst; usually there has been an uncovered isthmus connecting it with the "mainland." Mr. C. J. Staniland, R.I., who visited the mere in July 1887, described it as "the most impressive of the meres that we saw, lying in the midst of a wild scrubby heath, not a sound but the melancholy wailing of the peewit or the scream of a gull to break the silence; the dozen or so of fir trees on the peninsula standing up in solitary grandeur against the sky." Almost equally impressive is the large oval bed of this mere when it is dry, and one looks down upon it from the crest of the island knoll encompassed by it. At August-end the black-headed gulls have generally taken their departure from their inland summer haunts; but the stone curlew still breaks the silence of the lonesome brecks with its weird whistle, and maybe a late-lingering ringed plover utters its autumnal note as it flits across the stone-strewn wastes. Often as far as eye can see not a single human figure is visible on the wide heaths, which have the appearance of having been uninhabited ever since they were shaped out of the chaos of the waning glacial epoch; but we know that there was a time when primitive man found these barrens a fitting dwelling-place, and the skin-cloaked hunter often sought the red deer among the heather, and lay in wait for the waterfowl on the margin of the meres. And while the rays of the mid-day sun beat down on the browning bracken and withering bents, one rests in the shadow of the pines and tries to conjure up some vision of those early Breckland scenes.

Around the mere there is a settlement of rude dwellings—pit-dwellings with low flint walls, roofed with a rough thatch of dried turf and ling—and beyond it are small patches of cultivated ground, producing flax or a scanty crop of wheat. In and among the huts and around smouldering fires of logs and brushwood are moving women and children clad in coarsely woven linen or cloaks of skins, some of them wearing rudely fashioned ornaments in the shape of bead necklaces and pendants of stone and bone. Beside the fires are several hand-moulded clay bowls, some containing food for the mid-day meal, others water, which, as the coarse pottery will not stand the heat of a fire, is boiled by red-hot flints or "pot-boilers" being dropped into it. Most of the men seem to be absent from the settlement; but outside one of the pit-dwellings, in the midst of a litter of flint flakes, an axe-maker is at work, shaping, with a battered hammer-stone, an axe out of a large flake of black flint. Suspended from the low eaves of the huts are drying skins of bears, wolves, and red deer; other skins, more recently taken from slain beasts, are fastened fur-downwards to the ground with wooden pegs and being cleaned by the women with wooden-handled scrapers of flint. Near another hut, another flint-worker, who works with a stone or bone fabricator, is making some perfectly shaped barbed arrowheads, using for the purpose fragments of thin flint flakes, from which he continually presses tiny chips and flakes, gradually bringing the delicate implements into symmetrical form.

There are woodlands in the far distance, woodlands of sturdy oaks where the wolf lurks and the brown bear has its lair; but for many miles there is an uninterrupted view of richly coloured heathland, dotted here and there with settlements similar to that beside the mere. There is one near by, on the east side of Fowlmere; another on the plateau between the trackway and the northern slope of the river valley; while the smoke from the fires of more removed clusters of pit-dwellings rises above the crest of Bromehill, from the heaths beyond the river, and the far-off border of the great level of water and swamp which is now the Fenland. On the uninhabited tracts droves of great bustards are feeding; on a distant hillside some wild oxen are browsing; and at times a stag is seen standing at gaze on some knoll amid the heather. On the mere an old fisherman, paddling a coracle made out of a single tree trunk, is spreading a net weighted with sinkers of baked clay.

Towards sunset, when the shadows of the isolated

thorns and bird-sown elders lengthen upon the waste, and the whistling stone curlews commerce their evening flight towards the valley, the huntsmen of the settlement are seen returning from the chase, some coming by the old ridge trackway and bringing with them red and roe deer; others with wild boars from the woodlands; and yet others with cranes, ducks, and wild geese from the great fen lake. Most of these men are armed with bows and arrows, but some of them have sling-sticks in their hands and a pouch containing sling-stones hanging by their sides; and two or three, who have taken part in a boar-hunt, carry flint-tipped spears or javelins. These huntsmen, having handed over their prizes to the women, seat themselves around the fires, and presently they are joined by other men of their tribe, who, with picks fashioned of the antlers of the red deer, have been digging for flints in gloomy tunnels in the chalk. Just as the sun is setting, the short-horned oxen, horned sheep, and grunting hogs belonging to the settlement are driven into wooden stockades for the night; the dogs are turned loose to act as their guardians; and fresh fuel is heaped upon the fires, so that the leaping flames may prevent the intrusion of night-prowling beasts. For a while after nightfall the firelight occasionally reveals the face of some wakeful hunter or herdsman as he moves restlessly among the huts; but it is not long before the inhabitants of the heathland settlement are all asleep. And then the only sounds that break the silence of the dark barrens are the cries of the curlews in the valley, the piping of the plovers as they circle above the sleeping village, and the howling of the wolves in the distant woods.

A short distance from Langmere, on the other side of the Drove, is Ringmere, in the neighbourhood of which was fought the great battle between the armies of Ulfketyl and Thorkill. This mere lies close beside the road from Thetford to Wretham, so its wild life—chiefly interesting on account of the various species of duck occurring upon it—is usually less tame and undisturbed than that of Fowlmere. Like the Devil's Punch Bowl, Ringmere is a circular mere, and a plantation, chiefly consisting of silver birches, forms a background to it when it is seen from the northern edge of the crater-like pit.

Mention has already been made of the strange fluctuations of the water-level in these Wretham meres. In August 1905, both Langmere and the Devil's Punch Bowl were dry, while Fowlmere and Ringmere contained a fair quantity of water. During 1901 and 1902 all four of these meres were dry, and from an interesting paper contributed by Mr. W. G. Clarke to the *Transactions of the Norfolk and Norwich Naturalists' Society*,[1] it appears that during the last fifty years there have been rather remarkable changes in these picturesque lakelets, which have sometimes been quite full of water for years together, and then for several years have had little or no water in them. Mr. Clarke deals with this at length in his paper, and comes to the conclusion that " the rainfall is solely responsible for the fluctuations of the water in the meres, not as surface water—or why should ponds and wells on higher levels contain water when the meres are dry?—but so far as the rainfall affects the level of saturation in the Chalk." In this connection it may be mentioned that during the last dry period the bed of Fowlmere was ploughed and harrowed without any difficulty, and a good crop of swedes and cabbages grown there. On a previous occasion, when a similar state of things obtained, corn and vetches were grown in the bed of the mere.

Having reached Ringmere, we are on the verge of Roudham Heath, where the ancient trackway we have been following joins Peddars' Way, a characteristic

[1] Vol. vii. p. 499 *et seq.*

stretch of which runs parallel with the Thetford and Swaffham railway line on its east side between Wretham station and Roudham junction. On Roudham Heath, as on several others in Breckland, the ringed plover often nests, this being the most curious fact in connection with the bird life of the district, though it seems equally strange that the relics of a seaside flora, together with several species of coast-frequenting insects, especially beetles, should also be found on the South-west Norfolk and North-west Suffolk heaths and brecks, so far from the sea. It has been suggested that the plants occur here owing to the salts contained in the drift sands through the decomposition of felspar; but, as the Rev. W. M. Hind points out in his *Flora of Suffolk*, a marine flora is not found elsewhere, however rich districts may be in felspathic rocks, unless there are also indications of a comparatively recent presence of the sea. He thinks it possible that the insects may be attracted by the plants; but the latter he considers to be lineal descendents of plants which grew here when a salt or brackish arm of the sea extended to the border of Breckland across what is now the level of the Fens. A similar explanation may account for the presence of the ringed plovers which yearly nest on the stony brecks; but there is, of course, a possibility that many years ago some of the these shore-breeding birds were attracted to the district by the flint-strewn surface of the ground, which in many places bears a close resemblance to a pebbly beach. The earliest reference to the breeding of the species here appears to be that made in the MS. diary[1] of John Drew Salmon, F.L.S., who under date of February 16th, 1834, writes: " Six ring dotterels and one great plover on the warren (Thetford). Mr. Reynolds[2] says he heard some ringed plover soon after Christmas on Stanford Warren." Sir Thomas Browne,

[1] Preserved in the Norwich Castle Museum.
[2] A Thetford bird-stuffer.

though always on the alert for anything curious and "out of the common," makes no reference to their breeding here. The Breckland name for the ringed plover is "stone-hatch," owing to its habit of lining its nest with small stones.

Of the seaside plants occurring so far from the sea the commonest is the sand sedge (*Carex arenaria*), which flourishes amazingly on the sandy heaths on both sides of the Little Ouse, though it is more abundant, perhaps, on the Suffolk heaths. This sedge, as is well known, spreads rapidly by means of underground runners, and for this reason is locally known as "net-rein"; in several places it serves the same useful purpose here as among the sand dunes, where it helps to bind together the wind-heaped sand. The fact— referred to by Mr. Wallis—of rabbits disliking it is also, no doubt, in part responsible for its maintaining itself so well here, and it is noteworthy that where it occurs in any quantity very little else will grow. Another plant generally found growing beside brackish water, but which also occurs in Breckland, is the golden dock (*Rumex maritimus*), which in a dwarf form can generally be found in the bed of Langmere when that mere is dry. One or two seashore grasses have survived during many centuries the departure of the sea from the ancient shores of Breckland; also a dwarf form of the centaury.

In connection with the flora of Beckland, mention may be made—first, of two or three plants remarkably abundant here, but nothing like so plentiful in other parts of England; and, secondly, of some of the rarer plants found in the district.

Of the former, the most interesting species is an alien known as the Canadian fleabane (*Erigeron canadense*), a plant which, as its name implies, was introduced into this country from North America, and which has so taken possession of the broken soil in certain parts of the Breck district during the last half century, as to have become quite a pest. The flower-heads of this plant, which have a superficial resemblance to those of the common groundsel, have a pale yellow disc and, sometimes, faintly purple rays; but as a wild flower it cannot be described as attractive, and the farmers of the light-soil lands would undoubtedly be glad if someone discovered a method of exterminating it. But, like the thistles and dandelion, it bears seeds that are carried away in all directions by the wind, and by this means it has, since 1862,—when it was first recorded for this part of the country,—firmly established itself. The first seeds of the Canadian fleabane are said to have been introduced into England in a stuffed bird, which, on being damaged by moth, was thrown on to a rubbish heap near London. There the seeds took root, and in a very short time the plant became a common weed in the neighbourhood, from whence it has since spread into most of the English counties. It is doubtful, however, if it be anywhere so abundant as on some of the large brecks, especially on the Suffolk side of the Little Ouse, where Canadian fleabane and ragwort—the latter the most conspicuous autumn flower of the district —cover hundreds of acres of ground.

Another common Breckland species, the cut-leaved mignonette (*Reseda lutea*), is stated by Sir J. D. Hooker to be very rare in England; but it has been recorded for fifty-three of the counties and vice-counties recognised by the *London Catalogue* (ninth edition). It is a more attractive plant than the Canadian fleabane, and where, as is the case here, it grows in large quantities, covering many acres of sandy soil, the general effect of its innumerable greenish-yellow flowers is far from unpleasing. It is to be met with in all parts of Breckland; but was never more conspicuous in any one locality than in the early autumn of 1905, when it sprung up in remarkable abundance on Rushford Heath, after many acres of ground, which had been undisturbed for some years, were broken up by means of a scarifier. The common ling (*Calluna vulgaris*) imparts its rich colour to large tracts of the primitive heathland of the district; but, strange to say, its frequent companion moorland flower, the fine-leaved heath (*Erica cinerea*), is very rare.

Among the rarer plants of the district are the lesser meadow rue (*Thalictrum minus*), which has been recorded for several localities around Lakenheath and Mildenhall; the pasque flower (*Anemone Pulsatilla*), which seems to be almost extinct; three fumitories (*Fumaria densiflora, parviflora* and *vaillantii*); the maiden pink (*Dianthus deltoides*); the Spanish and conical catchflies (*Silene Otites* and *conica*); the perennial knawell (*Scleranthus perrennis*); the hairy broom (*Genista pilosa*), which has been found on the Suffolk side of the Little Ouse; the purple milk vetch (*Astragalus hypoglottis*), recorded for several Suffolk-side heaths and also for Mundford in Norfolk; the horseshoe vetch (*Hippocrepis comosa*), which was first recorded for Suffolk by the old herbalist Gerarde; the rupture-wort (*Herniaria glabra*), which is very rare on the Norfolk heaths, but not uncommon on those of North-west Suffolk; the quinsywort (*Asperula cynanchia*), which occurs frequently on the Icklingham and Mildenhall heathlands, and was first discovered in Suffolk by Dillenius; the field gentian (*Gentiana campestris*); the bastard toadflax (*Thesium humifusum*); and the dwarf orchis (*Orchis ustulata*).

In rambling along the ancient Drove road the traveller crosses some of the wildest tracts of Breckland, but he has to confine himself to the Norfolk side of the Little Ouse, and to be content with occasional glimpses of the wide stretches of Suffolk heathland and breckland equally characteristic of the district. On the Suffolk as on the Norfolk side of the river, there are many miles of primitive heathland where the stone curlew nests and rabbits abound, and hundreds of acres of stony breck where the ringed plover and the wheatear are often undisturbed by man for weeks together. Desolate lands they are, and under certain aspects more impressive by their dreariness than by their primitiveness; yet, as has been said, they have a certain fascination that seldom permits one to grow weary of them, and is often felt even the more strongly when one has left them for scenes of admitted loveliness and charm. One cannot look down upon these wastes of bracken, heather, and flint-strewn sand without feeling impressed by the fact that, deserted as they are to-day, there were periods of the remote past when they were peopled by some of the earliest inhabitants of England. This is not the place in which to deal with the remarkable discoveries of Palæolithic implements which have made the valley of the Little Ouse so widely famous among students of the earlier periods of the Stone Age; but even the knowledge that thousands of such implements have been found in the Breckland river gravels tends to increase the interest of the district for those who know it well. Great and almost unimaginable changes have taken place since those remote days when England was connected by a land-link with the Continent, and man dwelt here beside rivers which have long since vanished so completely that even their courses are unknown; but the relics of that human occupation of Breckland tell their tale to-day, though they tell it as might such relics strewn on the cold bleak surface of a dead world. A far more human interest attaches to those implements of the Later Stone Age which the rabbit, the mole, and the plough so frequently bring to light; also to the Neolithic flint quarries called Grimes Graves, where the deer-horn picks, stone axes, and rudely shaped chalk lamps of primitive man have been found lying in the dark subterranean tunnels in which he worked, perhaps twenty thousand years ago. Between the present and that long-gone time, when man knew of no harder substance than stone out of which to fashion his domestic implements and weapons of warfare and the chase, there remains an interesting link in the flint-knapping industry still carried on in the little Breckland town of Brandon, and which survived at Icklingham and in one or two other neighbouring villages until a few years ago.

On the Suffolk side of the Little Ouse the main road from Thetford to Brandon crosses Thetford Warren, to which some reference has been made in connection with the account of rabbit-trapping. This hilly warren, in all probability, was one of the resorts of King James I., who had a hunting-lodge in Thetford, and is well known to have been an enthusiastic falconer. That he amused himself with hawking while at Thetford is evident from a passage in the MS. diary of Hans Jacob Wurmsser von Vendenheym, who was with him there, and who refers to his having witnessed the taking of dotterels by means of a sparrow-hawk, though, as Professor Newton remarks,[1] whether the birds, after being frightened together by the hawk, were taken by hand or with a net is not clear. Dotterel-netting was, however, a common sport in Norfolk in the seventeenth century, and in Willughby's *Ornithology* (1678) it is mentioned, on the authority of a certain Mr. Peter Dent, "a gentleman of Norfolk," that it was the custom for six or seven persons to go in company in quest of these birds, which, when found, were driven into a net by their pursuers getting behind them and striking stones together. That they were easily secured, is suggested by some lines in Drayton's *Polyolbion*, where we read:

> "The Dotterel, which we think a very dainty dish,
> Whose taking makes much sport, as no man more can wish.
> For as you creep, or cower, or lie, or stoop, or go,
> So, marking you with care, the apish bird doth do;
> And acting everything, doth never mark the net,
> Till he be in the snare which men for him have set."

---

[1] "Hawking in Norfolk." Appendix to the *Fauna of Norfolk*, 1879 edition.

There is a tale told of a certain local parson who was so skilled in imitating the call-note of the dotterel, that he was able to provide exceptionally good sport for King James, and the King was so gratified that he promised to him preferment at the first opportunity. Time passed, however, and the reward was not forthcoming, so the parson went up to London with the view of jogging his Majesty's memory. He happened to arrive just as the King was passing through the city, and it occurred to him to whistle his famous dotterel-call, which his Majesty no sooner heard than he exclaimed: "Why, Lord! there's our old dotterel parson!" and he sent for him, and at once fulfilled his forgotten promise.

Kite-flying was a favourite branch of hawking with King James,[1] who must have had ample opportunities for practising it around Thetford. About the middle of the eighteenth century it was taken up by George, Earl of Orford, who employed a Dutch falconer, and flew his hawks at Eriswell, a heathland parish within the bounds

[1] Respecting the connection of Kings James I. and Charles I. with Thetford, Mr. W. G. Clarke informs me that in 1607 instructions were sent for the preservation of the King's game within a twelve-mile range of Thetford; while in 1611, Thomas Cockayne was appointed for life, keeper of the game at Thetford. In 1614, John Coward and his son were appointed keepers of the stags and hawks. In 1626 a warrant was issued to Sir Thomas Germaine to preserve the game of King Charles I. within five miles of Thetford, and a decade later similar authority was given to Sir Lionel Tollemache, the radius then being twelve miles, and the game "hare, pheasant, partridge, and other wild-fowl."

Hans Jacob Wurmsser von Vandenheym, whose Diary is quoted on page 89, also tells us that after the Duke of Wurtemberg (whom the diarist had accompanied to Thetford) had been with King James to watch the dotterel-hawking, he supped with his Majesty, "and upon rising from table they went in a coach to the river, where they saw cormorants, birds which at a sign given by the master who has trained them, plunge under the water and catch eels and other fish, and which at another signal were made to give them up and disgorge them alive." These cormorants were probably kept at Thetford for the King's amusement, for we read that when he visited the town in 1608 he was "welcomed . . . by three cormorants on the church steeple."—See *The King's House at Thetford.* By H. F. Killick; *Proceedings of the Norfolk and Norwich Archæological Society,* vol. xvi. p. 18.

of Breckland. At his death, Colonel Wilson (afterwards Lord Berners) became the leader of the Breckland falconers, and revived the almost-forgotten pastime of heron-hawking at Didlington, a few miles north of Brandon. A large heronry there generally provided the necessary quarries for this sport; but when herons were not available the hawks were hooded-off at rooks, stockdoves, and stone curlews. Lord Berners, as the chief of the local falconers, was succeeded by Edward Clough Newcome, of Hockwold, who, when the herons grew scarce, managed to induce a colony of rooks to establish themselves near his house. Of this enthusiast Professor Newton writes: "The open county around Hockwold, Wilton, and Feltwell was his most constant ground, and here, from the beginning of March until the corn was well grown, he might be nearly always met. He had a boy to carry the cadge, and occasionally to unhood a second hawk; but he was his own falconer both at home and afield. . . . Somewhat later in the season, Lakenheath and Wangford warrens in Suffolk were places of resort; and here stone curlews often furnished a flight, while sometimes the hawks were taken into the fens for a chance of a crow or of a pie. When the corn-fields were cleared he had some diversion with merlins, but herein he was not so very successful, for the larks, as soon as they had got over their moult, and were strong upon the wing, generally beat their pursuers—which, it must be remembered, were eyesses. I remember his once having a sparrow-hawk which was rather good at taking blackbirds, but I do not think he ever possessed a goshawk while I knew him, and indeed he viewed with contempt, that he was hardly at the trouble of disguising, the kind of flight which that bird affords. I happened to be present when William Barr, the well-known Scottish falconer, who was then travelling through England exhibiting his hawks wherever he could, came to Hockwold on a visit. I remember the surprise with which we all saw him carry a hamper on to the field, and produce from it one falcon after another. These, when let go, circled around, and obeyed each signal given by their master. Mr. Newcome was, however, greatly struck with the marvellous control over his birds exercised by Barr, who probably never exhibited their somewhat tame performance to a more appreciative company. So thoroughly docile were his hawks, that on one occasion Mr. Newcome and I went out snipe-shooting attended by Barr, who had a falcon flying nearly all the time to make the snipes lie to us—and lie they did, for it was almost impossible to make them rise."

On the lonely wastes of Breckland, as elsewhere, one may have experiences which make so deep an impression on the mind that in after days they stand out in clear relief among the recollections of past events and scenes. Two such experiences are still vividly impressed upon my mind. One was a noontide hour spent in a fir wood on the high ground of Bromehill. It was a gloomy autumn day, and while rambling over the brecks extending northward from the river valley, I had been watching at intervals the distant rain-storms sweeping across the valley and hiding the far-off level of the fens. Presently the midday gloom grew deeper, so that even the changing bracken seemed to lose its brilliant hues, and to escape the worst of the downpour that threatened, I took shelter in a fir wood bordered by a dense thicket of broom. There, not a glimpse could be had of the valley nor of the upland barrens of bent and bracken; but beneath the wide dark canopy of the tall firs avenues of seemingly lifeless silence could be seen stretching away into impenetrable depths of gloom. Over the bare floor of the wood not a creature moved; between the countless motionless boles not a bird took flight; for a while the stillness and silence of the scene suggested a haunted wood where no sound was ever heard but the melancholy hooting of the owl, and no movement ever stirred the air save the soft wing-beats of the flickering bat. Even the sound of the falling rain failed to enter the dark portals of that temple of silence, where everything seemed under an enchanter's spell. But presently, when the silence had grown so intense that one almost held one's breath, a breeze began to make mournful music among the myriads of fir needles, and the dark wood became filled as by the voices of a multitude singing a low, sweet, sighing song. At times it sounded so far away that it seemed to come from the remotest depths of the wood; then it rose gradually until one could imagine some vast procession of mourners slowly advancing along the dark woodland cloisters, chanting a dirge as they came. Then for a while the wind's song died away, and when it was heard again one could fancy it was being sung in another and less despondent key; for the breeze had strengthened and made the song a storm song, which was being sung among the crags and caverns of a wave-beaten coast. Like the distance-deadened voice of the sea it rose and fell, and as the strength of the breeze increased, and cool currents of air came stealing through the wood, the dim wood itself seemed to be a cavern which had never known the sunlight—a cavern beside the "echoing bay of Carmona."

The other experience was a summer-night visit to an isolated barrow on a small, high plateau near the verge of the Little Ouse valley. It was an hour after sunset when I climbed the valley slope, and I had hardly reached the high ground when the moon rose from behind a distant belt of woodland, filling the misty valley with silvery light, and revealing the dark outline of the barrow against the deep blue of the sky. As I approached the mound, two or three rabbits which had been frisking on its sides scampered away and vanished into their burrows, while a sleeping bird, probably a lark or a pipit, was startled from its nest or some hollow in the ground, and passed before me like the shadow of a bat. From the top of the barrow the surface of the flint-strewn plateau showed white in the moonlight, as though it were strewn with the bleaching bones of the men whose chieftain, perhaps, was buried in the heart of the ancient mound. Now and again a stone curlew uttered its wild whistle as it flew from the heathland to the valley, and once a rabbit shrieked as though a stoat had seized it; but apart from such occasional cries of wakeful wild life the only sound to be heard was the soft "sishing" of the breeze among the bents. All day the open barrens had been exposed to the heat of a blazing sun, which had made the flints on the brecks so hot that they could scarcely be held in the hand; but now the breeze, as it came to the barrow from across the valley, was pleasantly cool, and laden with the fragrance of heath grass and thyme. It was, indeed, an air such as in East Anglia can only be breathed on the dry uplands of Breckland, where the grass and flowers wither like the leaves on a broken oak branch, and the soil itself is sweet and clean as the seashore sand.

There was nothing in the night, perhaps, to make it more impressive than the other peaceful moonlight nights I have passed abroad in the lone places of the countryside; but it has a place apart from them in my memory, owing to that hour I spent on the lonely grave mound. A few men, such as he who sleeps on the Samoan hilltop, have been singularly fortunate in regard to the place of their interment, and among them I must reckon that unknown chieftain, if such he was, who many centuries ago was laid to rest in that high Breckland barrow. Forgotten he is, and even his race is unknown; but is he not more to be envied than the most famous man who rests under the cold marble of a cathedral tomb? On that lonesome breezy height mortality is seldom mocked by the careless footsteps of the unheeding quick, and the renewal of life continually going on around the warrior's grave is the true emblem of immortality. It seemed to me as I stood there, that far from being dead, he was still a part of the growing grass, the fragrant thyme; that the breath of his life was still in the passing breeze, that he was not dead nor even sleeping. To all around him he had been and was still akin; time for him was nothing, for he was it; he grew with the grass and thyme, and moved on the wings of the wind. In the mound was only the husk of his life, the cast-off integument of a season's growth, in which he had existed for a while, before entering upon a wider life. Now he was one with the moonlight and the breeze. "There is something," writes Jefferies, "beyond the philosophies in the light, in the grass-blades, the leaf, the grasshopper, the sparrow on the wall. Some day the great and beautiful thought which hovers on the confines of the mind will at last alight. In that is hope, the whole sky is full of abounding hope."

CHAPTER V

THE REED PHEASANT

IN an earlier chapter some reference is made to the lost breeding birds of East Anglia. There is, unfortunately, a rather long list of them—longer, in all probability, than any other English district of like size can show—but although the great bustard, the avocet, the ruff, the black tern, and several other species are lost to us, and not likely ever again to be numbered among our breeding birds, we find some satisfaction in the fact that as a result of protection a few species which appeared to be on the verge of extinction have re-established themselves, and there is no immediate fear of their being added to our "black list." But while congratulating ourselves on this, we must not imagine that the time has come when the advocates of bird protection can afford to pause in their good work. So long as the bird-netter is permitted to use his clap-nets on the Yarmouth Denes, so long as the kestrel and the owl are found nailed to the keeper's door, so long as the nests of the lapwing and redshank decrease in number in our marshes, and those of the black-headed gull are systematically raided every year, so long will the Wild Birds' Protection Acts be in need of amendment, or their local operation be in need of extension.

Among the birds that were threatened with extinction, but which of late years have benefited by protection, is the beautiful little bearded titmouse, better known to the dwellers in the Broads district, where it has its last British stronghold, as the "reed pheasant." The "gem of the Broads" it has been called, and well it deserves the name; for at the present time it is certainly, to observers who know where to look for it and how best to study its habits, the most attractive ornithological feature of that popular district.

More than two hundred years ago, when Sir Thomas Browne compiled his list of the birds of Norfolk, he was apparently unaware of the existence of the bearded tit in the county of his adoption, nor did he know that such a bird was to be found in England; but about two years after the completion of his list he seems to have heard of it for the first time; for in a communication to John Ray he mentioned the occurrence "in an osier yard" of a "little bird of a tawney colour on the back, and a blew head and yellow bill and black legs," which he called the silerella, and which was undoubtedly a bearded tit. But until Sir Robert Abdy re-discovered it in Essex it did not find its way into any authoritative catalogue of British birds. At no time does it appear to have had a wide distribution in this country, and Mr. J. H. Gurney, though he has discovered records of its occurrence in twenty-seven counties, finds that in the cases of several of them there have only been single occurrences, while in others there is no authentic record of breeding. In fact, as a breeding bird it seems to have been confined to the eastern counties, the eastern Midlands, and the southern counties as far west as Dorset and Hampshire. About the middle of the eighteenth century it was said to be not well enough known in England to have a name; but in his *Natural History of Belvoir* the poet Crabbe calls it the "bearded manica," and states that one was shot near Melton Mowbray, in Leicestershire. Subsequently it became known as the "bearded pinnock," and was supposed to be more common in the marshes bordering the Thames than anywhere else in England; but in 1830, Mr.

J. D. Hoy, of Stoke-Nayland, in Suffolk, contributed some valuable notes to the *Magazine of Natural History*, in which he rightly stated that the Norfolk Broads were the favourite places of the resort of this bird; adding, that during the autumn and winter bearded pinnocks were found distributed all along the Suffolk coast, wherever there were large tracts of reeds, and that he found them numerous, in the breeding season, on the skirts of Whittlesea, and not uncommon in the fenny district of Lincolnshire. He gave some interesting information about their habits, and asserted that in winter he had found them so intent on searching for the seeds of the reed, that he had been able to take them with a bird-limed twig attached to the end of a fishing-rod.

Strangely enough, Lubbock, in his *Fauna of Norfolk*, omits to mention this exquisite little bird; but among his MS. notes there was one in which he speaks of it as "a common resident among the Broads," but "fastidious in its choice of situation." This was written about sixty years ago, and about that time commenced the persecution of the species by bird and egg collectors which nearly resulted in its becoming extinct as a British breeding bird. From then until a few years ago it appears to have decreased in numbers almost yearly, until, in 1898, Mr. Gurney estimated that there were only about thirty-three nests in the whole of the Broads district. Since then there has been a marked increase in its numbers, and, provided that it continues to receive the protection it deserves, there now seems to be no reason why it should not survive as long as the district remains a suitable resort for it. Whether the Broadland bearded tits have their numbers increased from time to time by small flocks of immigrants from the Continent, is uncertain; but evidence from abroad points to these frail little birds being quite capable of crossing the sea. That there is no regular immigration seems fairly certain. At the time when it was considered to be quite non-migratory, some curious theories were advanced to account for its occurrence in England. Charles Kingsley, in his delightful essay on *The Fens*, suggests that its presence in this country tends to prove that it was formerly possible for it to make an overland journey from the Continent, across the wide tract of swamp and woodland which once connected England with Holland and Belgium. Buffon, however, did not credit it with having been so long established here, and affirmed that all the bearded tits found in England had sprung from a pair the Countess of Albemarle allowed to escape from a cage; but as it was not until 1743 that the Countess brought several of these birds from Copenhagen, this statement calls for no comment. Although commonly known as the bearded tit, it is very doubtful whether it be a tit at all. As Mr. Bowdler Sharpe points out, its plumage is unlike that of any Palæarctic tit, though its tail somewhat resembles that of the long-tailed tit. Dr. Gadow, judging from its internal structure, is disposed to consider it akin to the finches; while other ornithologists have looked upon it as an aberrant kind of bunting. As the best way out of a difficulty, family rank is now generally accorded to it, and it is placed next to the tits.

If one wishes to see the "reed pheasant" in its native haunts, a day should be chosen when there is scarcely enough breeze stirring to make a ripple on the water or a whisper among the reeds. You row your boat—a flat-bottomed marsh boat or a gun-punt for choice—down a dike just wide enough to permit of two wherries passing each other, and presently, though the channel is still narrow, you see that, instead of being bordered by a firm bank, it is widening into what was once a large sheet of water, but now is what is called a "grown-up" broad. On either side of you the young reeds are rising green amid the leafless yellow stems of last year's crop; intermingled with them are brown-topped reedmaces and the yellow blossoms of the greater spearwort; and beneath, as far as the eye can penetrate the dense lacustrine jungle, the silvery-white water-lily floats like a fairy boat on the surface of the still water. While you keep to the channel there is always a chance of a passing wherry reminding you that you are in a byway connected with one of the main waterways of the district; but at a point where in June a marsh islet is covered with the hyacinthine blossoms of the beautiful bogbean, you turn aside into a narrower dike leading into the watery wilderness. There, shut in on all sides by tall reeds and rank-growing swamp flowers, you have a feeling of complete isolation: nowhere is there a sign of even the occasional presence of man, and not a sound is heard out of harmony with the wild-life voices of primitive solitude. Every bend of the dike seems to bring you deeper into the heart of the fenny labyrinth.

It seems just the place to keep a secret—just the place one would come to in search of the relics of a vanishing flora and fauna. Pushing your way through the reed jungles and swamp flowers, you would hardly be astonished should you suddenly see before you the great fen ragwort, nor would the appearance of a great copper butterfly cause very much surprise; even now the beautiful swallow-tail butterfly often flutters like a wind-blown autumn leaf over the ragged reed-tops. Conceal yourself and your boat among the reeds, and if you keep still and silent, you will have many welcome glimpses of bird life. Sedge and reed warblers fly down into the boat and run about in it within reach of your hand; kingfishers come and fish close beside you; coots, notwithstanding their readiness to see and scent danger, venture out of the swampy cover and dive in the open water; even the great crested grebe, though more at home on the open Broads, sometimes brings its young into this narrow channel, carrying them, should they be tired, on its back like the swan.

In your reed-girt hiding-place, should the day be warm, you will probably be troubled by innumerable midges; but their attentions must be ignored if you wish to watch the reed pheasants. These, if you have previously made their acquaintance, will betray their presence by their unmistakable call-note—one of the most musical sounds to be heard in the Norfolk Lakeland. It is a low but ringing and metallic note which has been vocalised as *ping*, *ping* and *ching*, *ching*, and it has been likened to the clashing of tiny cymbals and a chord struck on a French mandolin. The late Lord Lilford, who was acquainted with the bird in its Norfolk haunts, stated that "its note once heard can never be mistaken for that of any other European bird"; while Mr. J. E. Harting has discovered that it can be imitated by balancing a penny on the middle finger of each hand and lightly touching the edges of the pennies together. When a little flock of reed pheasants is in possession of a reed-bed, the frequent repetition of this sweet chiming note is very pleasing, and whenever I hear it I cannot help imagining that I am listening to just such music as would be heard in fairyland.

Should the birds be near you when you hear this note, you will also hear intermittent rustlings and flutterings amid the reeds, and it may be that before a bird is seen you will notice little mouse-like movements among the reed-stems, and an occasional downward bending of a reed blade. Indeed, it may easily happen that a bird will pass before your eyes unnoticed, so harmoniously does its colouring blend with that of the dry and leafless reeds which have been standing all through the winter. But presently from the heart of the reed-bed there emerges a beautiful little grey-headed, orange-brown bird, which, by its black moustache, drooping downward like a Chinaman's, you recognise as a cock reed pheasant. It alights on the middle of a reed, which is set swinging for a moment by its feather-weight; but almost at once it begins running like a mouse up the stem, pausing now and again to search in the sheaths of the blades for grubs and insects, and at times going through a small acrobatic performance, hanging first head-downwards and then sideways on the reed. Its tail is as long as that of the long-tailed tit, a bird whose movements the reed pheasant frequently reproduces while searching for food; but as soon as it takes flight over a reed-bed or across an open space among the reeds, you understand how it came about that the Broadsmen gave it the name of reed pheasant. For there is no British bird whose short flights are so pheasant-like as those of the bearded tit.

All day long, when the days are fine and almost breezeless, the reed pheasants are active in their quiet haunts, and you may spend hours in watching them without wearying of their sweet music and charming ways. During the hour before sunset they seem more active than ever, probably because at that time the night-flying insects are becoming plentiful among the reeds; and even after the sun has set they are laggards in going to rest for the night. On calm summer evenings, while rowing quietly in a gun-punt along the reed-bordered channels of a "grown-up" Broad, I have often heard them creeping and rustling among the reeds even when it has been too dark to see them. At such times half a dozen reed pheasants will suddenly fill a silent reed-bed with restless life, and against the darkening sky you see the reed tops tremble as their stems are shaken by the unseen birds. Even by moonlight, should the moon rise soon after sunset, some of them may be seen flitting to and fro, silent save for the rustling they make in the reeds. Their orange-brown plumage then seems to have turned grey, and their movements, as they flit from reed to reed, are almost like those of great moths.

In winter the reed pheasants wander far and wide over Broadland, and there is a chance of meeting with them wherever reeds grow; but early in spring, before the earliest of the chiffchaffs and willow warblers have come back to us, they return to their breeding haunts, where there are young birds before, as we say in Norfolk, March is "out." The nest, a rather bulky structure for so small a bird, is never, as has sometimes been stated, suspended among the reeds, but is built among the sedgy undergrowth, and generally on a kind of platform of dead and down-bent stalks. It usually consists of dry reed leaves, which are rather loosely woven, and lined with fragments from the reed tops, locally known as "reed feather"; but occasionally dry marsh litter is used for the nest, and it is lined with soft grass. Rarely a nest is found in a dwarf thicket of sweet gale. The eggs, usually five or six in number, vary considerably in size and are rather large for the size of the bird; they are china-white in ground colour, with a pinkish tinge when newly laid, and are faintly dotted and scrawled with brown. The spots and scrawls are generally distributed over the surface, and there is no cluster of them round the larger end. As Mr. Richard Kearton remarks, it would be difficult to confuse them with those of any other species. Sometimes as many as nine eggs are found in a nest, and in one instance no less than twelve were found; but in this case there were two hens near the nest. Not infrequently eggs are laid before the nest is completed, and these are sometimes found covered over with a layer of nest lining.

The young birds, like the adult female, are without the black moustache which distinguishes the adult cock bird, and they can also be recognised by their having a black back and a black stripe on either side of the crown. According to the late Mr. E. T. Booth, the young males can be distinguished by their bills being more lemon-coloured. As a nestling the young bird is remarkable for having a deep pink mouth, on the roof of which are four rows of raised black and white dots, which Mr. Gurney compares to the contrasted colours of the bogbean flower. During the period of its helplessness it receives quite as much attention from the cock bird as from the hen. Up and down the reed stems he runs for hours together, industriously seeking insects and their larvæ, while as a change of diet for his growing offspring he often brings them a small succulent mollusc which has crawled a short distance up the stem of some swamp plant. From March until midsummer he has little time for rest; for scarcely has one little family relieved him of the responsibility of its maintenance than a second clutch of eggs is laid by his plain little mate, whom he again assists in their incubation. Indeed, the fact of nests with eggs having been found as late as the third week in July is suggestive of a third clutch being laid.

But by mid-August the time of parental responsibility is at an end, and there is a return of the restlessness which keeps the reed pheasants wandering about the Broadland all through the winter. At this time they gather together in flocks of from ten to twenty, which some have said are family parties, and their musical *chinging* is heard not only on the Broads, where the reeds grow in dense jungles, but on the upper and lower reaches of the rivers, where there are only reeds enough to make a scanty fringe on the margin of the ronds. Should you be afloat, or trudging along the river-wall at this season, you may sometimes encounter a lively party making its way, by a series of short flights, up or down the river. You will notice the birds at first, perhaps, in a reed-bed, where they will be feeding on the reed seeds and such edible morsels as can be found near the water-level, and they will be as active and musical as in their love-making days; but presently, as though at some understood signal, they will all take flight together to some neighbouring reed-bed, into which they drop suddenly and disappear from view. And no matter how sharp may be the winter, they will not forsake the Broads and rivers; for, notwithstanding their frail appearance, they are hardy little birds, and can generally manage to pick up a living there, even when the conditions are such that the reed buntings are glad to abandon the waterside and join the "wheat-pickers" in the farmyards and upland fields. But while they can endure the hardship of scanty fare, they can seldom avoid having their numbers sadly diminished by persecution at the hands of the marshland gunners, who, tempted by the bribes of thoughtless persons and bird-stuffers, are too often on the alert to shoot these dainty little birds. This, indeed, is an easy thing to do; for at this time of the year the reed pheasant shows very little objection to the presence of man, and you may often approach within a few feet of a feeding flock without disturbing them. Judging by the number of dead reed pheasants I have once or twice seen brought into a taxidermist's shop, there must sometimes be a wholesale "slaughter of the innocents," due, perhaps, to a habit of the species referred to by Lubbock, who states that in cold weather the bearded tits nestle together in a close ball upon the same reed. On one occasion, having asked a marshman to shoot some of these birds for him for preservation, he found that those brought to him were spoiled by having been killed with large shot. To prevent a repetition of this, he supplied the man with some of the smallest dust shot, of which, however, he accepted only two charges, observing, "This will be sufficient. I know where there are some reed pheasants. I shall watch for them just before dark, when they make a ball of themselves." The man subsequently brought to Lubbock six birds killed at one shot. That the birds brought to them are badly damaged owing to the size of the shot used, is a frequent matter of complaint by the bird-stuffers.

The question has been raised whether all the flocks of reed pheasants found scattered over the Broads district in winter consist of birds which have spent the summer there. Mr. Gurney, who discusses this question in his valuable monograph on the species, remarks that, "reasoning from the analogous case of the wild duck, snipe, and redshank, they probably are not," adding that the bird is said to be a summer visitant to some of its Dutch and German habitats, and migratory, "and there is a good deal in common between the Dutch Fens and the Norfolk Broads." He also mentions the occurrence during the winter in recent years of reed pheasants at Cley, Burnham, and Morston on the North Norfolk coast, and suggests that these may have been birds which had crossed the North Sea. "Frail as it is," he writes, "it is capable of an over-sea flight, as is proved by its turning up on six occasions in the Island of Heligoland." In the *Reports of the Migrations of Birds*, there is a note of a reed pheasant having been seen at the Landguard Lighthouse on the Suffolk coast on February 16th, 1887, and another note from Yarmouth stating that on November 13th a "nice lot of bearded tits are said to have come in at a great height, and from the east."

One of the most interesting papers dealing with the reed pheasant is that which Mr. J. Young contributed to the *Transactions of the Norfolk and Norwich Naturalists' Society*,[1] and which treats of the bird in confinement. It is, he says, by far the most interesting cage-pet of which he has any knowledge, and he thinks it would not be a difficult bird to breed in confinement, provided one could hit upon a suitable food for the young ones. At first it is shy and timid, but it soon acquires confidence, and becomes exceedingly tame. Owing to its possessing an affectionate disposition, it is advisable to keep a number together; for even during the breeding season quarrels among them are unknown. "Should one die," he writes, "the rest proclaim their grief by loud and incessant calls, nor do they cease calling for some days. It is almost impossible to keep one alone. The hen of a pair in

[1] Vol. iii. p. 519 *et seq.*

my possession having died, the cock was inconsolable, refusing to touch his food. Hoping to divert his attention, I allowed him to fly about the room, when he at once settled down in front of his own reflection in the looking-glass with every sign of delight. This little incident suggested to me the idea of hanging a small looking-glass in his cage: this I did, and he at once appeared perfectly happy, taking his food, and nestling close to the glass, uttering a series of low, soft, musical notes, eminently expressive of happiness. Whether he eventually discovered the deception I know not, but he did not long survive his loss."

CHAPTER VI

THE NORFOLK GULLERIES

IT was a windy day in the second week in June, and as the keeper quanted our flat-bottomed boat down the dike leading from the boathouse to Black Horse Broad, the rustling of acres of young reeds and gladden was at times so loud that we had almost to shout in making each other hear. Over the swampy "lows," where, after a few days' heavy and almost incessant rain, the rank marsh grasses had grown so high as to hide the pink-spiked orchids and dwarf sweet gale, the wind was sending grey-green waves rolling towards the reed beds, where they seemed to break with a pattering as of falling spray; but in the dike, which was sheltered by the tall growth of rush and sedge along its banks, the water was scarcely ruffled, and the gusts that were scattering the may-blossom all along the uplands roads and lanes passed over us without our feeling more of them than we should have done had we been sheltered by a high wall. In a few minutes we should be out on the open water, where we could see a welter of wavelets breaking against the rushy islets dotting the surface of the Broad. Meanwhile, in the interval of calm, we could notice the tender green of the marsh buckler fern growing beside the dike, the soft sheen of the young clubrush rods, the curious aloe-like leaf-clusters of the water soldier just covered by the clear shallow water, and the early blossoms of the bogbean opening in a green twilight of waving rush and swamp grasses.

At the dike-mouth the wind dealt us a boisterous buffet, and began to carry our boat towards a reed shoal stretching out some way into the Broad; but it was a westerly wind, warm and laden with the fresh fragrance of growing grass and blooming flowers, and we were well content to feel it on our faces when we brought the boat's head round and started rowing towards the nearest of the green islets of iris and rush. For by this time we were among the beautiful birds we had come in search of in order to see them at home; and all around us, their white breasts gleaming against the blue of the sky, they were flinging themselves to and fro in evident alarm at our presence so near their helpless young. Above the loud rushing of the wind we could hear their incessant wild screaming, and at times they swooped low towards us, doing their best to drive us away. As we drew nearer to the islet, their tumblings and swoopings became more frequent; while, warned by the cries of the parent birds, half a dozen or more little downy creatures scrambled from their nests and began swimming as quickly as possible towards the reeds bordering the Broad. But wind and water were against them, and though they swam strongly they could make little headway; for a moment we saw them on the crest of a wavelet, then they vanished from sight, to re-appear again, still struggling pluckily towards the haven of refuge amid the reed stems.

On the first islet we visited there were five nests, placed so close together that in the cases of three of them they might be said to overlap, their outer fragments of reed and sedge being intermingled; while the five nests together occupied a space of less than three square yards. Much of the material of which these "precarious lake-dwellings," as they have been called, were made, seemed to have been found ready "to hand" on the islet; some of it, indeed, consisted of down-bent rush and gladden still rooted in the little patch of swamp. Here and elsewhere there were nests that were little more than rafts of broken reed stems and dead reed leaves, and which had only the slightest suggestion of the saucer-shape in the centre; but others were rather more carefully fashioned, and in some cases there was a lining of dry swamp grasses. Of the five nests on the first islet, four were empty; but they may have been occupied by the young birds which swam away at our approach. The other nest contained two eggs and a newly hatched chick, too helpless to move when we touched its soft down. The nests were quite unconcealed by the vegetation of the islet, which, so far as could be ascertained so early in the summer, consisted only of the common clubrush or "bolder," the yellow iris or "gladden," and two or three plants of the somewhat rare cowbane or water hemlock (*Cicuta virosa*).

On the next islet, which we approached from landward, so as to intercept any young birds that might attempt to reach the reeds, there were over a dozen nests, and about half of them contained eggs or young birds. There was a scanty fringe of broken-down reeds around this islet, and among this withered growth were several chicks, the coloration of which—dark brown and buff, like polished tortoise-shell,—harmonised well with the amber of the dry reeds and the dark patches of shade where they crossed each other; but the youngsters generally betrayed themselves by movement—by paddling across little pools of open water, climbing over the horizontal reed stems, or pushing their way vigorously through the matted vegetation. One active little creature, while swimming sturdily along the margin of the islet, skirted the side of our boat, and when taken from the water and held in the hand made no effort to escape. It seemed surprisingly fat, and the keeper considered it to be about a week old. It was quite twice as big as the nestlings we saw in the nests still containing eggs. We placed it for a time on the triangular seat at the bow of the boat,

BLACK-HEADED GULLS FOLLOWING THE PLOUGH

where its movements were exceedingly awkward, and it soon crouched in the corner and, apparently, went to sleep; but, on being returned to the water, it promptly scrambled through and over a tangle of broken reeds and climbed into one of the nests, where it appeared to feel safe from harm or interference. In another nest, which seemed to be deserted, there was a dead and half-consumed young bird, probably the victim of one of the voracious rats, which are the worst raiders of the gull and tern colonies.

In 1905 there were about a hundred nests in all on Black Horse Broad and an arm of the water known as Pound Broad. A few years ago more than three times that number might have been counted here and on the neighbouring Great and Little Broads at Hoveton; and for many years subsequent to 1854, when Hoveton first became a regular resort of the black-headed gull during the breeding season, about two thousand eggs were collected yearly, without, it is said, having any disturbing effect on the birds. But of late years Hoveton Great Broad has been almost deserted by the gulls in favour of Black Horse Broad; and even here they have decreased in numbers, partly in consequence of floods and high tides having destroyed many of the rushy islets that were formerly dotted over the surface of the Broad. There is still a large tract of swampy ground suitable for nesting; but the gulls almost always prefer to nest on the islets, and the destruction of so many of these has undoubtedly caused some of the birds to abandon their Broadland haunts. Formerly the greater part of the Hoveton nests were made on the dry ronds, and it is probably due to the depredations of the rats that the birds now select sites surrounded by water.

On such a windy day as that on which we last visited Black Horse Broad, the black-headed gull is seen at its best. It seems to revel in the wind, and, unlike the great saddle-back, which in stormy weather rides for hours on almost motionless wings high above the cliffs, or seeks the quiet waters of some lake or estuary, it frolics tern-like above the ruffled water and rustling reeds, and is seldom at rest from dawn till dusk. It is the only seagull breeding in East Anglia, and as the "kitty" it is familiar, not only to the Broadsman, whose constant companion it is for several months of the year, but the ploughman, whom it often follows in such flocks as to whiten the furrows of the upland fields. When it comes to the Broads in early spring it is generally wearing its white winter cap; but as the days go by its head gradually darkens, until by the end of April it has assumed the deep brown hood from which its keen eyes look at us with a fixed gaze when we venture to disturb it in its marsh home. Its wild scream, heard far inland over the growing corn or the quiet waters of some lone lagoon, is as welcome a sound to the inland dweller as the murmur of the sea, and the gleaming of its white breast is as beautiful to see as the white gleaming of sea spray in the sunlight. And in winter, when for days together we see it hovering and circling over our harbours, often approaching so near to us as we stand on the quays that it seems to have a message for us we fain would understand, it shows nothing of that dislike of man's presence so manifest in the days of its parental cares. Rather it would seem to seek our company, and that with a confidence displayed by no other seagull. Even into the heart of London it comes, like a breath of sea breeze, and before the eyes of the dwellers in the great city conjures up visions of foam-flecked beaches and wide blue wastes of sea.

At the present time the Hoveton colony of black-headed gulls, which is distributed over Black Horse Broad and Hoveton Great and Little Broads, is the only one existing in the Broads district. Many years ago there was a large colony at Horsey, a coast parish about eleven miles north of Yarmouth; in the seventeenth century the gulls were so numerous there, that, according to Sir Thomas Browne, the country-folk sometimes brought them "in carts to Norwich" and sold them "at small rates." This colony was broken up early in the last century, in consequence of the draining of the swampy ground on which the nests were made. Another breeding-place was Rollesby Broad, which was deserted in 1855, when the Yarmouth Waterworks were erected by the side of the Broad. At Somerton, too, these birds used to nest, and even of late years a few pairs have occasionally attempted to re-establish a settlement there, but without success; and a like attempt at Hickling proved a failure owing to the nests being robbed. Other former nesting-places were some of the meres of South-west Norfolk, and there is evidence of colonies having existed in the neighbourhood of Blakeney and Wells.

A better-known gullery,—in fact one of the most famous in England,—is that on Scoulton Mere, a wood-girdled lake about two miles from Hingham, and adjoining the main road from Watton to Norwich. The colony here is undoubtedly of very ancient foundation; Stevenson was inclined to believe that it dates from prehistoric times; but the earliest mention of it is that of Sir Thomas Browne, who, in writing of "Larus alba or puets," tells us that "great plenty thereof have bred about Scoulton Mere, and from thence sent to London." Formerly the number of gulls breeding at Scoulton was far greater than it is now—at one time, indeed, the number of these birds nesting annually in Norfolk must have been simply amazing—and even when Lubbock visited the Mere—about the year 1840—he was so impressed by what he saw there that he wrote of the gulls as being present "in myriads." Since then, there has been a considerable decrease in their numbers; but even now they are numerous enough to constitute a very marked feature of the wild life of the locality during several months of the year.

No British gullery has been more frequently described than this one at Scoulton, the aspect of which during the time when the gulls are "in residence" must be familiar to almost everyone interested in British wild life. The Mere, which is about twenty-eight miles from the sea, is about seventy acres in extent, and the gulls nest on an island, called the "hearth," in the midst of the Mere. The date of their arrival there varies with the mildness of the spring; but they usually make their appearance during the first or second week in March, the first eggs being laid about a month later. According to Stevenson, "the nests, which vary considerably in height and general construction according to situation, are much flattened at the top, and loosely constructed of coarse flag and the withered stems of the last year's reeds, and are lined also with the dried leaves of the reed, partly obtained on the island itself, and partly from a stack of such materials left standing by the side of the Mere. In many cases, however, the eggs are deposited on some grassy tussock, a little lining only being placed in a depression at the top. The gulls will raise their nests, should the waters rise very much, and those situated near the edge of the island are commonly from half a foot to a foot in height. So closely are the nests placed in some parts of the 'hearth,' amongst the young reeds, that I have counted six or seven in a space of not more than three or four yards; and when one considers the general similarity of the eggs, and the still greater resemblance of the young when first hatched, the power that enables each parent bird unerringly to discover its own offspring is, with every allowance for the marvels of instinct, one of those things which no man can understand. A few years back (Stevenson wrote in 1871) a single pair built their nest in one of the small bushes on the island, and reared their young, but this eccentricity was neither repeated by them, or their example followed by others." In other breeding-places of the black-headed gull, similar departures from the usual nesting habit have been occasionally noted. In several instances nests have been built in trees, even at a height of seven or eight feet from the ground; and there is also a record of a nest having been made on a boathouse. Mr. W. G. Clarke relates that on Langmere, in Norfolk, a coot's nest was found on a Sunday in 1897 near the shore. On the following Sunday it was discovered that a log had been thrown across the coot's nest, a black-headed gull had built its nest on the log, and one egg had been laid. According to the Scoulton keeper, the same birds come back to the same spots on the " hearth" year after year.

Rats, stoats, and weasels, at Scoulton as elsewhere, make havoc among the young birds. Mr. Gurney mentions that on one occasion a hundred and fifty of the nestlings and eggs were destroyed by a stoat which swam across to the "hearth." On another occasion a fox secreted itself on the island, and did much damage. The voracious pike often takes toll of the downy mites when they first venture out on to the water, and even eels have been known "to attach themselves to these swimming puff-balls, and sink with them to the muddy depths of the Mere."

The farmers of Mid-Norfolk welcome the "Scoulton cobs" or "Scoulton puits," as they call them, to their fields, well knowing that the birds render them good service in clearing the ground of noxious grubs and insects. Equally useful they are, when opportunity offers, in reducing the numbers of mice and field voles, many of which, in some seasons, are brought to the Mere, probably for the delectation of their captors rather than the young birds. In the evening twilight the old birds may often be seen hawking for moths around the trees bordering the water, just as in Broadland they hunt for the moths to be found among the reed-beds. For an hour or more after sunset they flit to and fro through the deepening gloom; then one by one they settle quietly down upon the broken reeds to rest for the night.

As regards the number of eggs collected at Scoulton, Lubbock, whose remarks deal chiefly with the first half of the last century, states that at that time an average season produced more than 30,000 eggs, and that five years before the time of his writing (1845) there were collected, according to the keeper, no less than 44,000. In 1860, Mr. Gurney visited Scoulton on May 28th, and ascertained that about 16,000 had been gathered that season. Stevenson, writing in 1871, informs us that for the first month after the birds commenced laying, two men were employed to collect on three days in each week, picking up every egg they could find, and generally at the rate of from 1500 to 2000 a day; but when in full laying, and left undisturbed from Friday to Monday, between 3000 and 4000 had been taken in one day. In this manner, he adds, from 10,000 to 20,000 had been obtained in different seasons, and on one occasion even 40,000. In 1872, when Mr. Gurney again visited the Mere, only 4000 had been collected. This sad falling-off was attributed to dry seasons, but was probably due to the systematic raiding of the nests year after year. Mr. Seebohm states that in 1885 the colony consisted of about 8000 birds, and was said to be gradually increasing, though in 1875 it had dwindled to less than half that number in consequence of dry seasons and reckless shooting. In 1845, he states, the colony was estimated at upwards of 20,000 birds. More recent figures are given by Mr. Gurney in the *Zoologist* for April 1903, where he states that in 1898 the number of eggs collected was 5736; in 1899, 6618; in 1900, 7474; in 1901, 7654; and in 1902, only 900. In 1902, he says, the owner of the Mere limited the "take" of eggs to 1000, owing to many young birds having died from the drought during the previous summer. A Scoulton correspondent of the *Norwich Mercury*, however, attributed the need of this limitation to a different cause. In denying the accuracy of some published statements in regard to the gullery, he said: " I beg to contradict that statement (that only the first eggs are gathered), and also that the cause of the birds not returning as usual, and leaving so much earlier last season, was because they were frightened. . . . As to only the first eggs being gathered, I beg to state that this is not the case. Not only the first eggs are taken, but all eggs that can be found—till it is seen that some are being set upon. Then, as to laying last season, the birds seemed to be disgusted with the robbery of the eggs, for they did not stop to hatch off one young one. . . . As to being strictly preserved and protected, . . . what would our great game preservers say if their keepers sold all their early eggs? Would they expect they had preserved their pheasants, etc.? . . . Once the gulls occupied two-thirds of their island home, but now only one-thirtieth part is occupied by them. Does strictly preserving cause them to gradually waste? I think common sense will answer that question. It is a well-known fact to everyone who is familiar with the gulls and their habits, that they are gradually becoming fewer every year, so that where there are now a hundred birds there formerly were thousands."

CHAPTER VII

DENES, DUNES, AND MEAL MARSHES

THE likeness between the marshlands of Norfolk and the reclaimed lands of Holland is often emphasised by writers on the Broads district and the Fens. There is also a likeness, when we compare the greater with the lesser, between the long lines of dunes or sandhills which, on both sides of the North Sea, are often the sole barrier between the lowlands and the sea. North of Yarmouth there is a practically continuous line of sandhills, of varying height and breadth, as far as Happisburgh, where a line of crumbling cliffs begins and extends to Sheringham, a few miles west of Cromer. There the land dips down to the Weybourne marshes, and from Weybourne to the borders of Hunstanton there are miles of salt and meal marshes, which, like the marshlands of Broadland, are for the most part protected from sea incursions by the wind-heaped bastions of the tawny dunes. Along the Suffolk coast it is the same, the only change from the alternation of cliff and dune being an occasional ridge of high-banked shingle, the débris of a wasted and wasting coast. To Norfolk especially these sandhills are of inestimable value; for were it not for the resistance they offer to the waves, there would be nothing to prevent the sea, when swelled by an abnormally high tide, taking possession again of that wide-spreading tract of marshland between the coast and Norwich, which now represents part of its ancient bed. Indeed, geologists tell us that in course of time it must be the fate of the delightful Broads district to return to its ancient estuarine state; and when we know that there are many places where the marshes are from six to twelve feet below the sea-level at high water, and note how frail are some of the sandhill barriers, we cannot help believing that the time when that condition will obtain is not so very far away. For many centuries the sea has carried on an incessant siege of East Anglia, and though we have gains to count against our losses, the balance is far from being in our favour. Continually our cliffs keep wasting away, so that nearly every year fresh footpaths along their crests have to be trodden to take the place of those that are gone; and even our sandhills are constantly shifting, retreating step by step, as it were, before the advancing enemy.

In East Anglia we have dunes and denes, and although etymologists tell us that the terms are synonymous, we do not believe them, for most of us make a clear distinction between the two. With us, as with folk outside East Anglia, the dunes are the undulating lines of sandhills; but our denes are something quite different. In the first place, they are for the most part level ground, and as such are not subject to the constant mutations of the wind-blown sand of the dunes. In the second place, they have a curious and characteristic flora, how acquired it is hard to say, but possibly by adaptation to environment. These denes of ours, though of unusual interest, are of no very great extent; and I think I am right in saying that they occur only in the immediate neighbourhoods of Yarmouth and Lowestoft. Near the Norfolk town they are known as the North and South Denes, names which sufficiently indicate their position in relation to the town. Near Lowestoft, the one continuous tract is known as the Lowestoft, Gunton, or North Denes.

Geographically speaking, these denes are of very recent formation; they have come into existence, in all probability, within the last thousand or fifteen hundred years. In the case of the Yarmouth Denes, they are formed of the débris of the sea-wasted cliffs of the Norfolk coast, the disintegrated material having been carried southward by southward-flowing currents, and deposited across what was formerly the mouth of the great East Anglian estuary. To this destruction of the Norfolk cliffs Lowestoft also, in part, owes the formation of its denes, though in this case a considerable portion of the material was undoubtedly derived from the Suffolk coast between Gorleston and Corton. The only difference between the two tracts of denes is, that at Yarmouth they form part of the level ground on a portion of which the town is built, while at Lowestoft the material composing them seems to have been deposited at the foot of an ancient cliff-line from which the sea then receded. As the Ness Point is really a portion of the Lowestoft Denes, these denes constitute the most easterly land in England.

With the flora of the dunes most people who know any considerable stretch of English coast are familiar, for it is the same almost everywhere. The common maram grass constitutes the chief vegetation, giving a ragged fringe to the bold outlines of the sandhills, which sometimes rise to a height of fifty and sixty feet. At Caister it is intermingled with *Psamma baltica*, a variety or closely allied species, the only English localities of which are on the East Anglian and Northumberland coasts. In most of the coast parishes the beautiful grey-green, milky veined, blue-flowered sea holly is fairly plentiful; but near Yarmouth it is much rarer than it used to be, and from the Lowestoft dunes it has practically disappeared. This may be partly due to the men whom Sir Thomas Browne refers to as "eryngo diggers"; for the sea holly was formerly in considerable repute as a medicinal plant, and not very many years ago its roots were made in Suffolk into a candied sweetmeat. Even now quantities of it are gathered in places where it is fairly plentiful, the object of the gatherers being to sell it for decorative purposes. A rarer sandhill flower is the yellow-horned sea poppy, which has suffered a considerable decrease since the coast became popular with holiday folk, owing to their plucking the handsome flowers or carrying away the curious long seed pods; but the beautiful pink-and-white sea convolvulus is still a common flower on the dunes, as are two forms of the pink-blossomed restharrow. South of Southwold and on the North Norfolk coast, the dainty sea campion is in several places abundant; and Suffolk is the northern limit of the sea spurge on the east coast of Britain; but this is a plant which seems to be more at home in the shingle than on the dunes. This may also be said of the rare sea-pea, which occurs on the shingly beach between Aldeburgh and Orford, where it was seen by that eminent botanist, John Ray. His, however, is not the earliest record; for in Martyn's edition of Miller we find the following interesting note:

"We learn from the epistles of the learned Caius that the sea-pea was first observed in the year 1555, when, in a great scarcity, the poor people on the coast of Suffolk, about Orford and Aldeburgh, supported themselves with it for some time. This story is related by Stow and Camden, with the addition that they were supposed to spring up opportunely in that year of dearth, from a shipwrecked vessel loaded with peas; whereas the sea-pea differs from all the varieties of the garden or field pea in the length and continuance of the roots, the smallness and bitterness of its seed, and in the whole habit and appearance of the plant. It had probably grown a long time on Orford beach unobserved, until extreme want called it into public notice. The seed is so bitter that it could not be eaten, except in a want of better food, and it is certainly not used at present, though it might be gathered in sufficient quantity; nay, it is neglected by the very birds. The legend of the miraculous arrival of these peas in a time of extreme scarcity is still believed among the country people." From the above it might be imagined that the sea-pea grows only in the neighbourhood of Aldeburgh. That such is not the case, every botanist knows. It is, however, confined to nine of the 112 counties and vice-counties recognised by the ninth edition of the *London Catalogue*, and its localities are in Shetland, the east and south coasts of England, and in Kerry in Ireland. The rarest East Anglian dunes plant is the seashore variety of the lesser rue, the specific name of which is *Thalictrum dunense*. It has been recorded for Corton and Gorleston, where it is now extinct; but the Rev. G. H. Harris states that it is stlll to be found north of Yarmouth.

Among the common plants of the dunes are the purple sea rocket, the creeping sea purslane or sea sandwort, the lady's bedstraw, and the curious sand sedge, which, like the maram, helps to bind the sand of the banks with its creeping rootstock, which often extends to a length of several feet. Among the Benacre dunes there is an abundant growth of the Danish scurvy-grass, a small variety of the common scurvy-grass of the salt creek. In spring the pale blossoms of the scentless dog violet are found half hidden beneath the bending bents, at least two varieties of this variable flower occurring along the coast. At Palling the clammy groundsel (*Senecio viscosus*) grows freely on the landward slope of the sandhills, and in the same neighbourhood one finds the sea buckthorn, locally known as "wyebibbles." From Palling, too, we have records of the sea storksbill; but this rare plant does not seem to have been found there of late years. Tamarisk has been planted on the dunes in some places as a protection against the destruction of the banks. Next to the maram the commonest sandhill grass is the lyme grass; but the maritime varieties of the couch grass grow freely, as

DENES, DUNES, AND MEAL MARSHES 123

does the sea fescue. Here and there one meets with the sea barley.

Writing of the Yarmouth South Denes, the Rev. G. H. Harris says that "botanically, this small triangular strip of denes, bounded on the north by the town, by the sea on the east, and by the high land of Gorleston on its third side, and isolated therefore from any kindred soil, must be nearly unique." It may be compared with the Lowestoft Denes, which possess an almost identical flora. To mention all the plants indigenous to these two localities, and some of them to the Yarmouth North Denes, would be a lengthy task, and as some of them are familiar heath plants it is scarcely necessary that they should be named here. Other species are rare enough to make their occurrence on these denes of especial interest, while the fact of as many as twelve species of clover being met with in so restricted an area is certainly remarkable.

Some of these clovers are common kinds, such as may be found on almost any tract of waste land, but others are rather rare, especially the throttled clover (*Trifolium suffocatum*) and the burrowing clover (*T. subterraneum*). Both of these are of peculiar habit, the former, a very small tufted annual, having tiny flowers which grow in such close-packed heads as scarcely to permit each other to show a sign of bloom, while the latter has a curious way of burying its own seeds. Only less rare are the rough clover (*T. scabrum*) and the clustered clover (*T. glomeratum*). Each of these may be described as common on the denes, and at Lowestoft they are accompanied by *Lotus tenuis*, a rare form of the bird's-foot trefoil, and the slender hop trefoil (*T. filiforme*). There, too, and on the Yarmouth North Denes, grows the teesdalia; and another inconspicuous plant, known as the upright moenchia, may be found near the Warren House at Lowestoft. A characteristic denes plant is the pretty little English stonecrop, which resembles the common wallpepper, but has white star-like flowers.

Among the peculiarly maritime species or varieties are the sea pearlwort, sea sandwort or sea purslane (also common on the dunes), and sea sand spurrey. A far from common flower is the smooth cat's-ear, and the same may be said of the dwarf seaside centaury (*Erythræa littoralis*), both of which have been identified on the Lowestoft Denes. A puzzling plant, found at Yarmouth and Lowestoft, is a little Cerastium, which blooms as early as March. It seems to be a matter of dispute among botanists whether it be *Cerastium semidecandrum* or *C. tetrandrum*. At Lowestoft no one can help noticing the extraordinary abundance of the buck's-horn plantain. The most interesting of the denes grasses are the bulbous meadow grass, which constitutes the greater portion of the summer grass, and the grey corynephorus (*C. canescens*), which in England is confined to Norfolk and Suffolk.

Manship, the Yarmouth historian, writing of the denes in the early part of the seventeenth century, says: "Let me tell you, and that most truly, that albeit the Denes or Downs of Yarmouth be but short grass, by reason the same is overcharged with cattle (for being common, the poor there hath like privilege with the rich, so that the one may not exceed the other in the feeding of any sort of beasts of what kind soever to be put thereon), it cannot have growth accordingly. Yet, notwithstanding is the feed so sweet, and the sand so warm, whereon the beast does couch and rest itself, that it doth nourish and battle the same (be it horse, cow, or calf) in such wise that it will fat it as speedily, and causeth the milch cow there to give as much milk commonly, as any other the like beasts which do live in any of the countries adjacent."

Among the dunes one has excellent opportunities, both by night and day, of observing the wild life of the shore.

Shortly after two o'clock of a warm, misty morning in early June, when the crescent moon was low over the North Sea, and scarcely a sign of the approaching dawn had appeared in the east, there were larks singing high above the sandhills of the Suffolk coast. Hardly a breath of breeze was stirring along the shore, and the sea was so quiet that the dipping of a 'longshoreman's oar could be heard quite half a mile away; but broken masses of dark cloud were rolling up from the south, hiding the stars in the western sky, but drifting northward without hiding the face of the moon. Save for the singing of the unseen larks, the stealthy creeping of the wavelets up the beach, and the dipping of the drawnetter's oar, not a sound broke the silence of the shore; and as I lay crouched in a hollow among the sandhills I sought in vain for signs of life among the gloomy dunes and along the misty beach. Even the maram-grass on the dun ridges was motionless, every grey bending blade being weighted down with a chain of mist drops; and between the dunes and the sea a wide stretch of pebbly sand, strewn with dark tangles of stranded seaweed and boulder-like blocks of peat from the submerged land surface off the Covehithe shore, showed dimly through the mist a dreary aspect of desert desolation. Landward, the limited outlook was even more gloomy. There, under a starless sky, miles of marshland lay hidden under a close-drawn coverlet of dense fog. Yet high above this sombre scene the larks were cheerily heralding the dawn of day.

Slowly the ashen hue of the eastern sky grew lighter, and the outlines of near and distant objects more clearly defined. Through the thinning mist the 'longshore boats became visible, at first as though floating in air; presently their long lines of net-floats appeared rising and falling with the sluggish motion of the sea swell. Seaward, the outlook widened and revealed the last pale glimmer cast on the water by the fading moon, while northward and southward, the undulating sandhills emerged from obscurity and shaped themselves out of apparent formlessness. Away in the marshes a lapwing wailed; nearer, where the rich colouring of the patches of sheep's sorrel was brightening among the dunes, a meadow pipit cheeped; and presently a solitary curlew, looking unnaturally large in the still uncertain dawnlight, stole silently down a hollow among the sandhills and stood motionless by the tide-mark on the beach. Then the red rim of the sun appeared above the sea-mist, still dimming the horizon, and, as though it had awaited the dawn, a fresh breeze set streaks of silvery ripples running along the surface of the sea. For the first time since nightfall the air grew chill. Till then it had been warm and stagnant, laden with the marish odour of the lowland dikes and the strong scent of the heaps of sodden seaweed cast up along the shore.

Suddenly there was a movement among the grey and white of the pebbles strewn over the sands near the hollow where I was hidden among the dunes. It was a flitting movement, as though one of the stones had stirred from its place or the shadow of a flying bird had been cast for a moment on the beach. While I kept my eyes fixed intently on the spot, the movement was repeated, and, taking up my field-glasses, I saw a pair of ringed plovers, whose protective coloration had defied my unaided sight, making little darting runs to and fro on the pebbly sand. For quite ten minutes they kept darting about without travelling more than six yards from the spot where I had first observed them, and from this and the behaviour of the bird I took to be the female—though no difference between them could be detected from where I lay—I felt sure there must be young birds near them. As it proved, I was right in my conviction; for, a few minutes later, while I was still bringing my glasses to bear upon them, what looked like a tuft of down blown from a seeding salsify sped quickly towards the mother-bird and vanished from sight. I waited for the appearance of other chicks; but only one arrived, post-haste from behind a block of stranded peat, and vanished, like the other, by taking shelter beneath the parental wing. Meanwhile the male bird, after approaching his mate, and surveying her knowingly with head on one side, flitted down to the edge of the sea and began searching for food among the cast-up patches of purple and crimson weed.

Nothing could be more interesting than watching the crouching mother-bird apparently bent on making no movement that might disturb her sleeping chicks, yet at the same time turning her head from side to side, keeping a careful lookout for any sign of approaching danger. I hardly liked to alarm her; but, having no harmful intention towards either parents or chicks, I gratified my curiosity as to how she would behave when apparent danger threatened. Keeping my glasses to my eyes, I rose quietly to my feet and stood erect and still. I expected to see the old bird run or flutter off in the usual decoying fashion; but she did not stir, though I felt convinced that she saw me, for although she stayed covering her chicks she ceased moving her head, and it seemed to me that she had one eye fixed steadily on me. Apparently she was waiting for further evidence of my intentions; or it may be that the occasional appearance of a coastguardsman or beachman had taught her not to trouble herself unless the intruder came too near. Half a dozen steps down the slope of the hollow brought me to the level of the beach, where I paused and again looked for some sign of disquiet on the part of the plover; but still she did not move. At the first step I took on the level, however, her head was raised with a jerk, and I heard a soft sweet piping note. It was anything but an alarm-note, judging simply by the sound of it; but it was no sooner uttered than there were no youngsters under her wings, nor any sign of them around her.

It was like some clever trick of a conjuror: Hey, presto! and the chicks were gone! Directly afterwards the mother-bird made a running dash down the beach, darted as quickly towards the dunes again, only away from where she had started from, and then began tumbling and fluttering about like a winged bird trying to escape capture.

Having made a mark with my heel in the sand at the spot where the little family party had been resting, I walked slowly in the direction of the anxious parent, whose imitation of a disabled bird would have been wholly admirable had her acting been without intervals during which she betrayed herself by steady flight. As I approached her, she dashed off for a dozen yards or so, and then began tumbling again, repeating the performance until she was satisfied that she had lured me to a safe distance from her skulking young. Then with a cheerful whistle, that seemed to have a note of derision in it, she flew quickly away across the sandhills, to reappear, in company with her mate, some hundred yards or more along the beach.

Returning to the mark I had made in the sand, I now began seeking the young birds. Casual glancing over the surface of the beach is almost bound to prove a fruitless method of prosecuting such a quest; every inch of the ground must be carefully scanned, and that, perhaps, over and over again. Around the heel-mark there was no sign of them. Drawing on the sand with my walking-stick a circle about two yards in diameter, I first examined every pebble within it. Then I drew a larger circle, and went over the space enclosed between it and the smaller one. Still I sought in vain, though the return of the parent bird, and a recommencement of her decoying antics told me that, like a child playing hide-and-seek, I was getting " warm." A second search within the outer ring was attended with success; for on examining again a small group of pebbles I

THE RINGED PLOVER'S RUSE.

caught sight of a crouching chick pressing close against the side of a stone. I stooped over it; but its only movement was a slight ruffling of the down, which may have been caused by the breeze. Then I touched it gently with my finger; but still its only movement was an attempt to crouch even closer to the stone. I turned my eyes from it for a moment to watch the mother-bird, who was acting the cripple within a dozen yards of me, and when I looked again for the chick it was gone. Nor during about half an hour spent in searching could I locate both of the young birds at the same time. One of them I found quite twenty feet from the spot where it had rested under the mother-bird's wing.

Small colonies of ringed plovers are distributed nearly all along the Suffolk coast, where the beach is almost everywhere suited to their requirements, during the breeding season. Between Kessingland and Gorleston, however, no nest has, to my knowledge, been found for several years, and immediately north of Yarmouth nests are now far rarer than they used to be. But the farther north we go along the Norfolk coast, the more nests we meet with; and on the North Norfolk coast, thanks to the protection afforded to the birds and their nests, not only the ringed plover, but common and lesser terns, lapwings, and redshanks have increased in numbers as breeding birds. There the chief enemies of the shore birds are the rat and hooded crow, the latter being charged with eating most of the eggs that are laid before it takes its departure from our shores. Mr. J. H. Gurney in 1902 counted nine nests containing eggs of the ringed plover on one nesting-ground, as well as several of the so-called "cocks'-nest" or "play-holes." In regard to the recently hatched chicks, he noticed how neatly the shell had been divided into halves; this he believes to have been accomplished with the aid of the beak of the parent-bird. These fragments of shell are not allowed to remain in the nest. "It seems fairly evident," writes

Mr. Gurney,[1] "that directly the nestling is free the old plover must fly off with both pieces of egg-shell, and drop them at a safe distance, where they cannot betray her. It is clear," he adds, "that the young ringed plovers are not hatched quite simultaneously; it is also evident that when hatched their legs develop so rapidly that three or four hours suffice to give them strength enough to run. Most likely they return to the nest at night, and are sheltered under the warmth of the parent's breast; otherwise one hardly sees the necessity for such speedy removal of the egg-shells. Most of the nest-holes here are lined with broken cockle-shells, of which there are plenty in Norfolk, and while three exquisitely spotted eggs point inwards, the fourth is generally pointed sideways. I measured many of the nest depressions with a rule; some are larger than others, but the average circumference is fifteen inches, and the average diameter, four inches. The above were typical nests, and neither on this nor any other occasion have I found one constructed of bents of grass, as described and figured by Mr. Kelso."

In connection with Mr. Gurney's remark on the arrangement of the eggs in the nest, it may be interesting to read what Sir Thomas Browne has to say about the ringed plover. He calls it "Ringlestones, a small white-and-black bird like a wagtail, and seems to be some kind of motacilla marina, common about Yarmouth sands. They lay their eggs in the sand and shingle about June, and, as the eryngo diggers tell me, not set them flat, but upright like eggs in salt." As Mr. Southwell has pointed out, the concavity of the nest-hole, together with the disproportionate size of the larger end of the eggs, gives them the appearance of being placed in the way the eryngo diggers described. As regards the lining of the nests with fragments of shells, this is undoubtedly the case on the North Norfolk

[1] *Zoologist*, April 1903.

coast; but along some parts of the Suffolk coast nests so lined are rarely seen, owing to the scarcity of cockle and all kinds of shells on the beach.

Wild Birds' Protection Societies are often badly supported, notwithstanding that the good work they do is to the benefit of bird-lovers generally, as well as those of the immediate neighbourhood where protection is undertaken. Most of the promotors of these societies would probably be satisfied if they were supported in accordance with results; and in such case the Wells Wild Birds' Protection Society would be one of the most flourishing in the kingdom; for the change it has brought about in a few years is both gratifying and surprising. To appreciate its good work, one should pay a visit during the breeding season to the line of sand dunes extending eastward of Wells harbour between the meal marshes and the beach.

A few years ago the colony of common terns here had been reduced to about a dozen nests, while nests of the lesser tern were rarities, and those of the ringed plover hard to find. Now, from mid-May to mid-July, almost everywhere on the dunes and shingle patches one has to exercise continual caution to guard against treading on eggs or young birds. The scene here, indeed, is an extraordinary one, especially to those who can remember how deserted were the dunes such a short time ago. As you approach the breeding-grounds, hundreds of graceful terns leave their nests and hover over you, keeping up a constant creaking chorus of disapproval of your intrusion; while near by, and probably alarmed by the behaviour of their larger relatives, a score or more lesser terns rise in the air as though anxious to discover the cause of the sudden disturbance. And all the while you remain among them, both common and lesser terns keep up a continual clamour, with which is mingled the piping of the ringed plover, the oft-repeated alarm-note of the redshank, and the harsh screaming of the black-headed gull. Well it is for the terns if you have the watcher at your elbow; for while your attention is taken up by the graceful movements of the birds you may easily forget that you are walking over ground literally covered with nests. Cringle, the local watcher,—a good naturalist, skilled wild-fowler, and thorough sportsman,—estimated that in 1905 there were quite a thousand nests of the common tern and about forty nests of the lesser tern among the Wells dunes, to say nothing of innumerable and more widely distributed nests of the ringed plover and redshank; and I am inclined to think this was not an exaggerated estimate.

As regards the common tern, the nests I saw that year—and I saw some hundreds—were chiefly made on the patches of shingle among the dunes, where each had a scanty lining of blades of the maram-grass; but a good many were in sandy hollows of the sandhills, three or four being often made within a space of four square yards, while others were in fairly straight lines along the narrow crest of the dunes. Yet others were simply saucer-shaped depressions in level patches of close, short grass and sand-sedge, these last mentioned being without any lining, save what the growing grass and sedge provided. I saw no nest answering accurately to the description of some found lined and surrounded with fragments of shell; but the shingle patches were strewn with shells and shell-fragments, and Cringle, who had seen some of the shell-decorated nests, was of the opinion that sometimes the sitting birds amused themselves by drawing bits of shell close around their nests. The variation in the depth of the colouring of the eggs, and in the character and distribution of the markings, was very noticeable, and very darkly blotched eggs were quite as numerous as spotted ones. A year or two ago, a nest containing three eggs, "blood-red" in colour, and without any markings, was discovered; and for three years in succession a nest was made in exactly the same spot on one of the dunes, and contained each year abnormally dark eggs. In one nest on the shingle I noticed two eggs of normal colouring, and a white egg finely dotted with faint purple spots. The nests of the lesser tern were without any attempt at lining, consisting simply of saucer-shaped depressions in the sand; the eggs, so far as those I saw in June 1905, were concerned, were very uniformly marked, being of a greyish stone-colour, plentifully dotted with small reddish-brown spots.

The nests of the ringed plover are scattered over a rather wider area at Wells than those of the terns, and are to be found in various situations, such as on the beach on the seaward side of the sandhills, among the terns' nests on the shingle patches inside the banks, on the dunes themselves—where they are rather conspicious—and amid the bents and sand-sedge of the level ground. Several of them, especially those made in the finer shingle, contained a good many shell fragments; but these could scarcely be said to form a lining to the nest, being mixed up with the shingle in the same way as they are found away from the nests. In cases where the latter were made at some distance from the shell-strewn sands, it was a rare thing to find shell fragments in them; so it would seem evident that the plovers seldom take the trouble to collect them unless they are to be picked up in the immediate neighbourhood of the nests. In regard to the eggs of the ringed plover, I could find no variation of the ground colour in accordance with the character of their surroundings, nor was there any very noticeable difference in their markings. Neither the terns nor the ringed plover seemed to make any attempt to conceal their nests; but those of the redshanks nesting among the dunes were often well concealed and difficult to find, owing to the site selected being usually close under a tussock of maram-grass.

One nest was an especially beautiful object, being made in some fine grass, and completely covered by the bending leaves of the maram.

Although some of the redshank chicks are hatched off before the end of May, many of the terns' nests are at that time without their full clutch of eggs, and June is generally well advanced before any young terns are seen. Unlike the ringed plovers, which make their way down to the beach or into the meals very soon after they emerge from the shell, the baby terns, from the middle of June till the middle of July, are much in evidence around their nests, from which they crawl almost as soon as they are hatched. There, among the pebbles or on the scantily grassed sand of the dunes, they lie without attempting to hide, looking the most helpless creatures imaginable, their sole anxiety, apparently, being that they should be well supplied with food. This, chiefly in the shape of small fish, is dropped in front of them by their attentive parents, who at such times seem very indifferent to the presence of man.

Now that the birds are protected on the Wells dunes, a visit to the tern colony in late spring or early summer must be reckoned among the chief delights Norfolk has for the observer of wild life, and perhaps the next best thing to watching the birds is to sit in Cringle's houseboat and listen while that ardent watcher talks of the wild life of the North Norfolk coast. During the nesting season his houseboat is moored in a salt-water drain winding amid the meals up to the back of the dunes; and it was there, on a sunny day in early June, we sat watching the terns flying high above the sandhills and the hungry shore-crabs crawling in the drain. The air was filled with the wild crying of the shore and marsh birds; just outside the boat a redshank was feeding on a gleaming patch of ooze; and for a while we were so quiet that a pied wagtail, which was nesting near by, flew first on to the stern of the boat and then through the doorway on to the cabin floor. This, I found, had been its custom for some days past; and talking of the friendliness of the wagtail reminded Cringle that at that moment a starling had its nest in the cabin stove-pipe, no fire having been lighted in the stove for some weeks. A curious fact in connection with this nest was that it had been built while the houseboat was moored on the other side of the meals, and when the boat was brought about a mile and a half along the drain the starling made the journey with it.

The adventures of Cringle as a wild-fowler would fill a good-sized book, and I wish my memory served me well enough to enable me to set down some of them in detail. But once started upon relating his reminiscences, one incident so quickly suggested another that I soon gave up all hope of remembering them. Plain it was that the man was in love with the life he led, and that even its hardships gave an added zest to his existence; if he could have begun his life again he would have wished it to be little different from what it had been. Crouched in a duck-hole and shooting by sound on a dark night, paddling in his flat-bottomed punt after the fowl in the grey light of a misty autumn dawn, stalking some rare migrant along the dunes or amid the meal-marsh scrub, or going down at daybreak to take the fowl out of his stake-nets on the tidal flats, he had been living a life which had a strong fascination for him, and which no bribe would have tempted him to abandon for any other.

After an hour or two spent in the houseboat, we rambled again along the dunes, where we could see on the one hand the lug-worm gatherers on the sandy flats, and on the other the wide-spreading meals with their gleaming creeks and deep-cut drains. Once we paused at a spot where a black redstart had recently been shot, and again where Cringle had caught a glimpse of some strange birds which he believed were desert wheatears.

Here, too, only a few days before, a horned owl had been found in a rabbit-trap on the dunes, and at different times little gulls, Sabine's gulls, and a pure white dunlin had fallen to the fowler's gun. And presently our thoughts were given a somewhat gruesome turn; for in a hollow in the dunes there are pointed out to me some of the bleaching bones of a human skeleton—the saddening relics of some shipwreck tragedy—which had been uncovered by the drifting sand. Less grim, but equally suggestive to the imagination, was the knowledge that sometimes rotten brandy kegs are brought to light among the dunes when the sand is blown in clouds from the banks; for, in the old and stirring "free-trading" days, Wells was the headquarters of a daring smuggling crew, of whom strange stories are still told by the ancient loungers on the harbour quay.

BY THE SEA BANK AT FLIGHT-TIME.—"A BIT TOO HIGH"

CHAPTER VIII

DENES, DUNES, AND MEAL MARSHES—*Continued*

NOW, as in the past, the handsome sheld-duck nests in the rabbit burrows in the sandhills of the Norfolk coast, but not in such numbers as on Dersingham Heath. In East Anglia it restricts itself as a breeding species to the North Norfolk coast, many years having elapsed since it bred in the Winterton dunes, a few miles north of Yarmouth. A few pairs of stockdoves still frequent the dunes, where, like the preceding species, they inhabit the rabbit holes; but the stone curlew, which twenty years ago nested regularly on the Norfolk and Suffolk sandhills, has now ceased to do so. Of late years the wheatear or "burrow-bird" has deserted the dunes in the neighbourhoods of Yarmouth and Lowestoft, save as a passing migrant; but in quieter parts of the coast it still seeks the company of the sandhill conies. On the North Norfolk coast a good many rare migrants, chiefly warblers, have been secured by gunners on or near the dunes, especially where the sandhills are heaped up along the seaward side of the meal marshes. On the denes, more particularly on the North Denes at Yarmouth, not a few rare species have been taken in clap-nets by the bird-catchers; among these may be mentioned Richard's pipits, serin finches, and ortolan and Lapland buntings. Snow buntings are often abundant in the same locality, and with them are sometimes found considerable numbers of shore-larks. According to Mr. A. H. Patterson, the great snipe shows a decided preference for the sandhills rather than the marshes, and on the occasions of this country being invaded by flocks of sand-grouse, both denes and dunes proved very attractive to the Asiatic wanderers. An example of the rare Steller's duck is recorded to have been shot on the denes near Caister as long ago as 1830; and on October 18th, 1896, a great spotted cuckoo—the third for Great Britain—was there obtained.

Rabbits are plentiful among the sandhills, where they are said to grow larger than those frequenting the inland hedgerows; they feed, apparently, on the maram-grass and such rushes as occur on or near the banks. In 1897, when the sea broke through the dunes in several places along the coast, many rabbits were drowned; for, as the sea came up, they retreated to their burrows, where they remained until the waves scoured away the banks, when they fell out of the burrows into the wash of the sea. Their presence among the dunes attracts a good many stoats and weasels. Early one morning an old beachman at Horsey saw a small pack of stoats hunting about the "hills," no doubt a family party, of which the young ones were being trained to hunt their prey. "They were shrieking like anything," said the old man, "or I shouldn't have noticed 'em; and I watched 'em go up and down the hills and in and out among the grass just like a little pack of hounds." Rats are far too numerous in the sandhills, and are responsible for the destruction of some of the eggs of the tern and ringed plover. Moles are far from common, for there is little to tempt them in the banks; but occasionally, while descending the side of some maram-rampart, you may chance to stumble over a freshly turned-up mole heap. They are plentiful, however, in some of the tracts of level ground which in places lie between the banks and the marshes, and there, in the early morning, you may sometimes watch them above ground, industriously grubbing for worms among the grass roots. Young moles, at such times, are exceedingly tame, and you may touch and stroke them without their showing any sign of alarm. The common lizard or "swift" inhabits both denes and dunes; and the viper, which has a very local distribution along the coast of East Anglia, is so abundant just inside the sandhills at Eccles as to call for constant watchfulness on the part of a pedestrian.

The meal marshes of the North Norfolk coast extend several miles eastward and westward of Wells, and one can get a very good idea of their general aspect from the quayside of that ancient little town. From there one sees stretching away for miles beyond the harbour a tract of level land the like of which is to be found nowhere save along that particular coast. It bears practically no resemblance to what is generally understood by marshland, nor has it scarcely any feature in common with the denes, apart from being bounded on its seaward side by sandhills. It is, to a certain extent, reclaimed land, and although its creeks and drains are filled by every flood-tide, it is now a rare occurrence for the sea to overflow any considerable portion of it; but for all that it has the appearance of land still at the mercy of the waves, and at first glance suggests nothing so much as a tract of country which has recently been inundated by the sea. When the tide is high, and the creeks are full, it appears to be so water-logged that one might be excused for believing it to be a place where it is hardly safe to set foot; often a quivering sea haze combines with the gleaming of the water in the creeks and drains to create mirage-like effects as beautiful as they are bewildering; and when, as is often the case in autumn, a dense fog comes up like a moving white wall from the sea, the whole of the strange land lying seaward of the town vanishes as completely from sight as though the sea had won it to itself again. But at other times, when the haze is only noticeable as a wind-rippled, translucent veil over the distant meals, mile after mile of firm land is revealed richly coloured with the varied hues of an almost unique flora—crimson, gold, and purple melting one into the other as far as eye can see.

Especially towards the hour of sunset, when the slanting sunrays set the creeks afire, this far-spreading plain wears an alluring aspect; but should you be without a native guide among the winding drains and rough trackways, it is unwise to attempt to explore it unless you can devote to it several hours of daylight. For even native wild-fowlers have been known to lose themselves in the meals at night, or when a fog has come down upon them suddenly; and very easy it is for a stranger to wander for hours in a fruitless attempt to escape from a labyrinth of intersecting drains. But neither the bird-lover who hears the bird-cries of the meals, nor the botanist who wishes to account for the rich floral hues spread over the surface of the plain, is likely to be able to resist the fascination of what have been well described as "the moorlands of the sea."

Perhaps the most interesting plant, though one of the least attractive, growing in the meals, is the shrubby sea blite, which is fairly well distributed over the meal area, but is unusually plentiful just within the sandhills at Wells. This small shrub, which in Britain is confined to the eastern and southern coasts of England, is said by Sir Joseph Hooker to be met with only in Norfolk, Suffolk, Essex, and Dorset, but it is recorded for seven of the counties and vice-counties recognised by the *London Catalogue*. It attains a height of about two feet, and, like the common sea blite of the salt marsh, from which its size sufficiently distinguishes it, has thick, succulent, and nearly cylindrical leaves. In places what may be described as small thickets of shrubby sea blite are found, helping to form that meal marsh "scrub" to which the flocks of migrant warblers resort when they land on this part of the coast. There is a legend among the local gunners that this plant became established on the North Norfolk coast through some seeds being washed ashore from the wreck of a "Malay" ship—a story which has its counterpart in Suffolk in that of the introduction of the rare sea pea.

The most conspicuous portion of the meal flora is provided by the sea lavender, many acres of ground being covered in summer with its beautiful clusters of mauve blossoms. Three species of sea lavender occur here,[1] and of one of these, *Statice Limonium*, there are two varieties. The two most noticeable species are the one with the largest leaves, and a small kind, of similar prostrate habit to the common knotgrass. The full beauty of the blooming lavender is not revealed until July and August; but in early summer a rich colouring shows itself along the banks of the creeks and drains with the appearance of the crimson-tinted leaves of a dwarf kind of shrubby plant, which locally goes by the name of "crab-grass," but which botanists know as the sea orache, or sea purslane (*Atriplex portulacoides*). The leaves of this plant change their hue with the seasons: in spring and early summer they have a crimson tint, at midsummer they appear to be coated with a silvery frost, and in the autumn they turn bright yellow. An allied species, the stalked orache (*A. pedunculata*), is also to be found by careful searching, and is reckoned among the botanist's treasures because it grows only on the east coast of England. Another rather uncommon flower, locally distributed over the meals, is the little pink-blossomed sea heath, which, notwithstanding its humble habit, grows in places in sufficient quantity to give a pinkish flush to the ground over which it spreads. These are some of the plants contributing to the wealth of colour on the meals; but other better-known seaside

---

[1] The meal lavenders are *Statice Limonium* (*genuina* and *pyramidalis*, Syme); *S. occidentalis*, Lloyd; and *S. reticulata*, L.

species have a share in making the meals so attractive. Among these are the sweet-scented sea southernwood—as fragrant as the southernwood in an old country garden—the dainty thrift or sea pink, the ruddy marsh samphire or glasswort, the yellow-anthered sea plantain, and the mauve-flowered sea starwort or Michaelmas daisy.

The North Norfolk coast offers exceptional opportunities for observing wild birds during the periods of migration, and not a few of the rare birds included in the Norfolk lists were obtained by gunners on or in the immediate neighbourhood of the meal marshes. In the autumn especially, the passing migrants are much in evidence, and it has generally been at that season the rare warblers have been met with, the local gunners having of late years found it worth their while to keep a lookout for them. In most instances they have been secured during the month of September, when there is usually a great inrush of birds of this family along the North Norfolk coast. Cley and Blakeney are the parishes which have produced the majority of the rarities, among which were included several icterine, barred, and aquatic warblers. Writing of the occurrence of the barred warblers, Mr. Gurney says that one of these was watched for a considerable time, skulking in some low bushes of chenopodium, where there was not much to hide in; this was about half a mile from the shore, and near where the others were detected. When driven from this retreat and forced to double back over the mud, the grey tint of its plumage was very apparent. The bird had probably lately arrived and was tired, for its flight was laboured. It presently took refuge in the thick roots of the chenopodium. Two even rarer visitors were a yellow-browed warbler obtained at Cley in October 1894, and a Pallas's willow warbler shot in the same parish in October 1896. The latter, which was first described by Pallas in 1811 from Siberia, was a very beautiful, bright lemon-tinted little bird, scarcely larger than a gold-crest, for an example of which it was at first mistaken when seen among the long grass on the Cley sea-wall. Until a few years ago it was looked upon as strictly an Asiatic species; but it is now known to visit Central and Southern Europe in the autumn, though until the Cley example was secured it had never been recognised in the British Isles. Mr. H. E. Dresser, to whom it was submitted, stated that on comparing it with specimens from Siberia and the Himalayas, he found it to agree most closely with a fully adult bird from Siberia; and he added that it was an adult female in very fresh plumage, quite as bright in tinge of colour as any Siberian specimen he had seen.

Another rare visitor to the North Norfolk coast is the red-breasted flycatcher, the first Norfolk example of which was shot at Cley in September 1890, by Mr. F. Menteith Ogilvie, who, in describing how he met with it, says that he flushed it two or three times from the scrub of sea blite before he was able to secure it. The alarm-note of this flycatcher is said to be a *pink, pink*, like that of the chaffinch, only softer, clearer, and quicker; but the Cley bird was silent while it was being followed. Its flight was graceful and buoyant, and always at some height from the ground; in this it differed from the other birds—chiefly willow wrens and chiffchaffs — which were in the scrub, and which flew very low and were flushed with difficulty. Other red-breasted flycatchers have since been shot or seen in the neighbourhood of the meals.

September is also the month during which, in some years, considerable numbers of bluethroats are seen in the meals; while during the winter, snow buntings are generally to be found there, with them often consorting some Lapland buntings, which were especially numerous in the winters of 1892 and 1893. In September of the following year an immature male ortolan bunting, found in the company of some linnets, was shot at Cley, this being at a time when enormous numbers of this species were seen on Heligoland. A fairly regular winter visitor is the shore-lark, for which the creeksides and vegetation of the meals provide an abundance of suitable food; and in some years rock pipits are exceedingly abundant, occurring as autumn migrants and winter visitors. This pipit has not been proved to have nested in Norfolk, though a pair are suspected of having done so in 1880.

In the cases of some of the smaller rare birds, and especially the warblers, correct identification is practically impossible, unless the birds are shot or otherwise secured; but, while admitting that the desire of local ornithologists to increase the length of their county bird lists is a perfectly natural one, it must, I think, sometimes occur to bird-lovers to ask themselves whether, in view of many common and harmless birds being shot in the hope that one of them may prove to be a rarity, this slaughter of the migrant warblers has not gone quite far enough. Such, at any rate, is the opinion of Mr. W. T. Hornaday, the Director of the New York Zoological Park. He says: "The difficulty lies in studying them effectively without killing them. As for myself, I have not yet seen the day wherein I could find myself willing to slaughter from five hundred to a thousand of these exquisite little creatures for the sake of becoming sufficiently acquainted with them to name them *when they are dead!* I blush not in admitting that I have gone half-way through life knowing less than a score of warblers to the point of naming them, accurately, as they fly before me." Mr. Hornaday exhorts the readers of his *American Natural History* never to slaughter birds of any kind, merely to become acquainted with their names. Admittedly, he is writing for young people interested in bird life; but there are older people who might do well to give his remarks careful consideration. Surely, if in an immense country like North America the naturalists are beginning to

DENES, DUNES, AND MEAL MARSHES 145

feel that they can rest content with *seeing* an apparently rare bird, we in a small country like England can well afford to spare the warblers. Mr. Hornaday urges that "it is not at all essential that such tiny, inconspicuous creatures as warblers should be recognised and correctly named at sight," and when one comes to think of it, it really does not seem at all essential.

Years ago there was a colony of avocets in the Salthouse marshes, and even now one or two of these birds are occasionally met with in the neighbourhood of their former breeding-place; had they survived until to-day as a Norfolk breeding-species they would undoubtedly be as well protected as are the terns at Wells. Far rarer visitors are the cranes; but in April 1898, a gang of workmen enjoyed the sight of the arrival of four of these striking birds, which alighted on the Wiveton bank of the little river Glaven (which enters the sea at Cley), and remained for some time resting full in view. Subsequently they were seen to fly eastward, and they were afterwards known to have paid a visit to Weybourne, near Cromer, from whence, as from Wiveton, they were—remarkable to relate—permitted to depart unmolested. Indeed, they probably had the strange experience for rare birds of their size, of being allowed to leave England.

A list of all the rare birds which have been met with on or near the meals would be a long one, and this is scarcely the place for it; but it may be mentioned that among the birds shot, or otherwise "obtained," in recent years, are king eiders, ruddy sheld-ducks, broad-billed and buff-breasted sandpipers, Sabine's gulls (including one taken in a stake-net at Wells in October 1892), a great skua, a great shearwater, a black stork, a night-heron, a whiskered tern, gull-billed terns, and a Temminck's stint. This will prove that some fascinating glimpses of bird life are not infrequently to be enjoyed in the meal marshes; but they are chiefly such glimpses as reward only the resident observers and gunners, or such fortunate persons as are able to make Wells, Cley, or Blakeney their headquarters during the migration seasons. One remarkable feature of the wild life of the North Norfolk coast remains to be mentioned, and it is one that can usually be observed by anyone who visits the meals on any day between the end of October and early spring. I refer to the presence in the Wells neighbourhood of flocks of pink-footed geese. So far back as the oldest inhabitant of Wells can remember, large numbers of these fine birds have regularly put in an appearance as soon as sharp weather has compelled them to leave their northern breeding haunts. This has generally been about the last week in October; but the time varies a little with the weather, and in some years several hundred geese have arrived before the middle of the month. For two or three weeks their numbers appear to increase almost daily, and although no such enormous flocks are now seen as are recorded to have visited Norfolk in the early part of the last century—when they were mistaken for bean geese—they may still be counted at times by the thousand. These wild grey geese of Holkham, as they are called, divide their time during the winter between the fields and marshes around Wells and the sandbanks lying off the coast. Mr. Seebohm says that they only go out to the sandbanks after nightfall; but this is not the case, for almost every day, as soon as the tide ebbs from the sandbanks, flocks of geese may be seen flying high over the meals, on their way to the uncovered sands. Day after day they follow the same lines of flight, one of which crosses the meals a short distance eastward of Wells harbour; so one has only to ascertain the hour of tide-ebb to be almost sure of seeing one or more flocks in flight towards the sea.

I still have a vivid recollection of the circumstances under which I first made the acquaintance of the wild

PINK-FOOTED GEESE.

grey geese. It was a dismal morning in late October, and to escape being drenched by a heavy rain while I was down in the meals, I had taken shelter in a cramped little shelter of turf and hurdles built by some wild-fowler on the border of the marshes. There, seated on a rough wooden bench, and watching the water dripping from a hole in the roof, I was patiently waiting for the rain to cease, when I suddenly heard the unmistakable loud "honking" of wild geese. In an instant I was outside the shelter, and, looking inland, I saw at least two hundred geese approaching, flying high, for the most part in V-shaped lines, each line consisting of from thirty to sixty birds. A more clamorous flock of birds it would have been hard to find, save on the mud-banks of an estuary on a foggy night. While they were passing overhead it was impossible to hear anything save their cackling and trumpet-like cries. They passed right over the spot where I was standing, flying, apparently, slowly, and giving me a good opportunity of observing their outstretched necks, heavy bodies, and widespread wings and tail feathers; but probably they were moving faster than they appeared to be, for a seagull, although apparently in leisurely flight, will often make one hundred and twenty wing-beats in a minute. Like an aerial army they advanced across the meals and out to sea, until they were directly over the sandbanks, when they suddenly dropped, like dark flakes, from the sky, and, after wheeling around for a while, settled on the sands.

While the sandbanks are covered by the tide, the grey geese are generally to be found in the marshes or the barley and clover fields [1] lying inland of the meals,

[1] According to Mr. A. J. Napier, of Holkham, the geese seldom visit the wheat stubbles, although they are probably quite as fond of wheat as of barley. Possibly this is because the hard and sharp wheat stubbles prick their feet. Mr. Napier says he has seen geese settle on a wheat stubble "and spring up immediately as if they had alighted on hot coals." See *Wild-Fowl* (Fur, Feather, and Fin Series).

where, thanks to the protection extended to them by Lord Leicester, they seldom come to any harm; but in the dusk the local gunners often lie in wait for them among the sandhills, and occasionally one or two birds fall to their guns. In the early morning, too, according to Mr. A. J. Napier, the sea-wall which protects the Holkham marshes is often lined with gunners of all descriptions, "armed with every sort of weapon, from an 8-bore to a crow-keeping gun tied up with tarred line." Even then, however, the geese usually escape the gunners, for they have learnt how high to fly, and when they draw near the sea-wall they rise out of reach of any but very powerful guns. Of late years considerable numbers have been taken in the stake-nets set up on the Wells sands, into which the geese, like a good many gulls, are floated by the rising tide. These stake-nets, which have a two-feet mesh, are about 30 feet long and 7 feet deep, stretched on poles about 12 feet high, which are set up on the wide sandy flats over which the tide flows. They are to be seen not only at Wells, but also at Blakeney, Holme, and on the Wash near Lynn, and wherever they are used they are at times very destructive of bird life. Mr. F. J. Cresswell, of Lynn, used to set up nets of this kind extending a distance of at least a third of a mile, and it is on record that between 1859 and 1869 he netted no less than 3693 birds. These included owls, larks, golden and grey plovers, curlews, redshanks, bar-tailed godwits, woodcocks, knots, dunlins, oyster-catchers, storm petrels, sheld-ducks, mallard, wigeon, teal, black-headed kittiwake, common herring, and great black-backed gulls, grebes, guillemots, and razorbills. On one occasion as many as sixty dunlins were secured; on another, one hundred and forty birds, chiefly gulls; and yet again, sixty oyster-catchers. Seven grey geese were also taken by Mr. Cresswell in one night; they had "rolled themselves up in one little bit of net into such a ball that it had to be cut to pieces to get them out"; but this was nothing compared with the hauls sometimes made by the Wells netters, who, however, are chary of mentioning how many birds they catch, for fear of steps being taken to put a stop to their netting. Dark, boisterous nights are said to be the best for bird-netting, and the nets at daybreak often present a remarkable sight, owing to the various kinds of birds found entangled in them. Mr. Gurney mentions having seen 1 woodcock, 4 curlews, 15 knots, 3 golden plovers, 3 grey plovers, 1 bar-tailed godwit, 1 redshank, 2 oyster-catchers, 34 dunlins, and 17 gulls of different kinds dangling together in Mr. Cresswell's nets; and on another occasion 40 dunlins, 19 knots, 1 grebe, 1 guillemot, 1 razorbill, 5 gulls, and 1 golden plover. A remarkable thing about these nets is that, notwithstanding their large mesh, they will catch a lark as easily as they will a goose. "If a dunlin so much as touches with the tip of his wing, it is wound round in an instant," writes Mr. Gurney, "and there he hangs until he is taken out and killed." A good many waders caught alive by Mr. Cresswell were presented to the Zoological Gardens.

Although the local wild-fowlers sometimes find the net to be a more profitable means of taking wild geese than shooting them, some gunners have had considerable success. Undoubtedly the record bag was made by Lord Leicester and the Hon. Colonel Coke on January 13th and 26th, 1881, when, according to "Thormanby," they between them killed "seventy-six wild geese, all with shoulder-guns." "The best grey-geese shooting at Holkham," writes Mr. W. J. Pope, "is always obtained in stormy weather, when the ground is covered with snow; and the usual method of killing them is by 'flighting.' The gunners separate on the marshes, and go off in different directions to ascertain the line which the geese are following, and then find whatever shelter is available, behind which they hide themselves. A gate sometimes answers the purpose, and if there is snow on the ground the shooter usually envelops himself in a nightshirt or an overall, and a white cap, in order to make himself less liable to detection."[1]

No matter at what season of the year an observer of wild life visits the meals, he is likely to linger among them as long as he is able, and leave them with regret. There is a strange fascination about them, as there generally is about a primitive place where the works of man are little in evidence, and that fascination weaves such spells as are hard to break. For hours one may wander amid the meal scrub or by the side of the creeks and drains where the foot-marks of the wading birds make strange patterns on the mud, and yet there always seems to be something fresh to see. So that when one returns to the quay at Wells, and looks back across the harbour to the wide, wild plain with its dusk-darkened waters, one knows only too well that its wonderful wild life has been only half revealed, that it has many secrets, and keeps them well. Around the quay, where the sea-trout netters are just starting for their night's netting, and the fishermen are standing in little groups about their 'longshore boats, there is much to interest one; but it is the wide-spreading meals, beyond which the landmark steeple of Blakeney is fading from sight far off against the darkening sky, which appeal to the imagination with all the witchery of a wild-life wonderland.

[1] *Wild-Fowl* (Fur, Feather, and Fin Series), p. 166.

CHAPTER IX

SMELTS AND SMELT-NETTING

ALTHOUGH March is commonly said to "come in like a lion and go out like a lamb," there is seldom anything lamb-like about the winds that sweep across our eastern estuaries during the last week of the roaring month. On the sunny side of a high-banked river-wall there may be, perhaps, a little warmth, and there a few white flowers of the salt-loving scurvy-grass may be found in bloom; but away from the scanty shelter of the low-lying shore, in the stake-marked channel where the tide flows swiftly and strongly, one is often glad to undertake a stiff bit of rowing rather than crouch and shiver in the stern of a boat. Yet nowhere can the joy of living be better appreciated than on the racing tidal waters, and to feel that joy to the full one must be afloat on an estuary when it is flashing in the fickle sun-gleams of March, and a boisterous wind is whipping its surface into a welter of dancing wavelets. In the restless life of wind and water one becomes an active participant, and welcomes an amount of vigorous exertion which at another time it would be a hardship to endure. Amid gleaming ooze-flats and far-spreading marshes, suggesting the primeval times when the world was in making, one experiences a temporary reversion to primitive feelings and heedlessness of elemental changes.

I was conscious of some such feeling on a wild March day, when I found myself among a party of smelt-fishers on Breydon, the wind-swept estuary of the Yare and Waveney. For a day or two a gale had been blowing, and though its strength had slightly moderated, the mud-flats uncovered by the tide were alive with gulls, storm-driven from the sea. Migrating wigeon, too, were much in evidence on the shallow water above the flats just awash, and redshank and lapwing were piping and wailing above the bordering marshes. It was a day of sudden weather changes; sun-gleam and cloud-shadow followed each other in quick succession over water, marsh, and mud-flat; distant rain-storms at times obscured the far horizon of the marshes—storms that came sweeping over the lowlands and down upon us with surprising suddenness, to pass as quickly as they came.

The spring migration of the smelts into the fresh water was in progress, so all the smelters in the neighbourhood were on the alert to reap their annual harvest. Eight nets were being used, so twice that number of men and boys were afloat in shallow flat-bottomed boats, or congregated in the vicinity of some quaint black ark-like houseboats moored in a small artificial harbour banked by bastions of glue-like ooze. Since daybreak the netting had been going on; but it was nearly ten o'clock when, in response to a hail from the Burgh shore, a boat was sent to bring me into the midst of the estuarine flotilla. By that time the shallow boxes in some of the boats contained a fair number of the delicate golden-green fish, though the results of the early morning netting were described as being "only moderate," the smelts as yet having put in an appearance in small numbers. On more than one occasion, a haul had been made without the taking of a single fish.

During the winter months smelt-netting is carried on at intervals in the main channel of the estuary and the branch channels or "drains" between the mud-flats;

SMELTS AND SMELT-NETTING 153

but at the time of my visit the smelters were at work near the highest point at which they may legally net, which has a landmark on the bank of the Waveney in the lofty chimney of the Burgh Cement Works, less than a quarter of a mile from the spot where the river enters the estuary. Here the channel is comparatively narrow, so by mutual agreement among the fishermen each net is worked in turn. This means that when only three or four boats are present, each can spread and haul its net about once every hour, save at the turn of the tide; but when, as was the case at the time of my visit, eight nets are being used, each can be hauled only once in about two or two and a half hours. In order to see as much as possible of the operations, I jumped into the boat about to spread its net, and, having watched the hauling, hastened along the river bank to secure a seat in the boat having the the next turn. Occasionally, however, I missed a boat, owing to its having put off from the shore before the one in advance of it had quite finished hauling. My first companions were two young smelters, ruddy of cheek and remarkable for muscular development. They belonged to a family of which the men had been smelters for at least four generations, and which had five representatives in the little fishing fleet. Our first haul was with the ebbing tide, and as the mud-flats bordering the channel were of inconsiderable width, one end of the net was worked from the boat and the other from the shore.

A start was made by rowing to within a few yards of the landmark chimney, where the younger of the two smelters jumped ashore, taking with him the end of a rope about a hundred feet long, which was attached to one end of the net. As soon as he had landed, his brother began rowing out into mid-stream, letting the rope, and afterwards the hundred yards or more of draw-net, slip rapidly over the smooth-worn stern of the boat.

This net, which was buoyed with corks but weighted with enough lead to cause it to touch the bottom of the channel, was about eight feet in depth, stouter in make than those formerly used by the smelters, and with a mesh measuring five-eighths of an inch from knot to knot, the smallest mesh permitted by the law. By the time the net was spread, and a second length of rope paid out, the boat had almost reached the opposite side of the channel, and its rower, settling himself to steady pulling, commenced towing the net down stream. This, notwithstanding that the tide was still ebbing and so assisting the rower, seemed to be no easy work. Meanwhile the young smelter on the bank was ploughing his way through salt-pools and mud, into which he sank almost knee-deep at every step, dragging the other end of the net, but keeping some distance behind the boat in order that the latter might bring its end of the net round to the shore a good way ahead of him. All the while the drawing was in progress the net was entirely submerged, and could not be seen owing to the "colour" of the water, which was yellow with mud stirred up by the little waves breaking upon the flats.

With one end of the net worked from the shore only a short haul was possible, for before the net had been towed more than about three hundred yards the boat had to be brought round to the shore in order that the net might escape contact with the first of the worm-eaten stakes marking the entrance to the channel of the estuary. Having rowed hard on to the mud, my companion seized the net-rope and jumped out of the boat on to the oozy flat, where he at once began hauling in, his brother meanwhile quickening his pace along the shore and bringing up the other end of the net, which, freed of the strain upon it, now became visible as a long cork-dotted loop gradually decreasing in size as yard after yard of net was deposited in layers at the feet of the haulers on the flat. When only about twenty yards remained in the water, the hauling became slower and steadier, the bottom as well as the top of the net being grasped. By this time an occasional splash or gleam within the decreasing loop betokened that the surrounded smelts were becoming aware of an obstacle to their movements. While the last few yards were being drawn in there was quite a little commotion within the loop, which ended suddenly when top and bottom of the net were quickly brought together and the last of it deposited on the flat. One by one the fish were then taken out and thrown on to the mud a few feet from the water. There were fifteen smelts of marketable size, about half a dozen so small that they were thrown back into the water, two fair-sized flounders and a few tiny ones, some shore crabs, and a sharp-nosed eel about fourteen inches long.

My next trip was in the company of the father of my previous companions, a middle-aged man, who wore a yachtsman's cap and jersey, and who worked his net from a low-sided boat of wide beam, built especially for smelting, which was not the case with most of the boats belonging to the little fleet. There was just time for him to make his haul before the tide turned; but he had some difficulty about doing so, owing to his net catching against some obstacle in the bed of the channel. This is a frequent experience of the smelters, the wash of the river steamers often dislodging large masses of "hover" from the riverside ronds, while the tide sometimes brings up, or the current brings down, sunken logs. Our misadventure on this occasion may have affected our catch by letting some of the smelts escape under the net; the haul only produced seven fish, one of which was a flounder.

To pass away the time while the tide was at slack water, the smelters occupied themselves in cleaning out their boats, some of which were nearly half filled with water that had drained from the wet nets, while all were, like the slush-boots and breeches of the fishermen, liberally coated with drying ooze. Then some of the nets were washed by dipping them yard by yard in the river; and this done, most of the smelters entered their cramped little houseboats in order to rest a while, smoke a pipe, or eat the dinner which, in their case, was a moveable feast, the time for it being fixed by the tide.

On entering one of the houseboats, I found half a dozen men and boys lounging on lockers extending the full length of the cabin on either side of a glowing fire, which had raised the temperature of the interior of the boat to about the same height as that of the Tropical House at Kew. That the health of these men and boys is apparently unaffected by their frequent sudden changes from such a temperature to that of the chill flats and frozen marshes in midwinter, is a constant surprise to me; but they seem to be indifferent to such changes, and almost invariably enjoy the best of health. It may be that the weaklings are soon compelled to abandon smelting; at any rate, there were no weaklings among the party in the houseboat I entered, and I may add that in all my rambles among and encounters with marsh-folk, fishermen, and gipsies, I had never met with a party clad in so odd an assortment of garments. Each man and boy, of course, wore slush-boots reaching above the knee; but there, I think, the likeness between them ended. No two of them wore a similar headgear; their coats ranged from a pilot-jacket with brass buttons to a dilapidated and almost buttonless frock-coat which had been cut short for convenience; and their nether garments were so varied, and in some cases in such condition, as to defy description.

The fittings of the cabin were of the rudest kind, consisting, apart from the stove and lockers, of two or three shelves, on which were placed a number of empty marmalade jars. These, I soon discovered, served the purpose of cups and saucers, when cold tea was warmed in earthenware bottles over the stove. Plates and table knives were luxuries that could very well be dispensed with, so long as a pork bone could be picked with the aid of a clasp-knife and a sound set of teeth.

Chatting with an elderly man about the past and present of smelt-netting, it was not without surprise that I learnt that, in his opinion, smelting, though at all times an uncertain occupation, is as profitable a business now as he could ever remember it to have been. Since his "young time," he admitted, the area in which smelting can be done has become more restricted, not only on account of the netting regulations, but also owing to the increase in size and height of the Breydon mud-flats; but, so far as he was aware, there had been no diminution in the numbers of the smelts. Indeed, during the previous April (1904) he had made the record catch of his life, landing no less than eighteen score smelts by one haul of his net. Among these was a twelve-inch specimen weighing seven and a half ounces, while several others were ten inches long. This old man, who was born in a village adjoining Breydon, commenced smelting when only nine years old, by accompanying his father in his boat; and often on bitter winter mornings he was abroad and afloat by daylight, handling the wet and often frozen nets. The nets then differed from those at present in use, in being smaller and made of a thread so fine as to be practically invisible in the water. They were generally made by the wives of the smelters, whose fingers, when "chapped" in winter, were often severely cut by the fine thread—a painful experience even more common in the case of the smelters themselves. Afterwards such nets as these could be bought ready-made, and cost from £3, 10s. to £5 each; but they soon became useless, requiring far more careful handling than they usually got among the smelters, the sides of whose old boats often had a splinter which did serious damage to the fine-thread meshes.

The frosty mornings, the old man repeated, were "cruel" times for the smelting boys, who, however, generally welcomed a spell of sharp weather, because it brought considerable flocks of wild-fowl to the Breydon mud-flats, and for a time the smelters found punt-gunning more profitable than netting. This meant that the boys were able to stay in bed a few hours later in the mornings—in fact, until it was time for them to go down to the Breydon wall and bring home the fowl that had fallen to the big swivel guns. Afterwards they would sometimes ramble along the walls, seeking the wounded fowl which had managed to fly or swim beyond reach of the gunners. These wounded birds almost invariably made for the shore, where it was no rare thing for a boy to gather up in a morning as many as would fill a "ped" (wicker basket). But sometimes the boys were forestalled by the grey crows, which flocked to Breydon when punt-gunning was in progress, and were always on the alert to pick up and despatch the unfortunate "cripples" that crept into holes and hollows in the walls or the margin of the creeks. The "owd Denchmen," as the boys called the grey crows, always seemed to know when there was a good meal to be picked up; but at the same time they were generally far too wide awake to come within range of the fowler's gun.

Smelting in those days could be carried on at all times, there being no fishing regulations save those ancient ones which were seldom or never enforced. Wherever the smelts were to be found in any numbers, there the netters went in search of them, and no matter what might be the condition of the fish, as many as possible were taken. Now it is illegal to use a smelt-net on Breydon during the months of May, June, July, and August, when the water is often "alive" with young fry; and at no time may a net be used having a mesh measuring less than five-eighths of an inch from knot to knot. On the higher waters of the Yare and Waveney no net may be used for taking smelts except between the 10th March and the 12th May, and even then only at certain spots mentioned in the Fisheries Act.

While we were chatting, the tide had turned and the mud-flats were slowly disappearing. Already the smelters who had the next "turn" were preparing to haul, so, leaving the old man to finish his pipe, I descended again to the oozy waterside, and boarded one of two boats just putting off from the shore. Hauling with the flowing tide I found to be a slightly different proceeding to netting on the ebb, for a start was made lower down the channel where it was marked by a double row of tall stakes. These stakes prevented the working of one end of the net from the shore, so two boats were required to draw the net, one working within the stakes on each side of the channel. At the end of the draw, which terminated near the spot where a start was made while the netting was in progress on the ebb, the net was hauled up in a small muddy creek, the flats being now covered by the tide. About twenty minutes were occupied in spreading and hauling, and the catch was anything but satisfactory, only five smelts being taken. There were also a couple of atherines or "smolts," as the fishermen call them, the presence of which among the smelts working up the river to spawn being difficult to account for, seeing that the atherine spawns in the open sea. "Smolts," however, are frequently plentiful in Breydon, and it is a well-known fact that considerable numbers of them are sold by fishmongers as true "cucumber" smelts. But the characteristic smell of the true smelt is always enough to distinguish it from the atherine, which also has a differently shaped mouth and a beautiful iridescent band of violet along its sides.

Netting was continued until nightfall, but the catches were exceedingly light. At the close of the day the fish captured by the eight boats hardly numbered four hundred in all. A month later, the smelting season was at its best, and there were days when each boat took as many as the eight took during a day in March, and sometimes one haul resulted in the capture of from six to ten score of fish. A good deal depends upon the weather, a long spell of fine weather being in the favour of the smelters, who, however, do not object to just enough wind to ruffle the water, and thicken it with stirred-up mud.

In the river Ouse there has been for a great many years an important smelt-fishery, which is now subject to like regulations to those applying to Breydon and the Yare and Waveney, excepting that between the 1st April and the 31st August the taking of smelts is entirely prohibited. This fishery was undoubtedly carried on as early as the days of Queen Elizabeth, when an Act was passed fixing the size of the mesh used in the capture of smelts; and Sir Thomas Browne was evidently acquainted with it, for among his notes on Norfolk fishes we find mention of "spinachus or smelt, in greatest plentie about Lynne, but where they haue also a small fish calld a primme (? atherine), answering in tast & shape a smelt, & perhaps are butt the yonger sort thereof." Some interesting facts concerning the Ouse fishery are to be found in a paper written by Mr. C. W. Harding, of Lynn, which was submitted as a prize essay to the International Fisheries Exhibition of 1883. From observations of the habits of the smelt in the Ouse and other Norfolk rivers, Mr. Harding ascertained that the fish spawn where the water is fresh about the middle of April, the spawn being deposited on sticks and stones in the river, but not covered up, as with the larger members of the salmon family. The fry are soon hatched out, and by the end of summer have attained a length of between three and four inches. While in the brackish water of the river the smelts appear to feed in a great measure on the fry of sprats and herring, small shrimps, and the yellow goby (*Gobius auratus*), a little fish abounding in the Ouse and Wash. "I find," continues Mr. Harding, "that an average-sized female smelt contains 12,000 eggs, and from the large quantity which spawn in the Ouse every year, the river ought to teem with smelts, and would, but for the eight or ten trim or stow nets set for their capture. Last June (1882) the net set to catch samples was covered with young smelts a few days old. They were caught and destroyed in the meshes, and I counted as many as 800 in one square yard of it. The number destroyed every day by the huge nets set in the river must amount to tens of millions.... They are not of the slightest use either for food or bait at this age. In addition to the destruction caused by the fixed nets to the smelt fishery, myriads of shrimps, herrings, sprats, yellow gobies, anchovies, and whiting are daily destroyed." A trim net, as Mr. Harding explains, is a net set open to the tide by means of three poles; each pole is seventeen feet long, so that the mouth of the net is a large triangle seventeen feet on each side. Such a net is exceedingly destructive, catching fish, fry, and spawn. In the opinion of Mr. Harding, the great falling-off in the sole fisheries of the Wash was largely due to the destruction of the young smelts, sprats, and other small fish upon which the soles feed.

As regards the taking of smelts in the rivers Yare and Wensum, it is enacted by the Norfolk and Suffolk Fisheries Act of 1877 that no person shall attempt to use any net except a cast net or drop net in those rivers for the purpose of taking smelts between the 10th March and the 12th May, both days inclusive, and then only between the New Mills at Norwich or Trowse Bridge and the junction of the Yare and Wensum at a place known as Trowse Hythe, and between Hardley Cross and the junction of the Yare and Waveney. It is also enacted that no person shall use a cast net exceeding sixteen feet in diameter. The exception of the neighbourhood of the

New Mills and Trowse Bridge from the general provisions of the Act was made on account of the existence of an old-established fishery at Norwich, the New Mills—which scarcely deserve the name, seeing that they were first built in 1430—being the spot where the upstream progress of the smelts is barred. This fishery came under the notice of Lubbock, who remarks that the smelts taken in the pool of the New Mills are of the largest size; while the Norwich smelters, he was inclined to believe, excelled all England in the management of a cast net. "Their profits nowadays," he wrote in 1845, "are much curtailed, although the earlier smelts are sold in the market for five and six shillings a score. Formerly, twenty-five and even thirty score have been taken by one net in the course of a night. March is the time when this fishery begins, which lasts until the middle or end of April, and a smelter may be deemed the personification of patience; hour after hour does he persevere, moored exactly in the same spot, with a torch attached to the side of his broad flat-bottomed boat—for this is a nocturnal occupation—in flinging his immense casting net, dropping the near side of it at each throw within three inches of the torch. One fortunate cast, if smelts sell well, may recompense him for hours of fatigue, wet, and cold; and he waits, like the losing gambler, for the lucky throw which is to brighten his fortunes. The smelts taken are kept alive, and a tank full of these beautiful fish is a very pretty sight. Besides these, a few gudgeons are taken, and a good many lamperns (*Petromyzon fluviatilis*). These last are all sold to the eel-fishers for bait. It is a curious fact, that other fish greatly forsake the higher part of the river whilst it is occupied by smelts spawning. Roach and dace are at that time very scarce, although plentiful enough before the smelts arrive; they then remove farther down the river for a time, and, as they say here, 'the fish are down because the smelts are up.' I have known it at that time

SMELT-NETTING IN A MILL POOL

difficult to provide a few coarse fish for the sustenance of a tame heron."

Cast-netting for smelts in the New Mills pool seems to have come to an end when the New Mills were converted into a refuse destructor, municipal enterprise thus putting an end to an old-established local fishery; but in the mill-pool at Trowse, a Norwich suburb near the junction of the Yare and Wensum, two or three cast-netters may still be found in spring, industriously netting from dusk until late in the evening or early in the morning. Each boat contains two men, one of whom, by "back-watering" with his oars, keeps the boat from being carried downstream by the roaring outrush of water from beneath the old mill, while the netter, clad in yellow oilskins, held close about him by a large waterproof apron, stands at the stern on a little deck made of half a dozen boards Over one arm is slung the lead-weighted net, which from time to time, with a swaying turn and a sudden jerk, he casts upon the water in such a way that it expands to its full circumference as it falls, its contact with the water being sometimes accompanied by a gleaming of bluish phosphorescence. For a few moments the net is allowed to sink in the deep water of the mill-pool, and as it sinks its leads cause it to assume the shape of an inverted funnel; then it is carefully drawn towards the side of the boat, the funnel of net meanwhile closing as the leads come together, and by a quick final movement it is lifted on to the little deck at the stern of the boat. Time after time, and sometimes night after night, this performance is repeated without the capture of a single fish; but there is always a chance of a fair catch being made, or even a good one, which will reward the patient fisherman for many fruitless casts. In the twilight, when the netting begins, the movements of the boatmen can be seen from the mill-bridge or the riverside, and, occasionally, it may be, the pale gleam of a netted smelt is seen through the meshes of the net; but as the dusk deepens and a gloom settles under the tree-boughs overhanging the river, boats and boatmen gradually grow less distinct, until they are seen only as vague shadows slowly moving over the surface of the pool. Sometimes, when a rower lets a boat drift beneath the trees, it vanishes altogether; but when the net is cast the splash it makes is heard faintly even above the turmoil of the mill-water. Very few men take part in this fishing to-day, and those who do so complain that the draw-netters on the lower waters of the river, by netting almost night and day during the spring migration of the smelts, permit very few fish to work their way up the river.

CHAPTER X

THE EDIBLE FROG

ONE summer night, after a day spent in cruising on the Waveney, I sat on a locker in a water-bailiff's houseboat, chatting with its owner about marshland life and marshland lore. Presently the conversation turned towards the gipsies and their liking for certain far from popular dishes, and this reminded my companion that, when he was a young man working in the riverside cement works at Burgh Castle, a fellow-workman persuaded him to partake of hedgehog under the delusion of its being rabbit. He admitted that the hedgehog was "very good eating," and that he would have no great objection to eating another. I told him that Frenchmen were fond of eating frogs. He made a grimace; but said that he had heard of frogs being eaten in Norfolk, and, on my asking for particulars, told me that a good many years ago the late Squire Berney, of Morton Hall, invited a friend to dinner, and placed before him a dish of what appeared to be young birds. The guest ate of them with relish, and then asked what kind of birds they were. "They are not birds at all; they are 'freshers,'" was the reply, "fresher" being the name locally applied to young frogs.

It occurred to me when I heard the story, that the frogs referred to were probably an edible species; but it was not until some time after that I became aware of the late Mr. G. Berney having imported a large number of edible frogs into Norfolk. I then turned to the records of the edible frog as a British species. It was first discovered in Foulmire Fen, in Cambridgeshire, by Mr. Charles Thurnall of Daxford, whose discovery of the interesting amphibian is announced in a letter written by Mr. J. P. Wollaston and preserved in the Cambridge Museum. A short notice of the finding of the frog appeared in the *Zoologist* (1843), written by Mr. F. Bond, who stated that it occurred in considerable abundance in the fen, and that the male, when croaking, displayed "two large bladders, one on each side of the mouth," which gave it a very curious appearance. He expressed surprise that naturalists had not detected the frogs before, their croaking being quite different to that of the common frog; "the sound," he writes, "is more of a loud snore, exactly like that of the barn owl (*Strix flammea*). The whole fen was quite in a charm with their song!" He found the frog to be very timid, disappearing at the least alarm. Subsequently Professor Bell, the author of *British Reptiles*, sent to the *Zoologist* a letter in which he stated: "I have often heard my father, who was a native of these parts, say that the croak of the frogs there was so different from that of others, that he thought they must be of a different kind." Professor Bell added that the croaking was so loud and shrill as to have obtained for the frogs the name of "Cambridgeshire Nightingales" and "Whaddon Organs."

The late Dr. J. E. Taylor, curator of the Ipswich Museum, believed the edible frog to be rare, but indigenous in Cambridgeshire; and the late Charles Kingsley, in his delightful paper on "The Fens,"[1] quotes in support of the theory (now an admitted fact) that England was formerly connected by land with the Continent, the presence of the edible frog in Foulmire. "It is a moot point still with some," he says, "whether he was not put there by man. It is a still stronger argument against his being indigenous that he is never mentioned as an

[1] In *Prose Idyls*.

article of food by the mediæval monks, who would have known—Frenchmen, Italians, Germans, as many of them were—that he is as dainty as ever was a spring chicken. But if he be indigenous, his presence proves at once that he could either hop across the Straits of Dover or swim the German Ocean."

Although the discovery of edible frogs in Foulmire Fen aroused considerable interest among naturalists, no fresh discovery of the species was made for several years. It then happened that Professor Alfred Newton, whilst driving through a marshy district in Norfolk, heard a strange noise, which puzzled him, until he proved it to be the croaking of a considerable number of edible frogs. Through the courtesy of Mr. S. H. Miller, one of the authors of *The Fenland*, I am able to quote from a letter he received from Professor Newton, who wrote: " As to the edible frog in Norfolk, it was in 1853 that my brother and I found a colony at Rockland (near Attleborough). . . . Last May (1876) I found another at Stow Bedon —not very far off—and in the meanwhile it had not been observed by any naturalist so far as I know. But Lord Walsingham, who was with me on the second occasion, has since ascertained that it is pretty well established in the neighbourhood of Didlington."

As soon as Professor Newton found the frogs at Rockland, he made inquiries as to where they came from, and learnt from Mr. J. H. Gurney that in 1837, Mr. George Berney, of Morton Hall, imported a quantity of edible frogs; that, two years later, he imported two hundred more; and in 1841 and 1842, over a thousand were brought by him into Norfolk and deposited in the ditches and fields at Morton, some ponds at Hockering, and the fens at Foulden, near Stoke Ferry. These frogs were brought from France and Brussels. As Foulden is not far from Didlington, there seemed to be little doubt that the frogs mentioned by Lord Walsingham as being well established at the latter place were descendants of those liberated at Foulden, and it was at once taken for granted that such was the case. According to Mr. Gurney, those placed in the meadows soon betook themselves to the nearest ponds, where they gradually disappeared, and Mr. Berney came to the conclusion that the English climate did not agree with them. The discoveries made by Lord Walsingham and Professor Newton, however, seemed to prove that the alien amphibians were a long time in becoming extinct, and Professor Newton was satisfied that the species had "made good its existence in Norfolk for at least thirty-four years."

When naturalists heard of the experiment made by Mr. Berney, interest was re-awakened in the discovery made in Foulmire Fen, and as Mr. Berney's frogs were liberated in Norfolk six years before the Foulmire frogs were detected, it was suggested that some of the Norfolk frogs found their way to Foulmire. "Is it possible," asked Mr. Miller in *The Fenland*, "that some of these (the Norfolk frogs) travelled from Foulden to Foulmire, a distance of about forty miles?" He agreed that, while possible, this was not a probable explanation of the presence of edible frogs at Foulmire, as there was no record of any having been taken between the two places.

In 1874, Mr. Miller wrote to *Nature* asking for information respecting the naturalisation of the species. In reply, Lord Arthur Russell wrote that he had, some twelve years before, brought some edible frogs from Paris and placed them in a pond at Woburn Abbey. He added: "They thrived and multiplied there; but our summers are seldom hot enough to enable the tadpole to attain his full development before the cold autumnal nights set in . . . I believe that in our climate the young will pass the winter as tadpoles, and complete their transformation in the following spring. But this would require more accurate information before I can

THE EDIBLE FROG

affirm it with certainty." The experience of Mr. Doubleday, of Epping, who liberated some of the Cambridgeshire frogs in a pond near his house, was that "they soon migrated to another pond, and there made themselves perfectly at home." He does not say how long they were to be found there.

Ten years after the publication of Mr. Miller's letter, some valuable information concerning the edible frog in England was supplied by Mr. G. A. Boulenger, who in the meantime had been collecting information respecting its occurrence in this country. Mr. Boulenger made known the interesting fact that the frog which had been found in Foulmire Fen, in Cambridgeshire, at Stow Bedon, and between Thetford and Scoulton, and which was generally regarded as having been introduced from France and Belgium, was not the type species of the edible frog, but belonged to an Italian form, *Rana esculenta lessonæ*. The East Anglian frogs representing this Italian form were not, he felt convinced, descendants of any of those introduced into Norfolk by Mr. Berney, and he expressed a hope that descendants of Mr. Berney's frogs, which were of the type species (*R. esculenta*), would be discovered. "It is clear to me," wrote Mr. Boulenger in a note in the *Zoologist*,[1] "that all the specimens, the capture of which has hitherto been recorded, whether from Cambridgeshire or Norfolk, are not descendants of those introduced by Mr. Berney, but are of Italian origin. By whom and when they were introduced into this country, I cannot venture to suggest."

This new light on the subject of edible frogs in England led to a revival of interest in the Norfolk frogs, and the hope expressed by Mr. Boulenger was soon realised. On August 9th, 1884, he received from Norfolk two fine living specimens of the typical edible frog. These had been found at Foulden, one of the

[1] July 1884.

very spots where the frogs, of which they were undoubtedly descendants, had been turned out by Mr. Berney.

Previously to this, Mr. Boulenger had accompanied Lord Walsingham to Stow Bedon, where, on July 29th, they found the Italian form to be very abundant in small pools and pits, which, owing to an excessive drought, contained very little water. "They did not," writes Mr. Boulenger,[1] "indulge in their sonorous croaking on the occasion of our visit, and no tadpoles or spawn were to be seen. However, one full-grown tadpole was dredged from the bottom of a pit, but was so much injured that I could not preserve it. I was rather surprised to find that none of the specimens presented that beautiful green colour which is usual in *R. esculenta*; all were olive-brown, spotted and marbled with black, and provided with a pale yellow or pale green vertebral line; all had the enormous metatarsal tubercle. This accounts for the fact for which I was always at a loss to find an explanation, namely, the silence of the first discoverers of the edible frog in Cambridgeshire as to the green colour which, among other characters, so well distinguishes that species from the common frog. *R. esculenta lessonæ*, as occurring in England, is never green. Lord Walsingham informed me that he was making inquiries among the people of the neighbourhood as to how long the frogs had lived there, and that he had been assured that their existence could be traced as far as sixty years back."

Shortly after this, Mr. G. E. Mason visited Norfolk with the object of ascertaining the distribution of the edible frog in the county. On the common at Stow Bedon the form *lessonæ* appeared to be restricted to the north-west portion, and absent from all the ponds which are distributed over the remaining tract. An explanation of this was found in the fact that a good many water-

[1] *Proceedings of the Zoological Society of London*, 1884, pp. 573-576.

fowl had their home among the ponds from which the frogs were absent. A large number of recently transformed young were discovered; also some in the last stage of the tadpole. At Scoulton, nearly four miles from Stow Bedon station, Mr. Mason ascertained that examples of *lessonæ* had been easily found two or three years previously in nearly all the ponds on one estate; but since that time they had quite disappeared.

The two frogs sent to Mr. Boulenger from Foulden were typical edible frogs, grass-green in colour, and possessing only the moderate metatarsal tubercle. In the same fen Mr. Mason found other examples of the type species, and he satisfied himself that it was distributed over all the fenland in that part of Norfolk, where it was known as the "French frog." Before leaving the district, he liberated a few Foulden frogs in ponds at Brandon, a favourable locality from which both forms appeared to be absent. A fine adult example of the true edible frog was taken by him in Wereham Fen.

Mr. Boulenger sums up the whole matter as follows: "It is clear that the frogs of Stow Bedon and Scoulton (and Foulmire Fen, where they have disappeared for many years past) are quite distinct from those of Foulden and Wereham. Those from the latter places are certainly descendants of Mr. Berney's importations from Paris, Brussels, and St. Omer in 1837-42. Of the introduction of the other form we have no authentic record; but as they belong to a race known to occur only in Italy, we must come to the conclusion that they were imported from that country, and the suggestion of the late John Wolley, that they were introduced by the monks, appears the most plausible."[1] Baron von Hugel, however, thinks that they were probably introduced by the Romans, as their bones are met with in Roman middens.

The mystery attaching to these frogs is not yet

[1] *Proceedings of the Zoological Society of London*, 1884, p. 576.

quite solved. At the time when Mr. Boulenger wrote the above "summing up" he was not aware that the form *lessonæ*, instead of being confined to Italy, has a much wider distribution, it having been found not only in Austria, Hungary, Bavaria, and various other parts of Germany, but also by himself in Belgium and near Paris. "The supposed Italian origin of our frogs," writes Dr. H. Gadow,[1] "has naturally lost its interest by these recent discoveries, but nevertheless we must remember that there existed considerable intercourse between East Anglia and the monks of Lombardy, who, to mention only one instance, came regularly to the old priory of Chesterton in order to collect their rents. If the frogs were introduced by them for culinary purposes into various suitable localities, their descendants would remain as local as they actually are, and as are also the undoubtedly introduced French specimens of the *var. typica*. On the other hand, if we assume the *lessonæ* specimens to be the last living descendants of English natives, it is inconceivable why they should now be restricted to that eastern corner, while there are hundreds of other suitable places which, if on the Continent, would be perfect paradises for water-frogs. However, we know next to nothing about the œcology of these creatures. It is quite possible that the sporadic occurrence of the *var. lessonæ* is due to local adaptation and changes of the typical form, wherever the same favourable, or necessary, but to us unknown, conditions prevail. And, after all, the differences between these two varieties are not great, and in many specimens are even arbitrary, just as we might expect in actually changing forms. On the other hand, we know of a good many species which are either actually spreading, or which—and this may apply to the present case—are slowly but surely vanishing. In prehistoric times, *Emys*

---

[1] In the *Handbook to the Natural History of Cambridgeshire* (1904), pp. 106-107.

europæa, the pond-tortoise, was common in the Fens. It has now receded eastwards, being extinct in Belgium, Holland, and west of the Elbe; between this river and the Oder it is now in the vanishing stages, while it is still plentiful in Poland and Russia."

There is some evidence of the edible frog being an inhabitant of the Broads district. The Rev. Theodore Wood tells me that some years ago he came upon specimens in a lane at Brunstead, and Dr. Gadow states that he heard edible frogs in the pairing season of 1883 on Hickling Broad. On the same authority we have it that in the summer of 1901 a fine male was found among a number of grass-frogs which had been caught between Chesterton and Milton in Cambridgeshire for the Physiological Laboratory. He adds that great numbers have within the last few years been introduced from Germany, Belgium, and Italy, and liberated in Surrey, Hampshire, Oxfordshire, and Bedfordshire.

CHAPTER XI

AN UPLAND ROVER

I CAN never think of him without associating him with a hedgebank, so often have I seen him seated on such a bank, sheltering himself under woodbine and bryony from the glare of the summer sun. There is a certain tract of upland country — tame, flat country, divided into square fields which seem to be pegged down to the earth by churches and pollard oaks—of which he was as inseparable an adjunct as the carrier's cart which kept it in touch with the City of Churches; along its highways and byways he was a constant traveller, in its hamlets he was one of the most familiar figures, in the kitchen of every village and hedgerow alehouse he seemed to have a permanent place; but somehow there was always that about him which suggested his fitting environment to be the wind-swept uplands where the peewits fed among the furrows and the "wheat-pickers" flocked to the stubble fields. Yet you could never have mistaken him for a farm-labourer who found regular employment in such places, for, unlike the earth-bound farm-hand, who is ill at ease in strange company and away from his accustomed clods, he had the air of a freelance, eyes that could look one straight in the face, self-possession in all circumstances, and even a certain amount of cosmopolitism which is rarely met with in a rural district. He was plainly one of those who took life as it came, " the green and the grey of it, the summer and the winter," who had chosen the life that suited him best, "free to wander where he will, with no restraint of work and duty." For such men there is little scope to-day in rural England; most of them have vanished from the country-side, as the old tinkers, packmen, and reddlemen have vanished; but here and there, in isolate places where life still goes on at a jog-trot pace, such an one as he of whom I write may still be met with,—a careless, cheerful body, who, while always finding work when he is in want of it, partly from laziness, partly from independence of spirit, and partly from restlessness, persistently holds himself aloof from the routine of rural labour.

His manners, gestures, and briskness of movement distinguished him from the teamsters, horsemen, and ploughmen with whom he chiefly consorted; while his attire made it obvious that he not only lived a free and independent life, but did his best to make the fact evident to everyone. His beard was well frost-whitened by the years that had passed over his head; yet there was a suggestion of youthful dandyism about the cut of his green velveteen coat, the superabundance of pearl buttons on his corduroy leggings, the way in which he used his ground ash stick, and the angle at which he often tilted his home-made cap, the last-named evidently part of the skin of a brown retriever. The waistcoat he wore in summer—a yellow and black striped one, with bright horseshoe buttons—gave place in winter to one of moleskin, worthy of the proprietor of a travelling steam circus; while the crimson silk handkerchief he wore about his neck, and the curb-like silver watch-chain which swung in a double festoon from his waistcoat, and had a "lion" shilling for a pendant, were in keeping with a whole that was fantastic, individual, and more in harmony with the road-life of which Borrow has written, than with the characterless monotony of rural life at the end of the nineteenth century.

In the Census Returns, "Old Mowl," for so he was usually known, was probably described as a mole-catcher, and unquestionably the trophies of his skill as such were exhibited on many whitethorn hedges and solitary thorns; but he was also a kind of general messenger between farmers and their shepherds, when the latter were spending days and nights on the open uplands at lambing-time; and between kinsfolk residing in different parishes. During the Michaelmas sales of farming-stock, he would often make himself useful in the farmyard or at the village alehouse, either as ostler or "drawer"; and in the absence of the landlord of an inn he would often take charge of the kitchen for a day or two—an arrangement which, owing to his popularity with the inn's patrons, not infrequently meant a temporary increase of custom. Sometimes for days together he would be seen every night in a corner seat of the fireside settle of the Jolly Ploughman or the Dog and Duck, and from the joviality of his behaviour and the friendliness of his relations with all who met with him there, one would take him to be one of the most sociably inclined of human kind. But after a few nights his place would be found empty; the old restlessness had come over him; he had heard, perhaps, the rustling of the leaves of the upland oaks, or the whirring flight of a covey from the furrows, and he had taken to the road again. And it was then that, in the course of your ramblings along the old field footpaths or the winding lanes beside which the old high hedges still grew, you might chance to find him leaning listlessly against a field gate, or lounging idly on a hedge-bank, plainly quite as content to be amid the upland solitudes as with the rustic company in which he always found a hearty welcome. Or you might discover him, during the early months of the year, cheering for a while the nightly vigil of some lonely shepherd, sharing his hut with him, and helping him with his ewes and lambs; but you could never count upon finding him where you had last left him, even though he might have promised to meet you there; for when the inclination to wander seized him, he could not resist it, but must sling his canvas bag over his shoulder, take up his treasured ash stick, and be up and away.

Like the majority of his labouring friends, he seldom darkened the doorway of a church, yet he was more honest than many a churchwarden and regular payer of pew-rent, and I have yet to meet the man who can say he was ever wronged by him. It would seem that, like the average Romany, he had no religion; yet unconsciously he worshipped daily, and his temple had the whole sky for a roof. The very restlessness that compelled him to wander, and made the walls of a house a prison to him, came from a craving for something better than himself, which he found on the uplands where the breeze shrilled through the thorns; and though he would not have understood the meaning of the lines, one might, I think, rightly say of him what Hood had said of one akin to him:

> "To *his* tuned spirit the wild heather-bells
>   Ring Sabbath knells;
> The jubilate of the soaring lark
>   Is chant of clerk;
> For choir, the thrush and the gregarious linnet;
> The sods a cushion for his pious want;
> And, consecrate by the heav'n within it,
>   The sky-blue pool, a font."

Born to a higher state, and with fuller opportunity for following his bent and developing the best that was in him, he would have become one of those wild, wayward, most loveable of men, who are in love with all that is good in the world, but in whom, notwithstanding that their lives teach a lesson of which the age is sadly in need, the "unco' guid" can find no merit.

When first I knew him, some twenty years ago, there was not a streak of grey in his hair, and he thought nothing of walking twenty-five or thirty miles a day in execution of some self-imposed task, or to serve some old countryman or countrywoman who had a message for some distant friend or relation. At that time he was in the habit of turning up every year at the May Fair held in an old-fashioned little market town, where he generally received many invitations from the farmers to come and rid their fields and pastures of moles, or their outbuildings of rats—invitations he accepted or rejected as the whim seized him. He was even then a well-known figure in two or three upland Hundreds, and was held in some esteem as an amateur cattle doctor and herbalist. On the fair-ground everyone knew him, not excepting the owners of the roundabouts, swing-boats, and shooting galleries; and it was also noted that he rarely had any difficulty in getting upon good terms with strange horses and dogs. Mettlesome cobs would rub their noses against his sleeve while they were waiting for an opportunity to show off their paces to the buyers; while as for shepherds' dogs, even those which growled at the friendliest advances of strangers in general, came at a word to lick his hand. Dumb creatures seemed to have an instinctive knowledge that they had a friend in him, and the old sheep-dog which in those days was his constant companion, understood and obeyed him like a faithful human servant.

A pleasant trait in his character was his love of children, by whom his advent into a village was often heralded by loud acclamations. He appeared to have an inexhaustible supply of curious tricks and quaint sayings for their amusement; often he had a live furred or feathered pet for one of his favourite boys or girls; and when he had an hour or two to spare he would not infrequently spend it in making model windmills, willow-wand whistles, and popguns of bits of elder boughs. For the old women in the almshouses he would often pick up some of the broken branches with which the roads and woods were strewn after gales; once, at least, he was traced for over two miles by the trail left on the road by

AN UPLAND ROVER

a big bough he had dragged from a copse border to the cottage of an old woman who earned a precarious living by knitting worsted stockings for the local farm-hands. In the old country town where I first met him he would sometimes stay for a day or two in order to help an old man to dig over his allotment, considering himself sufficiently remunerated for his work by the gift of a cauliflower or a couple of lettuces, and these he would generally give to the first needy old man or woman he met with on the road. There were few country occupations to which he could not turn his hand when he felt so disposed; his advice was sought on subjects as different as the working of a pump and the cut of a moleskin waistcoat; while the problems he was called upon to solve by the patrons of the village inn kitchens would have puzzled even the Editor of the *Field*.

For fear of being accused of exaggerating the versatility of this random roamer, I will now, before going on to recount some of the country lore which fell from his lips in the course of the occasional interviews I had with him, content myself with mentioning that he had a considerable reputation as a singer, and was always called upon to assist at the impromptu concerts which were held at the inns after harvest and during the long winter evenings. Like most of the East Anglian rustics with musical pretensions, he was a chanter rather than a singer, and one of his favourite songs was that mysterious chant which the Rev. J. S. Orton heard sung at harvest festivals at Beeston-next-Mileham, but which is also to be heard in various parts of central Norfolk and High Suffolk, as well as along the coast; and which Canon Jessopp suggests had its source in the " Great O's of Advent," while Mr. S. O. Addy looks upon it as an ancient pagan hymn which, in the course of centuries, has gathered up fragments of Christian doctrine. However this may be, the chant was always rendered with marked solemnity, and though a somewhat rollicking turn was given to the last words of some of the lines, when the whole chant was repeated by the company by way of chorus, there was never a suggestion of a smile on any singer's face.

"I'll sing the one O,"

would chant Old Mowl, and with nothing in their tones to indicate that they were asking a question, the company would add—

"What means the one O?"

and finally altogether they would chant—

"I'll sing the twelve O's.
What means the twelve O's?
Twelve's the twelve Apostles O!
'Leven's the 'leven Evangelists.
Ten's the ten Commandments.
Nine's the gamble rangers.
Eight is the bright walkers.
Seven's the seven stars in the sky.
Six is the provokers.
Five's the thimble in the bowl.
Four's the Gospel makers.
Three, three's the rare O.
Two, two's the lily-white boys,
That's clothed all in green O!
And when the one is left alone,
No more it can be seen O!"

Encores are rarely demanded at the village "sing-songs," as they are called; but when he was in a musical mood the mole-catcher would always oblige by rendering, later in the evening, that popular old East Anglian ballad, "The Old Grey Mare," one of the many ballads which owe their popularity to a "folderol, folderol, diddle, dum, dey" kind of chorus.

As "long-settle" company, Old Mowl was much in demand, but I think it was while we were sitting together in the shadow of an upland oak on a summer day that I had the best of him. For there the pure breath of the upland air seemed to sweeten his mind, and his thoughts would be directed to those subjects only which, while commonplace enough, had the charm of the open countryside and something of the fragrance of sweetbrier and new-mown hay about them. On such subjects he would talk for hours if he had the opportunity. Then he would turn the conversation towards old country ways and lore, and, as he had little of the secretiveness which characterises the average East Anglian rustic, one would soon begin to understand how the farm-folk talked around the fire in the twilight, and what strange significance some of them still attached to simple and natural events and things.

Naturally enough he had something to say about moles and their ways. He gave them credit for a good deal of cleverness, and said he had known them to avoid, by making a fresh run round it, a trap in which a mole had been caught. For this reason he had never favoured the plan of some mole-catchers of scenting their traps with aniseed, for although the odour might at first attract the moles, they soon learnt that it meant danger to them, and would desert the field or pasture where the traps were set. When I first knew him, he always favoured the use of the old-fashioned noose, which was tightened by the springing of a bent stick; in fact, I believe he was never known to use the iron trap, which he looked upon as a clumsy contrivance in which a mole was only likely to be caught by accident. Poisoning he considered a bad method of ridding a field of moles, for although some of them might die, the majority of them soon deserted the field for a neighbouring one, where they became as troublesome as ever. He would undertake, he said, to capture all the moles in a field with the aid alone of the old-fashioned spring-stick nooses. But he must be allowed to choose his own time for doing this—a thing a good many farmers could not understand. As a rule, a farmer who employed a mole-catcher expected him to go to work at once; and complete his catching in a given time; he made no allowance for the fact that there were times when it was practically impossible to capture moles, such as when the ground was dry and the moles had to seek their food some distance from the surface. The best time to catch them was just after a good shower of rain. Then, if the catcher knew his business, he would not only set his traps, but visit the field as soon as possible after daybreak, when he would often be able to take young moles by hand as they were "rutting" among the weeds and corn on the surface of the ground.

He did not believe that all moles were blind, though there could be little doubt that the majority of them were. He had seen young ones that were "rutting" along the surface of the ground, carefully avoid coming in contact with large stones and other objects, the presence of which they could not have become aware of by their sense of smell; he had also held them in the palm of his hand and had noticed that they were careful not to crawl over the side of the hand; but the blindness of the average mole was very manifest if it were placed in a pail or box, when it would usually run its nose against the sides, and be quite unable to locate at first any edible substance which might be near it. In his opinion, however, the moles which were sometimes seen to swim across dikes, brooks, and narrow rivers, were in possession of fairly good eyesight; otherwise, he maintained, they would never venture to resort to swimming unless compelled to do so by sudden floods. Asked whether the mole swam like the water-vole, he said it did not, but generally made what he called "hard work" of it. It did not swim so fast as the water-vole, nor so deep in the water. Upland moles were not such good swimmers as the marsh moles, probably because it was a very rare occurrence for one of the former to take to the water, whereas the latter often choose to swim across a dike rather than tunnel beneath it. It was a fact, he said, that they sometimes tunnelled beneath the dikes; but as a rule they preferred to swim across them, or travel from marsh to marsh by way of the waggon-gateways, which were often undermined with their tunnels.

Referring to the popular belief among country-folk that the mole sometimes collects worms and keeps a store of them in its fortress as a precaution against a time of dearth, he admitted that he had frequently come across a few worms at the bottom of the kind of downward run often found beneath the mole-heaps, but he did not for a moment believe that the moles had placed them there. In his opinion, the worms burrowed into the runs in the same way that they came to the surface of the ground, and were unable to escape for the same reason that they were often unable to return from the surface into the earth, that is, because they had crawled to a spot where the ground was too smooth and hard for them to force their way into it. It was often the case that at the end of a mole-run the earth at the end and sides of the run was hardened by the moles just like the lining of a bird's nest; and when this was the case at the end of a downward run, it would often be impossible for a worm that once got into it to escape from it.

On several occasions he had trapped stoats and weasels in the moles' main runs, and he had no doubt that both of these animals preyed upon the moles, though they were not so fond of them as of field mice. He had heard it said that it was only the weasel that made its way into the runs, but that was incorrect, for not only did the stoat enter them, but it was no rare thing for the mole-catcher to find that a stoat had taken up its abode in a mole's nest, from which it had driven the rightful owners. Undoubtedly, however, the weasel was the chief enemy of the mole, and rendered good service to the farmer by destroying great numbers of them every year. He had good reason to believe, too, that a grey crow would occasionally make a meal of a mole which ventured abroad during the nights of late autumn and early spring. At any rate, he had found the fleshless skins of moles in the fields with the footprints of the grey crow all about them, and that this crow had a liking for moles was certain, for he had known it to feed on the dead ones he hung on the thorn bushes. Poaching cats might also be numbered among the enemies of the mole, for they would kill them, though they would not eat them.

In the marshland district of Norfolk, where ague was formerly very prevalent, the mole was supposed to possess valuable medicinal qualities, as was related by a writer in *Science Gossip*. According to an old countryman, "you must catch a mole, and it must be a male one, one of those little creatures they hang on trees. Well, sir, you must then skin it and dry the body in the oven, and then powder it, and you must take as much of the powder as will lie on a shilling every day in gin. You must take it for nine days running, and then miss nine, and then take it nine days more, and then miss nine. By this time you are cured." My old mole-catcher had never heard of this cure; but in his younger days it was no rare thing for countryfolk to come to him for a mole, so that they might cut off the feet and carry them about as a cure for rheumatism.

Talking to him one day about folk-lore, I found that he was one of the very few East Anglian rustics who had ever heard of fairies, for at no time do the "good little people" appear to have been much in evidence in our easternmost counties. The story he told me was not one of his own, but that of an ancient farm-hand who was not a native of East Anglia, and who seems to have brought a belief in fairies with him from a parish on the border of Dartmoor. But it was in a

High Suffolk parish that he first made the acquaintance of the " pharisees," and it came about in this way : " He had bin out in th' filds all day," said Old Mowl, " and had bin a-working there alone, trimming th' fencing and banking up th' sides o' a holl (dry ditch). He wor an owd man at th' time, getting on for eighty; but he lived alone in a little owd tumbledown cottage what stood about half-way down a lane what led to nowheres in perticler, 'cepting to some meddas where no one went 'cepting at haysel-time and arter th' musherumes. And it wor through these meddas he had to go arter he had finished his work for th' day, and as he didn't laave off ontil it wor nigh dark, and he had tree mile to go, th' mune wor up afore he got more'n half-way home. It wor, as he towd it, a claar munelight night, and when he got inter one o' th' meddas what had a small plantin aside it, and which wor full o' what they call fairy-rings, he could see right claar acrost th' medda, 'cepting where there wor shadda along th' side o' th' plantin. He worn't, as he said, a-thinking o' nuthin in perticler, when summat med him luke towards th' plantin, and there he saw what fared to him like a little blue fire a-burning in a dark place onder th' hedge. It fared, according to him, like a fire what hadn't no heat in it, and while he wor a-staring at it, ' I saw,' said he, ' as sure as I'm alive, a lot o' little fairies go a-chasing each other past th' fire, and arter a little while come back again. They worn't above half a foot high, and it fared to me as though they wor a-running a race, for they wor all a-going th' same way, and kept pretty close together. Ezactly what they wor like he couldn't say, for they didn't gin him a chance to watch them, but he knew directly they wor fairies, a-cause he had heerd o' sich things in Devonshire from folks as had seen 'em. But he couldn't git no one to belaave what he said. Th' parson, who heerd on it, said as how th' fire wor only some rotten touchwood from one o' th' plantin trees, and if you axed me what th' fairies wor, I should say as how they wor a pack o' stoats out a-hunting."

Old Mowl's love of Nature was inborn, but apparently not inherited, for his ancestors, so far as he knew, had never given a thought to matters which brought them no tangible and pecuniary benefit. During the years he wandered about the uplands he was always learning something which, at least, was new to him. He could see more in a roadside hedge than can a thousand travellers who believe their eyes to be fully open to what is going on around them. When the sun was shining brightly and warmly, he was quite content to lie for hours in the shade of a roadside tree; there he would watch the insects crawling over the wrinkled bark, the woodpecker tapping above his head, or a swarm of ants travelling to and fro along one of their chosen highways. Once I found him stretched out on the frame of a farm roller which was drawn up in the corner of a field. At first I thought he was asleep, but he proved to be very wide awake, and told me that while he had been lying there he had seen the spikelets open on a rye-grass stem and hang out their pollen-dusted anthers. Another time, he was lying at full length on a couch of heather on an upland common. His basket was lying beside him, and he was watching a little lizard sunning itself on the sheep-cropped turf. He remarked that there was more "pluck" in a six-inch lizard than in many creatures a hundred times its size, and to prove the truth of his statement he made a grab at the lizard and caught it between his fingers. It twisted its head round and bit his hand, and he let it scurry away amid the heather. Once I caught him observing closely something he had imprisoned in an old matchbox. It was a large-tailed wood wasp, and he told me that he knew a house where some of the larvæ of such a wasp had suddenly emerged from a piece of firwood furniture in which they must have been embedded for many months.

It was in his company that I went one night to visit an upland shepherd. Over the high ground of the newly-ploughed fields the north-east wind was blowing keenly, and the ridges between the dark, clean-cut furrows were white with frost. The rush of the cold air was felt rather than heard on the summit of the bolder bluffs, for it met with little resistance, except where a few stunted oaks, their rugged branches stretching westward in consequence of the rough training of the winter winds, were rooted in the narrow banks beneath the leafless hedgerows. The ploughmen had finished work for the day, and seagulls from the coast had settled with the rooks to search for grubs in the freshly-turned earth. The wind-gusts which ruffled their feathers as they hopped across the ridges had few other playthings on the upland heights, for the sparrows flew low under the lee of the ragged fences, the fieldfares kept to the cover of the red-berried bushes, and the silent larks seldom rose far from the ground as they flew in flocks across the fields. Pedestrians on the byroads intersecting the cultivated land escaped as quickly as possible from the exposed heights, and lingered to regain breath in the hollows, where the roads dipped down in conformity with the uneven surface of the ground.

Under the shelter of a wide-browed hill, the broad base of which stretched away to the south, a fairly level tract of pasture-land was protected by the hill from the chill wind. Here a flock of nearly two hundred ewes was penned in a spacious fold, three sides of which were enclosed by iron hurdles, while the fourth side consisted of a high quickset hedge. Under the hedge, at an angle of the fold, stood the shepherd's movable hut, ramised fro the ground on low wooden wheels. It was a compact but roughly-built structure without windows, light being admitted through the door only, save when the slides were drawn back from one or both of the small circular ventilators under the roof of the hut. A small iron stove, with a flue that disappeared through a hole in the roof, was secured to a thin sheet of metal fastened to the floor, and was the most noticeable feature of the interior. The great change of temperature this stove was capable of producing in the hut was not appreciated until the door was closed against the inrush of the cold air. A tattered straw mattress, half hidden by a pair of dark-coloured blankets, was spread in the corner opposite to that occupied by the stove; the rest of the furniture consisted of a milking-stood and an old sugar box, the latter intended to serve as a table. A couple of shelves, fixed high up on the walls, supported the shepherd's limited but invaluable stock of physics and applications, such as turpentine, Stockholm tar, and ginger.

The shepherd himself was out in the fold when we arrived, and was engaged in making stable one of the straw-covered hurdles erected for the shelter and comfort of the sheep; but he soon returned to the hut. He was no "knightly shepherd" of a romantic Arcadia, but a weather-beaten old man whose hair was fast becoming white, and who, far from "piping a merry tune," could hardly find breath enough to whistle to his dog. His face was as ruddy as that of a country-bred boy, but had a less variable colour than that of youth, and bore marks of long exposure to the weather wherever the skin was unconcealed by its straggling fringe of hair. He was tall and angular, his limbs were somewhat distorted, and his hands were stained by frequent handling of sheep drugs and dressings. He wore a long, heavy coat of dingy drabbett, with capacious pockets, and lined with a check-patterned woollen cloth. Round his neck was a warm plaid scarf, the ends of which disappeared beneath a sleeved waistcoat of some thick drab material. The tops of his heavy boots were covered by tightly buttoned leather leggings, and on his head was a dogskin cap with wide "flaps," upon which the hair was left to form a warm covering for the ears. At his heels, as he moved about the pasture, followed his dog, an intelligent-looking animal, in whose charge the flock could be safely left during the shepherd's occasional brief absences from the fold. It had been his companion for several years, and showed a ready understanding of, and prompt obedience to, his every word and gesture. At times, when the sheep were driven from one pasture to another, the dog was of great service to the shepherd, and when the route was a familiar one it invariably took up a position by such roadside gaps in the fences as might tempt the sheep to stray, or which led to the dangerous gravel pits. To such dogs the shepherds often owe immunity from such "pastoral tragedies" as that which Thomas Hardy describes in one of the opening chapters of *Far from the Madding Crowd*.

The old shepherd was a trusted servant of his employer, and though it might have been said of him that his "ambition's masterpiece flies no higher than a fleece," his knowledge of matters pertaining to his fleecy charges was both extensive and valuable. No one was better acquainted with the quality of "keep" in all parts of his particular district, and he would solve, at any rate to his own satisfaction, some of the breeding secrets of Altom and Bakewell, which had puzzled breeders for many years. He had a vivid recollection of the outbreak of sheep smallpox in 1847, for at that time he was the assistant of his father—an old Yorkshire dalesman, who was esteemed one of the best shepherds in the eastern counties. To an attentive listener he would talk learnedly of rot, red-water, scab, and the early symptoms of rickets; while he had his own prescriptions for many, if not all, of the ills that sheep are heir to. He preferred to concoct his own oils rather than resort to any of the "safe and sure" patent embrocations, no matter how widely advertised and guaranteed by weighty testimonials. As a shearer he could safely compete with most of the skilled hands of the district, and he would accept no advice in regard to "dipping" and "smearing" or the preservation and cultivation of wool. During the lambing season his work was almost incessant, and he had to snatch his hours for resting when and how he could. His nights were often sleepless, for the ewes required unremitting attention, and the lambs careful watching, in order that their young lives might be preserved through the times of winter snow and frost. In his hut you might often see two or three of the little creatures which had just been born, lying on a bed of hay or straw before the stove; and when they were returned to their dams there were generally others ready to take their places. There is an old saying in some rural districts that it is "the lambs which pay the rent," and the old man always protested against their being taken from the ewes before they had become properly accustomed to eat corn and oil cake. The milk-flesh, he would tell you, was soon lost, and if the lambs were separated from their mothers before they had learned to rely on dry food, serious losses were almost bound to ensue. Every day he had to see that the sheep had their required supply of turnips in the fold, and in thus providing for their needs he had the assistance of a sturdy son, who came to the pasture at certain hours to turn the handle of the turnip-cutter, which stood under the hedge near the shepherd's hut. During wet weather it was necessary to provide a certain amount of "dry feed" for the ewes, and at all times there were members of the flock needing special attention. Thus he had few idle moments, and during lambing-time, his wife, who lived in a little thatch-roofed cottage in the outskirts of the nearest hamlet, often saw nothing of "her man" for days together.

It was while the shepherd was attending to a sickly

lamb that he and Old Mowl began talking about snakes, and especially about the old belief that vipers swallow their young. That the vipers often performed this wonderful feat the shepherd had no doubt, and he declared that on one occasion, while tending sheep on a sandy heath, he had been a witness to such a performance. Old Mowl admitted that at one time he had felt equally sure about it, but after opening a viper into whose jaws a boy had seen, as he said, a young one descend, and finding in it a long-tailed (field) mouse, he had had his doubts about it. What he knew to be a fact, however, was that one viper would sometimes devour another; for he had seen lying among the furrows of a heath-bordered field a full-grown viper with the tail of a smaller one protruding from its mouth. He was inclined to believe that occasional acts of cannibalism might be in part responsible for the belief that vipers swallowed their young when danger threatened them. The old shepherd again declared that he had no doubt about their doing so; it was, he said, "as true as true could be." But while admitting that what he said was uttered in perfectly good faith, it would not do to accept all the strange tales he told. For he was equally convinced that sheep were sometimes bitten by lizards or "effets," as he called them, and that the only cure for such a bite was to cut the "fangs" out of the wound! Old Mowl had a theory that wherever running toads (natterjacks) were found, there you might find vipers if you looked for them. Both of them, he said, had a liking for sandy soil during the summer months. In this the viper differed from the common snake, which was seldom found very far from water, its favourite haunt being a farmyard dunghill, especially if it happened to be near a pond. Common snakes he had sometimes encountered in mole-runs, where they occasionally "laid up" for the winter; but whether these snakes preyed upon the moles, he could not say. He could not remember ever having met with a professional snake-catcher in the Eastern counties; he doubted whether there had ever been enough snakes in this part of England to find employment for such a man.

He had, however, met with some curious characters among the "road folk," for he could remember the time when there were several travelling tinkers who had their regular country rounds, herbalists who visited the villages to sell their decoctions and buy herbs, and "leechers," who in the summer journeyed many miles, especially in the Fen districts, in search of leeches. Such folk were familiar to the country people of fifty years ago; but one by one they disappeared from their accustomed itineraries, and no others found it worth their while to take their places. Two of the last of these rovers with whom Old Mowl had been acquainted, were an old man and his wife who went about "meal-bolting." They carried about with them a couple of bolting machines, and used to call at every cottage to see if the inmates had any meal for them to dress. They might usually be relied upon to put in an appearance soon after harvest; for the meal they dressed was the produce of the corn which the women and children had gleaned from the fields. But with the introduction of reaping and binding machines the travelling bolters found their occupation gone; for the new machines left no corn in the fields for the gleaners, and the latter in consequence had no meal to be dressed. The shepherd could remember the two old bolters, and added to the mole-catcher's remarks about them, that the country-folk who employed them used to declare, "behind their backs," that their machines had "pockets" in them, which retained some of the meal with which they were entrusted.

I left Old Mowl to keep company with the shepherd throughout the night, and for several years I saw no more of him. When I again met with him he had grown old and feeble, but he still persisted in his circumscribed roamings. It was only when he no longer had strength enough to walk more than a mile or so in a day, that he consented to settle down in an almshouse in his native village, and then he had less than a year left to him in which to lament the loss of the kind of life he loved.

CHAPTER XII

THE OLD FEN

SOME two hundred years ago, when the marsh reclaimers built on the Suffolk bank of the Waveney a certain broad-based wooden drainage mill to pump the surplus water out of the dikes intersecting several square miles of water-soaked marsh, there existed, about three-quarters of a mile from the river, at the foot of a gravelly upland slope which from time immemorial has been used as a sheep-walk, a fairly large tract of almost untraversable swamp. Formerly it had probably been a "Broad" —a reed-fringed lowland mere which had come into existence when the estuarine waters slowly retreated to the lower part of the river valley; but at the time when the drainage windmill was built it had "grown up," as some other Broads have done since, and become a treacherous morass, surrounding a few small pools in which eels grew to a fabulous size, and at March-end the water was "alive" with amorous frogs. Reeds still arose every year around the pools, and among them the cradles of the reed warblers were rocked by the wind; otters had their lairs there, and when weary of feasting on the eels, went down to the river to go a-fishing for roach and bream. Most of all was the morass loved by the water-rails, which, when they had made their nests of the reed leaves, betrayed their presence by noisily "sharming" during the quiet evenings of spring.

When the reclaimers first set the mill-sails turning, they were looking forward to a time when they would be able to send their cattle on to the marsh every May, to find there good pasture instead of a rank growth of sedge, rush, and fen flowers; and as time went on, such of them as survived saw a great change in the aspect of the marsh. Slowly but surely the water-logged peat became firmer and drier; gradually the reeds became dwarfed, until finally most of them disappeared. With them vanished the great spearwort, the tall marsh sow-thistle, and the fen ragwort; and then the sedge and rush made way for alien grasses and flowers. With the old fen flora vanished the old fen fauna. Most of the reed warblers went with the reeds, the water-rail with the rush and sedge, and the swallow-tail butterfly with the tall swamp flowers. A time came when there was no one left alive who could remember what the marsh was like in the days when the old mill first whirled its sails at the river end of the long fleet. Save the mill and the river, scarcely anything was as it had been; and in course of time the mill, which had become weather-beaten without and dilapidated within, made way for an ugly brick-cased steam pump.

But although miles of marsh were reclaimed, the tract of swamp which was formerly a "Broad" was scarcely affected by the diking and draining, and to-day it presents amid changed surroundings something of the old wild aspect of primitive fen. True, its pools have "grown up," and there is now hardly a yard of its surface upon which it is unsafe to set foot; but a man's weight on the bog-moss overgrowing the peat is enough to bring the water oozing through the moss, while to jump from hassock to hassock of swamp grass or tufted sedge is to cause the surface of the fen to shake and undulate like a floating hover beside a wind-ruffled stream. The sensation experienced at such a time is that of being afloat on a loosely-constructed raft; and when a summer breeze is making wind-waves among the tall grasses, a green sea seems to roll across the peaty raft and break in a foam of flowering meadow-sweet on the border of the fen. The marshmen say that the time will never come when the fen will be drained as dry as the surrounding marshes. Beneath it, they tell you, there are ever-flowing springs, which, in the days when peat was cut in the fen, used to fill the holes with water as soon as the "turves" were taken away. It was around these holes that, fifty years ago, the fickle flame of the marsh-fire used to waver and dance when a moonless night succeeded a sultry summer day—a mysterious phenomenon which gained for the fen a somewhat uncanny reputation, and kept all save the least fearful of marsh-folk from venturing upon it after nightfall. One pool, now entirely "grown up," was known as the "Lantern-man's Well," and the marshmen were agreed in describing it as bottomless!

My earliest recollections of the fen are of it on early summer days, when, as a change from bird-nesting expeditions along the upland lanes and field-borders, I went down into it to watch an old marshman and his son cut and carry away the rank crop of sedge and swamp grass to be sold and used as litter. I remember that the method of carrying away the crop struck me as being curious; but I have since seen a like method adopted in Wicken Fen, the only remaining tract of primitive fen in Cambridgeshire. No horse could tread with safety the swampy ground, and had a waggon or cart been drawn on to it, it would probably never have been got out again; so, when the fen crop had been mown with the scythe, it was tied up in sheaves or bundles, which were placed lengthwise across two long poles lying about a foot and a half apart on the ground. When as many bundles had been placed on the poles as old Ben, the marshman, and his son could comfortably carry, they would raise the poles by the ends, and march steadily away with the load to the bottom of a driftway leading down from the uplands to the fen.

There the load would be dropped by letting fall one of the poles, and later in the day a horse and cart would be driven down the driftway to convey a load of the fen crop to a piece of waste ground adjoining the marshman's cottage. Earlier in the year the reeds which grew in the wettest part of the fen were similarly harvested, the marshman and his son wearing slush-boots, for when they carried away the reed sheaves they often sank a foot or more into the oozy peat. With this winter and early spring work in the fen I did not become acquainted until I, too, was the proud possessor of a pair of slush-boots, the soles of which were plentifully studded with hob-nails. But before that time I was delighted by being presented with my first reed-warbler's nest—a nest of the previous year, whicn old Ben had found for me in a reed-bed in the fen.

In those early days I never thought of the fen without associating with it the old grey-bearded marshman whose life had been spent on the marshlands, and to whom every aspect of the fen was as familiar as the plaint of the peewit and the whisper and rustle of the reeds. He was a man of many occupations—the River Commissioners' marshman and millman, a farmer's cattle-tender and dike-drawer, a reed-cutter, an eel-catcher, and a flight-shooter—but whatever he might be doing he was seldom very far from the fen, which had for him the attraction of being a place of interesting possibilities. That this should be the case was scarcely surprising, for ever since the time when, as a boy, he had shunned its neighbourhood at night on account of the lantern-men, the fen, at not infrequent intervals, had received strange and unexpected visitors. Generally they arrived during the night, as was the case with a bittern, which at daybreak was heard booming among the reeds; and also with a big dog otter, which, after being trapped by the riverside, succeeded in dragging the heavy iron trap across the marshes to the fen; but sometimes they appeared during the day, as when a black-winged stilt was seen to alight on the bank of the fleet, and at once begin snapping at the "whirligig" beetles on the surface of the water. In late autumn, too, there would be days when the reed-beds were suddenly filled with a music like the chiming of bells in fairyland, which meant that a wandering flock of bearded titmice had come to feed for a while on the reed seeds and the larvæ in the sheaths of the leaves. Such visitors were fortunate if they were seen by old Ben at a time when his old long-barrelled muzzle-loader had been left at home, and they were wise if they took their departure before he had time to fetch it.

Several years have elapsed since old Ben, then almost a cripple with rheumatism, tottered down the driftway to see for the last time how the "segs" were coming up in the fen; but even now I never wander amid the pink marsh orchids and almond-scented meadow-sweet without thinking of the days when he was my companion there. I can still see him as plainly as ever, his wrinkled face half hidden beneath a peak-crowned Tyrolean hat, his moleskin waistcoat buttoned close up to the neck, but with the two bottom buttons always undone; his corduroy trousers carefully prevented, by a telescopic tuck, from coming in contact with boots dusted with golden pollen; and over all, should the weather be wet or cold, a soldier's overcoat, grey without and red-lined within. That overcoat, no matter what the weather might be like in the morning, always accompanied him down into the fen; and it had a great fascination for me, because it possessed a capacious inside pocket, the existence of which, though unsuspected when it was empty, was only too evident after the report of an ancient muzzle-loader had been heard in the fen. At times I found it best not to be too curious about the contents of that pocket, nor as to what became of certain pheasants which, notwithstanding that they were fed regularly in the coverts, seemed to find something more to their taste in the marshes; but not infrequently the pocket contained a prize for me. Out of it came grasshopper warblers' eggs and shrews' nests, crested newts and natterjack toads. These prizes, though highly valued, soon went the way of most of my boyhood's treasures; the eggs were smashed, the shrews' nests became shapeless tangles of grass, and the newts and toads generally came to a more or less unhappy end; but one reminder of the old marshman is hanging close beside me as I write. It is a rusty old otter-trap, made, I should say, by some village blacksmith who had for pattern one of those brutal man-traps that were used by game-preservers who attached a greater value to their pheasants than to the lives of their fellow-men. At first glance one might, perhaps, imagine the otter-trap a less cruel contrivance than the man-trap, for it is without the sharp teeth with which a man-trap in my possession is armed; but since I sprung the trap with a walking-stick, that stick has been three inches shorter than it used to be. The trap, in fact, is the one that the otter I just now referred to dragged all the way from the river to the fen, and I am glad to think that it is not likely to be used again as an implement of torture. Unfortunately there are others to be found in the hamlets around the fen, and too often they are set and baited by the river-side. It is time that the use of them is made as illegal as that of the barbarous man-trap.

On summer evenings, when the corncrakes—they seem to be rarer now—were *crek-creking* amid the long marsh grass, I used to sit on a wooden bench under the "living-room" window of old Ben's cottage and try to get the old man to talk about the wild life of the marshes and the changes he had seen. At times he was taciturn; but occasionally I was fortunate enough to touch upon something which set his thoughts flowing, and then there was no need for me to do more than let him see that he had my whole attention. He had lived a lonely life; often, when dike-drawing, spending weeks alone by the dikeside; but he had learnt much in his loneliness that is not to be learnt by those who constantly travel the highways of life.

It was seldom that he talked very long without making some reference to the old fen. When a young man, he had often cut peat there, which was the only fuel used in his father's cottage, and, indeed, in all the cottages on the marsh-border, where the fires were kept burning day and night all through the year. In those days there was an annual "peat-running," at which the men of the village decided where their turves were to be cut during the ensuing twelve months. This peat-running took place every tenth of May, on which day all the men who wished to cut turves met in front of an inn in the village street, and the rest of the villagers turned out to see the fun. "For th' way on it wor like this," said old Ben. "A line wor marked acrost th' road, and every man what wanted ter run had ter toe th' line jist as in a boys' race at a skule treat, ony each on 'em carried a spade in his hand. Th' parish constable wor th' starter, and as sune as he gin th' wud, they all started a-runnin' down th' driftway to th' fen as hard as they could put fut ter th' ground. When they got there, every man had ter stick his spade inter th' middle o' th' place where he wanted ter cut his turves, and a-course him as got there fust got fust chyce. Widders, owd maids, and owd men wor 'lowed to hev young chaps run for 'em. I can mind as how I used ter run for owd Betty Woodrow, what lived agin th' pound. It wor a rare sight ter see us a-runnin' wi' half th' willage at our haals—sich a sight as can't be seen nowadays nowhere." And he went on to say that, in addition to the turves, candle-rushes were cut in the fen for use as wicks in the tallow "rush-lights," which, save for the smouldering peat fire, provided the only light obtainable in the cottages after sunset. Waggon-loads of these rushes were sent up to Norwich, where there was annually a Rush Fair, at which the rushes were sold to the candle-makers. Another fen crop was black-weed (bur-reed), which grew in the pools and ditches, and was used in the making of the so-called straw horse-collars, now apparently almost entirely gone out of fashion, but which were formerly much in demand on account of their cheapness. But the most curious custom has become obsolete since the old man's father was a boy. Then it was by no means an uncommon thing for the hassocks, or tufts of matted rushes and grasses found in the boggy parts of the fen, to be dug out, trimmed into shape, and used as stools in the cottages, and even as kneeling hassocks in some of the marsh-bordering churches. Afterwards they gave place to "dosses," stuffed with hay or straw, and covered with plaited flags or rushes.

"Hob-o'-Lantern," or the "lantern-man," seems to have vanished from the fen when the pools "growed up." No one appears to regret this, for he is supposed to have been a dangerous sprite to encounter, and only foolhardy persons went out of their way to make his acquaintance. As old Ben once said, "If so be as how you went a-nigh him, he would 'come for you' like as though he wor a-goin' ter knock you down." This had not been his own experience, for he had always kept away from the fen when the lantern-man was in possession; but he had known a man to go down into the fen at night with a lantern, and have a lantern-man "go right tru him and take his breath right away." He had heard people say that the lantern-man was only a kind of marsh gas; but he did not believe it, for no matter in what direction the wind might be blowing, there were times when the light was seen going against it; in fact, it used to "marnder around" in all directions, and then suddenly go "a-slidderen orf as though it wor a flash o' lightnin'." Confirmation of this habit of the lantern-man may be found in the Rev. J. Denny Gedge's interesting "Experiences of a Fen Parson,"[1] where Mr. Gedge states that it was no infrequent thing for him to see, while taking lonely walks in the fens at night, "the *ignes fatui* come down long dim lanes of water, swimming towards one on the air, as it were, generally to make a sudden upward movement and vanish before they had approached closely enough for intimate inspection." A correspondent who contributed some notes on Will-o'-the-Wisps to the *East Anglian Daily Times*, said that an old man who saw one in a fen between Fakenham and Euston in north-west Suffolk, remarked that it "flew like an owl," and he believed it to be "the reflection of that bird's eye!" Many years ago this puzzling phenomenon was often seen on some low swampy ground in the parish of Syleham, in the upper part of the Waveney Valley. There the lantern-men were known as the "Syleham Lights"; but they are not to be seen now, though I have met an old man who could remember having watched three lantern-men

"Hovering and blazing with delusive light"

over the boggy ground not far from Syleham Mills. The neighbourhood of Horning on the Bure, where there is still a good deal of fenny land, was also one of the lantern-man's haunts, and he is said to have been very troublesome to farmers, whom he would dismount from their horses—presumably by frightening them—while they were on their way home from Norwich market. Nowadays he appears to be as extinct as the "farisees" who frolicked among the fairy rings in the moonlight; but I have a dim recollection of having once seen what may have been a Will-o'-th'-Wisp suddenly illumine a roadside ditch in a parish between Norwich and Bungay. I was a small boy at the time, and was riding home from Norwich in the heavy tilted van of the Bungay

[1] In the *Eastern Counties Magazine*.

carrier, which at that time was what Mr. Hardy calls a "moveable attachment" of the Norwich and Bungay road. Half asleep, I was crouched in a dark corner of the hooded van, when a gleam of bluish light appeared in a ditch by the roadside, and I heard an old countryman who was one of my travelling companions exclaim: "Look! There be a lantern-man!" I was wide awake in an instant; but the sudden glimmer of what may or may not have been *ignis fatuus* was all I saw before I lost sight of the ditch in consequence of the progress of the van.

With the lantern-men the natterjack toads seem to have taken their departure from the fen. A good many years ago, before the pools "grew up," the running toads, as the old marshman called them, used to spawn in the pools, from whence, later in the year, they dispersed over the sandy ground of the upland sheep-walks. They made their presence known at spawning-time by their curious trilling, a sound which made the air seem tremulous, and resembled the distance-deadened song of a nightjar, or a grasshopper warbler's "grinding" robbed of its metallic shrillness. "They've curous warmin," said old Ben, referring to their habit of feigning death when in danger. "You may see 'em layin' spread out flat beside th' deeks or on th' heth, lookin' jist as if someone had stamped on 'em and squashed 'em, and if you pick 'em up they 'ont mewve onless you gin 'em a tidyish nip; but if you laave 'em alone, and watch 'em, arter a little while they'll git up and maake orf as lively as you plaase." I asked him what was meant by the old Norfolk saying that "you can quiet a restive horse with the bone of a running toad"; but although he was familiar with the saying he could not say how it originated, nor had he ever heard of anyone attempting to quiet a horse with a bone of a toad.[1] He had noticed that

[1] Mr. W. Juby, writing in the *East Anglian Daily Times*, says that in Suffolk the villagers used to catch natterjacks and, after killing them, bury

during the spawning season large numbers of natterjacks were often killed by the herons, and on one occasion he had watched an "owd harnsee" striking and killing the toads "jist for sheer mischeeviousness," for it did not attempt to eat them. If one may judge by the number of mangled frogs and toads often found in a heap by the dikeside, this is a favourite amusement of the heron, and it must often happen that a breeding colony of these amphibians is decimated by a single ruthless bird. That the heron is the guilty party I have no doubt, for his footprints on the muddy dikeside are unmistakable.

Marsh and Montagu's harriers have been known to nest in the fen, but not of late years, and even the redshanks and peewits have decreased in numbers, chiefly because nearly all their eggs used to be taken every year and despatched to the London market. Lubbock mentions that in 1821 a single egger, residing at Potter Heigham in Norfolk, collected one hundred and sixty dozen lapwings' eggs on the adjacent marshes, and that at that time nearly a bushel of eggs, chiefly of that bird, but including those of the redshank, reeve, and various terns, were gathered by two men in a morning. Old Ben could quite believe this, for "in his young time" he never went down into the fen on a spring day without seeing the air suddenly filled with wheeling and crying plovers, and for years he used to collect several hundred eggs every season. These were sent by the carrier to a dealer at Yarmouth, who, in the height of the season, paid him half a crown a dozen for them; but for early eggs, he sometimes got as much as sixpence each. The eggs of the redshank also found a ready sale, the purchasers at the shops seldom distinguishing them from

them in the ground, where the ants would eat the flesh and leave the bones bare. The bones were then placed in a running stream, and if a bone "strove against the tide" it was kept as a charm. It was said that such a bone would be of use in stopping runaway horses on a waggon. Mr. Juby had heard of this being done at Whatfield and Hadleigh, and also by a man named Farrow, who lived at Elmswell.

those of the plover, notwithstanding the marked difference in their shape. Now not more than about two score lapwings' eggs are laid in the fen in a season, and the redshanks' nests can be counted on the fingers of one hand.

In mid-April there are abundant signs of spring along the borders of the driftway and in the upland plantations of larch, birch, and fir; but down in the old fen the tawny withered growths of the previous summer still hide the slender lady's smock, the first single leaf of the angelica, and the dark-brown spike of the sedge. Although the willow-wren is already busy among the sallows, and the yellow wagtail is flitting along the dike-side, the fen, for the most part, still wears its autumn aspect, chiefly because of the hardiness of its abundant growth of jointed rush, which has withstood the winds and snows of winter, and forms so dense a tangle over the swampy ground that even the bright green of the bog-moss is scarcely visible, and the blue-grey grass-like leaves of the marsh stitchwort are unseen until they are several inches high. New life there is in plenty—life that in a few weeks will transform the tawny swamp into a wild garden of brilliant and beautiful flowers; but as yet the old life seems loth to make way for it, and even the sapless skeletons of some of the dead flowers will linger until their seedling children are in bloom. In the intervals between the April showers, when a breeze already tempered by the warmth of the sun ruffles the pollen-dusted surface of the dike, the tapping together of the brittle stems of the dwarf reeds is like the rattling of dry bones. One has to look beneath the withered rush stems, where the saturated sphagnum is of every hue in amber and green, for the promise of the flowers that are to come, and one finds it in the spiny stars of crimson-edged leaves from which the tall marsh thistles will arise, the ruddy leaves of the meadow-sweet, the earliest shoots of the rare marsh vetchling, and the trifoliate leaves of the exquisite buckbean. Summer is here in making, and while watching its infancy in the lap of spring one anticipates its full ripe beauty; but this cannot blind one to the loveliness and perfection already attained. These are to be seen in the form and colouring of the thistle rosette, the fern-like grace and shapeliness of the angelica leaf, and the richly woven carpet of bog-moss. Beneath the faded vesture of the fen there is not only a green as vivid as that of the upland grass, but the glowing ruddiness of young, strong life.

Since the first week in March two couple of snipe have frequented the fen, and one nest with eggs has already been found among the withered swamp grasses near a low thicket of fragrant bog myrtle. The cocks have been a-wing at intervals since daybreak, sometimes flying low over the reeds and sweet gale, then soaring with rapid wing-beats high in the air, to fill the air as they descend with the vibrant drumming that has gained for them the name of "summer lambs," though the sound more resembles the bleating of a goat than the voice of a lamb. Down by the fleet you may see where they have been feeding, especially where the surface of the dike is covered with a green coating of duckweed fronds; but while the sun is shining they spend most of their time in soaring and drumming, resting occasionally on the top of a dead willow or the stake which marks the position of the plank bridge crossing the fleet. So far back as the marshmen can remember, the fen has never been without its breeding snipe; but, like the redshanks and plovers, they are scarcer now than they used to be, owing to the nest-raiding which has done so much to diminish the numbers of the marsh birds.

To-day, though few of the warblers have returned to their summer haunts, there are sunny hours when the cries, songs, and call-notes of the birds make the fen seem alive with bird-life. Now and again, while one snipe is drumming, the other is *a-chuck, a-chucking*, sometimes while on the wing, but not infrequently on the top of the willow or the stake. Meanwhile the lapwings are tumbling and wailing above the swampy ground where they nest, and two or three redshanks are uttering their musical love-notes as they wheel and hover around their mates. Larks are soaring and carolling above the fen, though their nests are generally found on the drier marshes; and the meadow pipit, which loves to make its nest in the bog-moss under a tussock of swamp grass, is repeating its brief song as it rises in the air, and its prolonged *see-see-see* as it descends. Already several yellow wagtails are back in their old haunts, and are calling softly as they take their dipping flights along the dikesides; and the first spring cuckoo is uttering its familiar note as it flies low across the fen. In a week or two there will be other voices, for soon the reed and sedge warblers will have returned, and the strange grinding song of the shy grasshopper warbler will be heard among the ruddy bog myrtles.

One of the earliest of the warblers is already here, as it always is before April is many days old, and if you stroll quietly along the fen border, where the gold and silver sallow catkins are being visited by humble and honey bees, you are likely to have a chance of watching him, for he is a friendly little bird, showing no aversion to human company. There is a dike dividing the fen from the lower edge of the upland slope, and its surface is covered with a thin coating of pollen blown and shaken from the catkins on its bordering alders and sallows. In the midst of this surface film are drawn tracks about two and a half inches wide and sometimes parallel with each other, but often ending suddenly, to be continued perhaps by an irregular succession of filmless spaces about the size of a golf-ball. These are the tracks left on the pollen-dusted surface of the dike by a swimming water-vole, and their abrupt ending at spots where there is no apparent obstacle to further progress, means that there the vole, startled, it may be, by a footstep on the dike-bank, dived suddenly, to leave no further trace of its progress save where it came to the surface for a moment and then disappeared again. In a week or two, when all the pollen will have been shaken from the catkins, the dusty film on the surface of the dike will be succeeded by a denser coating of duckweed. Then the vole tracks in the water will be no longer visible, for the tiny disks of duckweed, though pushed aside by the swimming vole, are pressed back by myriads of other disks into the places from whence they came.

It is here, where the garish marsh marigolds fringe the dike and the dark sedge shoots will soon be hanging out their golden anthers, that the sweet song of the willow-wren, beginning with a few high notes sung in quick succession, and ending with a descending scale of liquid melody, is heard ere the March winds have scarcely done blowing, and before the cuckoo-flowers are in bloom. You first hear the song—one of the sweetest to be heard in the marshlands—trickling out of the green leaf-spray flecking the low-growing alder scrub; then there is silence for a while, during which the little minstrel flits quietly on to a slender wand of a sallow bush growing opposite you on the other side of the dike, and there, heedless of your movements, though you may approach to the very edge of the dike, he remains for a minute in full view. In his soft colouring of blended green and yellow he is as beautiful as his song is sweet, while his movements, though suggesting those of blue-tit, flycatcher, and bearded titmouse, are more graceful, and at the same time more lively. No behaviour on the part of a wild bird, unless it be that of the robin which hops into a room through the open window, is more suggestive of confidence in you than the unconcerned way in which a willow-wren will flit about a sallow bush almost within arm's-length of you, and I can quite believe the tales that are told of hen birds permitting themselves to be lifted with their nests from the ground. The sedge warbler is friendly enough, appearing to love playing at hide and seek with you among the reeds, where I have known one to fly down into my gun-punt; but the willow-wren has the greater trustfulness, and I pity the man who could find it in his heart to harm so confiding a bird. If the old fen were robbed of all its birds, there is none I should miss more than this dainty warbler, whose flittings and music among the willow and sallow wands are a constant delight. And when it builds its snug little dome-roofed, feather-lined nest in a dikeside hollow, or the shelter of the long grass around a thicket of sweet gale, I would not rifle it for its weight in diamonds. I fancy that the willow wren, unlike some other birds, must feel it deeply when its warm little oven is raided, for when it is robbed it does not lay again.

Before April is "out," as they say in Norfolk, the willow-wren has two warbling companions in the fen. You stroll along the dikeside one morning during the third week in the month, and suddenly you hear the ever-welcome *chitty, chitty, cha, cha, chuck, chuck* of a cock sedge warbler, and you know that some time during the night the little russet-brown bird of the reeds and sallows completed the last stage of his long journey from Africa. He has not come alone, for there are others of his kind scattered over the fen, and among them is a grasshopper warbler, of which you hear more than you see as he lurks among the low thickets. Soon they will be joined by a pair or two of reed warblers, and then the chorus of the fen warblers will be complete. For nowadays one never hears of a great reed warbler being seen or heard in the fen, though they have been known to visit it within the recollection of some of the old marshmen, and I could give the names of two good naturalists who have seen great reed warblers in the neighbourhood. But unfortunately for the list-compilers, these good naturalists were content with seeing the birds, and the species has at present been lucky enough to escape inclusion in the local bird lists. This may also be said of the marsh warbler, the rich song of which has been heard in a sallow carr on the Herringfleet marshes.

The fauna of the fen can never again be what it has been; but I question whether there be any tract of land of like size in East Anglia where so great a variety of wild life can be seen as here during, say, a fortnight in late spring or early summer. You will look in vain for the harriers and the ruffs, as you will for the otters, now that the pools are gone; but hardly a day will pass without your seeing, in addition to the plovers, redshanks, snipe, and warblers, a kestrel hovering over the tawny tussocks, and a mallard rising from the fleet bordering the rushy ground where the hen has her nest. In the midst of the rushes, on a bed of bog-moss, you will find a hare's "form," warmed by the body of the startled creature which at your approach ran off at coursing speed; in the dikes, if you are careful, you may watch the water-hens; and there you may see in the sucked eggs signs of the presence of a stoat. Water-voles you need never have any difficulty in observing; but of the field-vole, or marsh mouse, as the marshmen call it, you will be lucky if you see more than the helpless young, though you may find the snug little nests made of swamp grass both near and away from the dikesides. Weasels are fairly common on and around the sheep-walk—where there are many rabbit holes—and they come down into the fen in search of the marsh mice; so, too, do the vipers, which are far too common on the dry wall between the upland slope and the fen. For hours together the air will be filled with the mingled songs of the warblers, and alive with wheeling swifts and swallows. From dawn till dusk there will be hardly a moment when the wild life of the fen is silent; and when night falls, the harsh screech of the owl and the weird churring of the night-jar will be among the fitting voices of this untamed tract of marsh wilderness.

By the end of June the promise of spring is in part fulfilled; for weeks the fen has been adding almost daily a new tone to its wealth of floral colour, and now the rank luxuriance of its rush and grass is such that one seeks for some of the plants of humbler habit in a marsh underworld where all day long a green twilight reigns. Down among the gleaming grass stems and flowering rushes, where the sunlight scarcely penetrates, and the leaves of the bog pimpernel and grass of Parnassus preserve all summer a tender green, the dewdrops glisten on the bog-moss at midday, and even after days of drought fresh fronds of the fragile marsh fern unfold. There, too, countless tiny moths are as active during the daytime as they are over the surface of the dikes at nightfall, and from dawn till dusk, and from dusk till dawn, the ruddy rosettes of the sundew take their toll of the winged insects for which, during their ephemeral existence, the world is a patch of moist moss shaded by leaves of meadow-sweet and angelica. Down in those cool depths of dim daylight, a myriad lives each day begin and end, and from spring till late autumn some of the loveliest wild flowers are blooming and dying unseen, and without adding an appreciable tinge of colour to the visible surface of the fen.

There is, indeed, so much to hide them. Just now there are thousands of wild orchids in bloom, purple-streaked, spotted orchids with leaves mottled like a snake's skin, pale pink marsh orchids, smaller green-winged orchids, and rank-growing twayblades, with tall slender spikes of greenish flowers suggesting an abnormal grass. Intermingled with them, where the water oozes through the richly coloured moss, is the beautiful bogbean, a flower which, if it were rare, would be highly prized for its loveliness; and floating above them like little sunlit clouds are clusters of meadow rue. More sparingly is found the lilac-blossomed marsh vetchling, a dainty flower which, owing to the draining of the swampy marshlands, is going the way of other rare fen flowers; here it grows in company with the dusky-purple marsh cinquefoil, the trailing marsh St. John's wort, and the single-flowered meadow thistle. But these, and even the flaunting yellow iris, are dwarfed by the tall cat valerians and handsome marsh thistles which, with the rare marsh sowthistle, are the floral giants of the fen. With such wild flowers all in bloom together, the fen is as rich in colour as an old country flower-garden, and in addition to their varied hues there is the delicate blush on the spike of the graceful reed grass, the sharply contrasted bright pink and dull purple of the red rattle, and the translucent rose of the seeding sorrel.

During June no bird in the fen attracts more notice than the cuckoo, three or four of which may often be seen or heard there together. In May they are more frequently seen in the driftway, which is bordered by pollard oaks; there the familiar call of the male bird and the "water-bubbling" note of the female are heard at intervals during the day, and more frequently towards the close of sultry afternoons; but as the end of the month approaches, and there are eggs to be disposed of, the fen seems to have greater attraction for them, probably because the nests of the pipits, yellow wagtails, and sedge warblers are more easily accessible than those of the birds which build in the thick hedges. Soon after this, during the first fortnight in June, you may, if in quest of cuckoos' eggs, look for them under the rush tussocks where the titlark nests, or among the sallows where the sedge warbler often makes its home; for these are the birds usually chosen by the fen-frequenting cuckoos as foster-parents for their young, though they occasionally select willow-wrens, yellow wagtails, reed warblers, reed buntings, or linnets which have built in the furze bushes in the drier parts of the fen. Even as late as the first week in July you may chance to find a newly-laid cuckoo's egg; but by that time the old cuckoos have generally taken their departure for the uplands, and by the end of the month they have disappeared altogether. But by that time there are young cuckoos abroad, and until early autumn, when they, too, take their departure, they may be seen in ungainly flight over the fen, still attended by their foster-parents, whose oft-repeated alarm-notes betray their surprise at the curious antics of their supposed offspring. Old Ben, who had many opportunities of watching the cuckoos, and who thought he knew all about them, used to say that he did not believe the young birds intentionally ejected the young of the foster-parents, though he thought it quite likely that the fact of the nest seldom being big enough for all of them was accountable for the smaller young birds being pushed out by the intruder. On more than one occasion he had picked up wagtail and pipit nestlings in the fen; but these were often found at some distance from the nests, and, in his opinion, an old cuckoo had dropped them there after depositing an egg in their nest. But, as a rule, one or more of the foster-parent's eggs were removed by the cuckoo when she placed her own egg in the nest. Once, indeed, he had known one cuckoo to remove another cuckoo's egg from a titlark's nest, and drop it on the " wall " on the border of the fen.

Nowhere is a cool breeze more welcome than in the fen on a cloudless day in midsummer; for, save under the two or three bare-topped willows beside the wall, you may search the level in all directions and find no patch of shade. On breezeless days at this season there is a moist sultriness there which causes a more noticeable feeling of lassitude than many miles of tramping along a hot, dusty highway, and very soon the heavy fragrance of the meadow-sweet grows sickly sweet. At noon, on such a day, there is no more silent spot on the marsh level than the old fen; scarcely a bird-note is heard, not a whisper comes from the reeds and sedge; the silence is like that brooding hush which comes before a thunderstorm. So stagnant is the air, so laden with the odour of the swamp flowers, and so humid with the moisture drawn from the dew-soaked moss, that sometimes one has a difficulty in breathing it; a feeling of suffocation comes from being surrounded by the dense growth of motionless stems and leaves. Even the birds seem listless, and should you disturb one resting on a reed or branch of bog myrtle, it simply drops down into the cover of a tangle of undergrowth and stays there. Only the insects display a marked activity, and seem to revel in the noontide heat. Countless meadow-brown butterflies flutter darkly among the fen flowers, five-spotted burnets wrap themselves round with a film of wing-beats, and dragonflies, their metallic glitter intensified by the bright sunlight, dart and hover everywhere "like flying gems."

All through the slumbrous summer afternoon this stagnant stillness often continues, and the fen, as seen from the uplands, lies drowsing in the undimmed sunlight; but towards nightfall, when the lowland dikes reflect the radiance of sunset, cool draughts of air, which have no connection with any rising night-breeze, set the reeds swaying and the fen sedge shivering audibly, as though it were suddenly awakened from a day-long sleep. For a while after the sun has sunk below the level line of the far-off horizon, the dikes which join the river westward are lanes of amber light, against which the bending rushes, upright plantain leaves, and floating lily-pads stand out clearly in black silhouette; but presently little wisps of mist are seen drifting slowly over the water, and these increase in density until the dikes are only visible as white bands of fog in the midst of the fen. As the dusk deepens these bands perceptibly widen, and slowly the surface of the fen is covered with a night-veil which by moonrise is as white as a misty sea. If you venture down among the fen flowers now, you are soon drenched by the mist drops, which, as you brush aside the tall meadow rue and valerian, patter down on to the dock leaves and sedge blades like drops of rain; and the air, now chill as on an autumn morning, is laden with an odour of primeval swamp. But at this hour it is safer to keep to the marsh wall, where, as you stumble among the sun-dried clods, you hear the sudden "plop" of the water-vole as it dives into the dike, and the intermittent serenade of the wakeful sedge warbler. There you are shut in on all sides by the white fog, out of which the great convolvulus hawk moths come flitting like bats, while above, where the sky has still an afterglow of daylight, the bats themselves fly to and fro. For this is the hour when the pipistrelle is tireless in its midge-chasing, and the great noctule bat, shrieking as it flies, and at times uttering a strange note like the snipping of a pair of scissors, circles high above the fen or swoops down from the clear heights into the sea of fog. Then, too, the nightjar, which spends the day in a fir plantation on the slope of the uplands, hawks up and down over the reeds and fen flowers, filling his crop with yellow underwings, and at times giving that loud cry which is as distinctive a note as its familiar jarring. And from the white marsh wilderness itself strange cries are heard, betokening the nocturnal wakefulness of the water-birds.

When midsummer is past and the days grow shorter, the misty nights become chillier and more frequent in the fen; but generally until late in the autumn there are days when the sun shines as warmly as in June on the rusting sedge blades and fading wild flowers. During the early days of September the little blue-backed whirligig beetles are more abundant in the dikes than at any other time of the year, and their restless gyrations on the surface of the open water spaces seem brisker than ever. But by the dikesides the tall marsh thistle is becoming topped with brown down, the long seed-pods of the willow-herb are splitting and curling backward to the stem, the drooping flower-heads of the dingy bur-marigold are almost rayless, and even the mauve florets of the fragrant water-mint are fading fast. On the patches of bog-moss the grass of Parnassus here and there holds up to the sunlight an untarnished cup-shaped blossom of creamy white, and there, too, the ruddy sundews are still taking toll of the midges; but the tall-stemmed fen parsleys are becoming flowerless skeletons, and the foam of the meadow-sweet has vanished from the marish sea. Of brilliant colouring there is still an abundance; but it is that of slow decay, and is to be seen in the crimsoning of the dock leaves and the gold and vermilion of the water-pepper with which the fen, in places, seems almost ablaze.

In the reed beds at midday there is silence, save when some reed bunting utters a feeble note or a foraging rat moves stealthily over the broken-down sedge and gladden; most of the reed warblers are gone, and even the lingering sedge warblers are quiet except on the warmest of early autumn days. Until the "blade" begins to fall, there is shelter among the reeds for large colonies of the smaller birds; but the "bushes," as the Broadsmen call them, are apparently almost untenanted from dawn till dusk, unless a wandering flock of bearded titmice should alight among them, to feed for a while on the reed seeds. As the autumn days go by, however, the reed beds are resorted to at night by some of the immense flocks of starlings which are often seen passing like clouds over the marshlands, and their arrival in the twilight of an autumn evening is as wonderful a sight as is to be seen in the fen during the

IN THE OLD FEN.—HERON AND STARLINGS

year. At times their number is so great that it can only be estimated in thousands, and the aerial manœuvering by which their settlement among the reeds is preceded, makes it difficult to form even so loose an estimate. Very rarely do they settle at once in their selected roosting-place, though they may circle over it as if about to do so; just as they seem to be on the point of dropping down, they will rise together as at an understood signal, and, after sweeping to and fro for a a while over the fen, settle for a few minutes on the alders at the foot of the upland slope. Then they will rise again, the sound of their wing-beats suggesting the tumult of a storm, and when at last they alight upon the reeds, four or five birds often settling upon a single stem, the whole reed bed will be bowed down by the weight of them and in an uproar with their chattering. Later on, when the reed-cutters begin their midwinter harvest, there will be complaints as to the damage done by the roosting starlings—damage in the shape of broken reeds which have snapped under the weight of the birds. Then, too, it may be some irate marshman will have his revenge upon one of the flocks, for which he will lay in wait just before nightfall or daybreak, and, after causing, by a sudden shout, the host of birds to rise from the reeds, will "cut a lane" right through them by a single or double discharge of his gun. As yet, however, the starlings may roost in peace, for until the reed stems grow brittle and the "blade" begins to fall, the flocks can do little harm to them.

Daintier birds than the starlings, and always pleasing to the eye of the autumn rambler in the fen, are the goldfinches, which come in small parties to feast upon the downy thistle-tops now scattering their wind-borne seeds. Seen in a cage, the goldfinch is a depressing sight, especially if it be a bird not born to captivity; but flashing to and fro over the bleaching fen grasses, or clinging like a bright-hued moth to a fen thistle, it is a beautiful bird, the more welcome because it is usually most in evidence here at a time when the marshlands are deserted by the summer birds. During the spring and summer little is seen of it on the open low grounds, for it then resorts to the upland orchards and fruit gardens, generally building its nest near the top of some apple or pear tree; but no sooner are the young birds able to fly and forage for themselves than parent birds and young betake themselves to the wide marsh levels, which they do not desert even though the snow be deep upon them. Of late years there has been no marked decrease in the number of goldfinches frequenting our marshlands in autumn and winter, the reason being, probably, that the bird-catcher, with his abominable clap-net, is seldom seen excepting in the neighbourhood of one or two of the larger towns.

Mild days in November see the dike-drawers at work in the fen, some with scythes and sickles to clear away the withered reeds, figworts, and willow-herbs, others with crome and dydle to make clean channels by drawing out the ooze and decaying water-plants. Often they work in a dense fog for days together, and the dark-bearded men become grey with the powdery drops of distilled mist; then a keen wind clears the air, and during the night a sharp frost whitens the fen and hardens the ooze heaps along the dikesides so that to walk there is like walking upon the boulders of a rocky shore. Two or three such nights, with cold days intervening, put an end to dike-drawing for a while, and the fen is deserted unless some gunner visits it in quest of duck or snipe. The fieldfares, too, which have been there for a month or more, are driven by the frost from the fen; but they often stay among the bordering alders or join the red-wings among the driftway hawthorns, now beautiful with ruby berries. There may also be seen many titmice and redpolls, the latter, however, being more in evidence on the alders overhanging the wide dike between the upland slope and the fen. And down the driftway comes at times the only green woodpecker that ever seems to visit the fen. Every day, at this season of the year, it makes at least one appearance on the fen border, and generally spares a few minutes to examine carefully the rotting trunk of an ancient willow which looms in a spectral fashion through the fog.

And so with frosty days and nights, and alternate spells of dark and dismal weather, the weeks slip by and bring us to midwinter, when, during days of bright sunshine, the general hue of the surface of the fen is like that of a field of ripe corn. Then begins the reed-cutter's harvest, for the blade has fallen from the reeds, which are now amber, brittle, and topped with the grey " feather " which supplies the warm lining of many a fen bird's nest. But the fen reed harvest is nothing now compared with what it once was, and almost every year the stack made of the reed sheaves seems smaller than that of the previous year. For, in spite of what the marshmen say, the old fen is gradually becoming less fen-like, and the time will come when it will be a fen only in name. It has seen the extinction of some of its wild flowers; others which still bloom there are numbered among those the botanists consider doomed to extinction; and, like the reeds, the bogbeans, sundews, and some of the orchids are less plentiful than they were a few years ago. But unlike the fenmen of the seventeenth century, the marshmen of to-day make no complaint when they see the swampy lowlands slowly changing into profitable pasture land. They know that the days when a good livelihood could be obtained by wild-fowling, egg-collecting, and other fen pursuits are gone never to return, so they behold unmoved the disappearance of the few—the very few—remaining tracts of sodden marsh which remind them of what has been. Indeed, they realise that the changes which have taken place and are still proceeding are to their benefit rather than otherwise, for where the wildernesses of reed and rush provided intermittent occupation for the wild-fowler, egg-collector, and reed-cutter, the reclaimed lands must be kept well drained and protected by marsh and river walls, or they cannot be preserved although they are won; and this banking and draining means frequent labour for many hands. So we must admit that the gain is greater than the loss, and that however much we may lament the loss of the wild life and primitive charm of the fen, others will be the better for the changes we deplore.

CHAPTER XIII

THE WATER-BAILIFF

IT was on a bright spring morning several years ago that I first met with the old Broadland waterbailiff. I was rambling along the river wall between Oulton and Somerleyton. The sun was shining warmly on the marshes; the sedge warblers had returned to their summer haunts, and were singing incessantly as they swung on the brittle stems of last year's reeds; and the banks of the dikes were lively with frogs which had left the water and were crawling among the sedges and cuckoo-flowers. A few wherries were gliding slowly seaward before a westerly breeze; here and there the white sail of a yacht or pleasure-boat betokened that cruisers had been tempted to risk the sudden weather changes of the fickle season; and the lowlands were dotted with cattle as far as the level line of the far-off horizon.

I had passed by a small steam pump-mill which drained the flood-water out of several miles of dikes, when, looking ahead along the river wall, I noticed signs of life amid a clump of sallows bordering a narrow creek. A human figure—the only one to be seen on the marshes—was moving among the sallows, and as I drew near the creek a dog appeared and advanced to meet me along the wall. He accompanied me to the bounds of a small enclosed garden patch on the landward side of the wall—a garden which was evidently cultivated by a grey-bearded, ruddy-cheeked, hale-and-hearty-looking old man whom I had seen among the sallows, and who now was seated in the stern of a houseboat moored in the creek.

The old man was glad to have someone to talk to out there in the midst of the marshes, for travellers were few along the river wall. I soon learnt that he was a water-bailiff having charge of the river between Oulton Broad and Breydon Water, and that from his earliest days he had lived in the Broadland. He made me welcome to his snug little houseboat, which, although small, slightly exceeded in size those used by the eel-catchers, and in it I afterwards enjoyed many delightful chats about the river, bird, and marshland life of Broadland.

Here let me describe, as faithfully as I can, the houseboat in which the old man spent the greater part of his time. It consisted of a nearly square cabin or hut built in a strong, heavy boat, not unlike those used by the North Sea trawlers for fish-ferrying. The entrance to the cabin was at the stern, from a small hollow or "well," and, excepting when the door was open, the interior was lighted only by a small window on each side. These windows had close-fitting shutters, which were kept closed at night so that fish poachers who might be on the river after dusk might not become aware of the presence of the water-bailiff through the lamplight shining out into the darkness. A stove was fitted into the bow end of the cabin, and along each side was a locker, one of which served the old man for a bed. Sundry cupboards contained his food, a small stock of plates, cups, and saucers, generally a bottle of catsup made from marshland mushrooms, and a jar of pickled bream. A double-barrelled gun hung in slings on the wall, with a leather wallet containing the bailiff's licence to act as guardian of the fish in the inland water-ways; sundry fishing rods and tackle were stowed in odd corners; the lockers sometimes contained a draw-net seized from a poacher, and invariably an assortment of clothes suited to the frequent weather-changes of the marshlands. In summer, when the heat of the sun on the unshaded marshes was almost unbearable, the cabin was a cool and pleasant retreat; in winter, when the keen winds blew from off the sea, and the ice had to be broken every morning in the creek, it was as warm and snug as the cosiest chimney corner.

Most of the old man's reminiscences of marshland and river life were related to me while we sat together in the little cabin or lounged in warm weather on the sun-scorched river wall. Once I spent a night with him in the houseboat, having come down to the creek to watch the bream at spawning-time, when they swarm up from the river at sundown and tide-ebb, to cleanse themselves, the water-bailiff said, in the fresh water flowing from the dikes. We sat and talked for hours, smoking our pipes meanwhile, and listening to the songs of the reed birds, the rustling of the rats in the hovers, and the crowing of the cock pheasants in the lush marsh grass. Midnight found us still talking; for one topic suggested another, and of the wild life of the marshlands who could say enough? At one o'clock in the morning we looked out of the cabin and saw the far-spreading marshes hidden by a dense white fog. It was a low-lying fog, and only hid the trunks of the willows and the lower part of a black windmill on the wall; above it the air was clear, and the light of the moon and stars undimmed. Then we turned in and slept, one on each of the long lockers, and I dreamt of the sea until, in a half-waking state, I realised that the rocking of the houseboat was caused by the swell from a wherry passing down the river. At four o'clock we were abroad to see the sun rise and watch the night-mist melting from the marshes. And the sedge warblers that were singing when the dusk came on, and which had sung all through the night, were chuckling in the reed beds at dawn.

Then, in the early morning hours, ere the sun had quite dispelled the mist, and while the breath of the cattle on the marshes rose like white smoke from their nostrils, we ate a frugal breakfast in the cabin; directly afterwards setting out in a slate-hued gunpunt on our homeward voyage. As yet there were few yachts moving from their moorings; but as we passed the entrance to Oulton Dike we saw the large dark sails of wherries sailing seaward from the inland towns, and an angler's boat drawn up near the reeds. By seven o'clock we had landed on one of the Oulton boatyards, where Broadsmen and boys were preparing boats and tackle for the anglers who were going out on to the Broad. There I took leave of my friend the water-gipsy, and he rowed back to his lonesome houseboat amid the marshes. But it was not long before I was with him again, and from time to time I made notes of some of his reminiscences.

He was born, nearly eighty years ago, in an out-of-the-way part of the parish of Reedham called Berney Arms, at the upper end of Breydon Water, where the rivers Yare and Waveney unite. In his early days Berney Arms was a queer place for children to be brought up in, for there was no church nor chapel there, and the nearest school was four miles away. Almost the only people the children saw besides their parents were the wherrymen who moored at Berney Arms staithe, and the smelt-fishers and punt-gunners who fished and shot about Breydon. There was no railway in the Broads district in those days, and all the fish landed at Yarmouth and Lowestoft had to be taken up to London by waggons built specially for the purpose. The old water-bailiff could remember that at that time a half-pennyworth of yeast often cost his mother fourpence halfpenny; for she had to cross the river for it, and the ferry charge was twopence each way. Sometimes, when the river was frozen, she could not get it

SETTING THE BOW-NET

even at that price. When the Berney Arms folk wanted coal they had to go three miles for it; and sometimes, when they were " frozen up," they had to go without a fire unless there happened to be an ice-bound coal wherry near the staithe.

The old man had seen many changes in the Broads district. When he first began fishing and shooting there was no local Act for the protection of the river fish, and no restrictions were placed upon the shooting of wildfowl; fishermen and gunners could do just as they pleased. The former used to trawl and draw-net the rivers to such an extent that if a stop had not been put to these practices the rivers would have been almost emptied of fish. On Oulton Broad alone seven draw-nets were worked regularly; and what the catches were like may be judged from the fact that the passing of the Fisheries Protection Act made a difference of three hundred pounds a year to one Lowestoft fish merchant. Much alteration has taken place, too, in some of the Broads. Expanses of water which, sixty years ago, could be rowed and sailed over, are now quite "grown up" with sedge and water-weeds; while others are fast " growing up." The marshes now are so well drained that there is hardly a spot where it is not safe to walk. Sixty years ago there were hundreds of acres of bogland where it was unsafe to set foot; now four-horse waggons are driven over them. The old water-bailiff once got " bogged" in one of these soft places, and it was only by supporting himself by means of his long-barrelled muzzle-loader, the ends of which were resting on firm hassocks of sedge, that he was able to extricate himself from the mud.

Speaking of punt-gunning, which was the chief occupation of several of the old-time Breydoners, the old man said that nothing like such quantities of fowl are seen on Breydon now as there used to be, though large flocks sometimes settle on the flats during hard winters. He himself had never owned a gun-punt while he lived by Breydon; but he had the use of two belonging to other men, and often managed to obtain good sport. One of these boats carried a gun throwing three-quarters of a pound of shot, while the other was charged with a pound. He could well remember the first birds he shot with a punt gun. He was waiting for some fowl to come by, when he caught sight of a pair of large cream-coloured birds some distance away, He sculled nearer to them; but before he got within gunshot they rose and flew away up Breydon. Twice they did this; but he followed them, and at last drew near enough to fire at them. Just as he pulled the trigger a heron "cut down" at the birds, and directly afterwards he found that he had killed two spoonbills and the heron and winged a gull quite forty yards away. He might, he said, have made a good price of the spoonbills; but he laid them down in his boat, and either their own blood or that of the heron so spoilt their feathers that the bird-stuffer to whom he took them would give him only two or three shillings for them. On another occasion, when there was a good deal of ice on Breydon, he saw a goosander, which tried to dive when he drew near it; but the ice prevented its doing so, so he shot it, "though his gun did not go off for quite a quarter of a minute after he pulled the trigger!"

Rather amusing were his experiences with a gentleman named W——, who came to him one day and asked to be taken out punt-gunning. It was arranged that they should start next morning; so about five o'clock they went down to the creek where the gun-punt was moored. Just as they were going on board, my Breydon friend produced the big gun, which was about nine feet long. The amateur did not like the look of it, and nothing would persuade him to go out with it; so they went out with shoulder-guns and had some fairly good sport. Next day it was the same; the stranger was anxious to go out punt-gunning, but the appearance of the big gun was too much for him. On the third morning, however, he steeled his nerves for the ordeal, and the two gunners rowed out on to Breydon to get a good place before the other gunners arrived. They took up their position some time before daybreak, and the stranger, chilled to the bone by the keen winds of the estuary, wished to row about for a while; but he was told that this was against the rules of Breydon. So they lay close under the wall until about seven o'clock, when a bunch of wigeon were seen feeding among some water-weeds. The gunners at once crouched down at the bottom of the boat; the Breydoner took off the leather guard, put the big gun on cock, and drew the boat up to within about ninety yards of the fowl. When he levelled the gun he could feel his companion shaking like a leaf, and the latter would not let him fire the gun until he had spread himself out flat at the bottom of the boat with the Breydoner on the top of him. Then the gun was fired, with the result that seven birds out of the nine in the flock were killed outright. Some time afterwards the nervous sportsman was persuaded to fire the gun, and he shot a red-breasted merganser, with which he was delighted, and vowed he would not part with it for five pounds.

About thirty years ago the late Mr. E. T. Booth was often to be seen on Breydon, where he engaged the professional gunners to keep a lookout for rare birds for him. One day when he was out with a local gunner a sea eagle was seen to alight on one of the stakes marking the channel. It was out of range, so Mr. Booth tried to draw his boat up nearer to the stake; but while he was doing so a wherry came sailing up. Knowing that the wherry would disturb the bird before he could get near enough to fire, Mr. Booth called to his companion, who was in a boat not far from the wherry, that he would give the wherryman three pounds if he would stop his wherry or sail it out of the way. Unfortunately the gunner could not make the wherryman understand this, and when the wherry approached the stake the eagle rose and flew away; but it settled again not very far away, and Mr. Booth followed it and shot it. When the wherryman heard of the offer made by the sportsman he was greatly disappointed, and declared he would have sailed his wherry all over Breydon for three pounds.

"The greatest number of birds I ever killed at one shot was eighty-four starlings," said the old man to me one day. And he went on to say: "A curious thing happened then. A mate of mine and I were down by the river, and we saw a large flock of starlings settle among some reeds. We had our guns with us, and agreed that we should both fire at the same moment. We fired—that is, I did, and I thought my mate did too, and so did he. Then we went and picked up the birds, and found there were eighty-four of them. We divided them between us, forty-two each, and set out for home. When we got there my mate's father came up to see what we had shot, and we told him what we had done. Then the old man looked at his son's gun, and said: 'Them birds is all Jimmy's,' meaning mine. 'What do you mean?' said my mate. 'I mean that your gun hain't bin orf,' said the old man; 'and you don't desarve any o' th' birds a-cause you hain't kept your gun clean.' He was quite right, too. My mate's gun had missed fire; but we both thought our guns went off together. There must have been a rare lot of starlings in the reeds for me to kill eighty-four at a shot; but large flocks of birds are to be seen in Broadland even now, though you don't often see so big a flock as that a man I know saw near the mouth of the Beccles River (the Waveney). I forget what birds they were; but the flock was such a long time in passing over, that the man, after killing one of the first birds that came to him, was able to re-charge his muzzle-loader and bring down one of the last birds of the flock."

Among other things, we chatted about otters and their ways. Otters, I was told, are not so plentiful in the Broads district now as they were forty years ago; but even now they are more numerous than most people imagine, and their tracks are not hard to find if one keeps a sharp lookout for them. The old water-bailiff had shot or trapped over a dozen, the largest weighing twenty-seven and a half pounds, and the smallest seven pounds. His largest otter was caught in a steel-fall trap set just under water about twenty yards from his houseboat; another was shot on a dark night in winter near a dike, and was found lying dead on the ice. A curious thing happened one night when he laid out an eel-line. When he went in the morning to draw in the line he could not find it, and seeing a man standing near the spot where he had laid it out, he accused him of having taken it. This the man denied, and the disappearance of the line seemed likely to remain a mystery, for no wherry had passed the spot during the night to drag it away. But at last the line was found on the river bank, and from its appearance it was evident that an otter had drawn it out of the water and eaten two eels off the hooks. A more sensational story was about an old fisherman who was nearly shot by a marshland gunner owing to the latter mistaking the fisherman's fur cap for an otter. The fisherman was in his boat, which was drawn up close to the rond, and only his fur cap was visible above the young reeds and sedge. Fortunately he raised his rod just as the gunner was about to fire, and thus prevented a tragedy.

CHAPTER XIV

SOME CELEBRATED TREES

THE Autocrat of the Breakfast Table always trembled for a celebrated tree when he approached it for the first time. Provincialism, he said, "has no scale of excellence in man or vegetable; . . . it is constantly taking second and third-rate ones for Nature's best." Consequently he had little faith in many of the stories told of enormous trees, and would never accept them until he had, on the unassailable evidence of the measuring tape, satisfied himself as to their correctness. This test of greatness would rob many famous trees of renown; but celebrity is not always due to height and circumference. Age often has much to do with it. So, too, have associations, as when a tree has been the meeting-place of a Hundred Court or has sheltered a fugitive king; while situation will sometimes lend a tree a certain distinction, either as a landmark, boundary-mark, or convenient place of rendezvous. But in the majority of cases it is girth that makes a tree famous, and here it is that the measuring tape has been the means of banishing illusions. As the Autocrat says: "Before the measuring tape the proudest tree of them all quails and shrinks into itself. All those stories of four or five men stretching their arms around it and not touching each other's fingers, of one's pacing the shadow at noon and making it so many hundred feet, die upon its leafy lips in the presence of the awful ribbon which has strangled so many false pretensions." Yet it may be that the stories were true once, though changes have made them sound like fables. For it does not follow that a tree which measures thirty feet in girth to-day cannot have measured thirty-three or thirty-five feet a hundred and fifty years ago. Indeed, we have conclusive evidence that more than one famous tree had formerly a considerably greater circumference than it has now. For an example we may take the Salcey Oak.

A description of the Salcey Oak, containing a table of its dimensions, was printed as long ago as 1797, by Mr. H. Rooke, F.S.A. In 1881, corresponding measurements were taken, and proved that considerable changes had taken place during the eighty-four years that had elapsed since the first figures were printed. The measurements may be compared in the appended table:

	1797.		1881.	
	ft.	in.	ft.	in.
Circumference at the bottom (where there are no projecting spurs)	46	10	42	0
At one yard from the ground	39	10	36	6
At two yards	35	9	35	4
At three yards	35	0	32	0
Circumference within the trunk, near the ground	29	0	33	6
At one yard from the bottom	24	7	27	0
At two yards	18	6	25	4
At three yards	16	2	25	0
Height within the hollow	14	8	11	0
Height of the tree, on the outside, to the top branch	39	3	30	0

The difference between these measurements, both external and internal, is, of course, due to decay. Externally, the loss of bark from the lower part of the trunk would be sufficient to account for a difference of from three to five feet; while internally the rotting of the tree would be accountable for the increase of the dimensions. In other cases a sinking of the tree into the ground, or an elevation of the ground around the trunk, has been responsible for an apparent decrease in girth. On the other hand, occasionally a celebrated tree has apparently increased in size remarkably during a period which must be looked upon as brief compared with the probable age of the tree; but this has been accounted for by the trunk becoming split, and widened by settling or the weight of the branches.

Norfolk and Suffolk have possessed, and still possess, many remarkable trees, and although, apart from Staverton Park in Suffolk, these counties retain no considerable tract of primitive forest, there can be little doubt that several of these trees have belonged to ancient woodlands. At no time, at any rate within the historic period, does either of the two easternmost counties appear to have contained a large forest; and when Sir Henry Spelman, the Elizabethan antiquary, compiled a list of the English forests, Norfolk and Suffolk were among the fifteen English counties without one. But a forest is not necessarily all woodland, and it is not unlikely that there may have been fairly extensive woodlands. Fuller, in writing of Norfolk in the early part of the seventeenth century, emphasised the fact that "all England may be carved out of Norfolk, represented, not only to the kind, but degree thereof," and he mentions among its features "woody" land; while his contemporary Reyce, in dealing with Suffolk, has a passage pointing to the existence of woodlands in that county. After mentioning that "necessity and want" of wood for fuel was "daily growing," he goes on to say: "So likewise for timber, I confesse now nothing so plentifull as of late dayes, what with multiplicity of curious buildings, variety of costly shipping, wherewith all along our ports our country is served most commodiously, with the endlesse wars of this latter age, and lastly with the continuall desire of Marchants in traversing all the countries and kingdomes of this inferiour world for gain, hath almost vtterly consumed our timber, a decay long since espied, butt hereafter will bee more bewailed, vnlesse there be some vniversall care some waies to repair so important a ruine, whereof there is noe great likelyhood, since generally there is more respect to a present private benefitt how smal soever, than to the great advantage of the comon wealth hereafter." The old woodlands, judging from the situation of the most ancient oaks, must have been in the central parts of the counties. A few fine old oaks are to be seen near the east coast, and on the North Norfolk coast there are some grand specimens in the King's park at Sandringham, which was formerly a part of Rising Chase; but westward, along the border of the fens, the country was, until about sixty years ago, almost entirely open heathland—a district subject to violent sandstorms, compared by Evelyn to those of the deserts of Lybia.

East Anglia is famous for its oaks, so it is not surprising that most of its celebrated trees are representatives of this sturdy species. In Staverton Park, the tract of primitive woodland before referred to, the finest trees are the oaks, several being of considerable girth. In Kimberley Park there is an ancient oak carr, of which several generations of the Wodehouses have been justly proud. So celebrated has it been as to give rise to an old election cry, " The Kimberley Oaks against the Holkham Purse," having reference to contests in which the respective candidates were members of the Wodehouse and Coke families. At Houghton there were formerly many magnificent oaks; but most of them were felled for ship-building in Nelson's day, just as the Houghton walnuts were cut down to furnish musket stocks for the British troops during the Peninsular War. Blickling Park lost a great many fine oaks some years ago during a violent gale; but it still possesses some splendid trees, and the same can be said of many other parks in Norfolk and Suffolk. The fine oaks, however, are not confined to the parks. Not a few are to be found by the roadside, especially on the widespread boulder clay; and some of the most delightful byways and lanes, such as Gainsborough's Lane near Ipswich, owe their charm chiefly to their bordering oaks.

Of our existing oaks the most famous is that which stands in the orchard of the Lodge Farm in the Norfolk parish of Winfarthing, about four miles from Diss. The history of this ruin of a grand old tree was written a year or two ago by Mr. H. F. Euren, in an interesting article entitled "The Oldest Living Thing in East Anglia." Winfarthing Oak is undoubtedly a relic of a vanished tract of ancient woodland, in which, in Norman times, Sir William de Munchensie had liberty to hunt the hare, fox, and wild cat. Afterwards this estate became known as "Winfarthing Great Park," belonging to the adjoining royal palace of Kenninghall Place; and early in the seventeenth century it was enclosed as a deer park by Philip, Earl of Arundel. It is suggested by Mr. Euren that the age of the oak is not less than sixteen hundred years, and that "we are at liberty to imagine that some of the Romans, who held this part of the land for the world-wide Empire, saw the Winfarthing Oak when it was a handsome tree of at least a hundred years old, and that it was in its prime when William the Norman parcelled out the land."

Measurements of Winfarthing Oak, taken at different times within the last hundred and seventy years, have been preserved. The earliest were taken by Robert Marsham, of Stratton Strawless, the correspondent of Gilbert White of Selborne: he states that in 1744 the circumference of the tree was 68 feet 7 inches. This measurement must have been taken at the base of the trunk, for, according to a plate which was affixed in 1820 above an opening giving access to the hollow trunk, "This oak in circumference at the extremities of the roots is 70 feet; in the middle 40 feet"; and James Grigor, who saw the oak in 1841, states in his *Eastern Arboretum*, that "the dimensions of the ruin are exactly as stated on the brass plate affixed to the tree." Previous to this, Samuel Taylor, in a letter written to Loudon, author of *Arboretum et Fruticetum Britannicum*, had described the oak as "now a mere shell—a mighty ruin, bleached to a snowy white; but it is magnificent in its decay. The only mark of vitality it exhibits is on the south side, where a narrow strip of bark sends forth the few branches . . . which even now occasionally produce acorns. It is said to be very much altered of late; but I own I did not think so when I saw it a month ago, and my acquaintance with the veteran is of more than forty years' standing: an important portion of my life, but a mere span of its own." In July 1873 the tree was measured again by Mr. T. E. Amyott, of Diss, who found that no alteration in its dimensions had taken place since 1841. But on measuring it again in 1894, Mr. Amyott discovered that during the previous twenty years it had lost 18 inches in its circumference, which had decreased from 40 feet to 38 feet 6 inches. From 1796 until 1874, he remarks, "time seems to have injured the fine old tree but little, but between 1874 and the present date (1894) much mischief has been done by storms, much of the upper timber has fallen into the interior, nearly filling the great cavity. The foliage this year is black with a 'smut,' and the acorns are small and few. I should state, however, that many other oaks in the neighbourhood are in a similar unhealthy condition."

In a meadow adjoining the orchard containing Winfarthing Oak there is the hollow, branchless trunk of another fine old oak, which, although of smaller girth, is higher and more imposing than the more famous tree. This second oak was also measured by Robert Marsham in 1744, and found to be 30 feet in circumference. It was again measured by Mr. Amyott in 1873, and proved to be unaltered in its dimensions. The trunk is 37 feet high.

In Huntingfield Park there is an ancient tree known as Queen Elizabeth's Oak, the Queen, it is said, having shot a buck with her own hand from beneath the tree. Of this oak the Rev. Charles Davy, rector of Onehouse, in Suffolk, wrote: " Its bulk was found to be nearly eleven yards in circumference at the height of seven feet from the ground; and if we may conjecture from the condition of other trees of the same sort in different parts of the kingdom, whose ages are supposed to be pretty well ascertained from some historical circumstances, I am persuaded this cannot be less than five or six hundred years old. The Queen's Oak at Huntingfield was situated in a park of the Lord Hunsdon, about two bowshots from the old mansion-house where Queen Elizabeth is said to have been entertained by this nobleman, and to have enjoyed the pleasures of the chase in a kind of rural majesty. The approach to it was by a bridge over an arm of the river Blythe, and, if I remember right, through three square courts. A gallery was continued the whole length of the building, which, opening upon a balcony over the porch, gave an air of grandeur with some variety to the front. The great hall was built round six straight massy oaks, which originally supported the roof as they grew; upon these the foresters and yeomen of the guard used to hang their nets, cross-bows, hunting-poles, great saddles, calivers, bills, etc. The roots of them had long decayed when I visited this romantic dwelling; and the shafts sawn off at bottom were supported either by irregular logs of wood driven under them, or by masonry. . . . Elizabeth is reported to have been much pleased with the retirement of this park, which was filled with tall and massy timbers, and to have been particularly amused and entertained with the solemnity of its walks and bowers; but this oak, from which the tradition is that she shot a buck with her own hand, was her favourite tree; it is still in some degree of vigour, though most of its boughs were broken off, and those which remain are approaching a total decay, as well as its vast trunk; the principal arm, now bald with dry antiquity, shoots up to a great height above the leafage, and being hollow and truncated at top, with several cracks resembling loop-holes, through which the light shines into its cavity, it gives us an idea of the winding staircase in a lofty Gothic turret, which, detached from the ruins of some other venerable pile, hangs tottering to its fall, and affects the mind of a beholder after the same manner by its greatness and sublimity." Queen Elizabeth's Oak is still in existence, though in an advanced state of decay. It is split into three sections, one of which is quite dead.

The ruin of another venerable oak stands, among many other fine old trees, near Henham Hall, the seat of the Earl of Stradbroke. Concerning it, Agnes Strickland, the author of the *Lives of the Queens of England*, wrote to Suckling as follows: "The story of Henham Oak, though a very picturesque legend, rests on a vague and doubtful foundation—that of oral tradition—handed down from village chroniclers of former days. . . . One of these worthies told me, many years ago, that there was a brave gentleman of the Rous family, in the great rebellion, whose life was preserved, when a party of the rebels came to Henham with a warrant for his arrest, by his lady concealing him in the hollow trunk of that venerable old oak, beneath the windows of the Hall. This tree being used by the family as a summer-house, was luckily provided with a door faced with bark, and which closed so artificially, that strangers not aware of the circumstance would never suspect that the tree was otherwise than sound. The hero of the tale was, I presume, the Cavalier baronet Sir John Rous, to whom King Charles II. wrote an autograph letter, thanking him for his loyal services. According to the story, the Roundhead authorities used threatening language to the lady to make her declare her husband's retreat, but she courageously withstood all their menaces. They remained there two or three days, during which time she, not daring to trust any one with the secret, stole softly out at night to supply her lord with food, and to assure herself of his safety. I fancy this conjugal heroine must have been the beautiful Elizabeth Knevitt (Knivett), whose portrait is preserved at Henham. It is possible, however, that the tradition may belong to a period still more remote. Our Suffolk peasants are not an imaginative race, therefore I should be inclined to think that the incident really did occur to a former possessor of Henham. In the course of my historical investigations, I have generally found that tradition, if not always the truth, was, at least, a shadowy evidence of some unrecorded fact; and I am always anxious to believe anything to the honour of my own sex. The oak was afterwards a noted resort for select Jacobite meetings of a convivial nature, when Sir Robert Rous, and two or three staunch adherents of the exiled House of Stuart, were accustomed to drink deep healths 'to the King over the water,' on bended knees." An ivy-grown trunk, about 12 feet high and 9 feet in diameter, is all that now remains of the Henham Oak; but the present Earl of Stradbroke can remember the time when its branches extended over a circle at least 25 yards in diameter. Then there were marks in the hollow trunk indicating that it had been divided into two rooms. The greater part of the tree broke away in July 1878, and the rest of it fell in 1904, leaving only the broken trunk. In its prime it must have been a fine tree, and some idea of its age may be gained from the fact that it was quite hollow in 1650.

A grand and finely proportioned Norfolk tree is the Thorpe Oak, which stands in Thorpe Wood, outside the ancient walled garden of the old Hall, where it is surrounded by lofty trees of various kinds. Its circumference at a foot from the ground is 21 feet 6 inches, and its height about 70 feet, while it has a clean trunk of 42 feet. It is in a vigorous state of health, and shows no sign of decay; but as a precautionary measure against the strain of storms, Lord Suffield has had its top lightened by the removal of some branches. Grigor tells us that this oak was sometimes called the "King of Thorpe," and he adds that in some respects it is "the oak of the county." "It is," he writes, "upright, lofty, and embowering; it is not only characteristic of strength and majesty, but it forms, in every respect, a beautiful tree. It reveals to us the perfect appearances of the species." A less celebrated tree is the Great Oak at Cretingham, in Suffolk. The hollow trunk of this tree was formerly used as a shelter for young neat stock, of which, it is said, about eight were kept there and foddered; while at other times the trunk was found convenient as a cart-shed and store for farm implements. An old woman, who was a servant on the Oak Farm, could remember having milked a cow inside this useful tree. The Great Oak is still in existence, though very decrepit, and having its arms supported by crutches.

Grigor mentions two trees in Norfolk which are traditionally connected with the great peasant rising of 1549, and each of which is known as Kett's Oak. One of these is at Ryston, near Downham Market: in 1841 it was 45 feet round, and had "a majestic head of boughs, bearing a just proportion to the immense size of its trunk." A better known Kett's Oak stands near the seventh milestone on the main road from Norwich to Wymondham. It has a trunk 10 feet high, and about 10 feet in circumference three feet from the ground. Among the giants with which we have been dealing, it must be reckoned a small tree; but it possesses unusual interest owing to there being a tradition that it was under this tree Robert Kett, the Wymondham tanner, and the leader of the great insurrection, pledged himself to lay down his life in the cause of freedom. Mr. Euren is of the opinion that at the time of the insurrection the oak stood in a wood; but early in the eighteenth century the turnpike road was made across the site of the old wood. The tree stands between the carriage way and a roadside footpath, and, as Mr. Euren remarks, the fact of its preservation in such a situation is evidence that it is a tree with a history. Evelyn, in writing of the oak, says: " I meet but one instance where this goodly tree has been in our country abused to cover impious designs, as was that of the arch-rebel Kett, who made an oak (under the specious name of Reformation, *Quercus Reformationis*) the court, council-house, and place of convention, whence he set forth his traitorous edicts." But the oak referred to by Evelyn—who wrote at a time when the motives of Robert Kett were not properly appreciated—was not the one still standing, but a tree which stood on Mousehold Heath, near Norwich.

Holy Oak Farm, near Combs Church, in Suffolk, takes it name from an ancient tree which, although almost dead, still has a few young branches bearing leaves. Its trunk, which is very gnarled and irregular in its circumference, is about 15 feet in its smallest measurement. Several vague traditions attach to the tree, as for instance, that the Druids worshipped beneath it; that processions were made to and from it in pre-Reformation days; and that during the reign of Queen Mary people used to assemble at night beneath it and listen to reading from a Bible which was kept chained to and concealed in its trunk. This tree may probably be included among the so-called " Gospel Oaks," of which there are others in Haughley Park, near Stowmarket, at Hawstead, near Bury St. Edmunds, and a better known example at Polstead, the Suffolk village famous for its connection with the "Red Barn Mystery." Of the Hawstead Oak it is said that under its shade " the clergyman and parishioners used to stop in their annual perambulations, and, surveying a considerable extent of a fruitful and well-cultivated country, repeat some prayers of the Gospel only, proper for the occasion."

Turning for a while from the oaks to some other trees, one of the most noteworthy is the famous Hethel Thorn, or " Witch of Hethel," which stands in a field adjoining Hethel Church, near Wymondham, in Norfolk. This notable whitethorn is one of the largest of its kind. At a foot from the ground it measures 12 feet 1 inch in girth, and at five feet from the ground, 14 feet; while the circumference of the space covered by its branches is 31 yards. Various ages have been assigned to it, and there is a popular tradition that it dates from the reign of King John; but botanists appear to be generally agreed that thorn trees hardly ever live more than two hundred years. In the cases of thorns permitted to grow untrimmed, this may be the case; but anyone tracing the foundations of the wall which surrounded the ruins of St. Benet's Abbey, in Norfolk, will notice that at fairly regular intervals there occur just outside the wall the stumps of ancient hawthorns. That these hawthorns were planted subsequently to the dissolution of the monasteries seems unlikely, and it is instructive to notice that, although most of the stumps have been cut down level with the ground, a few of them every year still shows signs of life in the form of young twigs with leaves. The Hethel Thorn, whatever may be its age, is still living. Another fine old thorn stands in the garden of Wortwell Hall, close beside the Waveney. Although an old tree, it is in vigorous growth, and in 1905 had every appearance of being equal to doubling its age. At four feet from the ground it measures 6 feet 7 inches in girth; but the lower part of the trunk is partly decayed. This tree is chiefly remarkable for its height, which exceeds that of the chimneys of the old Hall.

A big beech standing on the lawn in the gardens of Spixworth Park is remarkable on account of the extraordinary growth of the shoots that have sprung up in twenty-six different places around the parent tree from the unaided inlaying of branches which have touched the ground. The girth of the main trunk at three feet from the ground is 20 feet; the circumference of its spreading branches (measured in a leafless state) is 148 yards; while the spread of the longest branch from the main trunk is 33 feet. In an account of this tree which appeared in the *County Gentleman*, it is stated that "in summer the foliage is thick enough completely to conceal anyone under it from view, and a few years ago a party of eighty guests were having tea beneath it when a late arrival was ushered into the garden, and, failing to see anyone about, thought he must have mistaken the day, till he was reassured by the evidence—not of his sight—but of his ears." In the Park at Spixworth there is a horse-chestnut which has a branch stretching unsupported to a length considerably in excess of the height of the tree. The girth of this chestnut is 15 feet 8 inches at four feet from the ground; the branch, which leaves the trunk at seven feet from the ground, is 24 feet in girth near the trunk and is 56 feet long. The age of the tree is believed to be about 180 years.

Alders, though their rugged beauty adds greatly to the picturesqueness of some of the upper reaches of our rivers, seldom grow to very great size; but an exception is found in a magnificent tree in Haverland Park, in Norfolk. When Grigor wrote (in 1841), the height of this tree was 62 feet and its girth a foot from the ground 11 feet 7 inches; but a few years ago a gale robbed it of some of its branches, so that its greatest height is now 40 feet. During the sixty-four years which have elapsed since Grigor saw it, there has been no alteration in its circumference at a foot from the ground; it was measured for me by the gardener in May 1905, and proved to be exactly 11 feet 7 inches. Six feet from the ground the girth is 10 feet 5 inches. In girth this tree is beaten by another alder standing a few yards away from it, and which measures 18 feet 2 inches at a foot from the ground, while its height is 45 feet; but in the case of this tree the trunk branches into a crown about 3 feet from the ground.

Of trees noteworthy for their real or legendary associations, one of the most interesting is the ancient mulberry tree standing in the garden of the Old Vicarage in Stowmarket, Suffolk. The story is that this tree was planted by the poet Milton, who visited Stowmarket while his old tutor, Dr. Thomas Young, was in possession of the vicarage. At Barham, in the same county, there was an ancient oak known as Kirby's Oak, taking its name from the famous entomologist, the Rev. W. Kirby, who was rector of Barham. It stood between the church and Shrubland Park, but was burnt in November 1905, having been set on fire either by accident or through mischief. Yet other trees associated with a notable personage are the Stratton Strawless oaks, which were planted by Robert Marsham, the naturalist-correspondent of Gilbert White of Selborne. Robert Marsham, who died in 1797, was devoted to arboriculture, and in addition to the oak, he planted at Stratton Strawless several cedars, firs, hollies, and beeches, some of which have attained the dimensions of monarchs of their respective kinds. The fact of Marsham living to be ninety years of age helps to justify the remark of Evelyn, that planters of trees are often blessed with health and old age. In Suffolk especially there are some fine cedars, notably in the grounds of Claydon and Barking rectories. The latter are believed to have come from one of the oldest—if not the oldest—cedars in England, planted in the old palace grounds at Enfield.

Of the vanished oaks, one of the most celebrated was to be seen, until about sixty years ago, in the grounds of Bramfield Hall, in Suffolk. It was called the Bramfield Oak. In 1832 it had three main branches; but soon after one of these fell, and on June 15th, 1843, a sultry day without a breath of breeze, the tree fell from sheer decay, "with a most appalling crash, enveloping its prostrate form with clouds of dust." The dimensions of this tree have not been preserved; but, according to Suckling, it was said at the time of its fall that its bulk of sound timber would have been worth £80. This is a small sum compared with that paid for the Gelenos Oak, which stood near Newport, and which was bought for £405, the purchaser also having to pay £82 for labour in stripping, felling, and converting into timber. Bramfield Oak is mentioned in a ballad about Hugh Bigod and Bungay Castle, in which the flight of the Baron from London to Bungay in 1174 is described. This led Suckling to assume that the oak was over a thousand years old; but the ballad, which contains the lines—

> "When the Baily had ridden to Bramfield Oak,
> Sir Hugh was at Ilksall Bower;
> When the Baily had ridden to Halesworth Cross,
> He was singing in Bungay Tower,"

is not a very old one, and its author undoubtedly supplied the landmarks mentioned in it from his own knowledge of the road described, rather than from any ancient record of the Baron's flight.

In the Suffolk parish of Hoxne, a stone monument, surmounted by a cross, marks the spot where stood a famous oak, traditionally the one to which King Edmund, the Martyr King of East Anglia, was bound when he was shot to death with arrows by the Danes. According to an inscription on the monument, St. Edmund's Oak, as it was called, fell in August 1848; but in a letter written by Lady Kerrison it is stated that the tree fell on 11th September of that year. It was then apparently in vigorous health; but the weight of its foliage is supposed to have brought it to the ground. The trunk, which was shivered in the middle, was 20 feet in circumference, and the branches, which are described as having been of the size of ordinary oaks, covered an area 48 feet in diameter. Lady Kerrison tells us that the tree contained 17 loads of timber; but on another authority we have it that the trunk contained 6½ loads of timber, the limbs 9 loads, and the branches 4 loads of battens and 184 faggots.

A remarkable circumstance in connection with the fall of this tree was the discovery of what was supposed to be an arrow-head embedded in the wood about five feet from the ground. This discovery was naturally regarded as important evidence of the truth of the tradition that the tree was the one to which King Edmund was bound; but the references to the finding of the arrow-head are contradictory, Lady Kerrison asserting that it was covered " a little more than a foot thick with sound material," while Mr. Smythies, the agent to Sir Edward Kerrison, states that he found the arrow-head, partly corroded, projecting from the inside of the hollow part of the trunk," and that the wood around the arrow-head was " perfectly decayed." Lady Kerrison adds that " the arrow-head and wood have been shown to and approved by the Antiquarian Society of London."

Yet another famous oak, known as Thwaites Oak or Thwaites Tree, stood in the Norfolk parish of Tivetshall St. Margaret. Its main trunk was 19 feet in height, and had an average girth of 21 feet. This tree was sold a few years ago to a Cambridge firm of church-restorers for the sum of £40. A contemporary account of its felling states that when it was cut down four feet of the trunk was first removed, leaving twenty tons of solid oak lying half a mile from the road and sixty miles from its destination. To roll it down a half mile slope to the road was a fairly easy task; but even during the progress of this operation attempts to guide the rolling tree resulted in the snapping of wire ropes and heavy chains. After that the laborious task of hoisting the huge tree on to a platform of sleepers had to be undertaken; but eventually it was safely loaded and secured with wire ropes. It then took a day and a half for a 14 horse-power engine, assisted by the skill of about a dozen men, to convey the tree from the place where it was loaded to the high road, a distance of about fifty yards. A few days later it was conveyed by road to Cambridge by way of Attleborough and Thetford. It was subsequently found to be practically useless for the purposes for which it was intended, the wood being, to use the technical terms applied to it, "white" and "short," instead of "black" and "long."

Merton Park, the Norfolk seat of Lord Walsingham, formerly possessed a noble oak, which Loudon ranked next in size to Winfarthing Oak. It had a circumference of 63 feet 2 inches at the surface of the ground; 32 feet 4 inches at two feet from the ground; and 23 feet 4 inches at six feet. The height of the trunk to the fork of the branches was 18 feet 8 inches, and the total height of the tree, 64 feet. It was quite hollow, and was destroyed during a gale in January 1902. Another celebrated Norfolk tree was the Bale Oak, the trunk of which measured 36 feet in circumference. Grigor says he was unable to find any trace of it; but the author of a book entitled *English Forests and Forest Trees*, published in 1853, refers to it as standing near the village church; and I am told by a resident in the village that what remained of it in 1857 had so fallen into decay, that it was taken down and removed into a neighbouring park. The hollow trunk of the Bale Oak, the circumference of which can still be traced among the trees between the churchyard and the road, is said to have been capable of containing twenty men standing upright; and at one time it was inhabited by the village cobbler, who carried on his trade in it during one entire summer, after having cut a doorway in the side of the trunk. The branches of this tree seem to have been in proportion to the size of the bole; for one of them, which was lopped off during the latter part of the eighteenth century, extended to within three feet of the summit of the church tower, which is 54 feet high, and stands 72 feet distant from the site of the trunk of the tree. Blomefield has a note about this tree; but he puts the number of men it was capable of containing at twelve. A much smaller oak stood in Wayland Wood, near Watton, in Norfolk, and had some interest for the curious, owing to a local tradition that it was the identical tree under which the unfortunate " Babes in the Wood" were found dead and covered with leaves, Wayland Wood being the supposed scene of the tragic occurrence related in the old and popular ballad.

In Ketteringham Park, the seat of Lady Boileau, there was, until a few years ago, the ruin of a fine old walnut tree, planted by Lady Mary Heveningham in 1660, on the restoration of Charles II. Grigor, whose ear seems to have been deceived by the sound of a name, states that the tree was planted by Lady Mary Effingham, commemorative of the death of her husband, Sir Arthur Effingham, who suffered with many others for the support he gave to the cause of Oliver Cromwell; but Lady Boileau tells me that it was William Heveningham who suffered for the part he took against Charles I., and that his wife, who was a daughter of the Earl of Dover, went to London, not to ask for her husband's head, but to plead for his life, which was granted to him, and he was allowed to live in retirement at Ketteringham, where he died, and was buried in the parish church. The tree planted by Lady Mary Heveningham was standing until 1899, though the branches had so decayed that little save the stump remained, and as it seemed nearly dead, the late Sir Francis Boileau had it cut down. A small brick building now stands on the site of the tree, and into it is let a slab bearing the inscription: "On this spot flourished an immense Walnut Tree, from 1660 to 1899. Planted by the Lady Mary Heveningham, to commemorate the restoration of the Stuart Dynasty.

Cut down, when in an advanced state of decay, by Sir Francis Boileau, Bart. *Pereunt et Imputantur.*"

Until the year 1713, when, according to the local records of Hingham, it was destroyed by "a tarrible violent wind," there stood in the Norfolk parish of Deopham a gigantic lime, known as Deopham Great Tree. It is described by Evelyn in his *Sylva*, where he writes: "See what a Tilia that most learned and obliging person, Sir Thomas Browne, of Norwich, describes to me in a letter just now received: 'An extraordinary large and stately Tilia, Linden, or Lime-tree, there groweth at Depeham, in Norfolk, 10 miles from Norwich, whose measure is this: the compass, in the least part of the trunk or body, about two yards from the ground, is at least 8½ yards; about the root near the earth, 16 yards; about half a yard above that, near 12 yards in circuit; the height to the uppermost bough, about 30 yards. . . . To distinguish it from others in the country, I called it Tilia Colossæa Depehamensis.'" This tree, which was apparently a huge broad-leaved lime, is also mentioned by Sir John Pettus in his *Essays Explaining Metallick Words*, where, under the heading of "Petrifaction," he states that "at the bottom of this tree there is a spring of the like nature to that in Yorkshire (near Knaresborough Castle) for Petrifaction; now I wish that a graft might be carry'd from thence into Yorkshire, and planted near that petrifying well, by which it might be seen whether the tree gave any such virtue to the spring, or the spring to the tree from which, and other inquiries, I have still been diverted by publick imployments." On February 27th, 1713, Mrs. Gurdon, of Letton, wrote to her brother-in-law, Mr. Herne, of Mendham: "Ye great tree at Deepham was blown down wth ye high wind. I was at Sr J: Wodehouses last Munday, & yt morning he & my Lady Lemster had been to se it. He measur'd it, & it was 37 yds. high, & 16 about."

Blomefield, in his *History of Norfolk*, mentions that on Caston Common there was a tree which had grown in a very unusual manner. "It was first," he writes, "a large willow, on the head or tod of which an acorn, the key of an ash, an elder berry, and a hazel nut were lodged (probably carried thither by the birds), all of which took root in the dirt and rotten part of the tod, and so ran downwards till they reached the earth, and rooted in it, and continued growing till they split the body of the willow open, and so the first roots, which run from the tod to the earth, are become a tree, and, the outward rind of the willow being standing, there are five sorts of trees conjoined, viz. an oak, an ash, a willow, a hazel, and an elder." Grigor had his doubts as to whether such a curiosity ever existed; but it is no very rare occurrence for one tree to grow up within the hollow trunk of another, and it is quite possible that the Caston combination may have had a real existence. In Staverton Park there are two or three hollow oaks in the midst of which birches have taken root, and grown to be fairly large trees.

Until about half a century ago, Bury St. Edmunds also boasted of a famous willow, described as being "the largest willow in the kingdom." It was known as "The Abbot," or "The Abbot's Willow," and it stood within the wall which protected the famous Abbey of St. Edmundsbury from the frequent floods in the valley of the river Lark. In 1822 the girth of this tree was 18 feet 6 inches, its height 75 feet, the *ambitus* of the boughs 204 feet, and the girth of its two principle limbs 15 feet and 12 feet respectively. At that time the tree is said to have contained 440 feet of solid timber, and there was a popular belief that it was as old as the well-known Abbot's Bridge at Bury St. Edmunds, which dates from the twelfth century.

In the old days, when the "wooden walls" of England were to the Englishman what his ironclads are to-day;

our woodlands were sadly depleted, and, as Lord Nelson complained, very little planting was done to help towards making up for the losses our woods had sustained. Of late years we have heard a good deal about re-afforestation of certain parts of our country; but at present we are far behind several foreign countries in our attempt to bring about this very desirable end. In Norfolk and Suffolk, where nearly the whole of the land is under cultivation, little can be done in this direction; but so far as has been possible, East Anglia has set a good example to other parts of the country, and it is likely to keep well to the front, especially in cultivating quick-growing trees. In South-west Norfolk and North-west Suffolk the aspect of one of the wildest tracts of open country has undergone a great change through the planting of fir belts and large and small plantations; while in North Norfolk the King has accomplished around Sandringham what Thomas Coke, Earl of Leicester, brought about around Holkham a century and a half ago. So, as the famous old trees one by one decay and disappear, others will undoubtedly become famous owing to their associations, size, or antiquity. Even now no part of England has more or finer oaks than our two easternmost counties, and of late years so many trees have been planted by royal and distinguished personages in the Sandringham grounds, that Norfolk may well claim to be the county of famous trees.

CHAPTER XV

SWAN-UPPING

ABOUT the middle of August the Broadland cruising season is still at its height, and very few yachts, launches, and pleasure-wherries are lying idle by the Wroxham, Oulton, and Potter Heigham boat-yards. On the Broads and rivers the white sails of yachts are far more numerous than the dark sails of the familiar trading-wherries; the crowded river steamers throb noisily up and down the Yare, Bure, and Waveney; regattas and sailing matches are still in progress at one cruising centre or another; and at every waterside village the inn-keeper, boat-letter, and lodging-house keeper are busy reaping their annual harvest. By the wild life of the Broads there is preserved, it is true, a seasonable silence, and you may row or sail a mile or more along a river without hearing a bird's song or even a rustling in the hovers; but only on the upper reaches and narrow tributary streams is one afforded opportunities for the quiet enjoyment of nature. Nearly everyone afloat is manifestly "doing" the Broads, and that, apparently, as quickly as possibly.

In the midst of this season of somewhat strenuous pleasure-seeking, there assembles, almost unobserved, at Buckenham Ferry on the Yare, a little party of about half a score men, whose business has no connection with Broadland cruising or holiday pastimes. They arrive early in the morning, coming by rail or river from Norwich and other places on the Yare, and several of them bring with them curious-looking crooks, not unlike those used by shepherds, but with much longer handles. At the ferry they are met by the local water-bailiff and two or three Broadsmen in their marsh boats, and before the Ferry Inn is open to the public for the day, or the cruising folk are awake on the yachts moored by the riverside, these early visitors have squeezed themselves into an ancient steam-launch of somewhat cramped accommodation, the marsh boats are taken in tow, and the strange-looking flotilla moves slowly down the river towards Hardley Cross. Should a stranger inquire of some early-rising wherryman the meaning of these unwonted proceedings, he is told that the departing voyagers are "going arter th' swans," information that will satisfy him should he be acquainted with the ancient custom of the river, that the men he has seen are acting for a time as swanherds, and that they are about to commence the annual swan-upping. To make this matter clearer, let it be stated at once that they are the representatives of the various swan-owners who have swans on the river, and that they are about to catch and mark with the owners' swan-marks the cygnets which have been hatched off along the river during the year. At the present time the City of Norwich owns most of the swans frequenting the river Yare; but there are also a few private owners, who are usually represented at the annual upping.

Before giving some account of the customary proceedings during the upping, it may be explained that formerly, by an Act of Parliament passed in 1483, the privilege of keeping swans was confined to persons enjoying a freehold estate of the clear annual value of five marks. In order that each swan-owner might know his own birds, there was cut on the beak a distinctive mark, known as a "swan-mark"; and the swan-marks of the different counties were inscribed on rolls, each county having a separate roll, a copy of which was

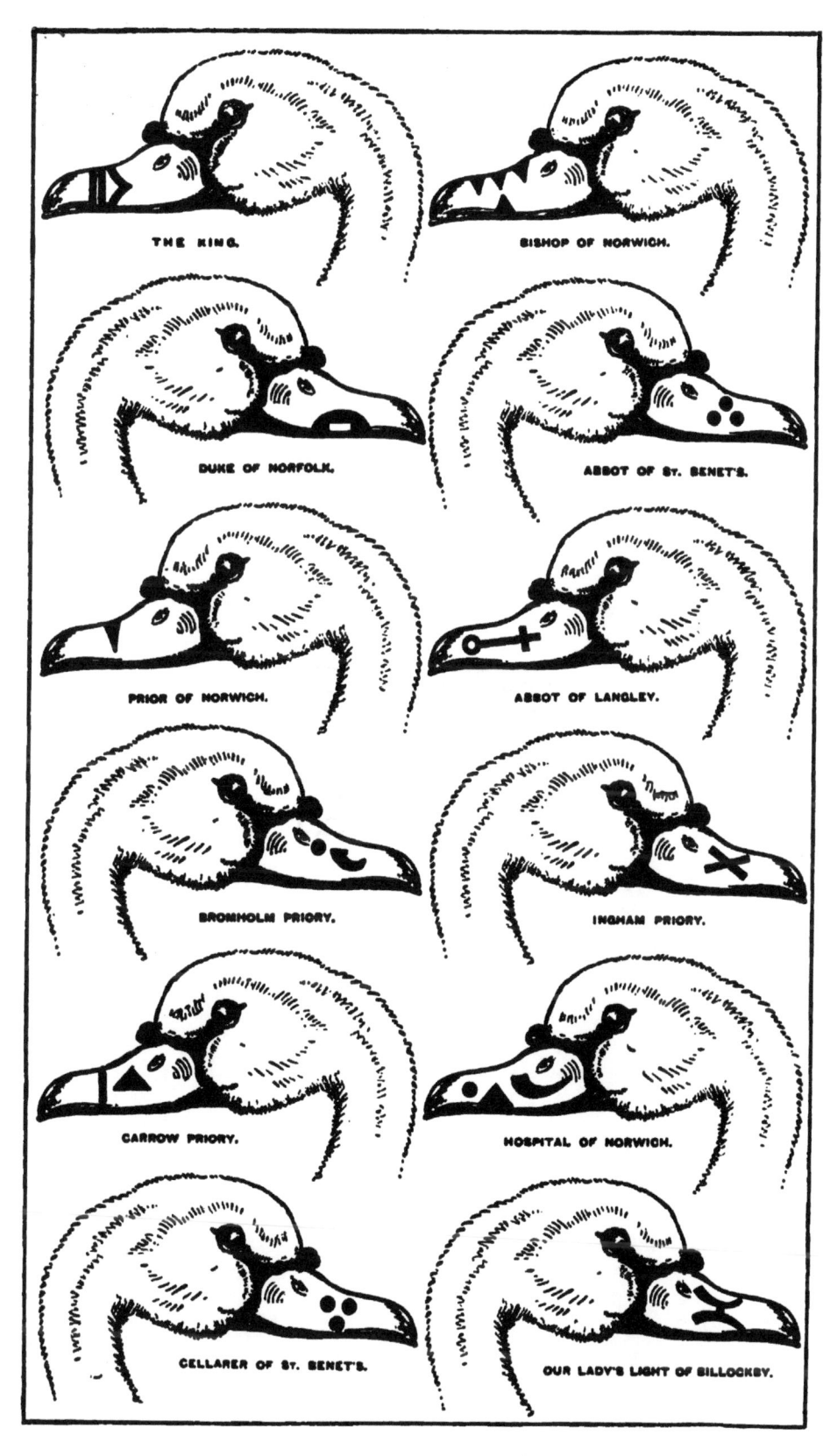

SOME NORFOLK SWAN-MARKS

THE NEW YORK
PUBLIC LIBRARY

ASTOR, LENOX AND
TILDEN FOUNDATIONS.

usually in the possession of each swan-owner. Some of these Rolls of Swan-marks, dating from the reign of Edward IV., are still in existence; but the majority of the existing rolls appear to have been made in the reign of Elizabeth. Some of the marks found in the Norfolk Rolls are reproduced in the accompanying plate, the particular document from which they were taken being a copy made of an ancient roll in 1837 by the Rev. Edward Wymer, vicar of Ingham, in Norfolk. The first mark shown in the roll is that of the King, which is immediately followed by those of the Duke of Norfolk, the Bishop of Norwich, the Earl of Surrey, and the Duke of Suffolk. Many of the monastic houses were swan-owners; among the marks being those of the Abbot of St. Benet's, the Abbot of Langley, and the Priors of Norwich, Bromholm, Ingham, and Carrow, the Cellarer of St. Benet's, and the Hospital of Norwich; there is also that of Our Lady's Light at Billockby. Some of these marks are simple affairs, consisting of bars, chevrons, triangular nicks or notches, dots, and crosses; but others must have necessitated considerable skill in cutting them, the operation being an unpleasant one for the swan. In a great majority of cases the mark was made on the upper surface of the beak; but, as shown in the Norfolk Roll, the King's mark, consisting of a chevron and two bars, extends to the lower surface, and similarly-extended marks occur in those of the Earl of Oxford, the Duke of Suffolk, and Martham Hall.

Swan-marks often changed hands, generally with the ownership of lands adjoining the rivers. A deed referring to the sale of a swan-mark in 1646 commences: "To all Christian people to whom this present writing shall come, greeting. Know ye that I, Robert Ladal's Baker, of Terrington St. Clements, in the County of Norfolk, Gentleman, for and in consideration of a certain sum of money to me in hand paid before then sealing hereof, by Anthony Williamson, of Kenwicke, in the parish of Tilney, in the said County, Gentleman;" and the document goes on to say that the disposer of the mark did sell, assign, and make over unto the said Williamson "all that my swan-mark commonly called the hammer-head and Roman R., with all other additions unto the same belonging or in any way appertaining." The mark in question appears on the "margent" of the deed.

In the year 1598 the City of Norwich was possessed of three swan-marks which had belonged to the Hospital of St. Giles. Referring to these, Blomefield, the Norfolk historian, says: "The city have three swan-marks on the narrow fresh-water streams in Norfolk, one called Blake's mark, belonging to the manor of Rokele's in Trowse; another called Paston's, or the Hospital mark, which belonged to Margaret, widow of John Paston, Esq., daughter and heiress of John Mautby, Esq., which she gave to Edmund, her second son (this should be her grandson Robert), and it was then called Dawbeney's mark, and was late Robert Cutler's, clerk; and in 1503, Geoffrey Styward settled it on Cecily his wife, for life, and then on his eldest son, who gave it to the City. The third is called the City mark, and formerly the King's mark, and was conferred on the City by Sir John Hobard in the grand rebellion." Elsewhere Blomefield refers to four marks belonging to the Mayor and City, namely: the City mark; St. Giles' Hospital mark, now the Mayor's; Rokele's Manor mark, late the Hospital, now the Mayor's; and the Hospital new mark, now the Mayor's.

To return to the upping. It is a still August morning with promise of midday heat. Hardly enough breeze is stirring to cause a whisper among the riverside reeds; the loosestrife at the water's edge is drooping until its purple spikes almost touch the water; the plovers are silent in the marshlands; and the countless cattle among which they are feeding move listlessly through the dew-drenched grass. The progress of the swan-herds' steam-launch is almost as listless, and as no swans are in sight, pipes are produced and reminiscences of other upping-days help to while away the time. These reminiscences are chiefly of the vagaries of former swan-herds, some of whom were known to vanish mysteriously in the midst of the day's proceedings, and to be discovered late at night seeking swans in the neighbourhood of some marshland inn. Of the festivities that marked the upping in earlier days, the present swanherds are without personal experience; they were abandoned too long ago. Then it was a regular occurrence for the Norwich Corporation officials to be present at the upping, which was preceded by a lavish breakfast at Coldham Hall; and not infrequently the Mayor of the City came down the river in his state barge to preside over the breakfast. In those days—which came to an end with the passing of the Municipal Reform Bill of 1835—the swanherds were distinguished by each wearing in his hat a snowy plume. And there was need for their being distinguished by some such adornment, for at that time the commencement of the swan-upping was a rural festival, people coming from far and near to watch the capture and marking of the swans.

The first swans, two old birds and five cygnets, are seen quietly feeding near the margin of a reed bed a little way above the wherry channel known as Langley Dike. The launch is stopped and moored by the "rond"-side; about half the swanherds remain on board her, while the rest, entering two of the boats, start in pursuit of the birds. The chase is quite without exciting incident. The boats are rowed slowly along in the wake of the swans, which are quietly driven towards the entrance of the dike; there one of the boats "heads them off," and, finding their passage up and down the river barred, the birds enter the *cul-de-sac* dike, from which they can escape only by taking to the land. Down the full length of this dike they are driven like sheep down a lane, and at the end of it they are enclosed in a space a few yards square by one of the boats being turned broadside across the channel. Then the long-handled crooks are brought into use, two of the cygnets being caught by the neck and drawn into the boats. The old birds, with the rest of the brood, make for the shore, where they are soon run down and caught by hand. A large rush basket called a "frail" is then produced, and from it are taken a number of old neckties. With these the legs of each captured bird are tied together above its back, and when all are thus secured two or three cygnets are selected to be taken up to Norwich, and there fattened in the old swan-pit for Christmas. The old birds' marks are then examined, and should they be found to bear the City or a private swan-owner's mark, the remaining cygnets— which are to be liberated again to help to keep up the stock on the river—are marked accordingly, the mark being cut in the bill with a sharp clasp-knife. In the event of one of the old birds belonging to the City and the other to a private owner, the cygnets are divided between the two owners, the ownership of any odd bird in the brood being decided by the simple expedient of "heads or tails." Another penalty those cygnets must pay for being permitted to remain at liberty is that they must undergo the painful operation of being pinioned, which is effected by cutting off a portion of the wing at the carpal joint.

The next brood, consisting of only three cygnets, is met with near the mouth of the tributary river Chet, a narrow, shallow stream which enters the Yare beside Hardley Cross, the ancient boundary-mark of the City of Norwich jurisdiction over the Yare. The Chet is navigable to wherries as far as the small town of Loddon, which is situated about four miles from Hardley Cross; and there is a legend to the effect that a party of swanherds, after securing at an early hour in the morning their first brood of cygnets near Loddon Staithe, adjourned to an inn called the Swan, and found the entertainment there so much to their liking that no more upping was done that day. The swanherds of to-day are more conscientious in the execution of their duties; for they show no inclination to drive the swans towards Loddon Staithe; indeed, they head them off and secure them within a hundred yards of the mouth of the tributary stream. Below Hardley Cross swans are seldom met with, probably owing to the brackishness of the water and the lack of suitable food below that point. So, having dealt with the second brood, the swanherds return to their launch, and, towing behind them the boat containing the cygnets for the swan-pit, make their way back to Buckenham Ferry and a substantial breakfast.

So far the swan-upping has been a simple affair; the birds have been on their best behaviour, and, taking into consideration the distance that has been covered, good progress has been made. But swan-upping along the river, where the swans have practically no chance of escaping, is very different to swan-upping on a Broad, and as the swanherds start for Rockland Broad as soon as breakfast is over, we cannot do better than keep in company with them, in the hope of seeing something more exciting than the early morning has afforded. At the mouth of Rockland Fleet the launch is again moored; the captured cygnets are taken out of the boat and allowed to rest—with their legs still tied together—amid the sedge by the fleet-side; and the swanherds enter three rowing boats, three of them occupying each boat. In the fleet, which is about three-quarters of a mile in length, no swans are encountered; but on reaching the open water of the Broad three broods are seen paddling quietly about the margins of the islets of reed, rush, and reedmace. A stranger to the business might imagine that one boat would go in pursuit of each brood; but on a Broad like Rockland, where, notwithstanding the "growing up" of some of its shallower parts, there are still considerable expanses of open water, the occupants of a single boat might spend hours in chasing the swans without effecting a capture. The only plan likely to be attended with success is for the swanherds to single out each brood in turn, and concentrate their attention upon it. By a series of careful movements it may then be possible to drive the swans into some creek or dike adjoining the Broad, and there catch them with the crooks.

An attempt is made to catch in this way a pair of old birds with six cygnets which have just emerged from a channel between two of the reedy islets, the aim of the swanherds being to drive them into a boathouse dike on the border of the Broad. One of the boats is rowed round the islet, so as to enter the channel behind the birds and prevent their returning by the way they have come; another closes in upon them with the object of keeping them from swimming out on to the open water; while the third is rowed to a point about a hundred yards beyond the entrance to the boathouse dike, where it waits in readiness to intercept the swans should they attempt to pass the dike-mouth. At the bow of each a swanherd stands, crook in hand, on the alert to secure any bird that may come within his reach. The old birds, it is evident, have been rendered uneasy by these preliminary movements, the cock bird especially showing an ungallant inclination to abandon his mate and offspring. For a while he swims backward and forward in an agitated manner, and when he is still about fifty yards from the dike-mouth, and while there remains a fairly wide space between the two boats that are closing in upon him, he decides to make a dash for freedom. Starting with a few powerful swimming strokes, he soon brings his pinioned wings into use, and with a rush, in

SWAN-UPPING

which the water is thrown up as by a miniature steam-launch, he dashes between the boats and is soon at safe distance from immediate pursuit. His deserted mate seems disposed to follow him, for with the cygnets crowding closely in her wake she heads towards the open water; but the swanherds have anticipated this, and by splashing the water with their crooks they drive her back towards the fringe of reeds bordering the Broad. On reaching the dike-mouth, however, she again shows signs of uneasiness, and although the dike seems to provide a way of escape from the troublesome intruders into her peaceful haunts, she cannot be persuaded to avail herself of it. Closer and closer the boats creep towards her, the third boat having by this time taken part in the manœuvring; but still she persists in turning her back upon the dike, the cygnets meanwhile flocking around her, much disturbed by such unwonted proceedings. Then she too decides to make a dash for liberty, and, notwithstanding that there are now only a few yards of open water between the boats, she defies the shouting and splashing swanherds, and, with her young ones close behind her, makes a frenzied rush between two of the boats and so baffles her pursuers.

Defeated in their first attempt to catch the brood, the swanherds now endeavour to drive the birds into another narrow channel on the opposite side of the Broad; but again their efforts are unsuccessful, the swans breaking away through the bordering reed beds, which are too dense to permit of the boats being forced into them. But shortly afterwards one cygnet, which has become separated from the rest, is discovered and secured in a shallow creek, and with this capture, and the birds taken in the early morning, the swanherds have to rest content for the day. For it is usually the experience at a swan-upping that when the swans are not taken at the first attempt they become for a time so shy that the occupants of a boat have great difficulty in approaching them. Towards the end of the afternoon not a single swan is to be seen on the Broad, both old and young birds having found shelter in the dense beds of reeds. But during the next day the pursuit of them is more successful, and by nightfall between thirty and forty cygnets have been transferred from the Yare and its Broads to the swan-pit.

The Norwich swan-pit, which is situated within the grounds of an ancient almshouse variously known as the Great Hospital, St. Helen's Hospital, and St. Giles' Hospital, was in existence at least as early as the year 1489, and probably had its origin in connection with one of the Norwich monastic houses. In the account rolls of the hospital there are entries dating from 1487 to 1501, from which it appears that the annual allowance to the keeper of the swans was 3s. 4d.; while during 1589-90 we find that the sum of 10s. was paid to two men for "dammyng and fyeng the cryck next to the swanyard," and 11s. to one of the men for eleven days' work "in pyling and casting the swanne pond at thospitall." In 1547 the hospital was granted by Edward VI. to the "mayor, sheriffs, citizens, and commonalty" of Norwich for use as an almshouse. Further information concerning the City's swans is found in the Court Books of the city of Norwich, some interesting notes from which have been edited by Mr. W. Rye.[1] We learn that in 1666 the "swanner" or "swanherd" was Goodman Swan, to whom there were delivered three rolls of marks "to mark the City breed." On November 6th, 1669, the swanner reported that 4 cock swans, 5 hens, 3 stags (birds in their second year), 4 blue-bills, and 10 brood swans were marked with the City mark. Within three years the number of birds had largely increased; for on July 20th, 1672, there were "in the river" and marked with the City

[1] *Notes from Court Rolls of the City of Norwich*, Edited by W. Rye, 1905.

mark, " 11 breeding swans, 23 birds, and 28 white swans." Two years later an order was made that "Mr. Sheriffs" should have three brace of swans whenever they choose to send for them; while on August 26th, 1676, the swanner was ordered "to take up four brace of cygnets of the City mark for Mr. Mayor's use." In 1680 there seems to have been some dissatisfaction at the way in which the swanner did his work; for he was instructed " to give a better account of the game of swans." The usual salary of the swanner at that time was 40s. a year, and until the passing of the Municipal Reform Act of 1835, the Corporation continued to have an official swanner—usually one of the mace-bearers—whose duty it was to mark the swans and deliver to the Master of the St. Helen's Hospital such birds as were required for fattening. Since 1835 the hospital has been under the control of the Corporation, and the management of the swan-pit has been undertaken by the Master, who employs a swanherd.

The swan-pit, which adjoins the pleasant old garden of the hospital, is a rectangular brickwork pond about 90 feet long, 30 feet wide, and 6 feet deep, the water in it being of an average depth of about 2 feet, though it varies slightly with the rise and fall of the river, with which it is connected by a sluice. Along the sides of the pond are floating wooden feeding-troughs which rise and fall with the water, and at one end is a wooden staging, by means of which the swans can enter an enclosed yard provided for them. Almost immediately after their arrival at the pond the cygnets make themselves quite at home there, and a few days after their capture the appearance of the swanherd or the governor of the hospital is a signal for every bird in the "pit" to swim towards him in anticipation of a handful of chopped grass or some other food. Grass is usually flung to them on the water, and is supplied in moderation from August to December; but the principal fattening foods are barley (of which each swan, while fattening, is said to consume a coomb) and well-soaked Indian corn. According to Stevenson, a cygnet begins to be fat in October, and keeps on improving in condition until December. In prime condition, a male cygnet then weighs about twenty-two or twenty-three pounds in the feathers, and the usual price of such a bird is two guineas. In addition to the City birds, a few cygnets belonging to private owners are sometimes sent to the swan-pit to be fattened; for these a charge of a guinea each is made. Several royal and distinguished persons have been presented with swans from the Norwich swan-pit.

For many years past it has been the custom to send out with every fattened bird the following rhyming recipe:

"To Roast a Swan.

Take three pounds of beef, beat fine in a mortar,
Put it into the Swan—that is, when you've caught her.
Some pepper, salt, mace, some nutmeg, an onion,
Will heighten the flavour in Gourmand's opinion.
Then tie it up tight with a small piece of tape,
That the gravy and other things may not escape.
A meal paste (rather stiff) should be laid on the breast,
And some 'whitey brown' paper should cover the rest.
Fifteen minutes at least ere the Swan you take down,
Pull the paste off the bird that the breast may get brown.

The Gravy.

To the gravy of beef (good and strong) I opine
You'll be right if you add half a pint of port wine:
Pour this through the Swan—yes, quite through the belly,
Then serve the whole up with some hot currant jelly.

N.B.—The Swan must *not* be skinned.

CHAPTER XVI

SOME OLD METHODS OF WILD-FOWLING

APART from the working of duck decoys and the use of stake nets on the North Norfolk coast, wild-fowling is rarely practised in East Anglia now without the aid of weapons of percussion, in the shape of swivel and shoulder guns; but years ago, when marketable wild-fowl, and especially the various species of duck, were far more plentiful than they are to-day, the professional fowlers, who must have been men well worth knowing, resorted to some curious means of wild-fowl capture, which nowadays are seldom or never heard of. Particularly was this the case in the Fen district, which, in the days before the drainage schemes were perfected, had an extraordinary abundance of resident water-birds, and in autumn and winter was visited by immense flocks of migrant fowl. Indeed, John Fuller, when writing of the Lincolnshire Fens about the middle of the seventeenth century, seems to have found it hard to credit the stories that were told concerning the skill of the local fowlers, for he quaintly says: "Lincolnshire may be termed the *Aviary* of England, for the *Wildfoule* therein; remarkable for their (1) *Plenty*; so that sometimes in the month of August, *three thousand Mallards*, with *Birds* of that *kind*, have been caught at one draught, so large and strong their *nets*; and the like must be the Reader's belief; (2) *Variety*; no man (no, not Gesner himself) being able to give them their proper names, except one had gotten Adam's *Nomen-*

clator of Creatures; (3) *Deliciousnesse*; *Wild-foule* being more *dainty* and *digestible* than *Tame* of the same kind, as spending their *grossie* humours with their activity and constant motion in flying." But in those days large tracts of the Fen country were in what Gough's Camden calls a "state of Nature," and the once famous East Fen was "a vast tract of morass, intermixed with numbers of lakes, from half a mile to two or three miles in circuit, communicating with each other by narrow reedy straits"; so there is nothing improbable in the statement as to the number of birds caught, and their abundance in the Fens. Indeed, the eccentric William Hall, who was born at Willow Booth, a small Lincolnshire Fen isle, in 1748, mentions the assertion of the old decoymen, that on a certain decoy-pond, three acres in extent, the ducks were at times present in such numbers, that "it was apparently impossible for an egg to be dropped without hitting one," while at a mile distance the tumult of their rising from the water was like the sound of distant thunder. Those were grand days for the Fen fowler, of whose origin and habits Hall gives us some idea in the curious lines he wrote, and which Mr. Southwell quotes in the *Transactions of the Norfolk and Norwich Naturalists' Society*:

> "Born in a coy, and bred in a mill,
> Taught water to grind, and Ducks for to kill;
> Seeing Coots clapper claw, lying flat on their backs,
> Standing upright to row, and crowning of jacks;
> Laying spring nets for to catch Ruff and Reeve,
> Stretched out in a boat with a shade to deceive;
> Taking Geese, Ducks, and Coots, with nets upon stakes,
> Riding in a calm day to catch moulted Drakes."

In crossing the Fen country by rail, one cannot help noticing the isolated situation of some of the farmsteads dotted here and there over the wide levels. In some cases the only road near them is the railroad, and even that is of little use to the dwellers on a farm, when their nearest station is eight or nine miles away.

From one week's end to another the farmer and his family see no human faces save those of their labouring folk; they have to send for their letters to some main-road cottage, which at times is hardly accessible, owing to the state of the rough trackway leading to it from the farm; and if they receive a daily newspaper it is thrown from a train by a travelling bookstall boy, who flings it every morning from a carriage window at a small white flag stuck up beside the line.

These few facts help to suggest the conditions under which a certain number of the Fen-folk live to-day, and by imagining that the well-drained levels around one of the isolated farmsteads are wastes of almost untraversable fen, and that the farmstead is a wild-fowler's clay-walled, sedge-roofed hut, almost as damp as though it were roofless, we may gain some idea of the conditions under which many of the Fenmen lived as recently as a century and a half ago. At that time a typical Fen wild-fowler and fisherman would have his home near one of the meres that were still undrained, and often this home, if not partaking of the nature of a lake-dwelling, would be built on soil so swampy that the walls soon "settled" into angles markedly out of the perpendicular, and often were only kept from falling by wooden props or stays. From his cottage door he would see, stretching away before him, an apparently limitless expanse of drained and undrained fen, dotted here and there with wooden windmills, low-roofed farm buildings, and crazy cottages like his own; far away, beyond a labyrinth of dikes and fen banks, a fen isle only, with a few trees and houses on it, would break the monotony of the level horizon. From the mere he would hear the seasonable wild-life voices of reed-birds or water-fowl; but often days would pass without his hearing a human voice save those of the members of his own family. In summer, however, the conditions under which he lived would not be unpleasant, for then there would be no hardships to endure; but in autumn and winter, when the chill fog came rolling up from the mere and dikes, or the icy wind swept furiously across the shelterless wilderness of water and fen, he would often be compelled to lead a far from enviable life; for hours together, while at work with his fishing and bird nets, he would be exposed to the roughest of weather. Early in life he would sow the seeds of diseases that would make a wreck of him ere he had scarcely passed middle age; for, as Dugdale says, "What expectation of health can there be to the bodies of men where there is no element of good? The air being for the most part cloudy, gross, and full of rotten harrs, the water putrid and muddy, yea, and full of loathsome vermin; the earth spongy and boggy, and the fire noisome by the stink of smoaky hassocks." The late Charles Kingsley, when he described the Fens as they were in the pre-reclamation days, pictured them as though they were the paradise of a wild-fowler's dream; but he said little about the dark side of the picture, and hardly suggested that there was one.

Yet notwithstanding its hardships, the old Fen life had a great fascination for many of those who lived it, and it was generally with indignation and always with regret that they saw first one mere and then another drained, and tract after tract of sedgy swamp converted into arable or pasture land. Writing of the old Fowl-mere, the Rev. A. C. Yorke says that when the Great Moor was enclosed and drained, the old folk looked back regretfully to the days when the waters covered the face of the moor, for then, they said, the labouring folk were better off than they are to-day. "Then everyone could keep a cow or two pastured on the common and the moor under the village herdman. Then a man out of work could always get a casual livelihood reed-cutting, or fowling, or leach-gathering, or frog-fishing. Then the labourer could put on his table ducks and geese of his own raising, as well as the wild water-fowl that homed and bred upon the Great Moor. And all affirm that to-day's advance in wages is not compensation enough for the free and common advantages of the old time, when George IV. was king."[1] The men who spoke in this way were the descendants of those "ruder sort of men," as Dugdale calls them, who in the earlier days of draining and embanking the fens put every obstacle they could think of in the way of the work of reclamation. For centuries their forefathers had by means of their fishing and fowling contrived to live an unfettered life, and to be robbed of the possibility of doing this seemed a hardship almost too great to be endured.

But to return to our mere-side fowler of a century or more ago. It is mid-October; the lush growths of the fens are withering, and boisterous winds have lately been making wild music among the reeds. For some days large and small flocks of fowl have been dropping in, among them being a considerable number of pochards, or, as the Fenman calls them, dun-birds. For these, as they are a favourite dish with the Fen-folk, the fowler has been lying in wait at nightfall, concealed in his boat among the reeds; and at daybreak, when they have been returning to the quiet spots where they rest during the day, he has been abroad and afloat again, taking toll of them as they collect together before taking wing. As a result, they have become shy and cautious, so he has decided to leave them undisturbed for a while and devote a day or two to plover-netting on one of the wash-lands bordering the river, this wash-land having been partly flooded by letting the water on to it through a sluice. He starts for the wash early in the morning, rowing thither down a dike, and carrying with him his net and some live lapwings to serve as decoy birds.

On reaching the wash-land he finds ten acres of it flooded to a depth of about eight inches, and on scanning the bordering lands, which are strewn with the stranded

[1] Rev. A. C. Yorke in *The East Anglian*, August 1903.

flotsam of a recent and more extensive flood, he soon detects some fair-sized flocks of lapwings, some golden plovers, and some wading birds feeding on the drying tracts and by the edge of the water. In the midst of the flooded portion is an artificial island made of sods of earth cut from a neighbouring dikeside: it is about twelve yards in length and two in breadth, and its surface is only a few inches above the water. To this island he wades, first with his net and its supporting poles, then with the wicker cage containing his decoy birds, and at once commences to fix the net in readiness for use. This he does by spreading it out flat on the island, where it is kept extended by poles about four feet in length, each pole having at one end a leather joint, by which it is attached to a stake driven into the ground, and by means of which it can be worked to and fro. One edge of the net—that which is fastened to the lower edge of the poles—is then pegged down to the ground near the shore of the little island, and the fowler proceeds to make fast to the other end of the poles two lengths of rope which pass through pulleys made fast to the ground, and are then connected with a long line, by means of which he can at any moment pull the net over upon such birds as come within its range. This done, he takes the decoy birds from their cage and tethers them with string to small pegs driven into the ground just beyond the range of the net. The trap is now set, and the fowler wades back to the dike bank, behind which he conceals himself, holding in his hand meanwhile the end of the line that works the net.

For a while the decoy birds, rendered inactive by their cramped confinement in the cage, remain almost motionless; but the fowler has tethered them in such a way as to afford them a certain amount of liberty, and after a time they begin to explore the muddy margin of the island, seeking the worms which have been drowned by the flood. Presently the fowler imitates a lapwing's

PLOVER-NETTING

cry, and it is repeated by one of the decoys, with the result that an answer comes from a lapwing flock feeding on the unsubmerged portion of the wash-land. Again the fowler whistles a loud *pee-a-wee*, and continues to do so at frequent intervals, until a small party of lapwings detach themselves from the distant flock, and, taking to wing, wheel erratically over the flood water. They have seen the decoy birds, and, it may be, have deduced from their presence on the island that they have discovered there some succulent food; at any rate, after wheeling and tumbling for a while above them, they dip down and alight beside them. Then the hidden Fenman, who has been watching their movements from behind the bank, cautiously raises his head above it and gets a tight grip on the net rope. He sees the strangers join the decoys on the shore of the islet, and his patience is tested by their being content to remain for some time in the company of the tethered birds and beyond the range of the net; but presently some of them move nearer to the centre of the island, and others, having helped to clear off the drowned worms and grubs, follow their example. With this movement the critical moment arrives. The fowler gives a quick steady pull at the rope, at the splash of which in the water the lapwings are alarmed, and at once rise from the ground; but before more than two or three of them are beyond the reach of the net, it comes sweeping over them and falls flat on the surface of the water, imprisoning them beneath it. Then the fowler springs to his feet, wades quickly towards the island, takes the captive birds one by one from beneath the net, and wrings their necks.

Before dusk descends upon the fens this method of plover-netting has been several times repeated, the decoy birds having meanwhile been kept active by fresh food being thrown to them after each cast of the net. And should lapwings continue to be plentiful around the wash-land, the net may be worked for several days, until, perhaps, a sharp frost drives the birds from the lowlands. Nor are lapwings the only birds taken. Golden plovers, ruffs, knots, redshanks, and dunlins also fall victim to the luring whistle of the Fenman and the innocent abetting of his decoys.

A spell of frosty weather, however, drives most of the birds from the frozen fens, and those that remain —a few duck, teal, and wigeon—can only be netted in an elaborately constructed decoy. But our friend the Fen wildfowler is too poor to possess a decoy, and now that the lapwings and most of the waders are gone, he must rely on his punt and his shoulder and swivel guns to fill his bag and provide fowl for the carrier when he crosses the fens on his weekly round. So, as long as there is open water on the mere he is afloat in his punt by moonlight and at dawn, creeping silently upon the feeding flocks. But night after night the frost grows keener, and at length, when he trudges down to the mere-side one morning about half an hour before dawn, he finds the ice so thick that he cannot get his punt afloat. The following night, and the next, the frost still "holds," and then a day dawns which finds the fowler ready with another device for getting at the fowl.

He has made a stalking sledge. In some respects this contrivance resembles the creeping-carriage by means of which some wild-fowlers approach fowl in the open, but instead of having wheels it is fitted with four marrow bones serving as runners. It consists of a long, low, raft-like framework, on which a swivel gun is mounted as in a gun-punt; at the fore end a screen of reeds is held together by pliant withies; and behind this the fowler kneels on some dry sedge litter and pushes the sledge along on the ice by means of two iron-pointed sticks.

Day is just breaking when he slides his sledge on to a frozen inlet of the mere, and begins to work his way cautiously along the edge of a reed bed extending some distance from the shore. His progress is slow and silent, for he is careful to keep on smooth ice, and avoid dry and broken reed stalks which might crackle beneath the runners of the sledge, nor does he make a sound when he touches the ice with his pointed sticks. At the extremity of the reed shoal he pauses, and scans the frozen surface of the wide lagoon. Eastward there is a brightening streak of pallid light along the horizon, against which the distant reed tops and a canvas-sailed windmill are gradually revealing clean-cut outlines; westward, where an undrained jungle of fen sedge represents a former extension of the mere, the shadow of night still lurks among the thickets of sweet gale and the frost-whitened blades of sedge. In the dawnlight the ice in the creeks is like dark glass through which the rotting water-weeds are seen; but away from the shore, where wind-rippled water has frozen around islets of reeds and rush, the ice has a white coating of rime. Hardly a breath of wind is now stirring—not enough to make the ice-crystals tinkle among the sedge—nor for a while does a sound break the silence of the mere; but before a rosy flush has spread along the pallid streak of dawnlight, an immense flock of starlings rises from the sedge fen, and the air is filled with the tumult of their wing-beats as with that of a wind-gust beating on a wood. But the flock, after sweeping upward and around as though it were caught in a great wind eddy, soon vanishes in the direction of the far-distant ploughed lands, and then there is silence again until some bearded titmice awake and make fairy music in a rimy tangle of reeds near the fowler's sledge.

For half an hour or more the Fenman crouches in his sledge, breathing now and again on his fingers, which are growing numb with cold; but after the starlings have vanished and the titmice have taken flight to a neighbouring creekside, the only birds he sees are three or four hooded crows which fly heavily over the mere. So presently he gets to work again with his pointed sticks, and slowly propels the sledge towards the nearest of the reed islets, round the edge of which he creeps until he gets a clear view of other islets lying beyond it. These he scans with the trained eye of an experienced fowler, and apparently is satisfied with what he sees, for he continues his slow progress over the ice until he reaches a clump of rushes, keeping his eyes meanwhile on an islet from which is heard at length the long-drawn quacking of mallard. Even now, however, he is not within range of the fowl, and to get nearer to them he has to venture out on to an open expanse of ice, and rely on his screen of reeds to cover his approach. So he resumes his stealthy stalk until he is within seventy yards of the duck, which he can now see resting quietly on the shore of the islet; then he stops the sledge, lays down his sticks, and takes careful aim at the unsuspecting birds through an opening in his screen of reeds. The great swivel gun flashes and booms, the sledge is jerked backwards by the recoil, and the wild-fowler, shoulder gun in hand, hastens over the ice towards his victims.

To take leave of the Fens and turn to the Essex marshes, we learn from Daniell's *Rural Sports* that years ago, when enormous numbers of pochards visited these marshes, they were taken by wild-fowlers with the aid of a decoy called a flight-pond and some curiously worked nets. These nets, which were fastened to poles from 28 to 30 feet long, were spread flat on the reeds beside the pond; but the bottom of each pole was weighted with a box full of stones in such a way that directly an iron pin was withdrawn, poles and nets rose upright in the air. Nets of this kind entirely surrounded the pond, and immediately within each was either a trench dug in the ground or a pen made of reeds about three feet high. The fowler's method of working these nets was to conceal himself near them at the time when the pochards generally visited the pond, and wait until a good number of them were disporting themselves on the water. He would then, by a sudden noise, cause them to take to flight, and as they, like other wild-fowl, flew against the wind, he would immediately unpin the poles of the net over which they were passing. The net at once rose up and swept the birds into the pen or trench beneath it, from which they were unable to rise owing to their numbers and the shape and shortness of their wings. No mention is made of the use of decoy birds in connection with this method of wild-fowl capture; but at the present time, when a similar method is resorted to in the taking of lapwing, both stuffed and live birds are used as decoys. As in the old days, the favourite spot for plover-netting is a small island in the midst of a flooded marsh, and, according to Mr. Nicholas Everitt,[1] "the meshes of the nets are coloured the same as their probable surroundings, and the pattern used is the ordinary clap-net—known to all bird-catchers—with the exception that one net only is used instead of two. Round the edge of the net stuffed peewits are set, and near the end nearest the fowler one or more live peewits are anchored down upon a small board, which, working on a pivot sunk into the ground, can be raised at the will of the string-puller some little height into the air. The decoy-birds are all placed head to wind, and the net is pegged down accordingly, so that when it is pulled over it will catch the birds as they are settling among the decoys. The poles of the net are about ten feet long, and the art of making a big haul is to allow the straggling part of the flock to pass and not to pull the net over until the thickest part of the flock can be reached."

This method of plover-netting is practically the same as that practised by the old-time Fenmen, and here it may be mentioned that plovers are netted in the Fens to-day in much the same fashion as a hundred years

[1] *Broadland Sport*, p. 223.

ago. The wild-fowler still constructs a long narrow island in the midst of a wash or a flooded marsh, but his decoy birds are usually tethered on separate islets about the size of mole-hills. On the main island there is seldom a live decoy, but here are strewn a number of worms, which keep the first-alighting plovers occupied until enough birds have settled beside them to make it worth the fowler's while to pull over the net. For his own accomodation he generally erects a small turf hut, around which a trench is dug to carry off the water in times of heavy rain. Outside this trench the excavated earth is heaped up in a kind of circular rampart, and the whole shelter somewhat resembles a model in miniature of a prehistoric camp. At the present time plover-netting in the Fens is usually carried on near a windmill pump, by means of which the decoy marsh can always be kept flooded.

In the days when several of the Fenland meres were still undrained, large numbers of fowl were taken in nets known as tunnels, the particular method of taking them being known as duck-driving. These tunnels were decoy-like nets spread in a horseshoe form over creeks or dikes adjoining a mere, and they were generally used at the time when the ducks were moulting and before the young birds or "flappers" were able to fly. It was by this method that, as Fuller relates, "three thousand mallards, with birds of that kind," were taken at one draught in Lincolnshire; and it is also on record that in Deeping Fen 4000 ducks were so captured in one day, 13,000 in three days, and, near Spalding, 2646 in two days. For duck-driving a day would be chosen when a considerable number of Fenmen could assemble and put out on to the mere in boats. They would then drive the fowl from the reeds and creeks on to the open water, where they would keep them together by splashing in the water with long sticks, and gradually get them to swim into the particular creek or dike which was arched over by the tunnel net. Once in the net, the birds were driven to the closed end of it, which was fashioned like the end of a decoy pipe; and there they would be taken out and killed. This reprehensible method of wild-fowl capture naturally resulted in a marked reduction of the numbers of ducks breeding on certain of the meres, and it is not surprising that in the reign of Queen Anne an Act was passed making it illegal to resort to this " pernicious practice," which was causing " great damage and decay of the breed of wild-fowl." By this Act duck-driving was prohibited between the 1st of July and the 1st of September, the penalty for breaking the law being a fine of five shillings for each fowl taken, and the destruction of the nets.

Another and simpler method of duck-killing, which was probably carried on at the same time that the tunnel nets were being used, is described by Mr. Christopher Merrett in a communication made to the Royal Society towards the end of the seventeenth century. He writes: " About Midsummer (when moultering time is) several Persons, some from Pleasure, others for Profit, go in small Boats among the Reeds, and with long Poles knock them (the ducks) down, they not being able to Swim or Fly from them."

CHAPTER XVII

SOME HEATHS AND COMMON-LANDS

OF all roads pleasant to travel, there is none, to my mind, to compare with the heath road. Let it be rough or smooth—a white highway over the chalk ridge or a winding trackway amid the ling and fern—there is always the wide wild about you and the wide sky above you; while the wind, no matter whence it blows, comes to you as fresh as a sea wind and fragrant with the scent of gorse and thyme. For the heath road is usually a hedgeless road, and while you are on it you have such a sense of freedom from all restraint as cannot be felt while you are between high banks or hedgerows; even where the gorse grows dense and high you can always see the blue sky or the clouds racing before the wind. While travelling the heath road, it is your own fault if you become footsore or weary of the way. Beside the true heath road there is always a footpath trodden on the yielding turf and a heathery knoll on which to rest. And if you choose, you can generally find good excuse for trespassing a little way to the right or left of the road. The heaths of East Anglia are not all common-lands, as they once were; but few of them are enclosed. The rambler does well to think before entering a forbidden game covert or crossing a pathless field; but he is a poor-spirited "child of the open air" who allows a threatening notice-board or the risk of an unpleasant encounter with a gamekeeper to prevent his enjoying the harmless pleasure of straying from the road on to the wild heathland. At one time and another I have wandered over most of the heaths and common-lands of East Anglia, and I reckon the days I have spent on them among the best-spent days of my life; I do not regret even the idlest of them. For even in one's idlest mood one can hardly help being the better for breathing the heathland air, listening to the singing and calling of the heathland birds, and hearing the storm-song of the wind among the firs on a heathland ridge. Our heaths, save in the north and east, are of no great area, but most of them are large enough to convey a sense of space and solitude; while our common-lands, around which there are often thatch-roofed cottages half hidden by their high garden-fences of hawthorn and wild plum, help to preserve to us something of the aspect the country wore in the coaching days. There you may still see the furze-cutter and the peat-cutter getting fuel for his cottage hearth; there the children still play the merry old games in which the "odd man" is "counted out" by curious old puzzling rhymes; and there at night the roving Romanies still gather around their flickering camp-fire.

Westleton Walks, a tract of about two thousand acres of sandy heathland, adjoining the ancient and sea-wasted village of Dunwich, presents in early autumn a glorious expanse of purple heath and ling; but it is seen at its best, perhaps, on an early May day, when a strong south-easterly wind is blowing, and the face of the heathland is checkered by sunlight and shadow; for a south-easterly wind on Westleton Walks is a sea wind, and its fresh-ness, when one faces it from the top of a heathery knoll or thorn-crowned ridge, is medicine for mind and body. There is one knoll there,—round as a barrow and brown in May as though spring had never a blossom to spare for it,—where there is a couch of moss and heather as soft as it is good for man to lie upon, and there one can lie in the sunshine, or the shade of a solitary thorn, and see, where the sandy cliffs dip low, the silken shimmer and wind-whipped shoal water of the sea. All around is the undulating heath, more varied in its colouring on a spring day than when the heather is in bloom, and as untamed in its aspect as it was in the Stone Age. Over hundreds of acres the gorse is ablaze with golden bloom; elsewhere are the browns of bloomless heather and withered bracken; and in the hollows where the new grass is slow in springing, the waving bents are as yellow in the sunlight as an autumn corn-field. At times some of the distant slopes are veiled by a quivering haze; but when the sun-gleams follow the cloud-shadows, glorious harmonies of colour reveal themselves like new creations, and while the distant slopes stand out clear the nearer ones grow dun.

While you lie here, sharing your couch with a pretty little lizard, which retreats into its sheltered underworld of heather whenever the sun lingers behind a cloud, you can watch the progress of the wind-gusts coming towards you from the sea. They give you fair warning of their coming. First you see a shuddering of the hawthorns on a ridge some hundreds of yards away, while the thorn above you is silent and unstirred. Then, the topmost sprays of a clump of flowering furze are set swaying as though they were being waved from beneath, and the whinchats, which a moment before were plainly visible against the sky, vanish into a thorny covert. By this time there is a sighing in the air which can be distinguished from the sound of the waves breaking on the beach—the sighing of the wind among the millions of wiry ling stalks and withered grass stems between the knoll and the cliff-brow. These, too, are seen to move, the ling stalks quivering and the grass stems bowing, as the wind-gust travels towards you. Then a bush, as tangled with woodbine stems as the gorse is at times with dodder, receives a buffet that sets every twig shaking, and a moment later the wind comes rushing up the side of the knoll, bringing with it the salt savour of the sea.

The gnarled and sturdy thorn above you has received such training from the sea winds, that it scarcely stirs when the gust flings itself upon it; for years it has, as it were, turned its back upon the sea and spread all its branches towards the west; now the wind can do nothing with it, save sing a storm-song among its stubborn branches and rustle the dry rags of lichen which cling to its boughs like grey seaweed to a rock. Hazlitt has said that to Wordsworth "an old withered thorn" was "weighed down with a heap of recollections;" this old thorn, so fixed in its growth to westward as to suggest a ragged and frozen pennant, tells the tale of many a battle with the storm. Sometimes it tells it in a low whisper, like that of a summer breeze among the heathland bents; but now, in the teeth of the sudden storm-wind, it shouts it like a proud warrior vaunting his victories; and because it is old its voice is sometimes shrill, even rising to a shriek as of an ancient crone who would play the witch upon some superstitious confidant. In East Anglia whitethorn and witches have a certain relationship, and the Norfolk folk call their most famous thorn the "Witch of Hethel."

Westleton Walks, with some adjoining tracts of sea-bordering heathland, was formerly a breeding-place of the wild-crying stone curlew, a bird now confined, as a Suffolk breeding species, to the wide barrens of Breckland. Even now you may occasionally hear its harsh whistle, or see one or two birds flying low over the heather before you when you have disturbed them in their daytime haunts; but this is generally in the spring or autumn, when the stone curlews are migrants resting here on their way to or from their summer quarters. Bustards, too, have been met with here; but they, of late, have been accidental visitors; for the great bustard, if it ever bred here, ceased to do so long before it became extinct on the western warrens. In 1863, and again in 1888, Westleton Walks had its share of the flocks of Pallas's sand-grouse which then distributed themselves over East Anglia. These beautiful birds, whose irregular irruptions into Western Europe have always excited interest in ornithological circles, used to frequent the sandy parts of the Westleton heathlands, where, according to one or two old men who can remember their visits, they would bask in the sun for hours together; but they went to feed in the neighbouring fields, which are also sandy—so much so, indeed, that on dry windy days the sand is blown about in clouds, and sand-drifts are heaped up along the stunted hedgerows. At that time the Act of Parliament making it a penal offence to destroy sand-grouse had not been passed, and as the birds were so tame that boys could often approach near enough to them to stone them, some of the local gunners had little difficulty in securing specimens, for which a good price was offered by the taxidermists. Both in 1863 and 1888, however, some of the early-arriving sand-grouse escaped through being mistaken for golden plover, notwithstanding that flocks of golden plover are seldom observed along the east coast during the spring migration, and are hardly ever seen in May, during which month the sand-grouse appeared. Strangely enough, too, one of these birds was mistaken by an old gunner on the Minsmere Level for a "kind of foreign pigeon," and as such he sold it to a more knowing person for two shillings.

To-day the wild-life voices of Westleton are familiar ones—the wailing of the lapwing, the unvarying song of the yellow bunting, the carol of the lark, the cheeping of the meadow pipit, and the *u-tack, u-tack* of the furze-haunting whinchat. Sea-gulls scatter themselves over the heath-bordering fields when the land is being turned by the plough, and on stormy days the greater black-backed gulls will ride for hours on motionless wings high up above the cliff-brow, waiting for calmer weather ere they return to the sea. On dark autumn nights the piping of migrant waders may often be heard here as they cross the heath on their southward journey; here, too, during the spring and autumn migrations, some of them come to grief through dashing against the telegraph wire which follows the course of a rough trackway not far from the edge of the cliffs. Beneath this wire I picked up a decapitated dunlin, which was lying on a ling tuft, its severed head not two feet away from it.

The rich colouring of such sea-bordering tracts of heathland as those around Westleton and Dunwich is so lavishly spread, that one may easily miss the loveliness of detail which only close observation reveals. On a spring day some of the low gravelly banks and hillocks are bright with the metallic glitter of thousands of minute sky-blue flowers of the early myosote, while on the same banks and hillocks there may be quite a frosty gleam from the massed florets of the vernal whitlow grass. There, too, the slender stems of the teesdalia bear perfectly arranged pagoda-shaped clusters of seed-pods, and closer to the short turf nestle the dainty blossoms of the spring vetch. A little later the blue blossoms of the milkwort and the golden Maltese crosses of the tormentil are scattered everywhere among the slender bents and silvery hair grasses, while the ruddy rosettes of two species of sundew appear on the bog-moss of some of the damp hollows. June sees the blooming of the daintiest of our wild roses, the pure white burnet rose, which I fancy must be the flower referred to as

> "The Dunwich rose, with snow-white blossom,
> Soft, pure, and white, as is the cygnet's bosom;
> This decks the stern and sterile cliff: and throws
> O'er its rough brow new beauty where it grows;"

though tradition says that the Dunwich rose, which gave its name to a once popular air called "Dunwich

Roses," was first planted here and cultivated by the monks of the sea-wasted town. A locally distributed plant occurring on these heaths is the mossy tillæa; and the botanist may even be fortunate enough to secure a treasure in the form of a green man orchis, of which Westleton is one of the few recorded East Suffolk localities.

Near the borders of one or two tracts of heathland in Norfolk, men still carry on the ancient industry of broom-tying; but they are few in number, and the day cannot be far off when they will find their occupation gone; for the demand for heather brooms is very small now compared with what it used to be. Thirty years ago there were as many as twenty broom-tiers in one Norfolk village, while in an adjoining village there were nearly thirty. At that time heather brooms were made by the thousand, and found a ready sale; while a good birch broom, such as may now be bought for twopence, cost from two shillings to three-and-sixpence. The broom-tiers of that day were a rustic folk quite distinct from the farm-labourers; for most of them had been village weavers, who, when there was no more work for their hand-looms, turned their hands to the making of heather brooms rather than the tilling of the ground. In their thatched-roofed cottages beside the heath roads you might still see their old looms, dusty and dilapidated, unless some of the women used them for weaving horsehair.

One old broom-tier I can well remember. I met him one day while he was ling-pulling on Marsham Heath, near Aylsham, and a figure more in harmony with the pristine aspect of the scene it would have been hard to find. His clothes were of a hue blending so well with that of the russet heathland that to all appearance they might have been woven of the fibres of its tawny growths; his cap was a home-made one of moleskins; and the crome-stick on which was slung a "frail"

SOME HEATHS AND COMMON-LANDS

or basket of plaited rushes, was fashioned from the stem of a heathland thorn. At first I thought he was cutting furze to burn on his cottage hearth; but on drawing near him I found that he was pulling up ling by the roots, and selecting only the longest of the wiry stems. Then I guessed he was a broom-tier, and it proved that he was one of the few men in the neighbourhood who did little else besides broom-tying for a livelihood.

Later in the day I saw him at work in a wooden lean-to shed against the end of his cottage. The corners of the shed were heaped with dry ling, and outside there was a small stack of heather, to which he had added the bundle he had pulled during the day. While working he sat astride of a low wooden bench, into the end of which an iron hook was driven. Taking up a handful of heather, he straightened the stems across his knees, laying each with its flowering end towards his left hand, and adding to them until he held enough to make a broom. Over one shoulder and under the other arm he then adjusted the loop of a short stout rope, with the loose end of which he made a single turn around the ling stalks, afterwards securing the end to the iron hook in the bench. Then by drawing his body backward he tightened the rope about the ling and worked the latter backward and forward until he had compressed the stalks into a close, round, faggot-like bunch. Next, into the root end of the bunch, which was naturally smaller than the flowering end, he pushed a twisted handful of waste ling to give it bulk, and the broom was then ready for tying. This was done with long pliant bonds of split bramble, which were wound tightly around the middle and root end of the broom, the ends of the bonds being secured by pressing them into the midst of the ling stalks, which were temporarily forced aside by a heavy, foot-long iron "needle." All that remained to be done was to trim the sweeping end with a sharp "hook" or chopper, and the broom was then ready for sale to the first person who offered twopence for it, while even a penny would not have been refused. Besides the bench hook, rope, needle, and chopper, the only tool used by a broom-tier is a comblike implement for "pithing" the brambles.

When one considered how small the demand for heather brooms must be, one could not help wondering how the old man contrived to live on the scanty proceeds of his industry, and not only maintain himself, his wife, and his youngest child, but also keep a donkey and cart. He himself could scarcely explain how he did it; but his garden helped him, as did his pigs and fowls; while the donkey had free grazing, I believe, on the heath. Not infrequently a week would pass without his selling a single broom; but this would be made up to him during the next week, perhaps, by the sale of a cart-load of brooms to some country shop-keeper or a travelling hawker, and occasionally he would receive an order for a dozen birch brooms for lawn-sweeping. These brooms, he explained, were made of twigs cut from the birches about Michaelmas, and they differed from the heather brooms only in material and being untrimmed at the sweeping end. There is an old country saying that "there is a trick in all trades except the broom-tiers', and they *always* put the small stuff in the middle." Considering that it takes half an hour to make a penny broom, it would hardly be surprising if there were many tricks in the broom-tiers' trade.

One tract of Suffolk common-land is associated with my earliest memories. I can remember it as it was at a time when its four hundred acres seemed to me a wild wilderness, not to be lingered on after dusk had fallen for fear of uncanny sights and sounds; but that was in the days when I was just tall enough to peep into the nests of linnets among the furze, and when I looked for a wren's nest I peered up into the hedge for it instead of down. Now I cannot help recognising

SOME HEATHS AND COMMON-LANDS

how inconsiderable is its area even when compared with some of our smaller heaths and commons; but even now it seems to me to possess certain attractive features not to be found in intimate association elsewhere. For Bungay Common—or Outney Common, as it is sometimes more correctly called—chiefly consists of a low promontory of alluvial gravel projecting into the midst of the picturesque valley of the Waveney, and around it the river, bordered by peaceful water-meadows and a steep wooded bank, has, in a horseshoe bend, one of the prettiest of its upper reaches. The river itself seems to love this quiet common; for not only does it engirdle it with peaceful waters, but divides itself for a while into two streams, as though to make the most of the flower-decked water-meadows. Quaint old wooden footbridges span the shallower stream, which is hardly anywhere so deep that the cattle cannot wade through it; and from May to October, when the cattle are turned on to the lush-grassed lowlands, you can never ramble along the riverside without coming upon pastoral scenes of tranquil charm and refreshing restfulness.

Years ago there was a water-mill on the river here, and at the foot of the steep wooded bank—which is known as the Bath Hills—there was a famous bath-house in connection with a spring that still trickles unseen through a tangle of underwood; but now the river flows unchecked by dam, and the site of the eighteenth-century baths is a marish spot where the water-vole creeps silently amid the sedge, and the grass snake glides among the purple orchids and the rough-leaved comfrey. The river here is narrow, and only navigable to rowing boats; but the reach between the old mill-house and the site of the vanished bath-house is without its equal along the course of the Waveney. On one side it is bordered by the common lowlands, amid the breezy levels of which are gravelly knolls whitened in spring by masses of saxifrage; on the other, the black poplars let ruddy catkins fall into the stream, and horse-chestnuts spread rugged boughs low over the water. Farther back, but close enough to convey an impression that they overhang the river, are the chestnuts, firs, and beeches of the hanger, some of them finding root-hold even where the bank is so steep as to be almost unclimbable. Seen from the common, the sweeping curve of this hanging woodland is like that of a vast sylvan amphitheatre; trees rise above trees in tier above tier, as though the curving hanger were an orchestra for the performance of the symphonies of the storms. But under this sheltering bank one usually hears the wind as a sibilant whisper only; here the sons of Astræus tread lightly, and "their soft steps deepen slumber."

On the common-land by the river one has the companionship of birds of the woodland, heath, and waterside, and often their songs are pleasantly mingled in a general chorus. From May to October scores of brown bank martins, which have their colonies in some neighbouring sand and gravel pits, are constantly skimming the surface of the water, chattering as they fly. Among the sallows is another chatterer, the sedge warbler, often accompanied, where the woodland thickets grow close to the water, by that sweeter singer the willow-wren. Quite as frequently one may hear the brief song and yellow-hammer-like twittering of the reed bunting, though the reeds bordering this narrow reach are few and far between. On the gravelly, gorse-grown knolls amid the water-meadows, whinchats continually repeat their familiar call-note, and linnets chuckle throughout the sunny hours. To mention all the birds to be met with along the borders of this river reach, barely half a mile in length, would be a lengthy task, and I will not attempt it; but to help to convey some idea of the interest it must have for every bird-lover, I will set down the names of the birds I saw or heard there in less than three hours of one

12th of May. On the common-lands: the whinchat, linnet, skylark, meadow pipit, yellow-hammer, rook, wood pigeon, and swallow; by the river: sedge warbler, willow-wren, reed bunting, yellow wagtail, moor-hen, swift, and bank martin; among the riverside trees and bushes: blue, cole, marsh, and long-tailed tits, blackbird, missel thrush, chaffinch, cuckoo, nightingale, and whitethroat; and in the hanger, besides several of the birds already mentioned, the gold-crest, tree creeper, green woodpecker, starling, robin, wren, hedge-sparrow, woodwren, and wryneck. Later in the day I saw a kestrel hovering over the water-meadows, and in the evening a landrail was *crekking* in the long grass near the river, a nightjar was moth-catching at the foot of the hanger, and a barn owl, which probably had its home in the hanger, emerged from its daytime retreat and was seen flying low over the common.

A remarkable thing about Outney Common is that the end of the promontory on which it is situated seems to have been cut off from the mainland by a fairly wide and deep ditch. Formerly this ditch was traceable right across the promontory; and I can remember the time when it was a favourite pastime of schoolboys to roll down its sloping sides; but part of the ditch was destroyed when the Waveney Valley railway was made, and of late years nearly the whole of the remaining portion has been filled up in order to level the ground. To what period this ditch should be assigned is doubtful; but I am inclined to think it was a prehistoric earthwork, and that, like some other similar ditches without a rampart, it may, as has been suggested by Messrs. A. J. and G. H. Hubbard in their *Neolithic Dew-Ponds and Cattle-Ways,* have served to protect a prehistoric settlement from being attacked by the packs of wolves which roved the country in Neolithic times. That the common is the site of a prehistoric settlement I have evidence by me as I write, in the form of a perfect polished flint axe, a beautifully chipped triangular flint knife, and a number of skilfully detached flint flakes, all of which I found on a sandy knoll on the common. With them were some human bones, which may also be prehistoric, though all traces of any barrow which may have existed on the spot have been obliterated by digging for sand. On Broome Heath, however, about a mile away on the Norfolk side of the Waveney, there are still the remains of two large barrows; but the rabbits have so honeycombed them with burrows that they are now almost shapeless, and unless steps are taken to preserve them they will soon be totally destroyed.

In North-West Norfolk there are several extensive tracts of heathland, especially in that delightful district where the King has his Norfolk home. Between Sandringham and Houghton, that ancient road, the Peddars' Way, skirts the large and undulating Harpley Common; also Anmer Mink, a stretch of wild gorseland. On both of these commons, which form part of a chalk ridge crossing the county from the neighbourhood of Hunstanton to that of Thetford, there are several round barrows, one of which, situated close beside the ancient Way on the verge of Harpley Common, is the finest and best preserved in North-West Norfolk. South of Houghton, on Massingham Heath, further traces of prehistoric man exist in a group of hut-circles, near which there appear to have been some Neolithic flint pits or quarries. On this heath, which has some high ground and fairly steep slopes, producing several interesting species of chalk soil flora, dainty purple milk vetch grows, a somewhat rare wild flower in East Anglia. Some wide views of the surrounding country can be enjoyed from the breezy heights of this heath; but they are scarcely so fine, perhaps, as that which can be had from the high ground of Dersingham Heath, which slopes down to the lowlands bordering the Wash, and is skirted by the main road from Hunstanton to Lynn. From the higher parts of this heath one has a view seaward of the wide waters of the Wash, between which and the foot of the slopes there are bright green levels of marshland, and, beyond them, miles of shimmering salt marsh.

It is due to the nearness of the flats and salt creeks that Dersingham Heath is a favourite resort of the sheld-duck during the breeding season. This handsome bird, which Sir Thomas Browne describes as "a noble coloured fowl," which bred about Northwold, seems to have formerly been fairly common in Norfolk, where it goes by the name of "burrow duck," owing to its habit of nesting in the rabbit-burrows; but it was long ago driven from most of its breeding grounds on account of the disturbing effect its presence is said to have had upon the rabbits. At Dersingham, thanks to the King having given orders for its protection there and elsewhere on his shooting, it has increased its numbers, so that at the present time it has, on this part of the coast, some fairly numerous colonies. On the seaward side of Dersingham Heath there are several small but steep clefts in the edge of the high ground, sloping down to the swampy level of Dersingham Fen; and it is in the rabbit-burrows in the sides and near the top of these clefts that most of the sheld-ducks lay their eggs. Around these burrows the ducks are conspicuous during the breeding season, the white of their plumage, in striking contrast to the dark patches of bloomless heather, making them visible a long way off. Every morning and evening numbers of them go down to the Wash, where even at midday Mr. J. H. Gurney counted as many as sixty swimming about at the mouth of one large creek. If such flocks are disturbed during the breeding season, they break up, Mr. Gurney says, into pairs, and in flying off the female as often takes the lead as the male. To get at a nest is no easy matter; for the eggs are often laid ten or twelve feet from the entrance to the burrow. Indeed, it is not easy, without watching the birds, to tell which of the burrows are occupied by them; for instinct, we are told, has taught the old duck that footprints on the sand at the mouth of a burrow may betray her, and consequently she flies straight into the hole without alighting. When the young are hatched, the old duck leads them down to the border of the Wash, a distance of over a mile. Sometimes this journey is interrupted by the little party meeting with an obstacle in the shape of wire-netting; and Mr. Gurney records in the *Zoologist* an instance of a sheld-duck having been seen to lead her brood down the village street at Dersingham in order to avoid the wire.

Records exist of the occurrence of the great bustard at Dersingham in the days when the native race of these grand birds was still with us; but in the latter years of their precarious existence in East Anglia the examples which visited this neighbourhood were probably stragglers from the drove which had its headquarters on the heathlands around Swaffham. Curiously enough, the tract of fen below Dersingham Heath is the only place in Norfolk where the curlew has been known to breed. Nests were found here in 1889 and 1890 by one of the King's keepers; but since 1890 no other has been met with.

Besides including a considerable portion of Breckland, Suffolk embraces, in its south-eastern corner, between the rivers Alde and Deben, some fairly extensive tracts of heathland in Sutton Walks and Sutton Common, while northward and southward of the two rivers several delightful tracts of heather and bracken remain to remind us of what a large part of the county was like in the days when it was said that, generally speaking, the land lying eastward of the London and Yarmouth coach road was sandy heathland, while that lying to the west of the road was clay-land. Along the coast especially we find, as at Westleton, such breezy open spaces, though almost everywhere they are being bit by bit enclosed or planted with quick-growing trees. Even as recently as a century ago the Suffolk "sand-lands," as they were called, were of considerable extent, and the heathy portions were largely utilised as sheep-walks; but the discovery of the valuable fertilising qualities of the coprolites found at the base of the Suffolk Red Crag—a discovery for which the county is indebted to the late Professor Henslow—resulted in vast quantities of this phosphatic deposit being used to improve these lands, large tracts of which have thus been converted into productive arable ground. But long before this the Suffolk Crag had been used for improving the soil, for in Kirby's *Suffolk Traveller* we read that "in a Farmer's Yard in Levington, close on the Left as you enter from Levington into the said Chapel-Field of Stratton Hall, was dug the first Crag or Shell, that has been found so useful for improving of Land in this and other Hundreds in the Neighbourhood. For though it appears from Books of Agriculture that the like Manure has been long since used in the West of England, it was not used here till this Discovery was casually made by one Edmund Edwards, about the Year 1718. This Man being covering a Field with Muck out of his Yard, and wanting a Load or two to finish it, carried some of the Soil that laid near his Muck, tho' it look'd to him to be no better than Sand; but observing the Crop to be best where he laid that, he was from thence encouraged to carry more of it next Year; and the Success he had, encouraged others to do the like." And Kirby then goes on to make the following interesting contribution to eighteenth-century geology:

"This useful Soil has been found in great Plenty upon the Sides of such Vales as may reasonably be supposed to have been washed by the Sea; towards which such light Shells might be naturally carried, either at Noah's Flood, or by the Force of the Tides to some Places since forsaken by the Sea. Whoever looks into any of these Cragg-Pits cannot but observe how they lie Layer upon Layer in a greater or less Angle, according to the Variation of the Tides. But when one considers that the Wells in Trimly Street, about a Quarter of a Mile distant from the Mill, are about 25 Feet deep, and that the Springs all rise in the Cragg, we can in no way account for this Cragg so many Feet under Ground, but from the universal Deluge."

Closely adjoining Norwich and Ipswich, the chief towns of Norfolk, and Suffolk, there are heaths which have been battlefields. It was on Mousehold Heath, near Norwich, that the great rising of the Norfolk peasantry under Kett, the Wymondham tanner, was crushed by the Earl of Warwick's troops—a rising largely due to the indignation of the peasants at seeing the common-lands one by one enclosed against them by the lords of the manors. For many years after this battle—the bloodiest, perhaps, that Norfolk has ever known—the character of the peasants' leader was persistently blackened by the historians; but justice is now done to his memory, and it seems only fitting that the famous heath which was the scene of his defeat should be preserved as an open pleasure resort for the Norwich citizens. For many years Moushold Heath was one of the chief East Anglian camping-grounds of the gipsies, and to-day it is not only noteworthy as being the scene of the sixteenth-century battle, but as the place where the hero of *Lavengro* and the gipsy Jasper Petulengro had that oft-quoted dialogue on life, death, and "the wind on the heath." The Suffolk battle-ground referred to is Rushmere Heath, which is crossed by the London Road just before it enters Ipswich from the north. There, so long ago as the early years of the eleventh century, Jarl Thorkill the Dane with his force of Viking raiders, fought Ulfketyl and his Saxon army at a spot afterwards known as "Wolfkettle," and some barrows are said to mark the scene to this day, though a like tradition attaches to some barrows at Snarehill in Breckland, where there were also conflicts between the Saxons and the Danes.

In Breckland, as stated in an earlier chapter, the area of heathland is probably greater now than it was a century ago; but almost everywhere else in Norfolk and Suffolk we are witnessing the gradual disappearance of heaths and commons. Some are being cultivated by the improved methods now in vogue; others have been, and are being planted with the various species of conifer which flourish so well in the dry sandy soil; while here and there, as on the heathery hills around Cromer, huge hotels and private houses have been built, and bricks and mortar have supplanted bracken and ling. Some of the heaths still appearing on the maps are heaths only in name, just as some of the commons are common-lands only in name, and almost every year sees changes that are not for the better, from the point of view of the lover of the heath road, the whin-birds, and the heather. To the town-dweller it may seem absurd that country-folk should be concerned about the preservation of open spaces; yet I think it will be admitted that there are counties which can no more afford to lose their remaining heathlands than London can afford to be robbed of its parks. And among these counties I am disposed to include Norfolk and Suffolk, two counties which may be said to have formerly consisted chiefly of wild heath and wild fen, but where we now see these conditions, so favourable to a varied and abundant wild life, surviving for the most part only in certain restricted areas.

CHAPTER XVIII

SOME OLD ACTS, RIGHTS, AND CUSTOMS

ALTHOUGH Acts of Parliament for the protection of such birds as were used in falconry were passed in the reigns of Edward I. and Edward III., no steps to make poaching illegal appear to have been taken until 1496, when an Act was passed "agaynst taking of Feasauntes and Partriches." In the preamble of this Act it was set forth that forasmuch as divers persons, having little substance to live upon, were in the habit of taking and destroying "feasauntes and partriches" by means of nets, snares, and other engines upon the lordships, manors, lands, and tenements without the consent of the owners, it was ordained that it should not be lawful for any person to do this upon the freehold of any other person, without the consent and special licence of the owner, upon pain of forfeiture of £10. Eight years later, herons were protected by an Act which provided that no one should take, outside his own ground, any heron by means of craft or engine unless it was by hawking or with a long-bow.

We find bird-netting mentioned again in an Act drawn up in 1533, with the view of bringing about a decrease in the numbers of "rooks, crowes, and choughs" which did daily (!) breed and increase throughout this realm, and devour wonderful and marvellous great quantity of corn and grain of all kinds in the sowing, as also at the "ripynge and kernelynge" of the same. These same rooks, crows, and choughs were also charged with "the marvellous destruction and decay of the covertures of thatched houses, barns, ricks, stacks, and such like." It was therefore enacted that all persons in possession of lands should do their best to destroy these birds, under penalty of "amerciaments" in Court Leets, Lawdayes, Rapes, or Courts; and that for ten years every parish should keep crow-nets in repair under survey of the Courts Leet.

In the eighth year of Elizabeth another Act for the protection of grain was passed, to revive that made in 1533. By this new Act it was ordered that in every parish the churchwardens, with other parishioners, to the number of six persons, should tax every owner of land or tithes, and the money so raised should be placed in the hands of "two honest & substantyall persons" in each parish, who should be named the "dystributors of the provision for the dystructyon of noyful fowells & vermyn." These distributors were authorised to pay a penny to every person who brought to them three crows', choughs', pies', or rooks' heads, and a penny for every six eggs or young birds. The same sum was to be paid for every twelve starlings' heads. "And for the heads of other ravenous byrds & vermyn as ar hereafter in this acte mentyoned, that is to say: for everye head of martyn, hawke, furskett, moldkytte, busard, schagge, cormorant, ryngtayle, ijd., & for everye two eggs of them, one penye; for everye jron or osprey's head, iiijd.; for the head of everye woodwall, pye, jay, raven, or kytte, one penye; for the head of everye byrd which is called the kyngfisher, one penye; for the head of everye bulfynche or other byrd that devourythe the blowthe or frute, one penye; for the head of everye fox or gray, xijd; and for the head of everye fytcheue, polcatte, wesell, stott, fayrebode, or wylde catte, one penye; for the head of everye otter, or hedgehogg, ijd.; and for the heads of three ratts or twelve myse, one penye. A small payment was also to be made for the heads of moles."

That the passing of this Act was the signal for the commencement of much activity among such countryfolk as were glad to earn an honest penny, is evident from the entries made on some old papers found several years ago in the church chest of the Suffolk parish of Bedingfield. These papers were much torn and dilapidated; but some, on which the writing was decipherable, proved to have belonged to a "boke made the fyrst day of March Ao dni 1568 for the destroying of noyfull fowles according to the statute in that case pvydd and made." From this book we learn that on Whitsunday the sum of four-and-eightpence was paid to divers persons for eggs and heads of vermin. Other entries supply details. Thus we find that twopence was paid to "Thoms Dranes boye" for a hedgehog; sevenpence to Thomas Revet for four young bullfinches, two old bullfinches, and three moles, "one halfpeny remayning yet unpayde"; fivepence to Samuel Payne for twelve crows' heads, twelve pies' heads, and seven crows' eggs; two shillings to John Hill for three score and six crows' and rooks' heads and one buzzard's head; twopence to William Liverych for a "ryngtayle"; tenpence to Philip Wolfe for two jays' heads and two polecats' heads; twopence to George Clerk for a weasel's head; a penny to Margaret Garrad and Anne Revet for a dozen "mese," and a penny to the "same Anne" for another dozen "mese." The list of payments, so far as it was decipherable, was printed by the Rev. J. W. Millard in *The East Anglian*. It consists of forty-four entries, dealing with —in addition to the payments made on Whitsunday— 1 harrier, 1 weasel, 1 rat, 2 buzzards, 2 polecats, 6 bullfinches, 9 jays, 13 snakes, 16 hedgehogs, 22 pies, 23 moles, 100 crows and rooks, and 147 mice (probably including voles), making a total of 343 "vermin." Seventeen crows' eggs were also taken. This account appears to have been kept by one Thomas Gonnell, for we find in it a memorandum that "I Thomas gonnell have taken three crowes & thre pyes wherefor I am to be alowed ijd."; also that "I Thomas gonnell toke ij appis (snakes) ijd." In order that there might be no "obtaining money under false pretences," the Act provided that all the heads and eggs brought to the distributors should be "sorthened in the presence of the said churchwardens & taxours, or of three of them, (and) burned, consumed, or cut in sondre."

Rather more than a century later, foxes seem to have been very troublesome at Bacton in Norfolk, for in the churchwardens' books for that parish, in the accounts for the year ending Easter 1686, we find that the sum of 11s. 6d. was paid for eleven foxes' heads and one badger's head, and in the following year 7s. was paid for seven foxes' heads. Coming down to comparatively recent times, there is an entry in the parish accounts of Pulham St. Mary the Virgin, that in 1760 the sum of £4, 18s. 4½d. was paid for 393 dozen and a half of sparrows. In ensuing years about the same amount was paid, until 1808, when £6, 6s. 8d. was paid. In 1818 the sum was £7, 8s.; in 1826 it was £8, 7s. 5½d.; and in 1838 it was £9, 5s. 10d. The highest number of birds killed in one year was 8920, the lowest 4723. During eighty-one years, remarks Mr. J. Calver, who made the calculation for *Eastern Counties Collectanea*, about 460,000 birds were killed. But tales, he adds, are current that the sparrows were dug up from the pits in which they were buried and made to do duty again.

Until 1534 no steps were taken to regulate the netting of wild-fowl. In that year an important Act was passed, in which it was set forth that there had formerly been within the realm great plenty of fowl, such as "dukkes, mallardes, wygeons, teales, wyldgeese, and dyverse other kyndes of wyldfowle," and the markets and households had been supplied with them; but now divers persons in the summer season, at such time as the old fowl were "mowted" and the young were not fully feathered, had, by means of nets and other engines, yearly taken such great number that the "brode of wyldefowle" had become wasted and consumed. It was therefore enacted that it should be unlawful for any person, between the last day of May and the last day of August, to take any such wild-fowl with nets or other engines upon pain of one year's imprisonment and the forfeiture of fourpence for every fowl so taken. This Act remained in force until 1550, when it was repealed owing to it "being notablye by daylye experience founde and knowen that there is at this present case plentye of fowle broughte unto the marketts than was before the makinge of the saide Acte, which ys taken to come of the punyshment of God, whose benefytt was therbye taken awaye from the poore people that were wont to live by their skill in taking of the sayde fowle, wherby they were wont at that time to susteyne themselves with their poor households, to the great savinge of other kynds of vyttaile, of which ayde they are now destitute to their great and extreame ympoverishinge."

In 1580 a further Act was passed for the protection of pheasants and partridges against netters; but it was provided that this Act should not extend to "lowbellers, tramellers," or others who should unwittingly take pheasants and partridges at night under any "tramell, lowbell, roadnette, or other engine," if they set at liberty every bird so taken. For the better execution of this and other laws an Act was passed in 1604, which, among other things, dealt with those "vulgar sort of men of small work," who made a living by breaking the laws in regard to the taking of game by means of guns, nets, crossbows, and other instruments. But it was provided that persons with £10 per annum freehold or £200 personalty, or duly authorised servants, might "take pheasants and part-

WILD-GOOSE SHOOTING

ridges in the daytyme with nets in and upon his and their owne, or his and their master's free-warren, mannor, and freehold, or on any parte of them, betwixte the Feaste of Sainte Michael the Archangel and the Feaste of the Birthe of our Lorde God yearlie." Other Acts, mainly intended to deal with poachers of game, were added to the Statute Book before and during the reign of Queen Anne, one, passed in 1710, having a special interest for the fen and marsh folk, inasmuch as it contained a clause reading: "And whereas very great number of wild-fowl of several kinds are destroyed by the pernicious practice of driving[1] or taking them with hayes, tunnells, and other nets in the Fens, Lakes, and broad waters where fowl resort in the molting time, and that at a season of the year when the fowl are sick and molting their feathers, and the flesh unsavory and unwholesome, to the prejudice of those that buy them, and to the great damage and decay of the breed of wild fowl," it is enacted that "if any person or persons whatsoever between the first day of July and the first day of September as they shall yearly happen shall by hayes, tunnells, or other nets drive or take any wild duck, teal, wigeon, or any other fowl commonly reported to be water fowl in any of the Fens, Lakes, broad waters and other places of resort of wild fowl in the molting season," he or they should be liable to a fine of 5s. for every fowl, and the justice should order his or their hayes, nets, or tunnells to be destroyed.

The method of taking eels by means of setts, which is still practised by several men on the Yare, Bure, and Waveney, is a very ancient one, dating back to before the reign of Henry VII., when, according to an old record, there were two kinds of fishing in the waters under the jurisdiction of the town of Great Yarmouth, one being for "flote fishes," and the other for eels with

[1] See pages 274-275.

setts and ground nets, which had been "of long tyme used." For the right to use a sett the fisherman had to pay the Yarmouth bailiffs a penny a year, and in the waters under the Yarmouth jurisdiction, which extended as far as Hardley Cross on the Yare, St. Olave's Bridge on the Waveney, and Waybridge (at Acle) on the Bure, there were no less than thirty-eight setts. Those on the Yare were situated at Norwich Water Mouth, Thorough Dike, King's Holme Bars, Gates-End, Stakes *alias* Parsons Fleet, Abraham's Bush, Reedham Key, Tildhouse, and Hardley Cross; those on the Waveney at Lady's Haven, Whitecote Bush, Burgh Castle, Highland, Michaelmas Dike, Fretton Sett, Umney Bridge, and Prior's Key; and those on the Bure and Thurne at the Barge House *alias* North Chains, Hugh's Fleet, Cross in the Sands, Caister Kills, Church Balls, Short Rack, Wessen Sett, Maltby Cote, Little Star Bush, Braborne Bush, Runham Score, Great Star Bush, Runham Dam, Little Sett, Herringby Bush, Cleer's Fleet, Tunstal Fleet, Stokesby Ferry, Muck Fleet, Pie Stakes, and Prior's Key.

There appears to have been some trouble at times in consequence of the number of fishermen being in excess of the number of setts, and owing to the fishermen failing to abide by the rule of holding each sett in rotation; but no serious dispute occurred until the year 1576, when the Yarmouth bailiffs obtained from Queen Elizabeth permission to farm out the setts to their water-bailiff, John Everist, at thirty pounds a year for thirty years. To this the fishermen seem to have offered strong objection, and their cause was championed by Clement and William Paston, who seem to have represented the riparian owners, to whom the fishermen had been in the habit of paying a tribute of eels for permission to use their lands for the staking, hauling, and drying of nets. This led the Yarmouth Assembly to make complaint to the Crown, and the Pastons were ordered to explain their conduct. They made the following defence:

In the three rivers concerned, the fishing for "float" fishes and eels had always been "in comon for all the fyshermen," without their making any payment, save a "reasonable composycion of eles" to the riparian owners for permission to stake and dry their nets on their lands. The custom among the fishermen was that every year on St. Margaret's Day the fisherman who first came to any of the eel-setts, and pitched a bough there, should have possession of that sett during the ensuing twelve months; but as there were only about thirty setts to be divided among a considerable number of fishermen, some contention had arisen "betwen some of the sayde fyshermen in the gettinge of the beste ele setts." This had furnished an excuse for the interference of the Yarmouth bailiffs, and a charge of a penny a year was made for the use of each sett. Subsequently the bailiffs, "perceivinge the said ele settes to be greatelie beneficiall unto the said fyshermen, dyd then yerelie beginne to exacte of the saide fyshermen for the assignment of the beste ele settes suche greate rewardes as were verie beneficiall unto them, whereby the saide fyshermen fynding themselves greved and greatlie abused, by reason of this yerelie exaccion," had neglected to resort to the bailiffs. The latter had therefore let the setts to their water-bailiff, John Everist, at a yearly rent of thirty pounds, a thing, the Pastons maintained, they had no right to do, though they did not deny that the Corporation had authority to correct misdemeanours committed on the rivers.

The dispute was finally settled by a Commission appointed by the Court of Chancery to meet at North Walsham. It was decided that the Corporation was entitled to all the rights it claimed, and that for each sett the fishermen should pay the owners of the lands adjoining one quarter of "Brewet" eels yearly. By this arrangement the unfortunate fishermen had to "pay out of both pockets." We find, however, that the revenue obtained by the Corporation for the leasing of the setts subsequently decreased; for in the Assembly Books there is noted an order, dated 18th August 1673, "that the lease to Mr. Dover ... of our sets and free fishing in our waters for fourteen Years at the yearly rent of twelve pounds shall be sealed."

The jurisdiction of the city of Norwich over the waters of the Yare dates from at least as early as the latter half of the fifteenth century. In a charter dated 4 Edward IV., we find the following: "We have granted to the same citizens, and their successors for us and our heirs, that the same mayor and sheriffs at all future times for ever, have search in the river of Wensum (below Trowse, now called the Yare) by all the length of the same river, that is to say, from a certain place on the north part of the city of Norwich called the Sheep Wash unto the cross called Hardley Cross, near Breydon, to survey and search all the nets, wears, and other engines for taking fish being found in the same water, and to take, carry away, retain, and at their pleasure burn all and singular the things which, as well by examination as inquisition, shall happen to be found, placed, or erected there against the form of any statutes passed, or to be passed, or to the destruction of young fish called Fry." In the reign of George II. this charter was supplemented by an Act making it illegal for any person to take or have possession of "any spawn, fry, or brood of fish, or any unsizeable fish, or fish out of season, or any smelt not five inches long." Under the above-mentioned charter and Act the fresh-water fisheries of the Yare above Hardley Cross were regulated until the passing of the North and Suffolk Fisheries Act of 1877.

Mr. Southwell, in a paper *On Some Ancient Customs with Regard to the Fresh-water Fisheries of*

Norfolk,[1] quotes the following regulations from the Norwich Assembly Book, where they appear under date " St Matthew the Apostle 3 & 4 Philip and Mary ":

"Regulations made for the Fresh-water Fishermen between the Tower at Conisforthe and Hardley Cross.

"No one to bete in the night for Perches or any other fish.

"No person shall use any 'Lambe nett' or wycker baskett . . . for destroying of small fishes.

"No person or persons shall have above vij Trammells wyde and narrowe and tenne Bowenetts.

"No person shall 'bushe' more than two days in the week, viz. upon the Monday and Thursday.

"No person shall lay any bokes or boke.

"No casting net be occupied between Ship washe and Hardley Cross.

"No man shall 'trolle' in the river.

"No person shall 'jobbe' in the river.

"Item that every man shall be bound to keep a dog to hunt the otter and to make a general hunt twice or thrice in the year or more at time or times convenient upon pain to forfeit ten shillings.

"No fisherman being a common fisher or victualler to market shall at any time fish with Flewe sett nette or any other engyne within the City bounds from the Chain to the New Mills.

"No fisherman shall put any long nette into the river to take fish there in spawning time, that is to say, three weeks before Chrowchmas (3rd May) and three weeks after Chrowchmas."

In writing elsewhere of the Norfolk Broads,[1] I have given an account of the ceremonies that attended the

---

[1] *Transactions of the Norfolk and Norwich Naturalists' Society*, vol. iv. p. 438.
[2] *The Norfolk Broads*, by William A. Dutt, 1903 (reprinted, 1905).

annual inquest of the river liberties undertaken by the Yarmouth bailiffs. Manship, writing in 1619, tells us that on the day when the bailiffs made their annual voyage up the Yare and Waveney, they carried with them "scales or 62 brass measures" with which "to try if the nets of the fishermen be lawful." At Norwich Water Mouth (where the Yare enters Breydon) the two bailiffs parted company, the senior bailiff going to St. Olaves, and the junior bailiff to Hardley Cross, where a proclamation was made by which the public were charged "that if you do know any person or persons that do frequent and use to fish any manner of unlawful craft, engine, or nets, other than is lawful and good, whereby the fry of fish in the said river and streams should be hindered, and utterly destroyed, to the great hindrance of the liege people, you shall do us to wit of them, and present their names." From the Yarmouth Assembly Book we learn that on March 1st, 1606, it was ordered: "that notice be given to them that fish with unlawful nets to cease so doing, and if after such warning any one do the like the nets to be seized by the chamberlains"; while on June 15th, 1631, four net reeves were appointed "to take care that no unlawful nets or engines be used in the sea or rivers within the liberties of the Burgh, for destroying the fry or breed of fish, according to his Majesty's proclamation." Previous to this, in 1587, by an extent and survey of the manor of Beccles, it was determined by a water-leet then held, "that if any fisherman whatever do fish in the said water of Beccles ... with any manner of net, the shale or meshes thereof not being in wideness two inches and a half of the rule (ground nets, wherewith they take eels only exempted), every such net is forfeit to the lord of the manor abovesaid, over and above twenty shillings in the name of a pain; and all the fish taken in the same unlawful net."

Turning from freshwater fishing to sea-fishing, we

find a curious custom surviving until about sixty years ago, in the payment to the rector of Lowestoft of a small sum of money in lieu of a tithe of the fish caught by each local fishing-boat. This tithe was formerly known as "Christ's half dole." There is a reference to it in a roll of the Proceedings in the Court of First Fruits, 9th Elizabeth, where it is shown, on the deposition of two Lowestoft men, "that there was a tythe of fyshe called Christ's dole, payde in this mannor, videlt, of every fisher bote goinge to the sea, halfe a dole. And of every ship that sayled to Islonde, halfe a dole, which doles about twenty yeares past dyd amounte to a seven pound, or more, yearely. For then there weare thirtene or fourtene doggers belongynge to the sayde towne, and now but one." Until about sixty years ago this dole was paid by the Lowestoft boat-owners; and in 1845 the rector succeeded in establishing before the magistrates his claim to a tithe which a boat-owner had refused to pay. Since that time, however, the payment has been allowed to lapse. At Yarmouth, in the reign of Edward III., "Christ's half dole" is said to have realised 700 marks, but in the reign of Henry VII. it had fallen to 60 marks. In the time of Charles I. the half-doles from the cod fishery were estimated to be worth nearly £300 a year.

In this connection it may be mentioned that at the time when the test case was tried before the magistrates, the profit-sharing system of doles provided that a fishing voyage should be divided into about 150 doles to each fishing-boat, and that these should be allotted as follows: Nets, 55 doles; boat, 28; master, 16; mate, 11; hawseman, 10; net-ropeman, 7; net-stower, 6; three capsternmen, 6 each; boy, 4½; and vicar, ½ dole. At the present time a somewhat similar custom prevails, the shares in the takings of each boat being thus divided: Nets, ½ share; boat and engine, 1 share; master, 1¾ shares; mate, 1⅛ shares; hawseman (or third hand), 1 share; net-ropeman, 1 share; net-stower, ⅞ of a share;

20

cast-off seizings,[1] ¾ share; driver, ¾ share; "all-works" hand, ⅝ of a share; and boy ½ a share.

Writing, in 1866, of the customs prevailing at Yarmouth at that time, Nall states that there was a system of dividing a fishing voyage into 180 doles, of which a 100 or 110 went to the boat and the remainder to the crew. In other cases there was an agreed scale of wages per last[2] of herrings caught. "By articles signed last voyage," he writes, "we found the scale in use to have been: master, 16s.; mate, 10s.; oarsman and whaleman, each 8s.; net-ropeman, 6s. 6d.; net-stower, 6s.; all-work man, 5s.; four capstan men, each 4s.; boy, 3s.—Total for the crew of twelve hands, £3 18s. 6d. The cost of victualling the boat, which is usually done on a liberal scale, averages £5 a week. Assuming the voyage to extend fourteen weeks and to realise fifty lasts, the outlay in provisions and wages will have been nearly £275, or £5 10s. per last, exclusive of outfit, capital invested, salt-curing, house plant, and wear and tear. The advantages of this arrangement are not reciprocal: when fish are scarce and the prices ruling are high, it operates more favourably to the merchant than the crew; when fish are plentiful and prices down, the gain is with the men, who receive the same amount although the sales may not cover the cost of catching."

[1] The man is here called after the nature of his work on the boat.
[2] 13,200 herrings.

CHAPTER XIX

WITH CRABBE AT ALDEBURGH

THE little fishing port of Aldeburgh, one of those sea-wasted towns met with at fairly frequent intervals along the Suffolk coast, cannot, from the point of view of the seeker after the picturesque, be said to have increased its attractiveness during the hundred and sixty years which have elapsed since George Crabbe was born. True, it still retains something of that primitive charm which dates from before the dawn of the era of railways, and its quaint old hamlet of Slaughden, with its houses like stranded derelicts cast up amid a waste of salt marsh and shingle, helps to preserve to the place a measure of that tragic suggestiveness which is not the least impressive attribute of a coast town which for centuries has had in the sea its greatest foe as well as its greatest friend; but in the somewhat glaring modernity of its present sea front, and certain architectural enormities which betoken a taste for the fantastic rather than the fitting, there is now something out of harmony with the associations of the place and the unchanged aspect of its surroundings. One has difficulty in realising that this is "The Borough" which provided Crabbe with many of the characters he portrays in the four-and-twenty cantos of the poem he completed here in the autumn of 1809; their fitting environment has to a large extent passed away with the conditions conducive to their existence. Not in Aldeburgh, more than in any other coast town dependent on what the sea attracts to it rather than on what the sea gives it, are there now apparent such conditions as are favourable to the production of that marked individuality of character Crabbe describes with such rare insight; only the beachmen, those silent heroes of many a fight with wind and sea, give the place a certain distinction, and they, too, have changed, and bear no resemblance to that "wild, artful, surly, savage race" with which the poet was familiar in the days of cargo-running among the creeks and inlets of the Alde and Deben.

To the naturalist who comes to Aldeburgh in the hope of finding here the scenes from which "Nature's sternest painter yet the best" drew his inspiration, the town will prove disappointing, until he remembers that it was not in Aldeburgh, but in the country around, that Crabbe sought for that wild life and scenery he has described so faithfully. With what wonderful fidelity he has depicted the country-side through which he rambled in the hard days of his youth, can hardly be appreciated until one has crossed the wild heathlands lying between Aldeburgh and Aldringham, strolled along the winding river-wall bordering the ooze-flats of the Alde, ventured down into the marsh land of wailing lapwings and rush-fringed pools of which one gets glimpses from the railway before the train enters the station, and wandered along the Crag Path to Thorpe or southward along that curious strip of shingly beach which for several miles diverts the river from its ancient outlet to the sea. When one has done this, keeping the while an observant eye on the details of the varied scenes through which one passes, the worthiness of Crabbe to be considered what Byron has called him, becomes strikingly manifest, as does the truth of the estimate made of his powers by one of his latest biographers, the late Canon Ainger, who writes: "It was undoubtedly to the observing eye and retentive memory thus practised in cottage gardens, and in the lanes, and meadows, and marshes of Suffolk, that his descriptions, when once he had found where his true strength lay, owed a charm for which readers of poetry had long been hungering. The floral outfit of pastoral poets, when Crabbe began to write, was a *hortus siccus* indeed. Distinctness in painting the common growth of field and hedgerow may be said to have had its origin with Crabbe. Gray and Goldsmith had their own rare and special gifts to which Crabbe could lay no claim. But neither these poets nor even Thomson, whose avowed purpose was to depict nature, are Crabbe's rivals in this respect."

Canon Ainger goes on to say that Byron's description of Crabbe as " Nature's sternest painter yet the best " would have been juster had he written that " Crabbe was the truest painter of Nature in her less lovely phases." Hazlitt more forcibly, but with characteristic exaggeration, puts it that " he desolates a line of coast with sterile, blighting lines," and that " the whole of Mr. Crabbe's *Borough* . . . is done so to the life, that it seems almost like some sea-monster, crawled out of the neighbouring slime, and harbouring a breed of strange vermin, with a strong local scent of tar and bilge-water." As " an exact facsimile of some of the most unlovely parts of creation," Hazlitt quotes from the author he criticises the following passage, which to my mind is one of the truest pieces of descriptive writing in English poetry:

> " Thus by himself compelled to live each day,
> To wait for certain hours the tide's delay;
> At the same times the same dull views to see,
> The bounding marsh-bank and the blighted tree;
> The water only when the tides were high,
> When low, the mud half-covered and half-dry;
> The sun-burnt tar that blisters on the planks,
> And bank-side stakes in their uneven ranks;
> Heaps of entangled weeds that slowly float,
> As the tide rolls by the impeded boat.
> When tides were neap, and in the sultry day,
> Through the tall bounding mud-banks made their way,
> Which on each side rose swelling, and below
> The dark warm flood ran silently and slow

>   There anchoring, Peter chose from man to hide,
>   There hang his head, and view the lazy tide
>   In its hot slimy channel slowly glide;
>   Where the small eels, that left the deeper way
>   For the warm shore, within the shallows play;
>   Where gaping mussels, left upon the mud,
>   Slope their slow passage to the fall'n flood:
>   Here dull and hopeless he'd lie down and trace
>   How side-long crabs had crawled their crooked race;
>   Or sadly listen to the tuneless cry
>   Of fishing gull or clanging golden-eye;
>   What time the sea-birds to the marsh would come,
>   And the loud bittern, from the bull-rush home,
>   Gave from the salt ditch-side the bellowing boom."

Here, except that the bittern no longer booms by the "salt ditch-side," we have a masterly description of the foreground of the scene presented from the river-wall bordering the mud-banks and tidal waters of the Alde, or, as Hazlitt would call it, "one of the most unlovely parts of creation." Unlovely, under some aspects, it may be, and as Crabbe depicts it we see it as it appeared to the wretched man who

>   "Loved to stop beside the opening sluice;
>   Where the small stream, confined in narrow bound,
>   Ran with a dull, unvaried, saddening sound,"

and who saw it while his soul was oppressed "with misery, grief, and fear"; but the fact that the picture is drawn by a careful and observant student of nature is obvious in every line of it. There is nothing here of morbid imagination, such as, in the case of Crabbe, might well have been the result of viewing such a scene in the days of his troubled youth, when uncongenial surroundings must often have aroused gloomy reflections; every detail is drawn "to the life," and the description is as "living" whether we read it beside the tidal Alde or far away, amid very different scenes. To-day, should one descend from the golf-links on to the river-wall, and stroll seaward towards Slaughden

Quay, one feels conscious every moment of treading in the footsteps of the poet; nothing is changed; nothing, could he see the scene now, would be unfamiliar to him. Even the ancient hulks with the tar blistering on their planks have the appearance of having lain half-embedded in the mud for more than a hundred years.

That such a scene as this, when viewed under a lowering sky, or even in the sultry glare of a midsummer noon, may appear stagnant and repellant, is undeniable; but seen under favourable conditions it is far from being without its charm. Of this, so observant a naturalist as Crabbe must have been fully conscious; and because the requirements of his subject necessitated his dwelling on the least attractive aspect of the scene, it should not be assumed that he was blind to its brighter side. On a breezy summer day there is a sparkle on the water in the channel of the Alde like the sparkle of a million flawless diamonds, and even when the tide is at ebb, and there are miles of weed-strewn ooze bordering the channel, these far-spreading flats shimmer in the sunlight with apparently translucent green and gold. Indeed, on such a day there are many far less desirable retreats than a grey-green hollow in the slope of the Alde river-wall, or some neighbouring knoll at the base of which the flood-tide sucks away the close-packed shells of the crumbling Crag. In the immediate foreground, among the water-worn pebbles and stranded tangles of dark-green bladderwrack and ribbon-like zostera, dainty little ringed plovers are seen running to and fro, or heard piping melodiously as they flicker over the flats. Along the margin of the channel, little parties of terns from the shingly beach beyond Slaughden are skimming and wheeling, at intervals dipping down to rest for a moment on the water while they seize some tiny fish or morsel of flotsam food ; while by the side of some brackish drain among the flats, a heron is standing motionless, his neck "reined out," as they say in Broadland, his whole attitude betokening alertness and expectancy. Farther away, where the flats seem as bright green as though they are clothed with springing grass, a flock of sea-gulls have settled in some quiet spot, and are standing as still as sentinels, each bird with its head to the wind. Intermingled with the creaking of the terns and the whistling of the ringed plovers, are the piping of redshanks and the wailing of lapwings in the salt marsh; and like the voice of summer itself, is heard the sibilant murmur of the breeze among the grey blades of the couch grass on the walls.

The wailing of the lapwing was a familiar sound to Crabbe in those early days, that were evidently in his mind when he wrote of the "Adventures of Richard," in the *Tales of the Hall*. Then, as he tells us was the habit of Richard, he

> "Loved to walk where none had walked before,
> Among the rocks that ran along the shore;
> Or far beyond the sight of men to stray,
> And take my pleasure when I lost my way;
> For then 'twas mine to trace the hilly heath,
> And all the mossy moor that lies beneath:
> Here had I favourite stations, where I stood
> And heard the murmurs of the ocean-flood,
> With not a sound beside except when flew
> Aloft the lapwing, or the grey curlew,
> Who with wild notes my fancied power defied,
> And mock'd the dreams of solitary pride."

These lines were written far away from Aldeburgh, amid scenes very different to those he described; but one needs no assurance that when he wrote them he was thinking of the heaths and moorlands near his boyhood's home. The *Tales of the Hall* contain many fine passages inspired by his recollections of the somewhat sterile country on the verge of which his native town stood sea-threatened and forlorn, and among them is that wonderful picture of an autumn landscape which Tennyson found it impossible to forget:

> "Early he rose, and look'd with many a sigh
> On the red light that fill'd the eastern sky;
> Oft had he stood before, alert and gay,
> To hail the glories of the new-born day;
> But now dejected, languid, listless, low,
> He saw the wind upon the water blow,
> And the cold stream curl'd onward as the gale
> From the pine-hill blew harshly down the dale;
> On the right side the youth a wood survey'd,
> With all its dark intensity of shade;
> Where the rough wind alone was heard to move,
> In this, the pause of nature and of love,
> When now the young are rear'd, and when the old,
> Lost to the tie, grow negligent and cold—
> Far to the left he saw the huts of men,
> Half-hid in mist that hung upon the fen;
> Before him swallows, gathering for the sea,
> Took their short flights, and twitter'd on the lea;
> And near the bean-sheaf stood, the harvest done,
> And slowly blacken'd in the sickly sun."

Landward of the Crag Path as you follow it towards Thorpe, you can see that scene to-day: the misty fen, the ruffled pools, the pine-hill with its silhouette of rugged, sombre, deep-breathing firs, the distant wood before which is drawn a thin veil of haze, the gathering swallows awaiting a fair wind before taking their oversea flight, and on the russet slopes leading down to the fen, the rows of bean-sheaves blackening in the sun. "Unlovely," we fancy we again hear the critic say; but here again we have truth to nature, a vivid presentment of a commonplace scene, given in a few lines, but with all the essential detail to make it a perfect picture.

Canon Ainger is probably right in saying that Crabbe's chief passion from early life until the time came when he was called upon to take Holy Orders was botany. This study was first taken up while he was living in Woodbridge in Suffolk, the flora of which neighbourhood is of a different character to that we find around Aldeburgh; but he afterwards pursued his favourite study with equal zeal at home. Later in life he contributed largely to the Suffolk list of plants in the *Botanist's Guide*; but his chief contribution to the natural history of his native county is a list of local plants to be found in Loder's *History of Framlingham*. "His Framlingham List," writes the Rev. W. M. Hind in his *Flora of Suffolk*, "includes 226 flowering plants and a few Cryptogams. Its importance chiefly consists in its being the first considerable contribution to the Botany of East Suffolk, and as adding nearly forty new species to the Flora of the County." At the time when he commenced this study he was an apprentice to a Woodbridge apothecary, and when he returned to Aldeburgh, and became a doctor in a small way, on his own account, it was his unfortunate experience to find that the fact of his being able to obtain medicinal herbs so readily was pleaded by some of his poorer patients as "reason why his fees need not be calculated on any large scale"; but, as Canon Ainger remarks, his absorbing pursuit did far more than serve to furnish Crabbe's outfit as a healer. It provided him with that knowledge of the appearance and habits of wild flowers which afterwards enabled him to give us, not simply impressions of nature, but nature herself, and so win for himself lasting fame. Time after time it came to his aid, with the result that we have many lines like those oft-quoted ones:

> "Lo! where the heath, with withering brake grown o'er,
> Lends the light turf that warms the neighbouring poor;
> From thence a length of burning sand appears,
> Where the thin harvest waves its withered ears;
> Rank weeds, that every art and care defy,
> Reign o'er the land, and rob the blighted rye:
> There thistles stretch their prickly arms afar,
> And to the ragged infant threaten war;
> There poppies nodding, mock the hope of toil;
> There the blue bugloss paints the sterile soil;

Hardy and high above the slender sheaf
The slimy mallow waves her silky leaf;
O'er the young shoot the charlock throws a shade,
And clasping tares cling round the sickly blade."

Of the flora of Aldeburgh itself, Crabbe appears to have had rather a poor opinion. There, he says,

"Fed by food they love, to rankest size,
Around the dwellings, docks and wormwood rise:
Here the strong mallow strikes her slimy root,
Here the dull nightshade hangs her deadly fruit:
On hills of dust the henbane's faded green
And pencill'd flower of sickly scent is seen;
At the wall's base the fiery nettle springs,
With fruit globose and fierce with poison'd stings;
Above (the growth of many a year) is spread
The yellow level of the stonecrop's bed;
In every chink delights the fern to grow,
With glossy leaf and tawny bloom below:
These, with our sea-weeds, rolling up and down,
Form the contracted Flora of our town."

But I have my doubts as to whether the poet ever found the deadly nightshade growing in his native town; for it is a very rare plant in Suffolk, and the nearest localities for which it has been recorded are Oakley Park and Framlingham. Formerly it grew around the walls of the grand old castle at Framlingham, where Crabbe added it to his local list; but it has been extinct there for several years, and at Oakley only one plant of deadly nightshade was ever found. Nor is the henbane now so familiar a plant as it was in the days when its leaves were a favourite remedy for asthma; but the henbane has been found in Aldeburgh in recent years, and Crabbe, no doubt, often came across it when he was "culling simples" for the benefit of his local patients. His reference to the nettle "with fruit globose and fierce with poisoned stings" is, however, to the botanist the most interesting detail of his description of the "contracted flora" of Aldeburgh; for here there can be no doubt he had in mind, not the common nor the small nettle, but the Roman nettle, one of the rarest of British plants, distinguished by its globular heads of female flowers and the virulence of its sting. This formidable nettle has, according to Sir J. D. Hooker, only been known to grow in waste places in the East of England, chiefly near the sea. To-day it would probably be sought in vain in Aldeburgh; but it was recorded for the town by Dillenius, the celebrated botanist who edited Ray's *Synopsis*, and it was again identified there in 1774 by Sir T. G. Cullum.

Within the bounds of "The Borough" Crabbe preferred to study human nature rather than plant life, and there he found a wide field for observation; but in his early days, whenever he could escape the drudgery of the excise work in which he helped his father at Slaughden Quay, he must, like the lover of whom he writes, have chosen to ramble

> "Through the green lane,—then linger in the mead,—
> Stray o'er the heath in all its purple bloom,—
> And pluck the blossom where the wild bees hum;"

and he would notice, as he rambled over the "sandy sheep-walks' slender grass," how

> "Dwarfish flowers among the gorse are spread,
> And the lamb browses by the linnet's bed."

Then presently, after crossing the brook by its rough rustic bridge, he would come to where he could see

> "The ocean smiling in the fervid sun—
> The waves that faintly fall and slowly run—
> The ships at distance and the boats at hand;"

and it is not unlikely that, after counting the number of those

> "Ships softly sinking in the sleepy sea,"

he would

> "Search for crimson weeds, which spreading flow,
> Or lie like pictures on the sand below."

But in wandering around Aldeburgh he could hardly go

far in any direction without finding himself in the neighbourhood of a "rushy moor" such as he describes in his "Lover's Journey," and which always had a great fascination for him, realising, as he did, that "all that grows has grace," and that bog, marsh, and fen "are only poor to undiscerning men."

For, as he says,

> "Here may the nice and curious eye explore
> How Nature's hand adorns the rushy moor;
> Here the rare moss in secret shade is found,
> Here the sweet myrtle of the shaking ground:
> Beauties are these that from the view retire,
> But well repay th' attention they require."

Time after time he returns to where

> "Our busy streets and sylvan walks between,
> Fen, marshes, bog, and heath all intervene;
> Here pits of crag, with spongy, plashy base,
> To some enrich th' uncultivated space:
> For there are blossoms rare, and curious rush,
> The gale's rich balm, and sundew's crimson blush,
> Whose velvet leaf with radiant beauty dress'd,
> Forms a gay pillow for the plover's breast."

Nothing escapes his eye, not even the samphire (*Salicornia*) nor the saltwort growing on the tidal verge of the salt-marsh.

Because he chose to linger amid such scenes as these, it is suggested that he had a preference for "the most unlovely parts of creation"; but where Hazlitt could see only muddy water full of "strange vermin," Crabbe saw the rosy sundew and the pink blossom of the bog pimpernel, and it may be truthfully said of him, as it was of George Borrow, that "he could draw more poetry from a widespreading marsh with its straggling rushes than from the most beautiful scenery." But his love of Nature was not confined to it in what one of his critics calls its "less lovely phases," nor was it only through the botanist's glasses that he saw the country-side. With the cries and habits of the sea and shore birds he seems to have been well acquainted, and he even has some claim to be considered an amateur lepidopterist. In dealing with the hobbies of some of the humble tradesmen of "The Borough," he includes among them that of his friend the weaver, of whom he writes :

> "Strong desires
> Reign in his breast; 'tis beauty he admires.
> See! to the shady grove he wings his way,
> And feels in hope the raptures of the day :
> Eager he looks; and soon, to glad his eyes,
> From the sweet bower, by nature form'd, arise
> Bright troops of virgin moths and fresh-born butterflies;
> Who broke that morning from their half-year's sleep,
> To fly o'er flowers where they were wont to creep.
> Above the sovereign oak, a sovereign skims,
> The purple Emp'ror, strong in wing and limbs;
> There fair Camilla takes her flight serene,
> Adonis blue, and Paphis silver-queen;
> With every filmy fly from mead or bower,
> And hungry Sphinx who threads the honey'd flower;
> She o'er the larkspur's bed, where sweets abound,
> Views every bell, and hums th' approving sound,
> Poised on her busy plumes, with feeling nice
> She draws from every flower, nor tries a floret twice."

This has been a chapter of quotations; but my aim has been to draw attention to the "truthfulness to nature" which entitles a somewhat neglected poet to be ranked above all his forerunners as a depicter of rural and coast scenery, and if my haphazard selection of descriptive passages from some of his best-known works should fail to convince some reader that Crabbe is what Byron called him, I must urge that reader to turn to Crabbe himself for conviction. But I cannot resist the temptation to make one more quotation—a somewhat lengthy one—but not without some relation to the wild life of the East Anglian coast :

> "But who . . .
> . . . shall paint . . . the sea?
> Various and vast, sublime in all its forms,
> When lull'd by zephyrs, or when roused by storms,

Its colour changing, when from clouds and sun,
Shades after shades upon the surface run;
Embrown'd and horrid now, and now serene,
In limpid blue, and evanescent green;
And oft the foggy banks on ocean lie;
Lift the fair sail, and cheat th' experienced eye.
  Be it the summer noon: a sandy space
The ebbing tide has left upon its place;
Then just the hot and stony beach above,
Light twinkling streams in bright confusion move
(For heated thus, the warmer air ascends,
And with the cooler in its fall contends);
Then the broad bosom of the ocean keeps
An equal motion; swelling as it sleeps,
Then slowly sinking; curling to the strand,
Faint, lazy waves o'ercreep the ridgy sand,
Or tap the tarry boat with gentle blow,
And back return in silence, smooth and slow.
Ships in the calm sea anchor'd; for they glide
On the still sea, urged solely by the tide:
Art thou not present, this calm scene before,
Where all beside is pebbly length of shore,
And far as eye can reach, it can discern no more?

 · · · · · · ·

  View now the winter-storm! above, one cloud,
Black and unbroken, all the skies o'ershroud:
Th' unwieldly porpoise through the day before
Had roll'd in view of boding men on shore;
And sometimes hid and sometimes show'd his form,
Dark as the cloud, and furious as the storm.
  All where the eye delights, yet dreads to roam,
The breaking billows cast the flying foam
Upon the billows rising—all the deep
Is restless change; the waves so swell'd and steep,
Breaking and sinking, and the sunken swells,
Nor one, one moment, in its station dwells:
But nearer land you may the billows trace,
As if contending in their watery chase;
May watch the mightiest till the shoal they reach,
Then break and hurry to their utmost stretch;
Curl'd as they come, they strike with furious force,
And then re-flowing, take their grating course,
Raking the rounded flints, which ages past
Roll'd by their rage, and shall to ages last.

 · · · · · · ·

  High o'er the restless deep, above the reach
Of gunner's hope, vast flights of wild-ducks stretch

Far as the eye can glance on either side,
In a broad space and level line they glide;
All in their wedge-like figures from the north,
Day after day, flight after flight, go forth.
In-shore their passage tribes of sea-gulls urge,
And drop for prey within the sweeping surge;
Oft in the rough opposing blast they fly
Far back, then turn, and all their force apply,
While to the storm they give their weak complaining cry;
Or clap the sleek white pinion on the breast,
And in the restless ocean dip for rest."

CHAPTER XX

A NIGHT WITH AN EEL-CATCHER

THE glowing embers of an autumn sunset had smouldered into grey ashes faintly edging a long bank of cloud fast becoming black as a pall. Against this cloud-bank the horizon was scarcely visible; but a westward stretch of river, bordered on one side by dark-plumed reeds and on the other by a low wide rond which had recently been mown, was still traceable by its surface dimly reflecting the leaden light that lingered in the sky. Here and there a dull glimmer of the same lifeless light came from some clean-cut dike at which the drawers had been at work, and beside which some willows were still bearing most of their yellowing leaves; but upon the wide levels through which the river flowed, and which the dikes intersected in every direction, the impenetrable gloom of a moonless autumn night had already rendered all outlines indefinable and the general aspect of the marshlands sombre and forbidding. At times the wail of a lapwing was heard; but even the lapwings seemed to be deserting the marshlands for the night, for at frequent intervals small flocks of them, moving onward in straggling flight, passed over the river, flying, rather lower than in the daytime, towards the ploughed lands. Two or three moorhens, after creeping through the stubble of the newly-mown rond, ventured to swim a short distance from the shore, but were soon lost sight of on the dusk-darkened water. The day had been warm for October, but just before nightfall a chill wind had sprung up, and now it was blowing in cold gusts down the river, causing the tall reeds to bow before it and whisper as though each had a secret to tell.

Before sunset I had crossed the marshes on the north side of the river, and now I was waiting to be rowed across the river by a marshman from whose cottage window came the only gleam of cheerful light which brightened the lonesome levels. In answer to my hail I soon heard above the rustling of the reeds the dull clank of a rowlock, and presently a boat emerged from a dike beside the cottage and came slowly up to a rickety landing-stage towards which there was a narrow banked-up footpath across the rond. A minute later I was seated in the boat, and the marshman, an old acquaintance in whose company I had spent several days among the marshes, soon brought it alongside a roughly-constructed staithe in front of his cottage. Then, having warned me to be careful in stepping ashore owing to the damage which had been done to the bank by the wash of the river steamers during the summer, he guided me among heaps of rond litter, driftwood, and empty eel-trunks towards his cottage. By daylight one could have seen that the cottage stood little more than a foot above the marsh level, and that its roof ridge had taken a marked dip downward at one end in consequence of the foundations of the house having " settled " in the marshy soil.

It had been arranged that I should spend the night with the marshman in the little houseboat he used when working his eel-sett, but as the tide in the river would not begin to ebb for nearly an hour, we entered the low-ceiled kitchen, in which a fire was burning, and, drawing a couple of chairs near to the grate, lit our pipes and chatted a while before starting for the river again. To my companion the fact that he was to be awake nearly all night after having been out in the marshes all day seemed a matter of indifference; while the eels were "running" it was his business to catch them, no matter how many sleepless nights it might entail. His life had been made up of like irregular occupations. For several weeks previous to my visit his daily cattle-tending had been varied by frequent trudges to the mushroom marshes; a few weeks hence he would be reed-cutting on, perhaps, four or five days of each week.

The weather and other conditions were, he considered, favourable for a successful night's eel-catching, though eels were "unaccountable" creatures, and the regularity of their migratory movements was not to be relied on. But during October a "fresher" of water, due to a heavy rainfall, was almost bound to set them running down the river, especially on dark or "misky" nights. On such a night the catch might amount to several stones in weight; but occasionally, when all the conditions seemed favourable for a good catch, the poke of the net, when raised in the morning, would be found practically empty. With the sett we were to use that night his biggest catch had been one of just over ten stones; but some years ago, when he had a sett placed just below the channel leading from a fairly large Broad, he had once caught twelve stones of eels. Nowadays, even the best-placed setts rarely take more than this in a night; but fifty years ago much larger catches are said to have been made. Mr. Christopher Davies has recorded an instance of 300 stones of eels having been taken in four nights in a sett at Hardley Cross on the Yare.

The pattering of raindrops on the kitchen window told us that the weather had not improved since we crossed the river, and when we ventured out of doors again we found the sky starless and an uncomfortable drizzle of rain accompanying the chill gusts of the wind. The night, indeed, was as dark a one as I had ever spent among the marshes, and as I followed the eel-catcher along a narrow footpath leading on to the river-wall, I could see neither the dike which bordered the path on the one hand nor the garden fence on the other. Beyond the far-spreading marshlands there was no visible horizon except where a dull light was cast up into the sky by the Yarmouth street lamps some nine miles away; and when we reached the top of the river-wall, which was some ten feet above the marsh level, we seemed to be moving along the crest of a narrow ridge sloping down on either side into a dark abyss. To my companion every inch of the ground was familiar, and by feeling with his feet the frequent hollows in the path he could have found his way along it even if he were blindfolded; but to one less accustomed to the narrow and elevated track the short journey of about two hundred yards between the cottage and the houseboat was rendered unpleasant by the likelihood of a slip resulting in a roll down the rain-soaked slope of the wall into the slough of a flooded rond. The danger of this I avoided to some extent by keeping close to my companion's heels; but none the less it was with considerable relief that I heard him say, "Here we are," and advise me to stand still for a minute while he entered the houseboat and struck a light.

The houseboat, as I was aware by previous knowledge of it rather than by what I saw of it that night, was a small ark-like craft, consisting of an almost square wooden hut roofed with boards and tarpaulin, built on an old smack-boat which had been bought at Yarmouth for a few shillings and towed at the stern of a wherry to its present moorings. Externally it had been made thoroughly watertight by several liberal coatings of tar; within it was, when closed, kept warm and air-tight by a lining of match-boarding. The cabin was entered from the stern of the boat by a low doorway, the door, like that of a stable, consisting of upper and lower halves, so that the lower part could be kept closed while the occupant of the cabin was watching his sett. On either side of the cabin a locker extended the full length of the interior, while at the bow end was a small stove from which a pipe passed upward through the roof. No window permitted the daylight to enter the cabin, but just under the roof, above each locker, was a narrow sliding shutter, the chief purpose of which was that of a ventilator. Some eel lines, a rush "frail" or basket, and a fisherman's guernsey hung on nails driven into the walls, and on some shelves across the bow end stood a small but varied collection of plates, cups and saucers, some empty bottles, two or three tins which sufficed for a larder, an earthenware teapot, and a small lamp, the last-named being fastened to the wall and overhung by the smoke-blackened lid of a biscuit tin.

In a few minutes wood and coal had been produced from one of the lockers, and a cheerful fire blazing in the little stove made a comfortable warmth in the cabin. By the time this was done the tide had turned, so we stepped out on to the bank beside the houseboat, and the eel-catcher slackened from a stake driven into the river bank the rope by means of which, and some blocks or pulleys, one end of the large net had been held down to the river bed during the day. That a part of the top of the net had risen to the surface of the water was signalled by the appearance of some wooden floats, which could just be seen by the light of the lamp shining from the open doorway of the cabin. Then, stepping into a marsh-boat lying beside the houseboat, the marshman rowed across the river in order to slacken another rope by means of which the rest of the net had been secured. When this was accomplished, a row of floats, curving like the bend of a gigantic bow, extended across the river almost from bank to bank, supporting a large, long net which formed a kind of network wall in the water, reaching from shore to shore and from the surface to the bed of the stream. On his way back to the houseboat the eel-catcher "felt" with an oar all along the bottom of the net to make sure that it rested everywhere on the river bed, to which it was weighted with sinkers. This precaution had sometimes proved very necessary, for occasionally sunken logs, branches of trees, or tins thrown overboard by yachtsmen, had been caught under the bottom of the net, raising a portion of it so as to permit of the passage of the eels beneath it.

His net, the eel-catcher explained, when he had returned to the cabin and we were seated facing each other on the lockers beside the open door, was a single-bosomed net, by which he meant that it possessed only one bow-net and poke for the eels to enter when they tried to find a way through the net. Along the wider reaches of the rivers it is usual for an eel-sett to have a two- or even a three-bosomed net and a corresponding number of bow-nets and pokes; but every eel-fisher has his own ideas as to the best kind of net, and my companion was in favour of one with a single bosom, because, he said, most of the running eels kept to the middle of the stream—a fact, he considered, which rendered a double-bosomed net less likely to catch them. Against this, however, we have the unquestionable fact that some of the largest "takes" have been made in double or three-bosomed nets. The poke, it should be explained, is the end of a kind of long bow-net expanded on wooden hoops and constructed at the entrance on the principle of a crab-pot. It extends downstream from the main net of the sett, the central curve or bosom of which guides the eels into it when they come in contact with it in the course of their journey down the river. The end of the poke is secured in such a way to a stake driven into the bed of the stream that it can be easily raised when the time comes for emptying it.

The eel-catcher had now commenced once more his nightly vigil, for while the net is raised or spread there can be no sleep for its owner, who must always be ready to lower it at the approach of a wherry or any other kind of craft which may be passing up or down the river. It was, he admitted, very unlikely that any wherry would be passing that night; but it would not do to run any risk of having his net damaged, for eel nets were "not to be bought for sixpence." It was usual, he added, for wherrymen to shout a warning to an eel-catcher when approaching a sett; but sometimes they forgot to do so, so there was need to be always on the alert. On glancing up the river, it seemed to me so densely dark that a wherry might have approached unseen; but my companion assured me that he would be able to hear one quite soon enough to allow of his lowering his net, and, as though to convince me of the truth of his assertion, he stretched himself at full length on one of the lockers and closed his eyes. At the same time he continued to chat about marshland life and his various occupations.

Like many of the marshmen, he had spent an unsettled youth, spells of marsh work, such as dike-drawing, wall-mending, and reed-cutting having alternated with wherrying and an occasional season with the drift-netters on the North Sea. Of eel-catching he had had some experience early in life, but only as a picker and babber, by which he meant that he had caught eels by means of an eel-pick or spear and with the aid of a lead-weighted bunch of worsted-threaded worms. At that time he was living with his father in a riverside village in the upper part of the Waveney Valley, and his picking had been chiefly done in the marsh dikes. In those days he had never thought of having an eel-sett, but the opportunity of buying one had been given to him some fifteen years ago, when at the death of one of the River Commissioners' marshmen, he had been given charge of a drainage windmill. Since then he had lived in the cottage by the river, and had worked the sett by which we were watching, having purchased it of the deceased marshman's widow. Its previous owner had, by his own account, made some "wonderful good catches" with the sett; but if all he said was true, eels were far from being so plentiful in the Broads and rivers now as they used to be, for such catches were unknown to the eel-catchers of to-day. For this the "growing up" of some of the Broads, the better drainage of the swampy marshlands, and the disturbance of the river bed by steamers, were probably each in part responsible. In the days when many of the Broads were surrounded by extensive tracts of swamp overgrown with reeds, rushes, and gladden, these untraversable margins were literally "alive" with eels, and in the migration season such numbers of them often came down the rivers that the setts could hardly stand the strain of their catches. Talking of this reminded me of the tales told of migrating eels knotting themselves into large balls, which came rolling down the rivers. My companion had never seen anything of the kind; but he had known the eels to come down in such numbers as to fill an empty poke in the course of an hour.

A marshman is seldom heard nowadays to give expression to the old belief that eels are "bred out of mud," much less do they credit the old-time assertion that chopped horse-hair will, if thrown into the water, turn into eels; but many of the eel-catchers are still of the opinion that eels are viviparous, and most of them are prepared to affirm that they have met with unborn young ones whilst cleaning eels for the table. So frequently does one hear this stated that there can be no doubt eels are often infested with some kind of worm-like internal parasite. Hardly a fisherman is to be found who will credit the now well-established fact that the eels spawn in the sea. With the phenomenon of the spring migration of the elvers up the rivers they are quite familiar, but they are convinced that the elvers are born in the estuaries, or, as a Broadsman will say, in Lake Lothing and Breydon. Equally certain are they that several kinds of eels inhabit the Broads and rivers. The best of these is, of course, the sharp-nosed eel which is taken in the setts during the autumn, and which is recognised by naturalists as the female, which has developed what is called a bridal coloration or "mating habit." This eel is known to the catchers as the "silver eel" or "streamer." Then there are "gluts" and "grigs," which are caught in the spring-time, both of these being broad-nosed eels, the former attaining a considerable size, while the latter is, according to Dr. Emerson, said to hang on to the weeds and seldom exceed half a pound in weight. Another variety is known as the "summer scarum," a very active kind, which, if dropped from between the teeth of an eel-pick, at once burrows into the mud.

That eels sometimes leave the water and travel some distance over land is a well-known fact. Dr. Emerson states that they do this when there is dew on the grass, as they find dewy grass easy to travel upon; but they have been known to crawl over the sun-hardened crest of an eight-feet-high river wall, and the locksmen of the upper waters of the rivers not infrequently notice them climbing up the perpendicular sides of the locks, supporting themselves on the wet green weed which clings to the brickwork. An old water-bailiff once told me that on one occasion he found three live eels lying in a wet marsh, and on looking into a stagnant dike near by, he discovered on its muddy margin the tracks made by them when they left the water. There is suggested here a probable reason for these occasional overland movements. At times the water in a marsh dike becomes so stagnant that eels find it difficult to live in it so should there be no waterway to another dike, they attempt a journey across a wall or marsh to find one. According to Dr. Emerson, however, eels sometimes leave the rivers in a like way, a movement on their part not easy to account for.

And here, perhaps, it may not be out of place if I quote from some remarks on eels and eel-catching, made by the above-mentioned old water-bailiff. I will give them as nearly as possible in his own words:

"In my young time—that is, over fifty years ago—nearly all the eels caught in the Broadland rivers used to be taken to Yarmouth, where they were sold for a penny, three-halfpence, and twopence a pound. There were not the means of getting them to London then that there are now; but now that they can be delivered almost everywhere while they are fresh, nothing like such quantities are caught as there used to be. That is due to the better drainage of the marshes, for it was out of the undrained boggy land that the eels used to come, and not out of the sea, as some folk would have us believe. Oh yes, I know what people have said on that subject; but it makes no difference to me, for I know what I have seen. When I was fifteen years old I thought nothing of catching three stone of eels in a day and selling them at Yarmouth for two shillings a stone. Some of the eel-catchers made great catches when the eels were running, and only a few years ago I took between twenty-five and twenty-six stone out of Leathes' Ham [1] in one night. Another time I took seventy-four stone out of the same place by putting a net across the sluice that opens into Lake Lothing, and if I had wanted them I could have taken as many more. They were all what we call 'summer-scarums,' and when they were put into a barrel we had to keep them covered up or they would have jumped out."

Speaking of eel-picking, he said: "Most of the picking is done in open weather; but frosty weather, when the dikes and rivers are covered with ice, does not altogether put a stop to it. Some of the pickers cut holes in the ice, and spear the eels that come there to breathe. Generally three or four holes are cut, and the picker takes each hole in turn. I once got a bushel-skep full of eels in that way out of an ice-hole near a sluice. Sharp frosts, however, are bad for the eels, and

---

[1] A small arm of Lake Lothing, now cut off by the railway and connected with the lake by a sluice.

A NIGHT WITH AN EEL-CATCHER

hundreds of stones of them die under the ice, so that you may see them lying six or eight inches thick on the bottom of the dikes. The worst times for eels are when the ice is overlaid with snow, and no air can get under the edge of the ice near the banks of the dikes and rivers. The ice is generally broken there, you know, so that the air can draw underneath. Sometimes, when I was a boy, I used to lay out eel-lines for my father, who was a Breydon smelter. When I was quite a small lad, I went out one night with two bigger lads to lay out some out Reedham way. We were told not to put them near a spot where some men had been sheep-washing; but my companions would pay no heed to what had been said to them nor yet to me, and they lay the lines out just where they had been told not to. In the morning the lines were all tangled up with sheep's wool, and we had a rare trouble to get them clear of it. In those days I often went eel-babbing. The best time to go is when the roach and bream are spawning, and you should choose one of their spawning-grounds, for the eels feed on the spawn, and always come to where there is plenty of it. Are there more eel-setts now than there were when I was a boy? Yes, on the North River (the Bure), but not on the Waveney. It is some time since I was up the North River; but so far as I can recollect there are seven setts worked there. They are at Mile Bars, Ant Mouth, Horning, Hoveton Little Broad, the Dydles, Hoveton Big Broad, and Wroxham. Then on the Heighman River (the Thurne) there are setts at Thurne Mouth, Grapes Dike, Candle (Kendal) Dike, Deep Meadow Dike, and Horsey; and there are some, too, on the Ant, and at Reedham, Somerleyton, and May's, above Geldstone."[1]

About these and kindred matters the eel-catcher and I chatted until nearly midnight, by which time the rain

[1] It may be interesting to compare these sett-stations with those given on page 300.

had ceased and a few stars were showing in the moonless sky. The wind, too, had moderated; but when I stepped out on to the river-wall the willows by a neighbouring dikeside were still shaking showers of pattering drops on to the water whenever their leaves were rustled by the breeze. In the intervals of the lessening wind-gusts not a sound broke the silence of the night save a slight rippling where the surface water of the ebbing tide came in contact with the floats of the set; over the miles of marshes surrounding the fisherman's lone houseboat not a single bird or beast seemed to be moving. Not for the first time I found myself wondering that I had never heard of any accident befalling any one of the eel-catchers who during the autumn months spend so many nights alone in the midst of the marshes. There were so many ways in which mishap might occur to them, and a man with a broken limb might lie for hours utterly helpless and exposed to the worst of weather. But the men of the marshes are a self-reliant folk, and most of them have grown so accustomed to lonesome living that it has nothing particularly distasteful, far less any terrors, for them. Until they are seventy or even eighty years old, some of them will continue to live a semi-aquatic and isolated existence, and among such old men I have yet to meet one who, if he could begin his life again, would choose to spend it very differently. There is in their veins, perhaps, some strain of the old Viking blood which has come down to them through a long line of marsh-dwelling ancestors, descended from some of those Norse settlers who in pre-Norman days established themselves along the borders of the East Anglian marshlands.

Returning to the cabin, I was advised by the eel-catcher to try and get a few hours' sleep, he promising to wake me at dawn in time to see him raise and empty the poke of the net. So I stretched myself on one of the lockers, and for some time attempted, unsuccessfully, to follow his advice. But for a while I could not help opening my eyes at intervals to make sure that my companion was still awake, and I was still in doubt about it when my drowsiness deepened into a somewhat restless repose—restless owing to the uncanny creaking and groaning of the houseboat as the falling tide brought her in contact with some stakes driven into the sides of the creek, and also in consequence of the chill draughts which came in at the open cabin door.

A grey dawn was breaking over the marshes when I awoke, to find the eel-catcher fast asleep on the other locker. My first thought was of the sett; but a glance told me that it had been lowered to the bed of the river, and I knew that my companion had continued his vigil until the turn of the tide. The fire had burned low, and the chill of the early morning was even keener than that of the night so, stealing out of the cabin, I climbed on to the river-wall and walked briskly to and fro for a while to get the stiffness out of my limbs and some warmth into them. From up the river I could see two or three wherries approaching, bound for Yarmouth with cargoes from the inland staithes; smoke was ascending from the chimneys of the scattered marsh farm-steads and marshmen's cottages; and here and there the millmen had set their windmills going to lower the water in the rain-swollen dikes. Within a hundred yards of the houseboat a heron was standing by a dikeside, and from its alert attitude it was evident that it was looking for its breakfast; while from the upper branches of an alder carr across the river came the *sack, sack* of some fieldfares, which presently flew down to some gnarled thorn bushes which were bright with red berries. Although a grey morning, owing to a thin cloud-drift through which the sunlight would probably break in a little while, there was no mist; but the storm had left every grass-blade on the marshes beaded with dew-like raindrops, and the finely netted hammocks of the marsh spiders were sprinkled with an aqueous dust.

I was still pacing the river-wall between the creek and the eel-catcher's cottage, when a hail from the houseboat told me that the eel-catcher was awake and ready to examine his night's catch. So in order to do this we entered the marsh-boat and rowed out into midstream, taking with us a tub shaped like half a fish barrel. When near the middle of the river, my companion leaned over the side of the boat and lifted from the water a small wooden buoy fashioned out of a piece of driftwood, to this was attached a rope made fast to the submerged poke of the eel-sett. Hauling in this rope, it was not long before the poke was brought to the surface, and we saw at once that the night's catch, though not large, was a fairly good one, for at the end of the poke was a squirming mass of eels, while others were imprisoned in the spaces between the hoops of the bow net. Thus twined around each other and the rubbish which had found its way into the net during the night, they certainly did not present an attractive appearance, and one could easily understand the Celtic aversion to them; but the eel-catcher spoke as though he had quite an affection for them, and with a " There you are, my beauties," untied the end of the poke and began shaking them into the tub. With them were three or four small flounders, one or two tiny smelts, a number of shore crabs, and quite a pint of sea shrimps. The presence of the last-named might have seemed strange to one who had had no experience of the working of an eel-sett; but it is no rare thing for considerable quantities of these shrimps to be taken by the eel-catcher, who occasionally boils them and sells them in the marshland villages. On a November night half a bushel of shrimps was caught in a Somerleyton sett, fourteen miles from the sea. Rarely however, do any fresh-water fish other than eels find their way into an eel-catcher's net. Some years ago, when there were many complaints concerning the diminution in size and number of the coarse fish in the Norfolk rivers, it was urged that the eel-setts destroyed considerable quantities of them, and it was even proposed that eel-netting should be prohibited; but investigation proved that the eel-catchers were not guilty, and when the Norfolk and Suffolk Fisheries Act was passed no restriction was placed upon their means of livelihood.

Having emptied the poke, the eel-catcher tied it up again and let it sink to the bottom of the river, there to remain until he made another haul. He then went back to his houseboat and drew from the creek a wooden eel-trunk, perforated with a great number of holes large enough to admit the water into it, but not so large as to permit the eels to escape. Already it contained the results of his previous night's netting, but even with his latest "take" added, the quantity was not large enough to make it worth his while to drive to the nearest station with his eels and despatch them to London. In a day or two, perhaps, he would have enough to send off, and in return he would expect to receive fivepence or sixpence a pound for them. Meanwhile they would take no harm in the trunk, provided there was not a thunderstorm, in which case, he said, they might all die and become worthless.

By the time the eels had been safely transferred from the tub to the trunk the marshlands were bathed in bright sunlight. As we made our way back along the river-wall to the cottage, a little flock of goldfinches rose from a clump of tall, down-topped marsh thistles, while among the upper branches of an alder growing near the cottage, we saw a party of lesser redpolls—dainty little birds, whose nests are sometimes found by the marshmen in the sallow carrs and amid the dense scrub of twigs which often fringes the alder boles. The lapwings were returning from the ploughed lands, and had for companions in the rain-soaked marshes some of the first arrivals of the host of hooded crows which descends upon the east coast in October and November, and adds a frequent raucous note to the wild-life voices of the marshlands during the winter.

CHAPTER XXI

SUFFOLK CLIFFS AND SHORE BROADS

THE longest line of cliffs of which the Suffolk coast can boast is neither impressive on account of its heights nor remarkable for its bird-life, for nowhere do the cliffs rise to a greater height than between seventy and eighty feet, while the sand-martin seems to be the only bird that has its home in them. Nor are these cliffs particularly imposing in outline; they run out into no bold headland, they are divided by no dangerous or picturesque ravine, and it is only when erosion loosens huge masses of boulder clay from the summit, and these are poised for a while as ledges and pinnacles half-way down the sandy slopes, that a certain ruggedness is lent to them which relieves them of monotony, and gives them a temporary semblance to rocky heights of more renown. For the geologist they have considerable interest, owing to the richly fossiliferous deposits at their base; town and parish councils have been troubled about them, because their constant crumbling has threatened and destroyed not a few houses that once seemed well removed from danger; one or two farmers, too, have watched helplessly the gradual shrinking and vanishing of some of their fields; but to the casual rambler along their crest or base the cliffs present no striking feature, and the stretch of coast they border has more than once been pronounced one of the least attractive in East Anglia. Long acquaintance, however, together with the memory of ideal days of idle rambling, tends to give most of us a liking for certain scenes or places not in the least wonderful, and to such acquaintance, and to odd hours of idle strolling, I owe it that I can always find pleasure in visiting this unimpressive line of Suffolk cliffs.

When I first used to ramble along that shingly beach which is so largely made up of alien rock fragments from the boulder clay, I often used to meet with an old beachman, who in his day was the chief fossil-hunter in the neighbourhood. Every day, as soon as the tide had ebbed from the base of the cliffs, he would prowl along the beach, scanning carefully the beds of clay, ooze, sand, and gravel, in the hope of finding a tooth or bone of some extinct monster which had inhabited the North Sea area in those pre-glacial times when England was linked by marsh and forest with the Continent; and though weeks and often months would pass by without his being rewarded by finding a presentable relic, he succeeded in the course of years in collecting a remarkable series of mammalian remains, several of which eventually found their way into the British and Norwich Museums. Some of these fossils came from the Chillesford Beds, which are generally exposed at the base of the cliffs; but the greater part and most interesting of them came from the famous Forest Bed deposits, which are seldom well exposed unless the cliffs and beach have been recently subjected to a violent scouring by the waves. Then it is that bones of the rhinoceros, hippopotamus, giant elk, and elephant are brought to light—remains which the beachmen used to believe were those of animals drowned in the Flood. I remember that the old fossil-hunter used sometimes to believe that he had found a human bone, and he would exhibit it as such until some geologist came along and undeceived him, by explaining that it was the bone of a deer. But although such bones will no longer pass muster as antediluvian relics, and so, to some people, may be robbed of much of their interest, the geologist has been able to deduce from them, and the beds in which they occur, facts and theories which help to make one of the most fascinating chapters in the geological record.

As has been already stated, most of these bones come from the so-called Forest Bed series, which are exposed occasionally, not only at the base of the Suffolk cliffs, but also along the coast in the neighbourhood of Cromer. Since the time when the geology of East Anglia first began to receive the serious attention of diligent and scientific inquirers, no local strata have excited more interest or been more carefully examined than these remarkable deposits. How they came by their somewhat misleading name is evident when we turn to some of the early descriptions of one of the beds. "It consists," wrote R. C. Taylor[1] in 1827, "of an apparently continuous bed of vegetable substances.... At some points this bed consists of forest peat, containing fir cones and fragments of bones; in others, of woody clay; and elsewhere of large stools of trees, standing thickly together, the stems appearing to have been broken off about eighteen inches from their base. They are evidently rooted in the clay or sandy bed in which they originally grew, and their stems, branches, and leaves lie around them, flattened by the pressure of from thirty to three hundred feet of diluvial deposits. It is not possible to say how far inland this subterranean forest extends; but that it is not a mere external belt is obvious from the constant exposure and removal of new portions at the base of the cliffs." Taylor then goes on to state—as incorrectly as when he speaks of the deposits marking the site of a "subterranean forest"—that these deposits indicate the southern boundary of a submarine forest which had long engaged the attention of geologists, and which could be traced across the Wash and the Fens, and along the Lincolnshire coast as far as the Humber.

[1] *The Geology of East Norfolk*, by R. C. Taylor (1827), pp. 21, 22.

Generally speaking, Taylor's conclusions were accepted by Sir Charles Lyell, who described the Forest Bed as consisting of the stumps of trees standing erect, with their roots penetrating the soil in which they grew. "They mark," he says,[1] "the site of a forest which existed there for a long time, since, beside the erect trunks of trees, some of them two and three feet in diameter, there is a vast accumulation of vegetable matter in the immediately overlying clays." But what might well puzzle geologists who accepted the existence of an ancient forest *in situ*, was the presence in the Forest Bed not only of remains of elephants, stags, hyenas, and cave-bears, but of such semi-aquatic animals as the hippopotamus and beaver, and marine mammals, as whales, narwhals, and dolphins. The finding of bones of such animals in deposits representing the remains of a forest was admitted to be most puzzling. Taylor, who seems to have been a Diluvialist, dismisses the subject with the conclusion that forest and animals were all buried at the time of a common catastrophe, namely, an "eruption of the waters." Sir Charles Lyell, after drawing attention to the fact of the Forest Bed being covered, in the cliffs, by a series of sands and clays representing alternations of fluviatile and marine strata, suggests that these imply that "the old forest land, which may at first have been considerably elevated above the level of the sea, had sunk down so as to be occasionally overflowed by a river, and at other times by the salt waters of an estuary." He assigned the deposits to the Post-Pliocene but Pre-Glacial period when Great Britain was united with the Continent.

The name of the Rev. John Gunn is inseparably associated with the elucidation of Forest Bed problems. Mr. Gunn was rector of Irstead, a small Broadland parish not far from the Norfolk coast, and he devoted many years of his life to securing the fine collection of Forest

[1] *The Antiquity of Man*, by Sir Charles Lyell (1863), p. 214.

Bed fossils now preserved at Norwich. In a paper read before the Geological Society, he stated that the earliest deposit or "first phase," as he called it, of the Forest Bed consists of an argillaceous sand and gravel, or a compound of both, which appears to have been deposited in an estuary. It was on this esturine soil, he believed, that the "forest"—everyone still took a forest *in situ* for granted—grew. This forest, according to Professor Boyd Dawkins, "covered a large portion of the area of the North Sea," and "was mainly composed of sombre Scotch firs and dark clustering yews, relieved in the summer by the lighter-tinted foliage of the spruce and the oak, and in winter by the silvery gleam of the birches, that clustered thickly with the alders in the marshes, and stood out from a dense undergrowth of sloes and hazels."

What does not seem to have struck any of the foregoing writers as strange, is Taylor's assertion that the trunks of the trees found in the Forest Bed appeared to have been broken off about eighteen inches from their bases, nor does it seem to have occurred to any one that an explanation was needed of the fact that most of the fossil bones discovered in these deposits were sharply fractured, and no complete skeletons were brought to light.

The probable significance of these facts is suggested by Mr. F. W. Harmer, who is intimately acquainted not only with the geology of East Anglia, but with that of Holland and Belgium. Without going into the technicalities of the subject, which are fully dealt with in his papers read before the Geologists' Association, it may be stated that Mr. Harmer considers that the presence in the Pliocene beds of East Anglia of certain mineral substances of a like character to those met with in the Rhenish drifts of Holland, indicates that at the time of the deposition of the Waltonian Crag and other later beds of the Pliocene period, Great Britain was connected with the Continent, and the channel of the Rhine extended from the neighbourhood of the present Hook of Holland to Walton in Essex, where it turned northward and traversed East Anglia, at one time crossing the district now represented by the valleys of Broadland, and afterwards, during the Forest Bed period, taking a course farther eastward. In his own words:[1] "During the period represented by the estuarine deposits of the Forest Bed the Rhine seems to have swung round in a great bend from Kessingland to Cromer, following more or less the present trend of the coast. It is on the convex bank of a stream, as the river yachtsmen of Norfolk know, that shoals and mud-banks accumulate. In such a position was the sediment of the great river deposited, and its wreckage stranded. In this way, I suggest, we may most reasonably explain the great abundance in one small area of tree-stumps, and of bones and teeth of elephants and other animals." The fact of the general character of the mammalian fauna of the Forest Bed being distinctly southern, and its being represented by isolated and often fragmentary bones and teeth, points, he adds, " to the remains being those of the fauna of some part of the Rhine valley towards the south, rather than that of East Anglia," and he suggests, as a possible explanation of their presence in the Forest Bed, that they may be those of herds of animals which were overtaken while browsing on the low grounds bordering the river, by sudden and violent floods. This would account for the fragmentary state in which they are found; also for the broken tree-trunks, and the indications they retain of having been drifted—for it is now generally admitted that the early geologists were mistaken in stating that the trees are found with their roots penetrating the soil in which they grew.

Identification[2] of many of the vegetable remains

[1] *Proc. of the Geol. Ass.*, vol. xvii. p. 449.
[2] Chiefly by Mr. Clement Reid.

found in the Forest Bed has enabled us to form some idea of the scenery and flora of the ancient Rhine banks of East Anglia and of the wide plain that connected England with the Continent in the days when the Rhine was an East Anglian river. Where we now see the North Sea there were forests of fir, spruce, yew, beech, elm, and oak, having an undergrowth of hawthorn, blackthorn, hazel, and dogwood. Bordering the river were wide marshes similar to those of Broadland to-day. There the alder, birch, and more than one species of willow flourished, the royal fern expanded its tall fronds, and the creamy meadow rue, golden buttercup, slender hog's fennel, and purple-flowered marsh woundwort bloomed. The river inlets and lagoons were fringed with reeds, and many of the same species of rush and sedge which are common in England to-day; while among the wild flowers that grew by the waterside were the gipsy-wort, forget-me-not, marsh marigold, and pink-belled bogbean. The broad leaves of the yellow water-lily covered the surface of the inlets, from the beds of which arose the bur-marigold, the water milfoil, and the curious mare's-tail, while beneath the surface the aquatic vegetation consisted largely of pond-weeds and hornwort.

What the mammalian fauna of these woods and plains was like, I have tried to show in the first chapter of this book. In the woods roamed roe deer and red deer, wolves, bears, and boars; squirrels frisked among the tree boughs, and martens lurked amid the undergrowth. On the plains were herds of wild horses; beavers built their dams across the narrow streams; voles made their tunnels in the banks. Contemporary with these still-existing species were the straight-tusked elephant and *Elephas meridionalis*, the latter a beast of enormous size; the cave bear, which was considerably larger than the brown bear; a magnificent elk or deer which must have rivalled in size the huge Irish elk; and three species of rhinoceros. With these existed the hippopotamus, a hyena identical with the existing South African species, the musk-ox, bison, and glutton. As regards the finding of remains of such animals as the hippopotamus, wild boar, and horse, intermingled with those of such northern species as the musk-ox and glutton, Mr. Harmer's suggestion that some of the remains represent "the fauna of some part of the Rhine valley towards the south," seems a reasonable one. The presence of nine species of marine mammals, including whales, the grampus, narwhal, and dolphin, may, as the same authority remarks, be due to shoals of these animals having made their way into the old estuary of the Rhine, and become stranded there when the water receded after high floods.

Mr. Harmer is content with tracing the course of the ancient Rhine as far as Norfolk. Cavaliere W. P. Jervis, the Curator of the Royal Italian Industrial Museum at Turin, has suggested, in a paper read before the Victoria Institute, that it can be traced much farther. Thirty-three miles north-west of Cromer and about fifteen miles east of Grimsby, there exists in the bed of the sea a "distinctly marked, tortuous, submerged river valley, 23 miles long by 2 miles broad, running towards the north." It is known to the North Sea fishermen as the Silver Pit, and Cavaliere Jervis is strongly of the opinion that it formed part of the ancient course of the Rhine, or, as he calls it, the "Palæorhine." That the rest of the submerged river channel should have become obliterated, he thinks not at all strange, "seeing that it ran principally through Tertiary strata with low banks." The Silver Pit, he suggests, may mark the passage of the river through chalk rocks. Nor is he content with this. The soundings of the North Sea enable him, he believes, to trace the Palæorhine northward as far as the Orkney and Shetland Isles, between which there is a deep-water channel that was also, in all probability, a part of the river which finally entered the Atlantic about fifty miles west of Shetland. This means that the

Rhine was at one time about double its present length; and Cavaliere Jervis looks upon the Scheldt, Thames, Humber, Forth, and Tay as being portions of its old tributaries! Enough has been written, I think, to prove the truth of my statement, that the Suffolk cliffs are connected with one of the most fascinating chapters in the geological record.

In summer the sand martins have large colonies in these cliffs, generally well out of reach in the upper part of some sheer face of middle glacial sand; and late in the summer a good many finches come to feed on the slopes, which are scantily clothed with ox-tongue, hawk-weeds, wild carrot, and other weeds produced by seeds that have fallen or been blown from the fields above; but as a rule it is only in autumn that the bird-life of this sea-wasted stretch of Suffolk coast is sufficiently interesting to attract more than passing attention. In September, some of the earlier of our winter visitors put in an appearance, and a few of them settle on the cliff slopes to rest for a while after their over-sea passage; about the same time, in some years, southward-bound waders may be seen working their way along the beach; but it is generally in October that the hosts of autumn immigrants begin to pour in, and many of them first alight on this part of the coast. Among them are not infrequently a good number of shore-larks, small parties of which may be encountered for days together, sometimes taking short flights to and fro along the sloping face of the cliffs, but more often feeding on the tiny shell-fish that are found amid the flotsam and seaweed stranded among the fallen masses of boulder clay. With them consort at times a few snow-buntings, easily distinguished by their black and white plumage, save when they alight upon the shingle; but these seldom stay long on this barren tract of coast, though they are often plentiful on the salt marshes to the south of it.

About midway between Pakefield and Kessingland there is a deep cleft in the cliffs, the sides of which are almost hidden by gnarled and stunted bushes. Occasionally during October this bushy cleft is alive with gold-crests, great numbers of which distribute themselves along this part of the coast during the early days of the month, soon to make their way inland to more congenial winter quarters. This, the tiniest of our wild birds, is a great favourite with the North Sea fishermen, upon whose boats flocks of gold-crests—or herring-spinks, as the fishermen call them—sometimes alight in foggy weather, and show a tameness and friendliness which is, no doubt, largely due to wing-weariness. That immense numbers of these brave little migrants come to grief while crossing the sea there can be little doubt, for only a few of them can be fortunate enough to find safety on the fishing boats when the fog rolls down upon them, or they encounter an adverse wind; but I cannot remember ever seeing a gold-crest among the dead birds washed up on the beach after a storm. But small birds are rarely numbered among these stranded victims of the storm and fog, probably because they are seldom overlooked by the vigilant gulls which are always scanning the surface of the sea for such tempting morsels of flotsam food. As for the plucky little gold-crests, not only do many of them come to grief while crossing the sea, but at times, when they reach land during dark or foggy nights, some of them dash themselves against the unseen cliffs and so kill themselves; while occasionally some tired mite of a bird dies of exhaustion after reaching the shore, and is found lying on some sandy cliff ledge, or on the open beach. And here it may be mentioned, that when the East Anglian coast had its share of the great immigration of painted lady butterflies which occurred in the autumn of 1903, hundreds of these butterflies were killed by dashing themselves against these Suffolk cliffs.

Larks and finches, fieldfares and redwings, and other autumn immigrants, often flock in unobserved, and we are

AUTUMN IMMIGRANTS.—HOODED CROWS AND SNOW BUNTINGS

not aware of their arrival until we see them in the hedgerows and coast-bordering fields. But it is not so with the rooks, crows, and jackdaws, straggling flocks of which come flying in day after day for a week or more, arriving in a leisurely fashion, apparently quite unwearied by their over-sea flight. This corvine immigration is usually most noticeable on the North Norfolk coast; but almost every year, large flocks of rooks and crows pass over this line of Suffolk cliffs on their way to the inland fields and marshes. Very few of them alight immediately on reaching land, and those that do so are almost invariably hooded crows, small parties and solitary examples of which spend the winter in scavenging up and down the shore, finding plenty of food along the tide-mark and on the salt marshes, and occasionally a daintier dinner in the shape of a dead rabbit on the sandhills. As soon as the tide begins to ebb, this harsh-voiced bird flies heavily down to the beach, where its footprints can sometimes be traced along the sand for a mile or more; and there is nothing eatable cast up by the sea which escapes its eye. But should a violent storm occur soon after its arrival on our shore, it frequents the beach all day long; for it is then that the tide-mark is often strewn with dead migrants, amid which Hoody is as happy as a ghoul among the tombs. And should the winged victim of some wanton gull-shooter float helplessly on the sea, or hop feebly up the beach to die in some hollow of the cliffs, it is Hoody who never fails to detect the cripple, and wait patiently for the meal the gunner has provided for him. But along the coast of easternmost England the hooded crow need never be in want of a dinner, for almost every wave that breaks upon the beach, casts up some flotsam food thrown overboard by the fishermen or the cooks of the steamships that are continually passing up and down the North Sea. For this reason, our winter visitor Hoody, ghoul though he be, is a useful bird—an unpaid scavenger, who only turns thief and poacher when times are hard with him. And he, too, notwithstanding the leisurely way in which he makes his autumn crossing, is sometimes glad to rest on a lightship or steamer, where, if the crew treat him well, he will meet their advances half-way, and come to them to be fed.

All through the winter, gulls may be seen working their way up and down this part of the coast, but it is only in the early morning, before the beachmen are abroad, that they alight on the beach at the foot of the cliffs, though they often do so along the quieter stretch of shore to the southward. Many of them appear to make regular journeys between Lowestoft Harbour and the sluice which drains the Benacre marshes, probably because there is generally plenty of floating food to be found either at the one place or the other. In the neighbourhood of the sluice, indeed, an interesting variety of sea and shore birds may often be met with, and among them, when they are feeding on the beach, are often a considerable number of rooks, which, in the autumn especially, fly daily down to this part of the coast from the Somerleyton woodlands. Crossing the line of cliffs, too, is one of the regular flight-lines of the gulls, which during the daytime feed on the coast and inland fields and marshes. Every day, save in stormy weather, for an hour or more before sunset, hundreds, and sometimes thousands, of these gulls may be seen passing seaward over the cliffs, and the herring-fishers say they are bound for the fishing grounds, where they will spend the night, feed on the herrings which fall from the nets, and return to the land in the morning. In stormy weather, should the wind blow from off the sea, a few greater black-backed gulls come inshore, and for hours together they will ride head to wind, on almost motionless wings, high up above the cliffs; but as soon as the wind moderates, they disappear. A farm-hand who had often noticed these " great gulls " while he had been ploughing the fields near the edge of the cliffs, told me that he once saw one of them die in mid-air. It was poised with others on wide-spread wings above the cliffs, when suddenly it "toppled over" in the air, and came down with closed wings, striking the beach below the cliffs with a thud. After striking the sand it did not move again, and an hour afterwards, when the farm-hand climbed down the cliffs to look at it, he found that it was dead. It was, he said, a "full-grown" bird, but in so poor a condition that he could "feel all its bones." It came down, he added, just as though it had been shot; but there was no gunner near at the time, nor could he find any sign of the bird having been in any way injured.

Southward of Kessingland there is another stretch of wasting coast, consisting of shingly beach, sandhills, fenny marshlands, small tracts of heathland, and, at Covehithe and Dunwich, other low lines of sandy and gravelly cliffs upon which the sea encroaches continually, so that almost every year a fresh footpath has to be trodden along the summit of the cliffs to take the place of one that has crumbled away. The country-folk often tell you of old wells being exposed as the cliffs fall away, and their stories of vanished homesteads, together with the historical evidence of the sea's destruction of towns and villages, tend to increase the lonesomeness of this somewhat sombre coast; but the archæologist tells us that these so-called wells were nothing more nor less than Roman middens, and that they belonged to the vanished villas of a Roman settlement which stood on the higher ground of Covehithe. And we hear from him, too, while he points to the human bones embedded in these Suffolk cliffs, the story of the destruction of Dunwich, that "mighty city of the East," with its massive walls and gates and many churches; and, again, as we journey southward with him, we hear of how at Walton, a Roman fortress which was probably as large as the great stone-walled camp at Burgh Castle, has vanished completely beneath the waves. Mingled with the sand and pebbles of the shore, on to which they have fallen from the cliffs, we can always find the stone implements of primitive man; and after winter storms we see the beach strewn with large masses of peat from the Neolithic land surface which now lies submerged by the sea. Everywhere there are signs that for ages the sea has been an insatiable destroyer, and everywhere there are signs that the story of its ravage is as yet only half told.

Along this stretch of coast between Kessingland and Southwold are the three Suffolk shore Broads, named Benacre, Covehithe, and Easton, after the respective parishes they most closely adjoin. In the case of the two last-named, only a hundred yards or so of beach separates them from the sea; but Benacre Broad, which is bordered by the marshlands of the Benacre valley, lies farther inland, and little is seen of it from the shore. None of the three has much resemblance to any of the well-known Norfolk Broads; Covehithe and Easton, indeed, being bordered on the seaward side by the beach, have considerable likeness to large salt pools left by the falling tide; while Benacre is much smaller now than it was twenty years ago, and is so "grown up" with reeds that very little water remains. Partly owing to this, but chiefly to the difficulty in securing the essential quietude, the Benacre duck decoy has not been worked of late years. Of the three, the largest and most interesting is Easton, in the immediate neighbourhood of which was the most easterly point of England until coast erosion robbed the parish of that distinction. This Broad, bordered on its landward side by a small tract of woodland, but open on every other to the winds of this bleak coast, has a certain wild beauty about it which is not without its charm. The water in this and Covehithe Broad is always more or less brackish, and both are probably partly fed by salt springs; while into both the sea waves break at times of abnormally high tides.

The largest flocks of wild-fowl I have ever met with

on the Suffolk coast have been those I have sometimes seen on Easton Broad, where as recently as the beginning of December 1905, there were assembled, at noon of a grey windless day, over two thousand duck, teal, grebes, and coots, Covehithe Broad, hardly half a mile distant, being at the same time quite deserted, save by a couple of herring gulls which were swimming on the open water, and a great black-backed gull which was foraging alone along its shores. Upon quite two-thirds of the surface of Easton the fowl were resting so closely together that there was scarcely a square yard without its bird, while among the fringing reeds, which sheltered several smaller pools, there were probably half as many more. On my approaching the north end of the Broad, a few of the coots made for the shelter of the reeds; but the majority of them, together with the duck and grebe, slowly made for the south end of the Broad, where they became so massed together as almost to hide the water. Such flocks are rare now on Easton, owing to the encroachment of the sea having brought the beach almost on to the edge of the Broad, and thus made a public way within a few yards of the water; but years ago some of the best wildfowling to be had along the coast was provided by the Broad. Now it is on account of the occasional glimpses of rarer wild life it often affords that Easton deserves greater attention from the naturalist than any other Suffolk Broad.

During the autumn passage of waders along the coast, many tired birds stop to rest and feed along the margin of the Broad, especially after dark, windy nights, during which many of them have probably spent hours in flying, dazzled and bewildered, above the Yarmouth and Lowestoft street lights; soon after daybreak, should you be awake and abroad early enough, you may chance to catch some of them sleeping, standing in quaint attitudes on the smooth flats of ooze and sand. The knots and dunlins are at such times the best of friends; for they feed and go to sleep together, though when alarmed they almost invariably part from each other and fly off in separate flocks. With them consorts, at this season of the year, the little curlew-sandpiper, which is a far commoner visitor to the Suffolk shore Broads than is generally imagined, but is often mistaken for a dunlin. Daintier birds than any of them are the tiny little stints, which reminds me that once—and only once—in October 1899, on creeping round a reed bed bordering Easton Broad, I caught a momentary glimpse of a small bird feeding amid some stranded refuse, and which I recognised, by the white on its tail, as a Temminck's stint.

Goosanders, smew, and a merganser are among the "hard weather" visitors which have been known to frequent for a while the quiet waters of the Suffolk shore Broads, and not all of them have been permitted to return again to the sea. On Covehithe a red-throated diver was known to remain for the greater part of a week, notwithstanding the greater attractions of Easton; only when disturbed by a stroller along the beach did it fly out to sea for a while and swim about within a few hundred yards of the shore. Grebes—great crested, red-necked, and Sclavonian—have been accounted for by shore-gunners during the autumn and winter, and not a few other "odd birds" have fallen to gunners who were on the look-out for duck; but at least one fine bird that favoured Easton with a visit, escaped unharmed from that part of the coast.

It was during the morning of a fine but grey winter day soon after Christmas that I approached Easton Broad from the north, keeping on the seaward side of the beach shingle bank so as to be able to get near the Broad without disturbing the fowl. On reaching a point opposite the Broad, I crept cautiously up a slight slope from which a good view of the open water could be obtained, and from this point of vantage I scanned the surface of the Broad in order to detect any strange visitor. Almost immediately I caught sight of a bird as big as a goose swimming well out in the midst of the open water, and with the aid of my field-glasses I was not long in convincing myself that it was a great northern diver. Around it were several hundred ducks and coots; but I noticed that they kept at a respectful distance from the big stranger, allowing him plenty of clear water whichever way he chose to go. And well they might, for even at a distance of a hundred yards or more, the sharp black bill of the diver had a formidable appearance, and that the bird can use it with damaging effect has been testified by more than one American gunner who has handled a wounded loon. For a quarter of an hour or more I watched the movements of the bird from behind the shingle ridge; but evidently it was resting, for it did not dive, nor did it swim with any vigour. Once it " sat up " on its tail and flapped its wings once or twice, and I hoped then to hear that wild cackling cry, " the laugh of the loon "; but it settled down again and contented itself with moving slowly in a kind of circle in the midst of the Broad, at the same time turning its head lazily from side to side.

As there was no chance of getting a nearer view of the bird, I made up my mind to reveal myself, trusting that its behaviour when alarmed would be more interesting than it had been while it was at peace. So I rose suddenly to my feet and stepped on to the crest of the ridge. The coots near the seaward side of the Broad at once began to swim towards the reeds, while a good many of the ducks took flight inland, afterwards doubling round the south end of the Broad and flying out to sea; but the diver, though the alarm of the fowl must have warned him of apparent danger, simply ceased swimming, and seemed at first in no way disconcerted. But in a few seconds I noticed that it seemed to be growing smaller, and with the aid of my glasses I could see that it was sinking in the water, and it went on sinking slowly until the water covered it between the neck and back, and only the ridge of the back was visible. Then I took a step forward towards the edge of the Broad, and in an instant the diver had vanished, scarcely leaving a ripple to mark the spot where it had disappeared. But I knew that it must soon come to the surface, for a pool like Easton is a very small place compared with the wild wide northern lakes where the loon has its home, and from the spot where it had dived it was hardly possible for it to swim more than fifty yards in any direction without coming into shallow water; so I watched the southern end of the Broad, where I looked for its reappearance. And there it rose again, scattering the frightened coots in all directions, and at once commenced to beat the water with its strong wings preparatory to taking flight. It was a long time in getting "under weigh," and the turmoil it made as it churned up the water was greater than that made by a score of scurrying coots; but, after beating along till it was within a few yards of the edge of the Broad, and leaving behind it a white trail of broken water which set ripples running towards the shore, it lifted itself from the water, and with strong, rapid, wing-beats rose in the air, gaining speed and ascending higher every moment, as it sped away over the sea. From the top of the ridge I watched its flight over the grey waves and under the grey sky, and it seemed to me that so long as it was in sight it kept rising higher and higher. And when it vanished it appeared to be in the sky rather than in the mist which hung over the sea.

APPENDICES

EAST ANGLIAN BIRD NAMES

A GOOD many of the bird names in this list have been already given in the following books: *Observations on the Fauna of Norfolk*, by the Rev. R. Lubbock (1879 edition, with notes by Mr. T. Southwell); *The Birds of Norfolk*, by Henry Stevenson (3 vols., the third completed by Mr. T. Southwell, 1866, 1870, and 1890); *Glossary of the Dialect and Provincialisms of East Anglia*, by J. G. Nall, 1866; *Birds, Beasts, and Fishes of Broadland*, by P. H. Emerson, 1895; *A Catalogue of the Birds of Great Yarmouth*, by A. H. Patterson, 1901; *Nature in Eastern Norfolk*, by A. H. Patterson, 1905; A List of the Vertebrate Animals found in the Neighbourhood of Thetford, by W. G. Clarke (*Transactions of the Norfolk and Norwich Naturalists' Society*, vol. vi., pp. 300–327); and *Broad Norfolk*, edited by C. H., 1893.

Air Goat—Common Snipe.
Alexandra or Alexandrine Plover—Kentish Plover.
Arps—Tufted Duck.
Awl Bird—Avocet.

Baldie Coot—Coot.
Banjo-bill—Spoonbill.
Bargoose—Sheld-duck.
Barley-bird—Nightingale.
Bay Duck—Sheld-duck.
Beam-bird—Spotted Flycatcher.
Beck—Shoveler.

Bee-bird—Spotted Flycatcher.
Bergander—Sheld-duck.
Betty-tit—Titmouse.
Big Razor-grinder—Nightjar.
Billy Whit—Barn Owl.
Black-breasted Plover—Grey Plover.
Blackcap—Reed Bunting and Marsh Tit.
Black Curlew—Glossy Ibis.
Black Duck—Common Scoter.
Black Goose—Bernicle and Brent Goose.
Black Poker—Tufted Duck.

Black Sandpiper—Green Sandpiper.
Black-toed Gull—Richardson's Skua.
Blood Linnet—Linnet.
Blood-olph—Bullfinch.
Blue Dar—Black Tern.
Bluegill—Scaup.
Blue Hawk—Merlin and Male Hen Harrier.
Blue-jacket—Montagu's Harrier.
Blue Pigeon, Blue Rocker—Stockdove.
Boatswain—Pomatorhine Skua.
Bottle-bump—Bittern.
Bottle Tom—Long-tailed Tit.
Bramble Finch—Brambling.
Brown Owl—Tawny Owl.
Bunt Lark—Common Bunting.
Burrow-bird—Wheatear.
Burrow Duck—Sheld-duck.
Butcher-bird—Red-backed Shrike.
Buttle—Bittern.
Buzzard Hawk—Common, Rough-legged, and Honey Buzzard.

Caddie or Cadder—Jackdaw.
Cambridge Godwit—Greenshank.
Car-Swallow—Black Tern.
Chit Perl—Lesser Tern.
Chummy—House Sparrow.
Clinker—Avocet.
Clod-bird—Common Bunting.
Cob—Common Gull.
Cobble-bird—Hawfinch.
Cobbler's Awl—Avocet.
Common Finch—Chaffinch.
Coney Chuck—Wheatear.
Cormorel—Cormorant.
Cow-bird—Yellow Wagtail.
Cracker—Pintail.
Cream-coloured Mow—Glaucus or Iceland Gull.
Crick or Cricket Teal—Garganey.
Cuckoo-leader or Cuckoo's Mate—Wryneck.

Danish Crow—Hooded Crow.
Deave-dipper—Little Grebe.
Denchman—Hooded Crow.
Devlin, Davelin, Develing, or Devilding—Swift.
Dickey-bird—Oyster-catcher.
Didlymot—Guillemot.
Didopper—Grebe.
Dipeere—Tern.
Dive-and-Dop or Divy-duck—Little Grebe.
Dobchick—Little Grebe.

Double Scoter—Velvet Scoter.
Double Snipe—Great Snipe.
Dow—Dove and Pigeon.
Dow Fulfer—Fieldfare.
Draw-water—Goldfinch.
Dun-bird—Pochard.

Easterling—Wigeon.
English Fulfer—Mistle Thrush.

Felt—Fieldfare.
Firetail—Redstart.
Flapjack—Lapwing.
Foreign Fulfer—Fieldfare.
Frank—Heron.
French Fulfer—Fieldfare.
French Heron—Bittern (Essex).
French Linnet—Twite.
French Mavish—Redwing.
French Partridge—Red-legged Partridge.
French Sparrow—Tree Sparrow.
Fulfer—Mistle Thrush.
Full-eyed Plover—Golden and Grey Plover.
Full Snipe—Common Snipe.
Furzechuck—Whinchat and Stonechat.
Furzehacker—Whinchat and Stonechat.

Game-hawk—Peregrine.
Gant—Gannet.
Gargle Teal—Garganey.
Gill-hooter—Barn Owl.
Golden-eye—Tufted Duck.
Gool-finch—Yellow Bunting.
Green Linnet or Green-olph—Greenfinch.
Green Plover—Lapwing.
Grey-back—Scaup.
Grey Crow—Hooded Crow.
Grey Duck—Gadwall.
Grey Goose—Grey-lag, Bean, or Pink-footed Goose.
Grey Gull—Immature Great Black-backed Gull.
Grey Linnet—Linnet.
Grey Mallard—Gadwall.
Grey Owl—Tawny Owl.
Ground Lark—Meadow Pipit.
Ground Oven—Willow Wren and Chiffchaff.
Guler—Yellow Bunting.
Gull-chaser—Skua.

Half-Curlew—Whimbrel.

APPENDIX I

Half-fowl—Teal and Wigeon.
Half-Snipe—Jack Snipe.
Hard Fowl—Scaup.
Harnsee—Heron.
Hart Duck or Heart Duck—Gadwall.
Hatcher—Hedge Sparrow.
Hayjack—Whitethroat and Blackcap.
Heave-jar—Nightjar.
Hedge Betty—Hedge Sparrow.
Hern, Hernsher—Heron.
Herring Loon—Great Northern Diver.
Herring Spink—Gold-crest.
Hobby-bird—Wryneck.
Holland Goose—Gannet.
Home-leg Goose—Grey-lag Goose.
Hornpie—Lapwing.

Jacks—Jack Snipe.
Jar—Nightjar.

Kentishman or Kentish Crow—Hooded Crow.
Kertlutock—Shoveler.
King Harry—Goldfinch.
Kitty—Black-headed Gull.

Land-Bunting—Corn-Bunting.
Laughing-Goose — White-fronted Goose.
Little Mealy Duck — Long-tailed Duck.
Little Rattlewing — Buffel-headed Duck.
Little Sandpiper—Common Sandpiper.
Long-legged Plover—Black-winged Stilt.
Long-tailed Caper—Long-tailed Tit.
Loon—Red-throated Diver.

Madge—Barn Owl.
Magloon—Great Northern Diver.
Marsh Owl—Short-eared Owl.
Martin-hawk—Montagu's Harrier.
Martin Snipe—Green Sandpiper.
Mavish—Song Thrush.
May-bird—Whimbrel.
Mealy Bird—Long-tailed Duck.
Meslin-bird—Fieldfare.
Molberry—Pomatorhine Skua.
Moor Buzzard—Marsh Harrier.
Morillon—Golden-eye.
Mouse Hawk—Short-eared Owl.
Mud Lark—Rock Pipit.
Mud Plover—Grey Plover.
Mud Snipe—Green Sandpiper.
Mullet-hawk—Osprey (Essex).

Musket — Male Sparrow-hawk (Essex).
Mussel Duck—Common Scoter.

Night Hawk—Nightjar.
Nope—Bullfinch.

Olph—Bullfinch.
Orstril—Osprey.
Oven-builder — Willow Wren and Chiffchaff.
Oxbird—Dunlin.
Ox-eye—Great Tit.

Parrot-beak—Puffin.
Partridge-hawk—Sparrow-hawk.
Peewit or Peeweep—Lapwing.
Penny Wagtail—Pied Wagtail.
Perl—Common Tern.
Pick—Godwit.
Pickcheese—Blue Tit.
Picker—Green Woodpecker.
Pied Wigeon—Garganey.
Pigmy-Curlew—Curlew-Sandpiper.
Pintail Smee—Pintail Duck.
Pit Martin—Sand Martin.
Pocka—Scaup (Lynn).
Poker or Pocka—Pochard.
Polly-Wash-Dish—Pied Wagtail.
Pudding-poke—Long-tailed Tit.
Puit-Gull—Black-headed Gull.
Purre—Stint.
Pywipe—Lapwing.

Rainbird—Green Woodpecker.
Rattle-wing—Golden-Eye.
Rattler—Golden-eye.
Razor-grinder—Nightjar and Grasshopper Warbler.
Red Godwit—Bar-tailed Godwit.
Red-headed Pocka — Common Pochard (Lynn).
Red Knot—Knot.
Redleg—Redshank.
Red-Olph—Bullfinch.
Red Linnet—Linnet.
Reed-bird—Sedge Warbler.
Reed-chucker—Reed Warbler.
Reed Pheasant—Bearded Tit.
Reed Sparrow—Reed Bunting.
Ring Dotterel—Ringed Plover.
Ring-Dow—Wood-pigeon.
Ringtail — Montagu's Harrier and Female Hen Harrier.
Robin Hawk—Crossbill.
Rock Dove—Stockdove.
Rodge—Gadwall.
Runner—Land or Water Rail.

Saddleback—Greater Black-backed Gull.
Sand Linnet, Sand Lark—Sanderling.
Sand Pigeon—Stockdove.
Sandpiper—Stone Curlew.
Sandy-head—Pochard.
Sawbill—Goosander.
Sawyer—Merganser.
Scammell—Godwit.
Scissor-grinder — Grasshopper Warbler.
Scotch Goose—Brent.
Scoulton Puit or Scoulton Gull—Black-headed Gull.
Scribbling Finch—Corn Bunting.
Sea Cob—Common Gull.
Sea Crow—Herring Gull.
Sea Lark—Ringed Plover.
Sea Parrot—Puffin.
Sea Pheasant—Pintail and Long-tailed Duck.
Sea-pie—Oyster-catcher.
Sea Swallow—Common Tern.
Sedge Marine—Sedge Warbler.
Shepherd-bird—Wheatear.
Shoe-awl—Avocet.
Shoeing-horn—Avocet.
Shovel-bill—Shoveler.
Shriek-owl—Swift.
Shrieker—Black-tailed Godwit, and Common Sandpiper.
Shrimp-picker—Tern.
Skeleton—Green Sandpiper.
Smee—Wigeon.
Snake-bird—Wryneck.
Snow-bird, Snow-fleck, Snow-man, Snow-sparrow—Snow Bunting.
Solitary Snipe—Great Snipe.
Speck or Woodspeck—Green-Woodpecker.
Spink—Chaffinch.
Spoonbill Duck—Shoveler.
Sprat Loon—Red-throated Diver.
Sprat-Mow — Herring Gull and Common Gull.
Stag—Wren.
Stan'gale Hawk—Kestrel (Essex).
Starn—Tern.
Steel Duck—Immature Merganser.
Stint—Dunlin.
Stonechuck—Stonechat.
Stone Falcon—Merlin.
Stonehatch—Ringed Plover.
Stone-runner—Ringed Plover.
Summer Lamb—Common Snipe.

Summer Snipe—Common Sandpiper.
Summer Teal—Garganey.
Swing-tree—Long-tailed Tit.

Tangle-picker—Turnstone.
Teapot—Gold-crest.
Terner—Tern.
Teuke—Redshank, Curlew, Whimbrel, and Godwit.
Thick-knee—Stone Curlew.
Thistle-finch—Goldfinch.
Titlark—Meadow Pipit.
Titmeg—Wren.
Tittereen—Wren.
Titterel—Whimbrel.
Tom Tit—Wren.
Turkey Buzzard—Common, Rough-legged, and Honey Buzzard.
Tyste—Black Guillemot.

Utick—Whinchat.

Vewer—Wigeon.

Wall-bird—Spotted Flycatcher.
Water-hen—Moor-hen.
Weasel Duck—Smew.
Wet-my-lip—Quail.
Wheatsel-bird—Cock Chaffinch.
Whew or Whewer—Wigeon.
Whiffling Pocka — Tufted Duck (Lynn).
Whilk—Scoter.
Whim—Wigeon.
Whistling Plover—Golden Plover.
White-eyed Poker — Ferruginous Duck.
White-nosed Day-Fowl — Female Scaup.
White Nun—Smew.
White Owl—Barn Owl.
White-rump—Wheatear.
Wilduck — Razorbill and Common Guillemot.
Willie—Guillemot.
Willie Reeve—Stone Curlew.
Willie Whit—Barn Owl.
Windfanner—Kestrel.
Windhover—Kestrel.
Woodcock Owl—Short-eared Owl.
Woodjar — Lesser Spotted Woodpecker.
Woodsprite—Green Woodpecker.

Yarwhelp—Black-tailed Godwit.
Yellow Fulfer—Mistle Thrush.

II

EAST ANGLIAN NAMES FOR WILD FLOWERS

SEVERAL of the names in this list have not, to my knowledge, appeared in print before. Others can be found in a *Glossary of the Dialect and Provincialisms of East Anglia*, by J. G. Nall, 1866; *Broad Norfolk*, by C. H., 1893; and some lists published from time to time in the " East Anglian Miscellany " of the *East Anglian Daily Times*.

Barber's Brushes—Teasel.
Birds'-eyes—Grey Field Speedwell and Germander Speedwell.
Black - weed — Common Bur - reed (*Sparganium ramosum*).
Blood-hilder—Dwarf Elder.
Boar Thistle—Cotton Thistle (*Onopordon Acanthium*).
Bolder—Common Clubrush (*Scirpus lacustris*).
Boodle—Corn Marigold.
Brakes—Bracken.
Brameberry—Bramble.
Brank—Buckwheat.
Bread and Cheese—Common Mallow.
Brush and Comb—Teasel.
Buck Holly—Holly without berries.
Buddle—Corn Marigold.
Bull Daisy—Ox-eye Daisy.
Bull - fice or Bull - fiest — Common Puffball.
Bullrush—Reedmace (*Typha latifolia* and *angustifolia*).
Bundweed—Knapweed.
Buns, Bunweed—Chicory.
Butter and Eggs—Common Toadflax.

Candles—Foxtail-grass.
Canker—Poppy.
Canker-weed—Common Ragwort.
Clote—Coltsfoot.
Cock Brumble—Bramble.

Cock Holly—Holly without berries.
Cock Sorrow—Common Sorrel.
Cockshead—Ribwort Plantain.
Copper Rose—Poppy.
Cornelian—Mezereon.
Cow Mumble—Cow Parsnip (*Heracleum Sphondylium*).
Creeping Sarah—Wall-pepper.
Cuckoo - flower — Common Bugle, Lady's-smock, and Early Purple Orchis.

Dane-blood—Dwarf Elder or Danewort.
Deal-tree—Scotch Fir.
Dick-a-dilver—Periwinkle.
Dindle—Common or Corn Sowthistle.
Drawk—Rye-grass.

Ebble—Aspen.

Fiddlesticks—Water Figwort.
Fish-leaf—Water Plantain.
Five-fingers—Oxlip.
Fliggers—Yellow Iris.
Fortune-teller—Dandelion.
Fug-Plant—Henbane (Essex).

Gargut-root—Hellebore.
Garland Flower—Mezereon.
Gatter-bush—Guelder Rose.
Gattridge—Dogwood.

Gentleman's Hair—Field Woodrush.
Ginger—Tansy.
Gipsy Rhubarb—Burdock.
Gladden—Yellow Iris.
Gold Cups—Crowfoots.
Golden-dust—Wall-pepper.
Goose Tansy—Silverweed.
Goslings—Sallow blossom.
Grandfather Greybeard—Traveller's Joy.
Green Gravel—Common Milfoil.
Guttrich—Dogwood.
Gutweed—Common or Corn Sow-thistle.

Harber—Hornbeam.
Haste-to-the-wedding—Rock Cress (*Arabis*).
Headache—Poppy.
Hogknife—Yellow Iris.
Hogweed—Knotgrass.
Hulver—Holly.
Hundred-leafer—Common Milfoil.
Huntsman's Cap—Yellow Iris.

Ife or Yfe—Yew.

Jack-go-up-your-arm—Wall Barley.
Jam Tarts—Hairy Willow-herb.
Jilster—A form of *Salix triandra*.
John-go-to-bed-at-noon—Common Goat's-beard.

Lady's Bonnets—Columbine.
Lady's Fingers—Common Arum and Kidney Vetch.
Lady's-frock—Lady's smock.
Lady's Hair—Quake-grass.
Lady's Pincushion—Field Scabious.
Lambs'-tails—Hazel Catkins.
Landberry—Dewberry.
Land Whin—Restharrow.
Luck—Kidney Vetch.

Milkmaids—Lady's-smock.
Mislen-bush—Mistletoe.
Muckweed—Goosefoot.

Naked Boys—Autumn Crocus.
Nathan-driving-his-chariot—Monks-hood.
Needle-weed—Shepherd's Needle.
Nep—Catmint.
Net-rein—Sand Sedge (Breckland).
New Year's Gift—Winter Aconite.

Nip—Catmint.
Nipnoses—Snapdragon.

Owl's Crown—Wood Cudweed.

Paigle—Creeping Crowfoot.
Pickcheeses—Common Mallow.
Pickpocket—Shepherd's-purse.
Pickpurse—Corn Spurrey.
Pig's Tootles—Bird's-foot Trefoil.
Pipperidge—Barberry.
Pochard-grass—*Chara aspera*.
Poker—Reedmace, Common Arum.
Popples—Willows.

Quann—Purple Willow (*Salix purpurea*).
Quicks—Couch-grass, Young Hawthorns.

Rassels—Restharrow.
Rattle Jack or Rattle-grass—Yellow Rattle.
Runaway Jack—Ground Ivy.

Salentine—Tansy.
Sandweed—Corn Spurrey.
Sauce Alone—Garlic Mustard (*Alliaria officinalis*).
Segs—Sedges.
Sention or Senshen—Common Groundsel.
Shepherd's-weather-glass or shepherd's sundial—Scarlet Pimpernel.
Shirt-buttons—Common Stitchwort.
Sleeping Beauty—Wood Sorrel.
Smartweed—Common Persicaria.
Soldier's Buttons—Red Campion, Herb Robert.
Suckling—White Clover, Honeysuckle.
Sweethearts—Cleavers.

Thistle-weed—Water Soldier (*Stratiotes aloides*).
Tinker-tailor-grass—Rye-grass.
Tittle-my-fancy—Field Pansy.

What's o'clock—Dandelion.
Wild Rhubarb—Butterbur.
Winter-weed—Ivy-leaved Speedwell.
Wire-weed—Common Knotgrass.
Witch-grass—Rye-grass.
Wret-weed—Sun Spurge (*Euphorbia helioscopia*).
Wye-bibbles—Sea Buckthorn (*Hippophæ rhamnoides*).

III
BIBLIOGRAPHY

Observations on the Fauna of Norfolk. By the Rev. Richard Lubbock. 1845. New Edition edited by Thomas Southwell, F.Z.S. 1879.

The Birds of Norfolk. By Henry Stevenson, F.L.S. 3 vols. (Vols. I. and II. issued in 1866 and 1870; vol. III. completed by T. Southwell, F.Z.S., 1890).

The Birds of Suffolk. By the Rev. Churchill Babington. 1884-1886.

Notes on the Natural History of Norfolk. By Sir Thomas Browne (1605-1682). Edited by Thomas Southwell, F.Z.S. 1902.

The Flora of Suffolk. By W. M. Hind, LL.D. 1889.

The Flora of Norfolk. By the Rev. Kirby Trimmer, A.B. 1866.

Suffolk in the XVIIth Century (The Breviary of Suffolk by Robert Reyce. 1618). With Notes by Lord Francis Hervey. 1902.

History and Antiquities of the County of Suffolk. By the Rev. Alfred Suckling, LL.B. 1847.

The Eastern Arboretum. By James Grigor. 1840-1841.

Handbook to the Natural History of Cambridgeshire. Edited by J. E. Marr, Sc.D., F.R.S., and A. S. Shipley, M.A., F.R.S. 1904.

Handbook to the British Mammalia. By R. Lydekker, B.A., F.R.S. 1896.

Birds, Beasts, and Fishes of Broadland. By P. H. Emerson, B.A., M.B. 1895.

Reminiscences of Fen and Mere. By J. M. Heathcote. 1876.

Wild-Fowl (Fur, Feather, and Fin Series). By L. H. De Visme Shaw and others. 1905.

Short Historical Notices of Burgh Water Frolic. By John Batley, M.D. 1889.

Nature in Eastern Norfolk. By A. H. Patterson. 1905.

Transactions of the Norfolk and Norwich Naturalists' Society, 1869-1905.

The Zoologist.

The East Anglian. Notes and Queries.

Glossary of the Dialect and Provincialisms of East Anglia. By J. G. Nall. 1866.

A Catalogue of the Birds of Great Yarmouth. By A. H. Patterson. 1901.

Broad Norfolk. Edited by C. H. 1893.

East Anglian Miscellany. Published weekly in the *East Anglian Daily Times*.

INDEX

Abbot's Willow, 249.
Abdy, Sir R., 97.
Addy, S. O., 179.
Ainger, Canon, 308, 309, 313, 314.
Albemarle, Countess of, 99.
Alces latifrons, 4.
Alder, Haverland, 242.
American Brook Trout, 30.
— Rose Perch, 27.
American Natural History, 144.
Amyott, T. E., 235.
Anchovy, 26, 161.
Angler (fish), 26.
Anmer Mink, 288.
Annual Plants in Breckland, 69, 70.
Antelope, Saiga, 5.
Arboretum et Fruiticetum Britannicum, 235.
Arctic Fox, 5.
— Glutton, 3, 4.
Atherine, 159, 160.
Auk, Little, 21.
Auroch, 5.
Avocet, 10, 11, 12, 16, 32, 38, 39, 145.

Babington, Rev. Churchill, 39, 40.
Badger, 297.
Baillon's Crake, 53.
Bale Oak, 246, 247.
Bank Vole, 4.
Barr, W. (falconer), 91.
Barrows, 60, 62, 288, 292, 293.
Basking Shark, 26.
Bat, 215.
Bear, 3, 7, 81, 343.
Bearded Seal, 3.
— Titmouse, 10, 16, 96–107, 271.
Beaver, 4, 7, 343.
— Giant, 4.
Beech, Spixworth, 241, 242.
Bell, Professor, 166.
Benacre Broad, 350.
Berkenhout, 52.
Berners, Lord, 91.
Berney, G., 165, 167, 168, 169, 171.
Bilney Moor, 5.

Bird, Rev. M. C. H., 37, 45.
Bird-netting, 44, 89, 96, 145, 148, 149, 267–270, 272–275, 294, 295, 297–299.
Birds of Suffolk, 39, 54.
Bison, 4, 344.
Bittern, Common, 10, 12, 13, 16, 32, 38, 40, 41, 197.
— Little, 41.
Blackbird, 19, 91, 287.
Black Horse Broad Gullery, 108–112.
Black-weed, 201.
Bleak, 25.
Bluethroat, 19, 143.
Boar-fish, 27.
Boar, Wild, 4, 7, 82, 342.
Boke of Kervynge, 34.
Bond, F., 166.
Bonito, 26.
Booke of Cookery and Housekeeping, 46.
Booth, E. T., 103, 227, 228.
Bos longifrons, 79.
— *primigenius*, 4, 7.
Boulenger, G. A., 169–172.
Boyd Dawkins, Professor, 341.
Brambling, 20.
Bramfield Oak, 243, 244.
Bream, 25, 27, 28, 29, 223.
Breckland, 7, 8, 31, 57–95.
— Flora of, 85–87.
Breviary of Suffolk, 66.
Breydon, 13, 14, 22, 25, 37, 38, 151–160.
British Birds, Butler's, 73.
— *Fishes*, 26.
— *Ornithology*, 50.
— *Reptiles*, 166.
Broad, Benacre, 350.
— Covehithe, 350, 351.
Broads District, 8–11, 12–14, 32–34, 36, 96–107, 108–113, 165, 194–220, 299–304, 321–336.
— Suffolk Shore, 350–354.
Broome Heath, 288.
Broom-tiers, 282–284.
Brown, Rev. J., 42.

INDEX

Browne, Sir Thos., 11, 12, 25, 26, 32, 34, 36, 38, 40, 46, 47, 52, 56, 74, 84, 97, 113, 120, 130, 160, 248.
Buckland, Frank, 29, 30.
Buffon, 99.
Bullfinch, 295, 296.
Bullhead, 24.
Bungay Common, 285-288.
Bunting, Common, 18.
— Lapland, 18, 21, 137, 143.
— Ortolan, 137, 143.
— Reed, 22, 213, 216, 286, 287.
— Snow, 18, 20, 24, 143, 345.
Burbot, 25.
Bustard, Great, 8, 12, 32, 53-56, 81, 279, 290.
Butterfly, Painted Lady, 346.
— Swallow-tailed, 100, 195.
Buzzard, Common, 50, 295, 296.

Caius, Dr., 121.
Calver, J., 297.
Canadian Fleabane, 65, 85, 86.
Candle Rushes, 200.
Cape Hunting Dog, 5.
Carp, 29.
— Speigel, 30.
Caston Willow, 249.
Cat, Wild, 7, 295.
Caton, Rev. R. B., 72, 73.
Cave Bear, 3, 343.
— Hyæna, 3.
Cedars, 243.
Centriscus scolopax, 26.
Cervus savini, 4.
— *sedgwicki*, 4.
Cetaceans, 4, 25.
Chaffinch, 18, 287.
Chant, East Anglian, 179, 180.
Charles the First, 52.
Chiffchaff, 143.
Chough, 294, 295.
"Christ's Half-Dole," 305.
Chub, 25.
Clarke, E., 17, 18.
— W. G., 60, 72, 77, 83, 115.
Cliffs, Suffolk, 338-349.
Clovers, Rare, 123.
Coke, Hon. Colonel, 149.
Continental Field Vole, 4.
Coot, 10, 16, 77, 78, 100.
Cormorant, 12, 52, 53, 295.
Corncrake, 199, 287.
Covehithe Broad, 350, 351.
Crab, Shore, 134, 155, 334.
Crabbe, G., 97, 307-320.
Crag, Red, 291, 292.

Craig Fluke, 27.
Crake, Baillon's, 53.
Crane, Common, 11, 12, 33-35, 82, 145.
Cresswell, F. J., 148, 149.
Crested Newt, 4.
Crossbill, 63, 64.
Crossbow, 33, 34.
Crow, Common, 12.
Crow, Hooded, 20, 129, 158, 184, 336, 347, 348.
Cuckoo, Common, 207, 212, 213, 287.
— Great Spotted, 138.
Cullum, Sir T. G., 316.
Curlew, Common, 22, 126, 148, 149, 290.
— Pigmy, 19.
— Sandpiper, 19, 352.
— Stone, 8, 58, 70-74, 80, 91, 137, 279.
— — Poaching by, 72-74.

Dab, Long Rough, 27.
Dabchick, 77, 78.
Dace, 162.
Davy, Rev. C., 236.
Decoys and Decoying, 15, 16, 31, 76, 350.
Deer, 4, 7, 80, 82, 343.
Defoe, Daniel, 12, 13, 31.
Denes, 119-124, 137.
Deopham, Great Tree, 248.
Dersingham Heath, 288-290.
Desman, 4.
Devil's Dike, 59.
— Punch Bowl, 75, 83.
Dictionary of Birds, 73.
Dillenius, J. J., 87, 316.
Diver, Great Northern, 12, 353, 354.
— Red-throated, 23, 352.
Dog, Cape Hunting, 5.
— Sheep, 189.
Dogfish, 26.
Dolphin, 344.
Dotterel-netting, 89.
Downes, J. D., 50, 51.
Dresser, H. E., 143.
Drove Road, 59.
Duck-driving, 274, 275, 297-299.
Duck, Steller's, 138.
— Tufted, 8.
Dugdale, 266, 267.
Dunes, 118, 119, 124-136, 137-139.
Dunlin, 19, 22, 23, 136, 148, 149, 281, 350.

Eagle, White-tailed, 12, 227.
Eastern Arboretum, 234, 235.

INDEX

Easton Broad, 350, 351-354.
Edmund, King, 62.
Eel, 24, 27, 115, 155, 323, 328-331.
Eel-catching, 27, 299-302, 322-336.
Egg-collecting, 204.
Eider Duck, 23.
— King, 145.
Elephant, Southern, 4, 343.
— Straight-tusked, 4, 343.
Elephas antiquus, 4.
— *meridionalis*, 4, 343.
Elk, 4, 343.
— Irish, 5.
Etruscan Rhinoceros, 4.
Euren, H. F., 234, 239, 240.
Evans, A. H., 20.
Evelyn, J., 233, 240, 243, 248.
Everitt, N., 273.
Extinct Fauna, 2-7, 338-344.

Fairies, 184-186.
Falcon, Peregrine, 23.
Falconers' Club, 49.
Fauna of Norfolk, 13, 26, 28, 48, 51, 98.
Fenland, The, 167, 168.
Fenman, Old-time, 265-272.
Fens, 33, 166-173, 196, 263-272, 273-275, 299.
Fieldfare, 11, 218, 333.
Finch, Serin, 137.
Fish, Coarse, Former abundance of, 28.
— Culture advocated, 29.
— Marine and Freshwater, 24-30.
— Tithe of, 305.
— Waggons, 224.
— -netting, 27, 38, 30, 150, 151-164, 225, 299-306, 322-336.
— -poaching, 28, 30.
— -snaring, 30.
Fisheries Act, Norfolk and Suffolk, 30.
Fleabane, Canadian, 65, 85, 86.
Flora, 85-87, 108, 110, 120-124, 140-142, 195, 205, 206, 211, 212, 216, 281, 282, 288, 314-316, 343.
Flora of Suffolk, 84, 314.
Flounder, 155, 334.
Flycatcher, Pied, 19.
— Red-breasted, 143.
Folk-lore, 184-186.
Forest Bed, 3-5, 339-345.
Fossil-hunting, 338.
Fowlmere, 74, 76, 77, 78, 83.
Fox, 3, 115, 295, 297.
— Arctic, 5.
Frog, Common, 4.

Frog, Edible, 4, 165-173.
Fuller, J., 232, 263.

Gadow, Dr. H., 99, 172, 173.
Gadwall, 8, 76, 77.
Gannet, 22, 23.
Garganey Teal, 76, 77, 78.
Gattorugine, 27.
Gedge, Rev. J. Denny, 202.
Gelenos Oak, 244.
Geology of East Norfolk, 9-10, 339-340.
George, Earl of Orford, 47, 49, 90.
Gerarde, 87.
Gilthead, 26.
Glutton, Arctic, 3, 4, 344.
Goby, Two-spotted, 27.
— White, 27.
— Yellow, 160, 161.
Godwit, Bar-tailed, 23, 148, 149.
— Black-tailed, 10, 16, 23, 24, 32, 38, 40.
Golden-eye, 16.
Goldfinch, 217, 218, 335.
Goosander, 226, 352.
Goose, Grey-lag, 53.
— Pink-footed, 8, 146-150.
Goshawk, 35, 36, 91.
Gospel Oaks, 240.
Grampus, 344.
Grebe, Great Crested, 16, 77, 100, 149, 352.
— Little, 77, 78.
— Red-necked, 352.
— Sclavonian, 352.
Grigor, J., 234, 239, 242, 249.
Grimes Graves, 61, 88.
Gudgeon, 24, 25, 162.
Guillemot, 149.
Gull, Black-headed, 77, 80, 108-117, 132, 148.
— Common, 148.
— Greater Black-backed, 148, 348, 349, 351.
— Herring, 148, 351.
— Kittiwake, 148.
— Little, 136.
— Sabine's, 136, 145.
Gulleries, 108, 117.
Gun, Introduction of the, 33.
Gunn, Rev. J., 340.
Gurnard, Streaked, 27.
Gurney, J. H., 19, 20, 37, 43, 45, 46, 51, 97, 98, 103, 105, 115, 116, 129, 130, 142, 149, 167, 168, 289, 290.
Gwilt, C., 54.

INDEX

Hall, William, 264.
Hammerhead, 26.
Handbook of British Birds, 46.
Harding, C. W., 160, 161.
Hare, 210.
Harmer, F. W., 2, 341, 344.
— S. F., 33.
Harpley Common, 288.
Harriers, 43, 204, 295, 296.
Harris, Rev. G. H., 123.
Harting, J. E., 36, 46, 50, 101.
Haverland Alder, 242.
Hawking, 33, 35, 47-49, 50, 51, 89-92, 294.
Hawstead Oak, 240.
Hazlitt, W., 309.
Hedgehog, 165, 295, 296.
Hedge Sparrow, 287.
Hele, Dr. N. F., 38.
Henham Oak, 237, 238.
Henslow, Professor, 291.
Herbalists, 192.
Hereward, 61.
Heron, 10, 12, 91, 163, 204, 226.
Herring, 160, 161.
— Fishery, Share System of, 305, 306.
Hethel Thorn, 241, 279.
Hind, Rev. W. M., 84, 314.
Hippocampus, 26.
Hippopotamus, 3, 344.
Hob-o'-Lantern, 201-203.
Holy Oak, 240.
Hooker, Sir J. D., 86, 140, 316.
— Sir W., 42.
Hoopoe, 12.
Hornaday, W. T., 144.
Horse, 4, 343.
— Steno's, 4.
Houseboats, 222, 223, 324, 325.
Hoy, J. D., 98.
Hubbard, A. J. and G. H., 287.
Hugel, Baron von, 171.
Hut-circles, 288.
Hyæna crocuta, 3, 344.

Ignis fatuus, 196, 201-203.
Irish Deer, 5.
Island Life, 5-6.

Jackdaw, 20.
James the First, 89, 90.
Jay, 20, 295, 296.
Jefferies, R., 95.
Jervis, Cavaliere W. P., 244, 345.
Jessopp, Canon, 179.
John, King, 33.
Juby, W., 203.

Kearton, R., 43, 103.
Kestrel, 19, 23, 210, 287.
Ketteringham Walnut, 247.
Kett's Oak, 239, 240.
King Edmund's Oak, 244, 245.
Kingfisher, 295.
Kingsley, C., 99, 166, 266.
Kirby's Oak, 243.
Kite, 47, 295.
— -flying, 90.
Knot, 22, 23, 148, 149, 351.

Lake-dwellings, 79.
Lambing-time, 187-190.
Lampern, 25, 162.
— Sea, 25.
Langmere, 79-82, 83, 85, 115.
Lantern-man, 196, 201-203.
Layton, Rev. J., 41.
Leechers, 192.
Leicester, Earl of, 148, 149.
Leopard, 5.
L'Estrange Household Book, 25.
Lilford, Lord, 101.
Lime, Deopham, 248.
Linnet, 23, 143, 213, 286, 287.
Lion, 5.
Lizard, Common, 139, 186, 191, 278.
Loach, 24, 25.
Lost Breeding Birds, 31-56.
Loudon, 235.
Lowe, Dr. J., 24, 26.
Lubbock, Rev. R., 13, 15, 26, 28, 30, 38, 39, 40, 41, 43, 44, 48, 50, 51, 55, 74, 98, 105, 113, 116, 162.
Lucioperca sandra, 28.
Lug-worm Gatherers, 135.
Lycaon pictus, 5.
Lydekker, R., 2, 3, 4.
Lyell, Sir Charles, 10, 340.
Lynx, 5.

Machærodus cultridens, 3.
Magazine of Natural History, 68, 98.
Mallard, 15, 16, 24, 76, 78, 148, 210, 272, 297.
Mammoth, 4, 5.
Manship, 124.
Man-trap, 199.
Marks, Swan-, 252-254.
Marsham, Robert, 234, 235, 243.
Marsham Heath, 292.
Marten, 3, 7, 343.
Martin, House, 23.
— Sand, 23, 286, 287, 345.
Meal-bolters, 192.
Meal Marshes, 139-150.

INDEX

Meres, Breckland, 75-85.
Merganser, 227, 352.
Merlin, 23, 91.
Merrett, Dr. C., 275.
Merton Oak, 246.
Migration, Bird, 17-24, 142-144.
Millard, Rev. J. W., 296.
Miller, S. H., 167, 168, 169.
Miller's-thumb, 25.
Milton's Mulberry-tree, 243.
Minnow, 24.
Mole, 4, 138, 139, 181-184, 295, 296.
Mole-catching, 181, 182, 295, 296.
Montagu, Colonel, 44.
Moor-hen, 77, 287.
Mouse, Wood, 4.
Mousehold Heath, 292.
"Mowl, Old," 174-193.
Mulberry-tree, Milton's, 243.
Munford, Rev. G., 50.
Musk Ox, 4, 344.

Napier, A. J., 147, 148.
Narwhal, 344.
Natterjack, 191, 199, 203, 204.
Natural History of Belvoir, 97.
Neolithic Dew-Ponds and Cattle-Ways, 287.
Nets, Stake, 148, 149.
Netting, Bird-, 44, 89, 96, 145, 148, 149, 267-270, 272-275, 294, 295, 297-299.
— Fish-, 27, 28, 30, 150, 151-164, 225, 299-306, 321-336.
Newcome, E. C., 39, 91, 92.
Newt, Crested, 4, 199.
Newton, Professor, 35, 36, 39, 40, 43, 47, 48, 51, 73, 91, 167, 168.
Night-heron, 145.
Nightingale, 287.
Nightjar, 63, 211, 215, 287.
Noctule, 215.
Norfolk Broads, The, 45, 46.
Norgate, F., 64.

Oak, Bale, 246, 247.
— Bramfield, 243, 244.
— Gelenos, 244.
— Hawstead, 240.
— Henham, 237, 238.
— Holy, 240.
— Kett's, 239, 240.
— King Edmund's, 244, 245.
— Kirby's, 243.
— Merton, 246.
— Polstead, 240.
— Queen Elizabeth's, 235-237.

Oak, Salcey, 231, 232.
— Thorpe, 238, 239.
— Thwaites, 245, 246.
— Wayland, 247.
— Winfarthing, 234, 235.
Oaks, Gospel, 240.
— Kimberley, 233.
— Stratton Strawless, 243.
Ogilvie, F. M., 143.
"Old Mowl," 174-193.
Orford, George, Earl of, 47, 49, 90.
Ornithology, Willughby's, 89.
Orthagoriscus mola, 26.
Orton, Rev. J. S., 179.
Osprey, 12, 295.
Otter, 3, 197, 229, 295, 303.
— -trap, 199.
Our Rarer British Breeding Birds, 43.
Outney Common, 285-286.
Ovis argali, 4.
— *savini*, 4.
Owl, Barn, 166, 287.
— Horned, 136.
— Short-eared, 19.
Ox, Celtic, 77.
— Musk, 4, 344.
— Wild, 7, 81.
Oyster-catcher, 8, 148, 149.

Packmen, 175.
Paget, C. J. and J., 14, 16, 26.
Palæolithic Implements, 88.
Panda, Giant, 5.
Partridge, 19, 294, 298.
Paston Letters, 35.
Patterson, A. H., 14, 21, 26, 27, 38, 137.
Payne-Gallwey, Sir R., 76.
Pea, Sea, 121, 122.
Pearlsides, 27.
Peat-running, 200.
Peddar's Way, 59, 83, 288.
Peewit (*see* Green Plover).
Pelican, 12, 32, 33.
Pelicanus crispus, 32, 33.
— *onocrotalus*, 32.
Perch, 24, 25, 27, 28, 29.
— American Rose, 27.
Peregrine Falcon, 23, 50, 51, 68.
Petrel, Storm, 148.
Pettus, Sir J., 248.
Pheasant, 19, 198, 223, 294, 298.
Pigeon, Wood, 287.
Pike, 24, 25, 27, 115.
— -perch, 30.
Pipefish, Worm, 26.
Pipistrelle, 215.

INDEX

Pipit, Meadow, 18, 23, 126, 207, 212, 213, 287.
— Richard's, 137.
— Rock, 23, 144.
Plover, Golden, 16, 148, 149.
— Green, 16, 23, 80, 129, 204, 205, 321.
— Grey, 22, 23, 24, 148, 149.
— -netting, 267-270, 273, 274.
— Norfolk, 8, 58, 70-74, 80, 91, 137, 279.
— — Poaching by, 72-74.
— Ringed, 22, 80, 84, 85, 126-133, 138.
Pochard, 8, 19, 76, 77, 267, 272, 273.
— netting, 272, 273.
Polecat, 295, 296.
Pollack, 27.
Polstead Oak, 240.
Polyolbion, Drayton's, 89.
Pond Tortoise, 173.
Pope, W. J., 149.
Porbeagle, 26.
Power Cod, 27.
Power, G. E. and F. D., 22.
Primitive Man, 79, 80-82, 88, 89, 287, 288.
Principles of Geology, 10.
Punt-gunning, 14, 158, 225-228, 270.

Queen Elizabeth's Oak, 235-237.

Rabbit, 6, 65-70, 138.
— Silver-grey, 67.
Rabbiting, 65-68.
Rail, Water, 10, 194.
Rat, Black, 6.
— Brown, 6, 111, 115, 129, 138.
Raven, 12, 51, 52, 295.
Ray, J., 97, 121, 316.
Ray, Cuckoo, 27.
— Sting, 27.
Razorbill, 149.
Red Deer, 4, 7, 80, 81, 82, 343.
Reddlemen, 175.
Redpoll, 218, 335.
Reid, C., 342.
Reindeer, 5.
Reports of the Migrations of Birds, 106.
Reyce, R., 66, 232.
Rhinoceros, 4, 5, 343.
— Woolly, 5.
Rhinoceros antiquitatis, 5.
— *megarhinus*, 5.
Ringmere, 62, 82, 83.

Rising, Mr., 41.
Roach, 24, 25, 27, 28, 162.
Robert of Swaffham, 31.
Robin, 287.
Rockling, Four-bearded, 27.
Roe Deer, 4, 7, 82, 343.
Roller, 12.
Rook, 20, 91, 287, 294, 295, 296.
Rudd, 25, 28.
Ruff, 10, 11, 12, 13, 16, 23, 44-47, 204.
Ruffe, 24, 25.
Rural Sports, 272.
Rush Fair, 201.
Rushmere Heath, 292.
Russell, Lord A., 168.
Rye, W., 260.

Sabre-toothed Tiger, 3, 5.
Saiga Antelope, 5.
Salcey Oak, 231, 232.
Salmon, J. D., 84.
Salmon, 25, 29.
Sanderling, 24.
Sand-grouse, 138, 280.
Sandhills, 119, 124-136, 137-139.
Sandpiper, Broad-billed, 145.
— Buff-breasted, 145.
— Common, 19, 22.
— Green, 23.
Sand-storms, 65, 66.
Saunders, Howard, 34.
Savi's Warbler, 41-43.
Sawfish, 25.
Scombresox saurus, 26.
Scoter, Common, 22.
Scoulton Mere Gullery, 113-117.
Seal, Bearded, 3.
— Common, 25.
Sea Pea, 121, 122.
Sea Woodcock, 26.
Seaside Flora in Breckland, 84, 85.
Seebohm, Mr., 116, 146.
Selous, E., 74.
Shag, 295.
Shark, Basking, 26.
Sharpe, R. Bowdler, 99.
Shaw, L. H. de Visme, 77.
Shearwater, 23.
Sheep, Wild, 4.
Sheld-duck, 8, 137, 148, 289, 290.
— Ruddy, 145.
Shepherd, Old, 187-192.
Shorelark, 21, 137, 144, 345.
Shoveler, 8, 76, 77.
Shrews, 4, 199.
Shrimp, 161, 334.

INDEX

Siberian Vole, 4.
Silurus glanis, 28.
Siskin, 20.
Skipper, 26.
Skua, Great, 12, 145.
Skylark, 17, 18, 20, 23, 24, 125, 148, 207, 287.
Smelt, 24, 151-164, 334.
— -netting, 27, 151-164.
Smew, 352.
Smith, Bosworth, 51.
Smuggling, 136.
Snake, Common, 4, 191, 192, 296.
Snares, Fish, 30.
Snipe, 10, 13, 16, 206, 207.
— Great, 137.
Sole, 161.
Southwell, T., 12, 25, 27, 32, 33, 34, 40, 41, 56, 64, 130, 264, 302.
Sparrow, 19, 297.
Sparrow-hawk, 20, 23, 91.
Speigel Carp, 30.
Spelman, Sir H., 232.
Spixworth Beech, 241, 242.
Spoonbill, 10, 11, 12, 16, 36-38, 226.
Sporting Tour through the Northern Parts of England, 48, 49.
Sprat, 160, 161.
Squirrel, 4, 6, 343.
Stake-nets, 148, 149.
Stalking Sledge, 270-272.
"Stanticle," 25.
Starling, 20, 135, 216, 217, 228, 271, 287, 295.
Staverton Park, 232, 249.
Steno's Horse, 4.
Stevenson, H., 16, 40, 42, 50, 73, 113, 114, 116.
Stilt, Black-winged, 198.
Sting Ray, 26.
Stint, 16.
— Little, 19, 22, 24, 352.
— Temminck's, 145, 352.
Stoat, 115, 138, 183, 186, 210, 295.
Stockdove, 68, 91, 137.
Stork, 12.
— Black, 145.
Stow-nets, 161.
Stradbroke, Earl of, 238.
Strickland, Agnes, 237.
Suffield, Lord, 239.
Suffolk Traveller, 291.
Sunfish, 26.
Sutton Walks, 290.
Swaffham, Robert of, 31.
Swallow, 17, 22, 23, 24, 287.

Swallow-tailed Butterfly, 100, 195.
Swan-marks, 252-254.
— -pit, 260-262.
— Tame, 19, 251-262.
— -upping, 251-260.
— Wild, 12, 16, 77.
Swift, 210, 287.
Swordfish, 26.
Syleham Lights, 202.

Tapir, 5.
Taylor, J. E., 166.
— R. C., 9, 339, 340.
Teal, 11, 15, 16, 24, 76, 148, 297.
Temminck, 42.
Tench, 25, 27.
— Golden, 30.
Tern, Black, 11, 16, 22, 32, 38, 39.
— Common, 11, 23, 129, 131-134.
— Gull-billed, 145.
— Lesser, 23, 129, 131-134.
— Whiskered, 145.
Thorkill, 62, 82, 292.
"Thormanby," 149.
Thorn, Hethel, 241, 279.
— Wortwell, 241.
Thornton, Colonel, 48.
Thorpe Oak, 238, 239.
Thrush, Mistle, 287.
— Song, 18, 19.
Thurnall, C., 166.
Thwaites Oak, 245, 246.
Tiger, Sabre-toothed, 3, 5.
Tinkers, 175.
Tipes, Rabbit, 66, 67.
Tithe of Fish, 305.
Titmouse, Bearded, 10, 16, 96-107, 271.
— Blue, 287.
— Cole, 287.
— Long-tailed, 287.
— Marsh, 287.
Toad, 4.
— Running, 191, 199, 203, 204.
Topknot, Müller's, 27.
Tortoise, Pond, 173.
Tree Creeper, 287.
Trees, Celebrated, 230, 250.
Trimmers, 30.
Trim-nets, 161.
Trout, 24, 25.
— Brook, 30.
— Great Lake, 30.
Trygon pastinaca, 26.
Tuck, W. H., 64.
Tufted Duck, 8, 16, 76, 77.
Tunny, 26.

INDEX

Turnstone, 22.
Twite, 20.

Ulfketyl, 62, 82, 292.
Uplands, 174-192.
Upping, Swan-, 251-260.
Ursus spelæus, 3.

Vendenheym, H. J. W. von, 89, 90.
Vermin, Act for the Destruction of, 295-297.
Viper, 4, 139, 191, 210.
Vole, Bank, 4.
— Continental Field, 4.
— Field, 115, 210.
— Siberian, 4.
— Water, 207-208, 215.

Wagtail, Pied, 22, 23, 134.
— Yellow, 207, 212, 213, 287.
Wallace, Dr. A. R., 5-6.
Wallis, A., 68, 69.
Walnut, Ketteringham, 247.
Walrus, 3, 4.
Walsingham, Lord, 167, 168, 170.
Warbler, Aquatic, 142.
— Barred, 18, 142.
— Grasshopper, 199, 207, 209.
— Great Reed, 209.
— Icterine, 142.
— Marsh, 210.
— Pallas's Willow, 142-143.
— Reed, 100, 209, 213.
— Savi's, 41-43.
— Sedge, 100, 209, 212, 223, 286, 287.
— Willow, 22, 143, 208, 209, 113, 286, 287.
— Wood, 287.
— Yellow-browed, 287.
Wasp, Large-tailed Wood, 186.
Water-bailiff, 221-229.
Water-hen, 16, 77, 287.

Waxwing, 12.
Wayland Oak, 247.
Weasel, 115, 138, 183, 210, 295.
Wells Wild Birds Protection Society, 131.
Westleton Walks, 277-282.
Wheatear, 19, 22, 137.
— Desert, 135.
Whimbrel, 22, 23.
Whinchat, 22, 286, 287.
Whiting, 161.
Wigeon, 15, 22, 24, 148, 227, 297.
Wild-fowling, 14, 31, 148, 149, 150, 158, 225-228, 263-275, 297-299.
Will-o'-th'-Wisp, 196, 201-203.
Willow, Abbot's, 249.
— Caston, 249.
Wilson, Colonel, 68, 91.
Windham, Katherine, 46.
Winfarthing Oak, 234, 235.
Wolf, 3, 6, 81, 343.
Wollaston, J. P., 166.
Wolley, J., 171.
Wood, Rev. T., 173.
Woodcock, 11, 20, 148, 149.
Wood Mouse, 4.
Woodpecker, Great Black, 64, 65.
— Green, 19, 63, 219, 286.
Woolly Rhinoceros, 5.
Wortwell Thorn, 241.
Wren, Common, 287.
— Willow, 22, 143, 208, 209, 213, 286, 287.
— Wood, 287.
Wretham Great and West Meres, 79.
Wryneck, 287.

Yarmouth, Sketch of the Natural History of, 26.
Yarrell's *British Fishes*, 26.
Yellow-hammer, 289.
Yorke, Rev. A. C., 266.
Young, J., 106.

Printed by
MORRISON & GIBB LIMITED,
Edinburgh

A CATALOGUE OF BOOKS PUBLISHED BY METHUEN AND COMPANY: LONDON 36 ESSEX STREET W.C.

CONTENTS

	PAGE		PAGE
General Literature,	2-19	Little Blue Books,	27
Ancient Cities,	19	Little Books on Art,	27
Antiquary's Books,	20	Little Galleries,	28
Beginner's Books,	20	Little Guides,	28
Business Books,	20	Little Library,	28
Byzantine Texts,	21	Miniature Library,	30
Churchman's Bible,	21	Oxford Biographies,	30
Churchman's Library,	21	School Examination Series,	30
Classical Translations,	21	Social Questions of To-day,	31
Commercial Series,	22	Textbooks of Science,	31
Connoisseur's Library,	22	Textbooks of Technology	31
Library of Devotion,	23	Handbooks of Theology,	31
Standard Library,	23	Westminster Commentaries,	32
Half-Crown Library,	24		
Illustrated Pocket Library of		Fiction,	32-36
Plain and Coloured Books,	24	The Shilling Novels,	37
Junior Examination Series,	26	Books for Boys and Girls	38
Junior School-Books,	26	Novels of Alexandre Dumas,	38
Leaders of Religion,	27	Methuen's Sixpenny Books,	39

JULY 1906

Belloc (Hilaire). PARIS. With Maps and Illustrations. *Cr. 8vo.* 6s.
*MARIE ANTOINETTE. With many Portraits and Illustrations. *Demy 8vo.* 12s. 6d. net.
 A Colonial Edition is also published.
Bellot (H. H. L.), M.A. THE INNER AND MIDDLE TEMPLE. With numerous Illustrations. *Crown 8vo.* 6s. net.
 See also L. A. A. Jones.
Bennett (W. H.), M.A. A PRIMER OF THE BIBLE. *Third Edition. Cr. 8vo.* 2s. 6d.
Bennett (W. H.) and Adeney (W. F.). A BIBLICAL INTRODUCTION. *Third Edition. Cr. 8vo.* 7s. 6d.
Benson (Archbishop) GOD'S BOARD : Communion Addresses. *Fcap. 8vo.* 3s. 6d. net.
Benson (A. C.), M.A. See Oxford Biographies.
Benson (R. M.). THE WAY OF HOLINESS: a Devotional Commentary on the 119th Psalm. *Cr. 8vo.* 5s.
Bernard (E. R.), M.A., Canon of Salisbury. THE ENGLISH SUNDAY. *Fcap. 8vo.* 1s. 6d.
Bertouch (Baroness de). THE LIFE OF FATHER IGNATIUS. Illustrated. *Demy 8vo.* 10s. 6d. net.
 A Colonial Edition is also published.
Betham-Edwards (M.). HOME LIFE IN FRANCE. Illustrated. *Fourth Edition. Demy 8vo.* 7s. 6d. net.
 A Colonial Edition is also published.
Bethune-Baker (J. F.), M.A. See Handbooks of Theology.
Bidez (M.). See Byzantine Texts.
Biggs (C. R. D.), D.D. See Churchman's Bible.
Bindley (T. Herbert), B.D. THE OECUMENICAL DOCUMENTS OF THE FAITH. With Introductions and Notes. *Cr. 8vo.* 6s.
Binns (H. B.). THE LIFE OF WALT WHITMAN. Illustrated. *Demy 8vo.* 10s. 6d. net.
 A Colonial Edition is also published.
Binyon (Laurence). THE DEATH OF ADAM, AND OTHER POEMS. *Cr. 8vo.* 3s. 6d. net.
*WILLIAM BLAKE. In 2 volumes. *Super Royal Quarto.* £1, 1s. each.
 Vol. I.—THE BOOK OF JOB.
Birnstingl (Ethel). See Little Books on Art.
Blackmantle (Bernard). See I.P.L.
Blair (Robert). See I.P.L.
Blake (William). See I.P.L. and Little Library.
Blaxland (B.), M.A. See Library of Devotion.
Bloom (T. Harvey), M.A. SHAKESPEARE'S GARDEN. Illustrated. *Fcap. 8vo.* 3s. 6d.; leather, 4s. 6d. net.
 See also Antiquary's Books

Blouet (Henri). See Beginner's Books.
Boardman (T. H.), M.A. See Textbooks of Science.
Bodley (J. E. C.), Author of 'France.' THE CORONATION OF EDWARD VII. *Demy 8vo.* 21s. net. By Command of the King.
Body (George), D.D. THE SOUL'S PILGRIMAGE : Devotional Readings from his writings. Selected by J. H. BURN, B.D., F.R.S.E. *Pott 8vo.* 2s. 6d.
Bona (Cardinal). See Library of Devotion.
Boon (F. C.). See Commercial Series.
Borrow (George). See Little Library.
Bos (J. Ritzema). AGRICULTURAL ZOOLOGY. Translated by J. R. AINSWORTH DAVIS, M.A. With 155 Illustrations. *Cr. 8vo. Third Edition.* 3s. 6d.
Botting (C. G.), B.A. EASY GREEK EXERCISES. *Cr. 8vo.* 2s. See also Junior Examination Series.
Boulton (E. S.), M.A. GEOMETRY ON MODERN LINES. *Cr. 8vo.* 2s.
Boulton (William B.). THOMAS GAINSBOROUGH With 40 Illustrations. *Second Ed. Demy 8vo.* 7s. 6d. net.
SIR JOSHUA REYNOLDS, P.R.A. With 49 Illustrations. *Demy 8vo.* 7s. 6d. net.
Bowden (E. M.). THE IMITATION OF BUDDHA : Being Quotations from Buddhist Literature for each Day in the Year. *Fifth Edition. Cr. 16mo.* 2s. 6d.
Boyle (W.). CHRISTMAS AT THE ZOO. With Verses by W. BOYLE and 24 Coloured Pictures by H. B. NEILSON. *Super Royal 16mo.* 2s.
Brabant (F. G.), M.A. See Little Guides.
Bradley (J. W.). See Little Books on Art.
Brailsford (H. N.). MACEDONIA. Illustrated. *Demy 8vo.* 12s. 6d. net.
Brodrick (Mary) and Morton (Anderson). A CONCISE HANDBOOK OF EGYPTIAN ARCHÆOLOGY. Illustrated. *Cr. 8vo.* 3s. 6d.
Brooke (A. S.), M.A. SLINGSBY AND SLINGSBY CASTLE. Illustrated. *Cr. 8vo.* 7s. 6d.
Brooks (E. W.). See Byzantine Texts.
Brown (P. H.), LL.D., Fraser Professor of Ancient (Scottish) History at the University of Edinburgh. SCOTLAND IN THE TIME OF QUEEN MARY. *Demy 8vo.* 7s. 6d. net.
Browne (Sir Thomas). See Standard Library.
Brownell (C. L.). THE HEART OF JAPAN. Illustrated. *Third Edition. Cr. 8vo.* 6s.; also *Demy 8vo.* 6d.
 A Colonial Edition is also published.
Browning (Robert). See Little Library.
Buckland (Francis T.). CURIOSITIES OF NATURAL HISTORY. Illustrated by H. B. NEILSON. *Cr. 8vo.* 3s. 6d.

GENERAL LITERATURE 5

Buckton (A. M.) THE BURDEN OF ENGELA: a Ballad-Epic. *Second Edition. Cr. 8vo. 3s. 6d. net.*
EAGER HEART: A Mystery Play. *Fourth Edition. Cr. 8vo. 1s. net.*
Budge (E. A. Wallis). THE GODS OF THE EGYPTIANS. With over 100 Coloured Plates and many Illustrations. *Two Volumes. Royal 8vo. £3, 3s. net.*
Bull (Paul), Army Chaplain. GOD AND OUR SOLDIERS. *Second Edition. Cr. 8vo. 6s.*
A Colonial Edition is also published.
Bulley (Miss). See S.Q.S.
Bunyan (John). THE PILGRIM'S PROGRESS. Edited, with an Introduction, by C. H. FIRTH, M.A. With 39 Illustrations by R. ANNING BELL. *Cr. 8vo. 6s.*
See also Library of Devotion and Standard Library.
Burch (G. J.), M.A., F.R.S. A MANUAL OF ELECTRICAL SCIENCE. Illustrated. *Cr. 8vo. 3s.*
Burgess (Gelett). GOOPS AND HOW TO BE THEM. Illustrated. *Small 4to. 6s.*
Burke (Edmund). See Standard Library.
Burn (A. E.), D.D., Rector of Handsworth and Prebendary of Lichfield.
See Handbooks of Theology.
Burn (J. H.), B.D. See Library of Devotion.
Burnand (Sir F. C.). RECORDS AND REMINISCENCES. With a Portrait by H. v. HERKOMER. *Cr. 8vo. Fourth and Cheaper Edition. 6s.*
A Colonial Edition is also published.
Burns (Robert), THE POEMS OF. Edited by ANDREW LANG and W. A. CRAIGIE. With Portrait. *Third Edition. Demy 8vo, gilt top. 6s.*
Burnside (W. F.), M.A. OLD TESTAMENT HISTORY FOR USE IN SCHOOLS. *Cr. 8vo. 3s. 6d.*
Burton (Alfred). See I.P.L.
Butler (Joseph). See Standard Library.
Caldecott (Alfred), D.D. See Handbooks of Theology.
Calderwood (D. S.), Headmaster of the Normal School, Edinburgh. TEST CARDS IN EUCLID AND ALGEBRA. In three packets of 40, with Answers. 1s. each. Or in three Books, price 2d., 2d., and 3d.
Cambridge (Ada) [Mrs. Cross]. THIRTY YEARS IN AUSTRALIA. *Demy 8vo. 7s. 6d.*
A Colonial Edition is also published.
Canning (George). See Little Library.
Capey (E. F. H.). See Oxford Biographies.
Careless (John). See I.P.L.
Carlyle (Thomas). THE FRENCH REVOLUTION. Edited by C. R. L. FLETCHER, Fellow of Magdalen College, Oxford. *Three Volumes. Cr. 8vo. 18s.*

THE LIFE AND LETTERS OF OLIVER CROMWELL. With an Introduction by C. H. FIRTH, M.A., and Notes and Appendices by Mrs. S. C. LOMAS. *Three Volumes. Demy 8vo. 18s. net.*
Carlyle (R. M. and A. J.), M.A. See Leaders of Religion.
*****Carpenter (Margaret).** THE CHILD IN ART. Illustrated. *Cr. 8vo. 6s.*
Chamberlin (Wilbur B.). ORDERED TO CHINA. *Cr. 8vo. 6s.*
A Colonial Edition is also published.
Channer (C. C.) and Roberts (M. E.). LACEMAKING IN THE MIDLANDS, PAST AND PRESENT. With 16 full-page Illustrations. *Cr. 8vo. 2s. 6d.*
Chapman (S. J.). See Books on Business.
Chatterton (Thomas). See Standard Library.
Chesterfield (Lord), THE LETTERS OF, TO HIS SON. Edited, with an Introduction by C. STRACHEY, and Notes by A. CALTHROP. *Two Volumes. Cr. 8vo. 12s.*
*****Chesterton (G. K.).** DICKENS. With Portraits and Illustrations. *Demy 8vo. 7s. 6d. net.*
A Colonial Edition is also published.
Christian (F. W.). THE CAROLINE ISLANDS. With many Illustrations and Maps. *Demy 8vo. 12s. 6d. net.*
Cicero. See Classical Translations.
Clarke (F. A.), M.A. See Leaders of Religion.
Cleather (A. L.) and Crump (B.). RICHARD WAGNER'S MUSIC DRAMAS: Interpretations, embodying Wagner's own explanations. *In Four Volumes. Fcap 8vo. 2s. 6d. each.*
VOL. I.—THE RING OF THE NIBELUNG. *Third Edition.*
VOL. II.—PARSIFAL, LOHENGRIN, and THE HOLY GRAIL.
VOL. III.—TRISTAN AND ISOLDE.
Clinch (G.). See Little Guides.
Clough (W. T.). See Junior School Books.
Coast (W. G.). B.A. EXAMINATION PAPERS IN VERGIL. *Cr. 8vo. 2s.*
Cobb (T.). See Little Blue Books.
Cobb (W. F.), M.A. THE BOOK OF PSALMS: with a Commentary. *Demy 8vo. 10s. 6d. net.*
Coleridge (S. T.), SELECTIONS FROM. Edited by ARTHUR SYMONS. *Fcap. 8vo. 2s. 6d. net.*
Collingwood (W. G.). See Half-Crown Library.
Collins (W. E.), M.A. See Churchman's Library.
Colonna. HYPNEROTOMACHIA POLIPHILI UBI HUMANA OMNIA NON NISI SOMNIUM ESSE DOCET ATQUE OBITER PLURIMA SCITU SANE QUAM DIGNA COMMEMORAT. An edition limited to 350 copies on handmade paper. *Folio. Three Guineas net.*
Combe (William). See I.P.L.

Cook (A. M.), M.A. See E. C. Marchant.
Cooke-Taylor (R. W.). See S.Q.S.
Corelli (Marie). THE PASSING OF THE GREAT QUEEN : *Fcap. 4to.* 1s.
A CHRISTMAS GREETING. *Cr. 4to.* 1s.
Corkran (Alice). See Little Books on Art.
Cotes (Rosemary). DANTE'S GARDEN. With a Frontispiece. *Second Edition. Fcap. 8vo.* 2s. 6d.; *leather,* 3s. 6d. *net.*
BIBLE FLOWERS. With a Frontispiece and Plan. *Fcap. 8vo.* 2s. 6d. *net.*
Cowley (Abraham). See Little Library.
Cowper (William), THE POEMS OF. Edited with an Introduction and Notes by J. C. BAILEY, M.A. Illustrated, including two unpublished designs by WILLIAM BLAKE. *Demy 8vo.* 10s. 6d. *net.*
Cox (J. Charles), LL.D., F.S.A. See Little Guides, The Antiquary's Books, and Ancient Cities.
Cox (Harold), B.A. See S.Q.S.
Crabbe (George). See Little Library.
Craigie (W. A.). A PRIMER OF BURNS. *Cr. 8vo.* 2s. 6d.
Craik (Mrs.). See Little Library.
Crashaw (Richard). See Little Library.
Crawford (F. G.). See Mary C. Danson.
Cross (J. A.). A LITTLE BOOK OF RELIGION. *Fcap. 8vo.* 2s. 6d. *net.*
Crouch (W.). BRYAN KING. With a Portrait. *Cr. 8vo.* 3s. 6d. *net.*
Cruikshank (G.). THE LOVING BALLAD OF LORD BATEMAN. With 11 Plates. *Cr. 16mo.* 1s. 6d. *net.*
Crump (B.). See A. L. Cleather.
Cunliffe (Sir F. H. E.), Fellow of All Souls' College, Oxford. THE HISTORY OF THE BOER WAR. With many Illustrations, Plans, and Portraits. *In 2 vols. Quarto.* 15s. *each.*
A Colonial Edition is also published.
Cunynghame (H.), C.B., See Connoisseur's Library.
Cutts (E. L.), D.D. See Leaders of Religion.
Daniell (G. W.), M.A. See Leaders of Religion.
Danson (Mary C.) and Crawford (F. G.). FATHERS IN THE FAITH. *Fcap. 8vo.* 1s. 6d.
Dante. LA COMMEDIA DI DANTE. The Italian Text edited by PAGET TOYNBEE, M.A., D.Litt. *Cr. 8vo.* 6s.
THE PURGATORIO OF DANTE. Translated into Spenserian Prose by C. GORDON WRIGHT. With the Italian text. *Fcap. 8vo.* 2s. 6d. *net.*
See also Paget Toynbee, Little Library and Standard Library.
Darley (George). See Little Library.
D'Arcy (R. F.), M.A. A NEW TRIGONOMETRY FOR BEGINNERS. *Cr. 8vo.* 2s. 6d.
Davenport (Cyril). See Connoisseur's Library and Little Books on Art.

Davey (Richard). THE PAGEANT OF LONDON. With 40 Illustrations in Colour by JOHN FULLEYLOVE, R. I. *In Two Volumes. Demy 8vo.* 7s. 6d. *net.* Each volume may be purchased separately.
VOL. I.—TO A.D. 1500.
VOL. II.—A.D. 1500 TO 1900.
Davis (H. W. C.), M.A., Fellow and Tutor of Balliol College, Author of 'Charlemagne.' ENGLAND UNDER THE NORMANS AND ANGEVINS: 1066-1272. With Maps and Illustrations. *Demy 8vo.* 10s. 6d. *net.*
Dawson (A. J.). MOROCCO. Illustrated. *Demy 8vo.* 10s. 6d. *net.*
Deane (A. C.). See Little Library.
Delbos (Leon). THE METRIC SYSTEM. *Cr. 8vo.* 2s.
Demosthenes. THE OLYNTHIACS AND PHILIPPICS. Translated by OTHO HOLLAND. *Cr. 8vo.* 2s. 6d.
Demosthenes. AGAINST CONON AND CALLICLES. Edited by F. DARWIN SWIFT, M.A. *Fcap. 8vo.* 2s.
Dickens (Charles). See Little Library and I.P.L.
Dickinson (Emily). POEMS. *Cr. 8vo.* 4s. 6d. *net.*
Dickinson (G. L.), M.A., Fellow of King's College, Cambridge. THE GREEK VIEW OF LIFE. *Fourth Edition. Cr. 8vo.* 2s. 6d.
Dickson (H. N.). F.R.Met. Soc. METEOROLOGY. Illustrated. *Cr. 8vo.* 2s. 6d.
Dilke (Lady). See S.Q.S.
Dillon (Edward). See Connoisseur's Library and Little Books on Art.
Ditchfield (P. H.), M.A., F.S.A. THE STORY OF OUR ENGLISH TOWNS. With an Introduction by AUGUSTUS JESSOPP, D.D. *Second Edition. Cr. 8vo.* 6s.
OLD ENGLISH CUSTOMS: Extant at the Present Time. *Cr. 8vo.* 6s.
See also Half-crown Library.
Dixon (W. M.), M.A. A PRIMER OF TENNYSON. *Second Edition. Cr. 8vo.* 2s. 6d.
ENGLISH POETRY FROM BLAKE TO BROWNING. *Second Edition. Cr. 8vo.* 2s. 6d.
Dole (N. H.). FAMOUS COMPOSERS. With Portraits. *Two Volumes. Demy 8vo.* 12s. *net.*
Doney (May). SONGS OF THE REAL. *Cr. 8vo.* 3s. 6d. *net.*
A volume of poems.
Douglas (James). THE MAN IN THE PULPIT. *Cr. 8vo.* 2s. 6d. *net.*
Dowden (J.), D.D., Lord Bishop of Edinburgh. See Churchman's Library.
Drage (G.). See Books on Business.

GENERAL LITERATURE

Driver (S. R.), D.D., D.C.L., Canon of Christ Church, Regius Professor of Hebrew in the University of Oxford. SERMONS ON SUBJECTS CONNECTED WITH THE OLD TESTAMENT. *Cr. 8vo.* 6s.
See also Westminster Commentaries.

Dry (Wakeling). See Little Guides.

Dryhurst (A. R.). See Little Books on Art.

Duguid (Charles). See Books on Business.

Dunn (J. T.), D.Sc., **and Mundella (V. A.).** GENERAL ELEMENTARY SCIENCE. With 114 Illustrations. *Second Edition. Cr. 8vo.* 3s. 6d.

Dunstan (A. E.), B.Sc. See Junior School Books and Textbooks of Science.

Durham (The Earl of). A REPORT ON CANADA. With an Introductory Note. *Demy 8vo.* 4s. 6d. *net.*

Dutt (W. A.). A POPULAR GUIDE TO NORFOLK. *Medium 8vo.* 6d. *net.*
THE NORFOLK BROADS. With coloured Illustrations by FRANK SOUTHGATE. *Cr. 8vo.* 6s. See also Little Guides.

Earle (John), Bishop of Salisbury. MICROCOSMOGRAPHIE, or A PIECE OF THE WORLD DISCOVERED. *Post 16mo.* 2s *net.*

Edmonds (Major J. E.), R.E.; D.A.Q.-M.G. See W. Birkbeck Wood.

Edwards (Clement). See S.Q.S.

Edwards (W. Douglas). See Commercial Series.

Egan (Pierce). See I.P.L.

Egerton (H. E.), M.A. A HISTORY OF BRITISH COLONIAL POLICY. New and Cheaper Issue. *Demy 8vo.* 7s. 6d. *net.*
A Colonial Edition is also published.

Ellaby (C. G.). See The Little Guides.

Ellerton (F. G.). See S. J. Stone.

Ellwood (Thomas), THE HISTORY OF THE LIFE OF. Edited by C. G. CRUMP, M.A. *Cr. 8vo.* 6s.

Epictetus. See W. H. D. Rouse.

Erasmus. A Book called in Latin ENCHIRIDION MILITIS CHRISTIANI, and in English the Manual of the Christian Knight.
From the edition printed by Wynken de Worde, 1533. *Fcap. 8vo* 3s. 6d. *net.*

Fairbrother (W. H.), M.A. THE PHILOSOPHY OF T. H. GREEN. *Second Edition. Cr. 8vo.* 3s. 6d.

Farrer (Reginald). THE GARDEN OF ASIA. *Second Edition. Cr. 8vo.* 6s.
A Colonial Edition is also published.

Fea (Allan). BEAUTIES OF THE SEVENTEENEH CENTURY. With 100 Illustrations. *Demy 8vo.* 12s. 6d. *net.*

FELISSA; OR, THE LIFE AND OPINIONS OF A KITTEN OF SENTIMENT. With 12 Coloured Plates. *Post 16mo.* 2s. 6d. *net.*

Ferrier (Susan). See Little Library.

Fidler (T. Claxton), M. Inst. C.E. See Books on Business.

Fielding (Henry). See Standard Library.

Finn (S. W.), M.A. See Junior Examination Series.

Firth (C. H.), M.A. CROMWELL'S ARMY: A History of the English Soldier during the Civil Wars, the Commonwealth, and the Protectorate. *Cr. 8vo.* 6s

Fisher (G. W.), M.A. ANNALS OF SHREWSBURY SCHOOL. Illustrated. *Demy 8vo.* 10s. 6d.

FitzGerald (Edward). THE RUBAIYAT OF OMAR KHAYYÁM. Printed from the Fifth and last Edition. With a Commentary by Mrs. STEPHEN BATSON, and a Biography of Omar by E. D. Ross. *Cr. 8vo.* 6s. See also Miniature Library.

FitzGerald (H. P.). A CONCISE HANDBOOK OF CLIMBERS, TWINERS, AND WALL SHRUBS. Illustrated. *Fcap. 8vo.* 3s. 6d. *net.*

Flecker (W. H.), M.A., D.C.L., Headmaster of the Dean Close School, Cheltenham. THE STUDENT'S PRAYER BOOK. THE TEXT OF MORNING AND EVENING PRAYER AND LITANY. With an Introduction and Notes. *Cr. 8vo.* 2s 6d.

Flux (A. W.), M.A., William Dow Professor of Political Economy in M'Gill University, Montreal. ECONOMIC PRINCIPLES. *Demy 8vo.* 7s. 6d. *net.*

Fortescue (Mrs. G.). See Little Books on Art.

Fraser (David). A MODERN CAMPAIGN; OR, WAR AND WIRELESS TELEGRAPHY IN THE FAR EAST. Illustrated. *Cr. 8vo.* 6s.
A Colonial Edition is also published.

Fraser (J. F.). ROUND THE WORLD ON A WHEEL. With 100 Illustrations. *Fourth Edition Cr. 8vo.* 6s.
A Colonial Edition is also published.

French (W.), M.A. See Textbooks of Science.

Freudenreich (Ed. von). DAIRY BACTERIOLOGY. A Short Manual for the Use of Students. Translated by J. R. AINSWORTH DAVIS, M.A. *Second Edition. Revised. Cr. 8vo.* 2s. 6d.

Fulford (H. W.), M.A. See Churchman's Bible.

C. G., and F. C. G. JOHN BULL'S ADVENTURES IN THE FISCAL WONDERLAND. By CHARLES GEAKE. With 46 Illustrations by F. CARRUTHERS GOULD. *Second Edition. Cr. 8vo.* 1s. *net.*

*****Gallaher (D.) and Stead (D. W.).** THE COMPLETE RUGBY FOOTBALLER. With an Account of the Tour of the New Zealanders in England. With Illustrations. *Demy 8vo.* 10s. 6d. *net.*

Gallichan (W. M.). See Little Guides.

Gambado (Geoffrey, Esq.). See I.P.L.

Gaskell (Mrs.). See Little Library and Standard Library.

Gasquet, the Right Rev. Abbot, O.S.B. See Antiquary's Books.

Messrs. Methuen's Catalogue

George (H. B.), M.A., Fellow of New College, Oxford. BATTLES OF ENGLISH HISTORY. With numerous Plans. *Fourth Edition.* Revised, with a new Chapter including the South African War. *Cr. 8vo.* 3s. 6d.
A HISTORICAL GEOGRAPHY OF THE BRITISH EMPIRE. *Second Edition. Cr. 8vo.* 3s. 6d.
Gibbins (H. de B.), Litt.D., M.A. INDUSTRY IN ENGLAND: HISTORICAL OUTLINES. With 5 Maps. *Fourth Edition. Demy 8vo.* 10s. 6d.
A COMPANION GERMAN GRAMMAR. *Cr. 8vo.* 1s. 6d.
THE INDUSTRIAL HISTORY OF ENGLAND. *Eleventh Edition.* Revised. With Maps and Plans. *Cr. 8vo.* 3s.
ENGLISH SOCIAL REFORMERS. *Second Edition. Cr. 8vo.* 2s. 6d.
See also Commercial Series and S.Q.S.
Gibbon (Edward). THE DECLINE AND FALL OF THE ROMAN EMPIRE. A New Edition, edited with Notes, Appendices, and Maps, by J. B. BURY, M.A., Litt.D., Regius Professor of Greek at Cambridge. *In Seven Volumes. Demy 8vo.* Gilt top, 8s. 6d. each. Also, *Cr. 8vo.* 6s. each.
MEMOIRS OF MY LIFE AND WRITINGS. Edited by G. BIRKBECK HILL, LL.D. *Demy 8vo, Gilt top.* 8s. 6d. Also *Cr. 8vo.* 6s.
See also Standard Library.
Gibson (E. C. S.), D.D., Lord Bishop of Gloucester. See Westminster Commentaries, Handbooks of Theology, and Oxford Biographies.
Gilbert (A. R.). See Little Books on Art.
Gloag (M.). See K. Wyatt.
Godfrey (Elizabeth). A BOOK OF REMEMBRANCE. Edited by. *Fcap. 8vo.* 2s. 6d. net.
Godley (A. D.), M.A., Fellow of Magdalen College, Oxford. LYRA FRIVOLA. *Third Edition. Fcap. 8vo.* 2s. 6d.
VERSES TO ORDER. *Second Edition. Fcap. 8vo.* 2s. 6d.
SECOND STRINGS. *Fcap. 8vo.* 2s. 6d.
Goldsmith (Oliver). THE VICAR OF WAKEFIELD. *Fcap. 32mo.* With 10 Plates in Photogravure by Tony Johannot. *Leather,* 2s. 6d. net. See also I.P.L. and Standard Library.
Goodrich-Freer (A.). IN A SYRIAN SADDLE. *Demy 8vo.* 7s. 6d. net.
A Colonial Edition is also published.
Goudge (H. L.), M.A., Principal of Wells Theological College. See Westminster Commentaries.
Graham (P. Anderson). See S.Q.S.
Granger (F. S.), M.A., Litt.D. PSYCHOLOGY. *Third Edition. Cr. 8vo.* 2s. 6d.
THE SOUL OF A CHRISTIAN. *Cr. 8vo.* 6s.

Gray (E. M'Queen). GERMAN PASSAGES FOR UNSEEN TRANSLATION. *Cr. 8vo.* 2s. 6d.
Gray (P. L.), B.Sc. THE PRINCIPLES OF MAGNETISM AND ELECTRICITY: an Elementary Text-Book. With 181 Diagrams. *Cr. 8vo.* 3s. 6d.
Green (G. Buckland), M.A., late Fellow of St. John's College, Oxon. NOTES ON GREEK AND LATIN SYNTAX. *Cr. 8vo.* 3s. 6d.
Green (E. T.), M.A. See Churchman's Library.
Greenidge (A. H. J.), M.A. A HISTORY OF ROME: During the Later Republic and the Early Principate. *In Six Volumes. Demy 8vo.* Vol. I. (133-104 B.C.). 10s. 6d. net.
Greenwell (Dora). See Miniature Library.
Gregory (R. A.). THE VAULT OF HEAVEN. A Popular Introduction to Astronomy. Illustrated. *Cr. 8vo.* 2s. 6d.
Gregory (Miss E. C.). See Library of Devotion.
Greville Minor. A MODERN JOURNAL. Edited by J. A. SPENDER. *Cr. 8vo.* 3s. 6d. net.
Grubb (H. C.). See Textbooks of Technology.
Guiney (Louisa I.). HURRELL FROUDE: Memoranda and Comments. Illustrated. *Demy 8vo.* 10s. 6d. net.
Gwynn (M. L.). A BIRTHDAY BOOK. New and cheaper issue. *Royal 8vo.* 5s. net.
Hackett (John), B.D. A HISTORY OF THE ORTHODOX CHURCH OF CYPRUS. With Maps and Illustrations. *Demy 8vo.* 15s. net. p
Haddon (A. C.), Sc.D., F.R.S. HEAD-HUNTERS BLACK, WHITE, AND BROWN. With many Illustrations and a Map. *Demy 8vo.* 15s.
Hadfield (R. A.). See S.Q.S.
Hall (R. N.) and Neal (W. G.). THE ANCIENT RUINS OF RHODESIA. Illustrated. *Second Edition, revised. Demy 8vo.* 10s. 6d. net.
A Colonial Edition is also published.
Hall (R. N.). GREAT ZIMBABWE. With numerous Plans and Illustrations. *Second Edition. Royal 8vo.* 21s. net.
Hamilton (F. J.), D.D. See Byzantine Texts.
Hammond (J. L.). CHARLES JAMES FOX. *Demy 8vo.* 10s. 6d.
Hannay (D.). A SHORT HISTORY OF THE ROYAL NAVY, Illustrated. *Two Volumes. Demy 8vo.* 7s. 6d. each. Vol. I. 1200-1688.
Hannay (James O.), M.A. THE SPIRIT AND ORIGIN OF CHRISTIAN MONASTICISM. *Cr. 8vo.* 6s.
THE WISDOM OF THE DESERT. *Fcap. 8vo.* 3s. 6d. net.
Hare (A. T.), M.A. THE CONSTRUCTION OF LARGE INDUCTION COILS. With numerous Diagrams. *Demy 8vo.* 6s.

Harrison (Clifford). READING AND READERS. *Fcap. 8vo.* 2s. 6d.
Hawthorne (Nathaniel). See Little Library. HEALTH, WEALTH AND WISDOM. *Cr. 8vo.* 1s. *net.*
Heath (Frank R.). See Little Guides.
Heath (Dudley). See Connoisseur's Library.
Hello (Ernest). STUDIES IN SAINTSHIP. Translated from the French by V. M. CRAWFORD. *Fcap 8vo* 3s. 6d.
Henderson (B. W.), Fellow of Exeter College, Oxford. THE LIFE AND PRINCIPATE OF THE EMPEROR NERO. Illustrated. *New and cheaper issue. Demy 8vo.* 7s. 6d. *net.*
AT INTERVALS. *Fcap 8vo.* 2s. 6d. *net.*
Henderson (T. F.). See Little Library and Oxford Biographies.
Henley (W. E.). See Half-Crown Library.
Henson (H. H.), B.D., Canon of Westminster. APOSTOLIC CHRISTIANITY: As Illustrated by the Epistles of St. Paul to the Corinthians. *Cr. 8vo.* 6s.
LIGHT AND LEAVEN: HISTORICAL AND SOCIAL SERMONS. *Cr. 8vo.* 6s.
DISCIPLINE AND LAW. *Fcap. 8vo.* 2s. 6d.
Herbert (George). See Library of Devotion.
Herbert of Cherbury (Lord). See Miniature Library.
Hewins (W. A. S.), B.A. ENGLISH TRADE AND FINANCE IN THE SEVENTEENTH CENTURY. *Cr. 8vo.* 2s. 6d.
Hewitt (Ethel M.) A GOLDEN DIAL. A Day Book of Prose and Verse. *Fcap. 8vo.* 2s. 6d. *net.*
Heywood (W.). PALIO AND PONTE: A Book of Tuscan Games. Illustrated. *Royal 8vo.* 21s. *net.*
Hilbert (T.). See Little Blue Books.
Hill (Clare). See Textbooks of Technology.
Hill (Henry), B.A., Headmaster of the Boy's High School, Worcester, Cape Colony. A SOUTH AFRICAN ARITHMETIC. *Cr. 8vo.* 3s. 6d.
Hillegas (Howard C.). WITH THE BOER FORCES. With 24 Illustrations. *Second Edition. Cr. 8vo.* 6s.
A Colonial Edition is also published.
Hirst (F. W.) See Books on Business.
Hobhouse (Emily). THE BRUNT OF THE WAR. With Map and Illustrations. *Cr. 8vo.* 6s.
A Colonial Edition is also published.
Hobhouse (L. T.), Fellow of C.C.C., Oxford. THE THEORY OF KNOWLEDGE. *Demy 8vo.* 10s. 6d. *net.*
Hobson (J. A.), M.A. INTERNATIONAL TRADE: A Study of Economic Principles. *Cr. 8vo.* 2s. 6d. *net.*
PROBLEMS OF POVERTY. *Fifth Edition. Cr. 8vo.* 2s. 6d.
Hodgkin (T.), D.C.L. See Leaders of Religion.

Hodgson (Mrs. W.) HOW TO IDENTIFY OLD CHINESE PORCELAIN. *Second Edition. Post 8vo.* 6s.
Hogg (Thomas Jefferson). SHELLEY AT OXFORD. With an Introduction by R. A. STREATFEILD. *Fcap. 8vo.* 2s. *net.*
Holden-Stone (G. de). See Books on Business.
Holdich (Sir T. H.), K.C.I.E. THE INDIAN BORDERLAND: being a Personal Record of Twenty Years. Illustrated. *Demy 8vo.* 10s. 6d. *net.*
A Colonial Edition is also published.
Holdsworth (W. S.), M.A. A HISTORY OF ENGLISH LAW. *In Two Volumes.* Vol. I. *Demy 8vo.* 10s. 6d. *net.*
Holland (Canon Scott). See Library of Devotion.
Holt (Emily). THE SECRET OF POPULARITY: How to Achieve Social Success. *Cr. 8vo.* 3s. 6d. *net.*
A Colonial Edition is also published.
Holyoake (G. J.). THE CO-OPERATIVE MOVEMENT TO-DAY. *Fourth Edition. Cr. 8vo.* 2s. 6d.
Hone (Nathaniel J.). See Antiquary's Books.
Hoppner. See Little Galleries.
Horace. See Classical Translations.
Horsburgh (E. L. S.), M.A. WATERLOO: A Narrative and Criticism. With Plans. *Second Edition. Cr. 8vo.* 5s. See also Oxford Biographies.
Horth (A. C.). See Textbooks of Technology.
Horton (R. F.), D.D. See Leaders of Religion.
Hosie (Alexander). MANCHURIA. With Illustrations and a Map. *Second Edition. Demy 8vo.* 7s 6d *net.*
A Colonial Edition is also published.
How (F. D.). SIX GREAT SCHOOLMASTERS. With Portraits and Illustrations. *Second Edition. Demy 8vo.* 7s. 6d.
Howell (G.). See S. Q. S.
Hudson (Robert). MEMORIALS OF A WARWICKSHIRE PARISH. Illustrated. *Demy 8vo.* 15s. *net.*
Hughes (C. E.). THE PRAISE OF SHAKESPEARE. An English Anthology. With a Preface by SIDNEY LEE. *Demy 8vo.* 3s. 6d *net.*
Hughes (Thomas). TOM BROWN'S SCHOOLDAYS. With an Introduction and Notes by VERNON RENDALL. *Leather. Royal 32mo.* 2s. 6d. *net.*
Hutchinson (Horace G.) THE NEW FOREST. Illustrated in colour with 50 Pictures by WALTER TYNDALE and 4 by Miss LUCY KEMP WELCH. *Large Demy 8vo.* 21s. *net*
Hutton (A. W.), M.A. See Leaders of Religion and Library of Devotion.
Hutton (Edward). THE CITIES OF UMBRIA. With many Illustrations, of which 20 are in Colour, by A. PISA. *Second Edition. Cr. 8vo.* 6s.
A Colonial Edition is also published.

ENGLISH LOVE POEMS. Edited with an Introduction. *Fcap. 8vo. 3s. 6d. net.*
Hutton (R. H.). See Leaders of Religion.
Hutton (W. H.), M.A. THE LIFE OF SIR THOMAS MORE. With Portraits. *Second Edition. Cr. 8vo. 5s.* See also Leaders of Religion.
Hyett (F. A.). A SHORT HISTORY OF FLORENCE. *Demy 8vo. 7s. 6d. net.*
Ibsen (Henrik). BRAND. A Drama. Translated by WILLIAM WILSON. *Third Edition. Cr. 8vo. 3s. 6d.*
Inge (W. R.), M.A., Fellow and Tutor of Hertford College, Oxford. CHRISTIAN MYSTICISM. The Bampton Lectures for 1899. *Demy 8vo. 12s. 6d. net.* See also Library of Devotion.
Innes (A. D.), M.A. A HISTORY OF THE BRITISH IN INDIA. With Maps and Plans. *Cr. 8vo. 6s.*
ENGLAND UNDER THE TUDORS. With Maps. *Demy 8vo. 10s. 6d. net.*
Jackson (C. E.), B.A. See Textbooks of Science.
Jackson (S.), M.A. See Commercial Series.
Jackson (F. Hamilton). See Little Guides.
Jacob (F.), M.A. See Junior Examination Series.
Jeans (J. Stephen). See S. Q. S. and Business Books.
Jeffreys (D. Gwyn). DOLLY'S THEATRICALS. Described and Illustrated with 24 Coloured Pictures. *Super Royal 16mo. 2s. 6d.*
Jenks (E.), M.A., Reader of Law in the University of Oxford. ENGLISH LOCAL GOVERNMENT. *Cr. 8vo. 2s. 6d.*
Jenner (Mrs. H.). See Little Books on Art.
Jessopp (Augustus), D.D. See Leaders of Religion.
Jevons (F. B.), M.A., Litt.D., Principal of Bishop Hatfield's Hall, Durham. RELIGION IN EVOLUTION. *Cr. 8vo. 3s. 6d. net.*
See also Churchman's Library and Handbooks of Theology.
Johnson (Mrs. Barham). WILLIAM BODHAM DONNE AND HIS FRIENDS. Illustrated. *Demy 8vo. 10s. 6d. net.*
Johnston (Sir H. H.), K.C.B. BRITISH CENTRAL AFRICA. With nearly 200 Illustrations and Six Maps. *Third Edition. Cr. 4to. 18s. net.*
A Colonial Edition is also published.
Jones (R. Crompton), M.A. POEMS OF THE INNER LIFE. Selected by. *Eleventh Edition. Fcap. 8vo. 2s. 6d. net.*
Jones (H.). See Commercial Series.
Jones (L. A. Atherley), K.C., M.P., and **Bellot (Hugh H. L.).** THE MINERS' GUIDE TO THE COAL MINES REGULATION ACTS. *Cr. 8vo. 2s. 6d. net.*
*COMMERCE IN WAR. *Demy 8vo. 21s. net.*
Jonson (Ben). See Standard Library.

Julian (Lady) of Norwich. REVELATIONS OF DIVINE LOVE. Edited by GRACE WARRACK. *Cr. 8vo. 3s. 6d.*
Juvenal. See Classical Translations.
'Kappa.' LET YOUTH BUT KNOW: A Plea for Reason in Education. *Cr. 8vo. 3s. 6d. net.*
Kaufmann (M.). See S. Q. S.
Keating (J. F.), D.D. THE AGAPE AND THE EUCHARIST. *Cr. 8vo. 3s. 6d.*
Keats (John). THE POEMS OF. Edited with Introduction and Notes by E. de Selincourt, M.A. *Demy 8vo. 7s. 6d. net.* See also Little Library, Standard Library, and E. de Selincourt.
Keble (John). THE CHRISTIAN YEAR. With an Introduction and Notes by W. LOCK, D.D., Warden of Keble College. Illustrated by R. ANNING BELL. *Third Edition. Fcap. 8vo. 3s. 6d.; padded morocco, 5s.* See also Library of Devotion.
Kempis (Thomas à). THE IMITATION OF CHRIST. With an Introduction by DEAN FARRAR. Illustrated by C. M. GERE. *Third Edition. Fcap. 8vo. 3s. 6d.; padded morocco. 5s.*
Also Translated by C. BIGG, D.D. *Cr. 8vo. 3s. 6d.* See also Library of Devotion and Standard Library.
Kennedy (Bart.). THE GREEN SPHINX. *Cr. 8vo. 2s. 6d. net.*
A Colonial Edition is also published.
Kennedy (James Houghton), D.D., Assistant Lecturer in Divinity in the University of Dublin. ST. PAUL'S SECOND AND THIRD EPISTLES TO THE CORINTHIANS. With Introduction, Dissertations and Notes. *Cr. 8vo. 6s.*
Kestell (J. D.). THROUGH SHOT AND FLAME: Being the Adventures and Experiences of J. D. KESTELL, Chaplain to General Christian de Wet. *Cr. 8vo. 6s.*
A Colonial Edition is also published.
Kimmins (C. W.), M.A. THE CHEMISTRY OF LIFE AND HEALTH. Illustrated. *Cr. 8vo. 2s. 6d.*
Kinglake (A. W.). See Little Library.
Kipling (Rudyard). BARRACK-ROOM BALLADS. *73rd Thousand. Twenty-first Edition. Cr. 8vo. 6s.*
A Colonial Edition is also published.
THE SEVEN SEAS. *62nd Thousand. Tenth Edition. Cr. 8vo. 6s.*
A Colonial Edition is also published.
THE FIVE NATIONS. *41st Thousand. Second Edition. Cr. 8vo. 6s.*
A Colonial Edition is also published.
DEPARTMENTAL DITTIES. *Sixteenth Edition. Cr. 8vo. 6s.*
A Colonial Edition is also published.
Knight (Albert E.). THE COMPLETE CRICKETER. Illustrated. *Demy 8vo. 7s. 6d. net.*
A Colonial Edition is also published.

General Literature

Knowling (R. J.), M.A., Professor of New Testament Exegesis at King's College, London. See Westminster Commentaries.

Lamb (Charles and Mary), THE WORKS OF. Edited by E. V. LUCAS. Illustrated. *In Seven Volumes. Demy 8vo. 7s. 6d. each.*
THE LIFE OF. See E. V. Lucas.
See also Little Library.

Lambert (F. A. H.). See Little Guides.

Lambros (Professor). See Byzantine Texts.

Lane-Poole (Stanley). A HISTORY OF EGYPT IN THE MIDDLE AGES. Fully Illustrated. *Cr. 8vo. 6s.*

Langbridge (F.), M.A. BALLADS OF THE BRAVE: Poems of Chivalry, Enterprise, Courage, and Constancy. *Second Edition. Cr. 8vo. 2s. 6d.*

Law (William). See Library of Devotion and Standard Library.

Leach (Henry). THE DUKE OF DEVONSHIRE. A Biography. With 12 Illustrations. *Demy 8vo. 12s. 6d. net.*
A Colonial Edition is also published.

Le Braz (Anatole). THE LAND OF PARDONS. Translated by FRANCES M. GOSTLING. Illustrated in colour. *Crown 8vo. 6s.*

Lee (Captain L. Melville). A HISTORY OF POLICE IN ENGLAND. *Cr. 8vo. 3s. 6d. net.*

Leigh (Percival). THE COMIC ENGLISH GRAMMAR. Embellished with upwards of 50 characteristic Illustrations by JOHN LEECH. *Post 16mo. 2s. 6d. net.*

Lewes (V. B.), M.A. AIR AND WATER. Illustrated. *Cr. 8vo. 2s. 6d.*

Lewis (Mrs. Gwyn). A CONCISE HANDBOOK OF GARDEN SHRUBS. Illustrated. *Fcap. 8vo. 3s. 6d. net.*

Lisle (Fortunée de). See Little Books on Art.

Littlehales (H.). See Antiquary's Books.

Lock (Walter), D.D., Warden of Keble College. ST. PAUL, THE MASTERBUILDER. *Second Edition. Cr. 8vo. 3s. 6d.*
THE BIBLE AND CHRISTIAN LIFE. *Cr. 8vo. 6s.*
See also Leaders of Religion and Library of Devotion.

Locker (F.). See Little Library.

Longfellow (H. W.). See Little Library.

Lorimer (George Horace). LETTERS FROM A SELF-MADE MERCHANT TO HIS SON. *Fourteenth Edition. Cr. 8vo. 6s.*
A Colonial Edition is also published.
OLD GORGON GRAHAM. *Second Edition. Cr. 8vo. 6s.*
A Colonial Edition is also published.

Lover (Samuel). See I. P. L.

E. V. L. and C. L. G. ENGLAND DAY BY DAY: Or, The Englishman's Handbook to Efficiency. Illustrated by GEORGE MORROW. *Fourth Edition. Fcap. 4to. 1s. net.*

Lucas (E. V.). THE LIFE OF CHARLES LAMB. With numerous Portraits and Illustrations. *Third Edition. Two Vols. Demy 8vo. 21s. net.*
A Colonial Edition is also published.
A WANDERER IN HOLLAND. With many Illustrations, of which 20 are in Colour by HERBERT MARSHALL. *Fifth Edition. Cr. 8vo. 6s.*
A Colonial Edition is also published.
THE OPEN ROAD: a Little Book for Wayfarers. *Ninth Edition. Fcap. 8vo. 5s.; India Paper, 7s. 6d.*
THE FRIENDLY TOWN: a Little Book for the Urbane. *Second Edition. Fcap. 8vo. 5s.; India Paper, 7s. 6d.*

Lucian. See Classical Translations.

Lyde (L. W.), M.A. See Commercial Series.

Lydon (Noel S.). See Junior School Books.

Lyttelton (Hon. Mrs. A.). WOMEN AND THEIR WORK. *Cr. 8vo. 2s. 6d.*

M. M. HOW TO DRESS AND WHAT TO WEAR. *Cr. 8vo. 1s. net.*

Macaulay (Lord). CRITICAL AND HISTORICAL ESSAYS. Edited by F. C. MONTAGUE, M.A. *Three Volumes. Cr. 8vo. 18s.*
The only edition of this book completely annotated.

M'Allen (J. E. B.), M.A. See Commercial Series.

MacCulloch (J. A.). See Churchman's Library.

MacCunn (Florence A.). MARY STUART. With over 60 Illustrations, including a Frontispiece in Photogravure. *Demy 8vo. 10s. 6d. net.*
A Colonial Edition is also published. See also Leaders of Religion.

McDermott (E. R.). See Books on Business.

M'Dowall (A. S.). See Oxford Biographies.

Mackay (A. M.). See Churchman's Library.

Magnus (Laurie), M.A. A PRIMER OF WORDSWORTH. *Cr. 8vo. 2s. 6d.*

Mahaffy (J. P.), Litt.D. A HISTORY OF THE EGYPT OF THE PTOLEMIES Fully Illustrated. *Cr. 8vo. 6s.*

Maitland (F. W.), LL.D., Downing Professor of the Laws of England in the University of Cambridge. CANON LAW IN ENGLAND. *Royal 8vo. 7s. 6d.*

Malden (H. E.), M.A. ENGLISH RECORDS. A Companion to the History of England. *Cr. 8vo. 3s. 6d.*
THE ENGLISH CITIZEN: HIS RIGHTS AND DUTIES. *Fifth Edition. Cr. 8vo. 1s. 6d.*
A SCHOOL HISTORY OF SURREY. Illustrated. *Cr. 8vo. 1s. 6d.*

Marchant (E. C.), M.A., Fellow of Peterhouse, Cambridge. A GREEK ANTHOLOGY. *Second Edition. Cr. 8vo. 3s. 6d.*

Marchant (C. E.), M.A., and Cook (A. M.), M.A. PASSAGES FOR UNSEEN TRANSLATION. *Third Edition. Cr. 8vo. 3s. 6d.*

Marlowe (Christopher). See Standard Library.

Marr (J. E.), F.R.S., Fellow of St John's College, Cambridge. THE SCIENTIFIC STUDY OF SCENERY. *Second Edition.* Illustrated. *Cr. 8vo.* 6s.

AGRICULTURAL GEOLOGY. Illustrated. *Cr. 8vo.* 6s.

Marvell (Andrew). See Little Library.

Masefield (John). SEA LIFE IN NELSON'S TIME. Illustrated. *Cr. 8vo.* 3s. 6d. net.

ON THE SPANISH MAIN. With Portraits and Illustrations. *Demy 8vo.* 10s. 6d. net.

A Colonial Edition is also published.

Maskell (A.). See Connoisseur's Library.

Mason (A. J.), D.D. See Leaders of Religion.

Massee (George). THE EVOLUTION OF PLANT LIFE: Lower Forms. Illustrated. *Cr. 8vo.* 2s. 6d.

Massinger (P.). See Standard Library.

Masterman (C. F. G.), M.A. TENNYSON AS A RELIGIOUS TEACHER. *Cr. 8vo.* 6s.

Matheson (Mrs. E. F.). COUNSELS OF LIFE. *Fcap. 8vo.* 2s. 6d. net.

May (Phil). THE PHIL MAY ALBUM. *Second Edition.* 4to. 1s. net.

Mellows (Emma S.). A SHORT STORY OF ENGLISH LITERATURE. *Cr. 8vo.* 3s. 6d.

Methuen (A. M. S.). THE TRAGEDY OF SOUTH AFRICA. *Cr. 8vo.* 2s. net. Also *Cr. 8vo.* 3d. net.

A revised and enlarged edition of the author's 'Peace or War in South Africa.'

ENGLAND'S RUIN: DISCUSSED IN SIXTEEN LETTERS TO THE RIGHT HON. JOSEPH CHAMBERLAIN, M.P. *Seventh Edition. Cr. 8vo.* 3d. net.

Michell (E. B.). THE ART AND PRACTICE OF HAWKING. With 3 Photogravures by G. E. LODGE, and other Illustrations. *Demy 8vo.* 10s. 6d.

Millais (J. G.). THE LIFE AND LETTERS OF SIR JOHN EVERETT MILLAIS, President of the Royal Academy. With many Illustrations, of which 2 are in Photogravure. *New Edition. Demy 8vo.* 7s. 6d. net

A Colonial Edition is also published.

Millin (G. F.). PICTORIAL GARDENING. Illustrated. *Cr. 8vo.* 3s. 6d. net.

Millis (C. T.), M.I.M.E. See Textbooks of Technology.

Milne (J. G.), M.A. A HISTORY OF ROMAN EGYPT. Fully Illustrated. *Cr. 8vo.* 6s.

Milton (John), THE POEMS OF, BOTH ENGLISH AND LATIN, Compos'd at several times. Printed by his true Copies. The Songs were set in Musick by Mr. HENRY LAWES, Gentleman of the Kings Chappel, and one of His Majesties Private Musick.

Printed and publish'd according to Order. Printed by RUTH RAWORTH for HUMPHREY MOSELEY, and are to be sold at the signe of the Princes Armes in Pauls Churchyard, 1645.

See also Little Library, Standard Library, and R. F. Towndrow.

Minchin (H. C.), M A. See R. Peel.

Mitchell (P. Chalmers), M.A. OUTLINES OF BIOLOGY. Illustrated. *Second Edition. Cr. 8vo.* 6s.

Mitton (G. E.). JANE AUSTEN AND HER TIMES. With many Portraits and Illustrations. *Second Edition. Demy 8vo.* 10s. 6d. net.

A Colonial Edition is also published.

'**Moll (A.).**' See Books on Business.

Moir (D. M.). See Little Library.

Money (L. G. Chiozza). RICHES AND POVERTY. *Second Edition. Demy 8vo.* 5s. net.

Montaigne. See C. F. Pond.

Moore (H. E.). See S. Q. S.

Moran (Clarence G.). See Books on Business.

More (Sir Thomas). See Standard Library.

Morfill (W. R.), Oriel College, Oxford. A HISTORY OF RUSSIA FROM PETER THE GREAT TO ALEXANDER II. With Maps and Plans. *Cr. 8vo.* 3s. 6d.

Morich (R. J.), late of Clifton College. See School Examination Series.

Morris (J.). THE MAKERS OF JAPAN. With many portraits and Illustrations. *Demy 8vo.* 12s. 6d. net.

A Colonial Edition is also published.

Morris (J. E.). See Little Guides.

Morton (Miss Anderson). See Miss Brodrick.

THE MOTOR YEAR-BOOK FOR 1906. With many Illustrations and Diagrams. *Demy 8vo.* 7s. 6d. net.

Moule (H. C. G.), D.D., Lord Bishop of Durham. See Leaders of Religion.

Muir (M. M. Pattison), M.A. THE CHEMISTRY OF FIRE. Illustrated. *Cr. 8vo.* 2s. 6d.

Mundella (V. A.), M.A. See J. T. Dunn.

Munro (R.), LL.D. See Antiquary's Books.

Naval Officer (A). See I. P. L.

Neal (W. G.). See R. N. Hall.

Newman (J. H.) and others. See Library of Devotion.

Nichols (J. B. B.). See Little Library.

Nicklin (T.), M.A. EXAMINATION PAPERS IN THUCYDIDES. *Cr. 8vo.* 2s.

Nimrod. See I. P. L.

Norgate (G. Le G.). SIR WALTER SCOTT. Illustrated. *Demy 8vo.* 7s. 6d. net.

General Literature 13

Norregaard (B. W.). THE GREAT SIEGE: The Investment and Fall of Port rthur. Illustrated. *Demy 8vo.* 10s. 6d. net.

Northcote (James), R.A. THE CONVERSATIONS OF JAMES NORTHCOTE, R.A., AND JAMES WARD. Edited by ERNEST FLETCHER. With many Portraits. *Demy 8vo.* 10s. 6d.

Norway (A. H.). NAPLES. With 25 Coloured Illustrations by MAURICE GREIFFENHAGEN. A New Edition. *Cr. 8vo.* 6s.

Novalis. THE DISCIPLES AT SAIS AND OTHER FRAGMENTS. Edited by Miss UNA BIRCH. *Fcap. 8vo.* 3s. 6d.

Oldfield (W. J.), Canon of Lincoln. A PRIMER OF RELIGION. *Fcap 8vo.* 2s. 6d.

Oliphant (Mrs.). See Leaders of Religion.

Oman (C. W. C.), M.A., Fellow of All Souls', Oxford. A HISTORY OF THE ART OF WAR. Vol. II.: The Middle Ages, from the Fourth to the Fourteenth Century. Illustrated. *Demy 8vo.* 10s. 6d. net.

Ottley (R. L.), D.D. See Handbooks of Theology and Leaders of Religion.

Overton (J. H.). See Leaders of Religion.

Owen (Douglas). See Books on Business.

Oxford (M. N.), of Guy's Hospital. A HANDBOOK OF NURSING. *Third Edition. Cr. 8vo.* 3s. 6d.

Pakes (W. C. C.). THE SCIENCE OF HYGIENE. Illustrated. *Demy 8vo.* 15s.

Palmer (Frederick). WITH KUROKI IN MANCHURIA. Illustrated. *Third Edition. Demy 8vo.* 7s. 6d. net.
A Colonial Edition is also published.

Parker (Gilbert). A LOVER'S DIARY. *Fcap. 8vo.* 5s.

Parkes (A. K.). SMALL LESSONS ON GREAT TRUTHS. *Fcap. 8vo.* 1s. 6d.

Parkinson (John). PARADISI IN SOLE PARADISUS TERRESTRIS, OR A GARDEN OF ALL SORTS OF PLEASANT FLOWERS. *Folio.* £4, 4s. net.

Parmenter (John). HELIO-TROPES, OR NEW POSIES FOR SUNDIALS, 1625. Edited by PERCIVAL LANDON. *Quarto.* 3s. 6d. net.

Parmentier (Prof. Leon). See Byzantine Texts.

Pascal. See Library of Devotion.

Paston (George). SOCIAL CARICATURES IN THE EIGHTEENTH CENTURY. *Imperial Quarto.* £2, 12s. 6d. net. See also Little Books on Art and I.P.L.

Paterson (W. R.) (Benjamin Swift). LIFE'S QUESTIONINGS. *Cr. 8vo.* 3s. 6d. net.

Patterson (A. H.). NOTES OF AN EAST COAST NATURALIST. Illustrated in Colour by F. SOUTHGATE. *Second Edition. Cr. 8vo.* 6s.

NATURE IN EASTERN NORFOLK. A series of observations on the Birds, Fishes, Mammals, Reptiles, and stalk-eyed Crustaceans found in that neighbourhood, with a list of the species. With 12 Illustrations in colour, by FRANK SOUTHGATE. *Second Edition. Cr. 8vo.* 6s.

Peacock (N.). See Little Books on Art.

Pearce (E. H.), M.A. ANNALS OF CHRIST'S HOSPITAL. Illustrated. *Demy 8vo.* 7s. 6d.

Peel (Robert), and **Minchin (H. C.),** M.A. OXFORD. With 100 Illustrations in Colour. *Cr. 8vo.* 6s.

Peel (Sidney), late Fellow of Trinity College, Oxford, and Secretary to the Royal Commission on the Licensing Laws. PRACTICAL LICENSING REFORM. *Second Edition. Cr. 8vo.* 1s. 6d.

Peters (J. P.), D.D. See Churchman's Library.

Petrie (W. M. Flinders), D.C.L., LL.D., Professor of Egyptology at University College. A HISTORY OF EGYPT, FROM THE EARLIEST TIMES TO THE PRESENT DAY. Fully Illustrated. *In six volumes. Cr. 8vo.* 6s. each.

VOL. I. PREHISTORIC TIMES TO XVITH DYNASTY. *Fifth Edition.*
VOL. II. THE XVIITH AND XVIIITH DYNASTIES. *Fourth Edition.*
VOL. III. XIXTH TO XXXTH DYNASTIES.
VOL. IV. THE EGYPT OF THE PTOLEMIES. J. P. MAHAFFY, Litt.D.
VOL. V. ROMAN EGYPT. J. G. MILNE, M.A.
VOL. VI. EGYPT IN THE MIDDLE AGES. STANLEY LANE-POOLE, M.A.

RELIGION AND CONSCIENCE IN ANCIENT EGYPT. Illustrated. *Cr. 8vo.* 2s. 6d.

SYRIA AND EGYPT, FROM THE TELL EL AMARNA TABLETS. *Cr. 8vo.* 2s. 6d.

EGYPTIAN TALES. Illustrated by TRISTRAM ELLIS. *In Two Volumes. Cr. 8vo.* 3s. 6d. each.

EGYPTIAN DECORATIVE ART. With 120 Illustrations. *Cr. 8vo.* 3s. 6d.

Phillips (W. A.). See Oxford Biographies.

Phillpotts (Eden). MY DEVON YEAR. With 38 Illustrations by J. LEY PETHYBRIDGE. *Second and Cheaper Edition. Large Cr. 8vo.* 6s.

UP ALONG AND DOWN ALONG. Illustrated by CLAUDE SHEPPERSON. *Cr. 4to.* 5s. net.
A volume of poems.

Pienaar (Philip). WITH STEYN AND DE WET. *Second Edition. Cr. 8vo.* 3s. 6d.
A Colonial Edition is also published.

Plarr (Victor G.) and **Walton (F. W.).** A SCHOOL HISTORY OF MIDDLESEX. Illustrated. *Cr. 8vo.* 1s. 6d.

Plato. See Standard Library.

Plautus. THE CAPTIVI. Edited, with an Introduction, Textual Notes, and a Commentary, by W. M. LINDSAY, Fellow of Jesus College, Oxford. *Demy 8vo.* 10s. 6d. *net.*

Plowden-Wardlaw (J. T.), B.A., King's College, Cambridge. See School Examination Series.

Podmore (Frank). MODERN SPIRITUALISM. *Two Volumes. Demy 8vo.* 21s. *net.*
A History and a Criticism.

Poer (J. Patrick Le). A MODERN LEGIONARY. *Cr. 8vo.* 6s.
A Colonial Edition is also published.

Pollard (Alice). See Little Books on Art.

Pollard (A. W.). OLD PICTURE BOOKS. Illustrated. *Demy 8vo.* 7s. 6d. *net.*

Pollard (Eliza F.). See Little Books on Art.

Pollock (David), M.I.N.A. See Books on Business.

Pond (C. F.). A DAY BOOK OF MONTAIGNE. Edited by. *Fcap. 8vo.* 3s. 6d. *net.*

Potter (M. C.), M.A., F.L.S. A TEXTBOOK OF AGRICULTURAL BOTANY. Illustrated. *Second Edition. Cr. 8vo.* 4s. 6d.

Power (J. O'Connor). THE MAKING OF AN ORATOR. *Cr. 8vo.* 6s.

Pradeau (G.). A KEY TO THE TIME ALLUSIONS IN THE DIVINE COMEDY. With a Dial. *Small quarto.* 3s. 6d.

Prance (G.). See Half-Crown Library.

Prescott (O. L.). ABOUT MUSIC, AND WHAT IT IS MADE OF. *Cr. 8vo.* 3s. 6d. *net.*

Price (L. L.), M.A., Fellow of Oriel College, Oxon. A HISTORY OF ENGLISH POLITICAL ECONOMY. *Fourth Edition. Cr. 8vo.* 2s. 6d.

Primrose (Deborah). A MODERN BŒOTIA. *Cr. 8vo.* 6s.

Pugin and Rowlandson. THE MICROCOSM OF LONDON, OR LONDON IN MINIATURE. With 104 Illustrations in colour. *In Three Volumes. Small 4to.* £3, 3s. *net.*

'Q' (A. T. Quiller Couch). See Half-Crown Library.

Quevedo Villegas. See Miniature Library.

G. R. and E. S. THE WOODHOUSE CORRESPONDENCE. *Cr. 8vo.* 6s.
A Colonial Edition is also Published.

Rackham (R. B.), M.A. See Westminster Commentaries.

Randolph (B. W.), D.D. See Library of Devotion.

Rannie (D. W.), M.A. A STUDENT'S HISTORY OF SCOTLAND. *Cr. 8vo.* 3s. 6d.

Rashdall (Hastings), M.A., Fellow and Tutor of New College, Oxford. DOCTRINE AND DEVELOPMENT. *Cr. 8vo.* 6s.

Rawstorne (Lawrence, Esq.). See I.P.L.

Raymond (Walter). A SCHOOL HISTORY OF SOMERSETSHIRE. Illustrated. *Cr. 8vo.* 1s. 6d.

A Real Paddy. See I.P.L.

Reason (W.), M.A. See S.Q.S.

Redfern (W. B.), Author of 'Ancient Wood and Iron Work in Cambridge,' etc. ROYAL AND HISTORIC GLOVES AND ANCIENT SHOES. Profusely Illustrated in colour and half-tone. *Quarto,* £2, 2s. *net.*

Reynolds. See Little Galleries.

*Rhodes (W. E.). A SCHOOL HISTORY OF LANCASHIRE. Illustrated. *Cr. 8vo.* 1s. 6d.

Roberts (M. E.). See C. C. Channer.

Robertson (A.), D.D., Lord Bishop of Exeter. REGNUM DEI. The Bampton Lectures of 1901. *Demy 8vo.* 12s. 6d. *net.*

Robertson (C. Grant), M.A., Fellow of All Souls' College, Oxford, Examiner in the Honours School of Modern History, Oxford, 1901-1904. SELECT STATUTES, CASES, AND CONSTITUTIONAL DOCUMENTS, 1660-1832. *Demy 8vo.* 10s. 6d. *net.*

Robertson (C. Grant) and Bartholomew (J. G.), F.R.S.E., F.R.G.S. A HISTORICAL AND MODERN ATLAS OF THE BRITISH EMPIRE. *Demy Quarto.* 4s. 6d. *net.*

Robertson (Sir G. S.), K.C.S.I. See Half-Crown Library.

Robinson (A. W.), M.A. See Churchman's Bible.

Robinson (Cecilia). THE MINISTRY OF DEACONESSES. With an Introduction by the late Archbishop of Canterbury. *Cr. 8vo.* 3s. 6d.

Robinson (F. S.). See Connoisseur's Library.

Rochefoucauld (La). See Little Library.

Rodwell (G.), B.A. NEW TESTAMENT GREEK. A Course for Beginners. With a Preface by WALTER LOCK, D.D., Warden of Keble College. *Fcap. 8vo.* 3s. 6d.

Roe (Fred). ANCIENT COFFERS AND CUPBOARDS: Their History and Description. Illustrated. *Quarto.* £3, 3s. *net.*

OLD OAK FURNITURE. With many Illustrations by the Author, including a frontispiece in colour. *Demy 8vo.* 10s. 6d. *net.*

Rogers (A. G. L.), M.A. See Books on Business.

Roscoe (E. S.). ROBERT HARLEY, EARL OF OXFORD. Illustrated. *Demy 8vo.* 7s. 6d.
This is the only life of Harley in existence.
See also Little Guides.

GENERAL LITERATURE

Rose (Edward). THE ROSE READER. Illustrated. *Cr. 8vo. 2s. 6d. Also in 4 Parts. Parts I. and II. 6d. each; Part III. 8d.; Part IV. 10d.*

Rouse (W. H. D.). WORDS OF THE ANCIENT WISE: Thoughts from Epictetus and Marcus Aurelius. Edited by. *Fcap. 8vo. 3s. 6d. net.*

Rowntree (Joshua). THE IMPERIAL DRUG TRADE. *Second and Cheaper Edition. Cr. 8vo. 2s. net.*

Rubie (A. E.), D.D. See Junior School Books.

Russell (W. Clark). THE LIFE OF ADMIRAL LORD COLLINGWOOD. With Illustrations by F. BRANGWYN. *Fourth Edition. Cr. 8vo. 6s.*
A Colonial Edition is also published.

St. Anselm. See Library of Devotion.

St. Augustine. See Library of Devotion.

St. Cyres (Viscount). See Oxford Biographies.

St. Francis of Assisi. See Standard Library.

'Saki' (H. Munro). REGINALD. *Second Edition. Fcap. 8vo. 2s. 6d. net.*

Sales (St. Francis de). See Library of Devotion.

Salmon (A. L.). A POPULAR GUIDE TO DEVON. *Medium 8vo. 6d. net.* See also Little Guides.

Sargeant (J.), M.A. ANNALS OF WESTMINSTER SCHOOL. Illustrated. *Demy 8vo. 7s. 6d.*

Sathas (C.). See Byzantine Texts.

Schmitt (John). See Byzantine Texts.

Scott (A. M.). WINSTON SPENCER CHURCHILL. With Portraits and Illustrations. *Cr. 8vo. 3s. 6d.*
A Colonial Edition is also published.

Seeley (H. G.), F.R.S. DRAGONS OF THE AIR. Illustrated. *Cr. 8vo. 6s.*

Sells (V. P.), M.A. THE MECHANICS OF DAILY LIFE. Illustrated. *Cr. 8vo. 2s. 6d.*

Selous (Edmund). TOMMY SMITH'S ANIMALS. Illustrated by G. W. ORD. *Fifth Edition. Fcap. 8vo. 2s. 6d.*

Settle (J. H.). ANECDOTES OF SOLDIERS. *Cr. 8vo. 3s. 6d. net.*
A Colonial Edition is also published.

Shakespeare (William).
THE FOUR FOLIOS, 1623; 1632; 1664; 1685. Each *Four Guineas net*, or a complete set, *Twelve Guineas net*.
Folios 3 and 4 are ready.
Folio 2 is nearly ready.

The Arden Shakespeare.
Demy 8vo. 2s. 6d. net each volume.
General Editor, W. J. CRAIG. An Edition of Shakespeare in single Plays. Edited with a full Introduction, Textual Notes, and a Commentary at the foot of the page.

HAMLET. Edited by EDWARD DOWDEN, Litt.D.
ROMEO AND JULIET. Edited by EDWARD DOWDEN, Litt.D.
KING LEAR. Edited by W. J. CRAIG.
JULIUS CAESAR. Edited by M. MACMILLAN, M.A.
THE TEMPEST. Edited by MORETON LUCE.
OTHELLO. Edited by H. C. HART.
TITUS ANDRONICUS. Edited by H. B. BAILDON.
CYMBELINE. Edited by EDWARD DOWDEN.
THE MERRY WIVES OF WINDSOR. Edited by H. C. HART.
A MIDSUMMER NIGHT'S DREAM. Edited by H. CUNINGHAM.
KING HENRY V. Edited by H. A. EVANS.
ALL'S WELL THAT ENDS WELL. Edited by W. O. BRIGSTOCKE.
THE TAMING OF THE SHREW. Edited by R. WARWICK BOND.
TIMON OF ATHENS. Edited by K. DEIGHTON.
MEASURE FOR MEASURE. Edited by H. C. HART.
TWELFTH NIGHT. Edited by MORETON LUCE.
THE MERCHANT OF VENICE. Edited by C. KNOX POOLER.
TROILUS AND CRESSIDA. Edited by K. DEIGHTON.

The Little Quarto Shakespeare. Edited by W. J. CRAIG. With Introductions and Notes. *Pott 16mo. In 40 Volumes. Leather, price 1s. net each volume.* Mahogany Revolving Book Case. *10s. net.*
See also Standard Library.

Sharp (A.). VICTORIAN POETS. *Cr. 8vo. 2s. 6d.*

Sharp (Cecil). See S. Baring-Gould.

Sharp (Mrs. E. A.). See Little Books on Art.

Shedlock (J. S.) THE PIANOFORTE SONATA. *Cr. 8vo. 5s.*

Shelley (Percy B.). ADONAIS; an Elegy on the death of John Keats, Author of 'Endymion,' etc. Pisa. From the types of Didot, 1821. *2s. net.*

Sheppard (H. F.), M.A. See S. Baring-Gould.

Sherwell (Arthur), M.A. See S.Q.S.

Shipley (Mary E.). AN ENGLISH CHURCH HISTORY FOR CHILDREN. With a Preface by the Bishop of Gibraltar. With Maps and Illustrations. Part I. *Cr. 8vo. 2s. 6d. net.*

Sichel (Walter). DISRAELI: A Study in Personality and Ideas. With 3 Portraits. *Demy 8vo. 12s. 6d. net.*
A Colonial Edition is also published.
See also Oxford Biographies.

Sime (J.). See Little Books on Art.

Messrs. Methuen's Catalogue

Simonson (G. A.). FRANCESCO GUARDI. With 41 Plates. *Imperial 4to. £2, 2s. net.*

Sketchley (R. E. D.). See Little Books on Art.

Skipton (H. P. K.). See Little Books on Art.

Sladen (Douglas). SICILY: The New Winter Resort. With over 200 Illustrations. *Second Edition. Cr. 8vo. 5s. net.*

Small (Evan), M.A. THE EARTH. An Introduction to Physiography. Illustrated. *Cr. 8vo. 2s. 6d.*

Smallwood (M. G.). See Little Books on Art.

Smedley (F. E.). See I.P.L.

Smith (Adam). THE WEALTH OF NATIONS. Edited with an Introduction and numerous Notes by EDWIN CANNAN, M.A. *Two volumes. Demy 8vo. 21s. net.*
See also English Library.

Smith (Horace and James). See Little Library.

Smith (H. Bompas), M.A. A NEW JUNIOR ARITHMETIC. *Crown 8vo. 2s. 6d.*

Smith (R. Mudie). THOUGHTS FOR THE DAY. Edited by. *Fcap. 8vo. 3s. 6d. net.*

Smith (Nowell C.). See W. Wordsworth.

Smith (John Thomas). A BOOK FOR A RAINY DAY: Or Recollections of the Events of the Years 1766-1833. Edited by WILFRED WHITTEN. Illustrated. *Demy 8vo. 12s. 6d. net.*

Snell (F. J.). A BOOK OF EXMOOR. Illustrated. *Cr. 8vo. 6s.*

Snowden (C. E.). A HANDY DIGEST OF BRITISH HISTORY. *Demy 8vo. 4s. 6d.*

Sophocles. See Classical Translations.

Sornet (L. A.). See Junior School Books.

South (Wilton E.), M.A. See Junior School Books.

Southey (R.). ENGLISH SEAMEN. Edited by DAVID HANNAY.
Vol. I. (Howard, Clifford, Hawkins, Drake, Cavendish). *Second Edition. Cr. 8vo. 6s.*
Vol. II. (Richard Hawkins, Grenville, Essex, and Raleigh). *Cr. 8vo. 6s.*
See also Standard Library.

Spence (C. H.), M.A. See School Examination Series.

Spooner (W. A.), M.A. See Leaders of Religion.

Staley (Edgcumbe). THE GUILDS OF FLORENCE. Illustrated. *Royal 8vo. 16s. net.*

Stanbridge (J. W.), B.D. See Library of Devotion.

'Stancliffe.' GOLF DO'S AND DONT'S. *Second Edition. Fcap 8vo. 1s.*

Stead (D. W.). See D. Gallaher.

Stedman (A. M. M.), M.A.
INITIA LATINA: Easy Lessons on Elementary Accidence. *Ninth Edition. Fcap. 8vo. 1s.*
FIRST LATIN LESSONS. *Ninth Edition. Cr. 8vo. 2s.*
FIRST LATIN READER. With Notes adapted to the Shorter Latin Primer and Vocabulary. *Sixth Edition revised. 18mo. 1s. 6d.*
EASY SELECTIONS FROM CÆSAR. The Helvetian War. *Second Edition 18mo. 1s.*
EASY SELECTIONS FROM LIVY. The Kings of Rome. *18mo. Second Edition. 1s. 6d.*
EASY LATIN PASSAGES FOR UNSEEN TRANSLATION. *Tenth Edition Fcap. 8vo. 1s. 6d.*
EXEMPLA LATINA. First Exercises in Latin Accidence. With Vocabulary. *Third Edition. Cr. 8vo. 1s.*
EASY LATIN EXERCISES ON THE SYNTAX OF THE SHORTER AND REVISED LATIN PRIMER. With Vocabulary. *Tenth and Cheaper Edition, re-written. Cr. 8vo. 1s. 6d. Original Edition. 2s. 6d.* KEY, 3s. *net.*
THE LATIN COMPOUND SENTENCE: Rules and Exercises. *Second Edition. Cr. 8vo. 1s. 6d.* With Vocabulary. 2s.
NOTANDA QUAEDAM: Miscellaneous Latin Exercises on Common Rules and Idioms. *Fourth Edition. Fcap. 8vo. 1s. 6d.* With Vocabulary. 2s. Key, 2s. *net.*
LATIN VOCABULARIES FOR REPETITION: Arranged according to Subjects. *Thirteenth Edition. Fcap. 8vo. 1s 6d.*
A VOCABULARY OF LATIN IDIOMS. *18mo. Second Edition. 1s.*
STEPS TO GREEK. *Second Edition, revised. 18mo. 1s.*
A SHORTER GREEK PRIMER. *Cr. 8vo. 1s. 6d.*
EASY GREEK PASSAGES FOR UNSEEN TRANSLATION. *Third Edition, revised. Fcap. 8vo. 1s. 6d.*
GREEK VOCABULARIES FOR REPETITION. Arranged according to Subjects. *Fourth Edition. Fcap. 8vo. 1s. 6d.*
GREEK TESTAMENT SELECTIONS. For the use of Schools. With Introduction, Notes, and Vocabulary. *Fourth Edition. Fcap. 8vo. 2s. 6d.*
STEPS TO FRENCH. *Seventh Edition. 18mo. 8d.*
FIRST FRENCH LESSONS. *Seventh Edition, revised. Cr. 8vo. 1s.*
EASY FRENCH PASSAGES FOR UNSEEN TRANSLATION. *Fifth Edition, revised. Fcap. 8vo. 1s. 6d.*

General Literature

EASY FRENCH EXERCISES ON ELEMENTARY SYNTAX. With Vocabulary. *Fourth Edition. Cr. 8vo. 2s. 6d.*
KEY. *3s. net.*
FRENCH VOCABULARIES FOR REPETITION: Arranged according to Subjects. *Twelfth Edition. Fcap. 8vo. 1s.*
See also School Examination Series.

Steel (R. Elliott), M.A., F.C.S. THE WORLD OF SCIENCE. With 147 Illustrations. *Second Edition. Cr. 8vo. 2s. 6d.*
See also School Examination Series.

Stephenson (C.), of the Technical College, Bradford, and **Suddards (F.)** of the Yorkshire College, Leeds. ORNAMENTAL DESIGN FOR WOVEN FABRICS. Illustrated. *Demy 8vo. Third Edition. 7s. 6d.*

Stephenson (J.), M.A. THE CHIEF TRUTHS OF THE CHRISTIAN FAITH. *Cr. 8vo. 3s. 6d.*

Sterne (Laurence). See Little Library.

Sterry (W.), M.A. ANNALS OF ETON COLLEGE. Illustrated. *Demy 8vo. 7s. 6d.*

Steuart (Katherine). BY ALLAN WATER. *Second Edition. Cr. 8vo. 6s.*

Stevenson (R. L.) THE LETTERS OF ROBERT LOUIS STEVENSON TO HIS FAMILY AND FRIENDS. Selected and Edited by SIDNEY COLVIN. *Sixth Edition. Cr. 8vo. 12s.*
LIBRARY EDITION. *Demy 8vo. 2 vols. 25s. net.*
A Colonial Edition is also published.
VAILIMA LETTERS. With an Etched Portrait by WILLIAM STRANG. *Fifth Edition. Cr. 8vo. Buckram. 6s.*
A Colonial Edition is also published.
THE LIFE OF R. L. STEVENSON. See G. Balfour.

Stevenson (M. I.). FROM SARANAC TO THE MARQUESAS. Being Letters written by Mrs. M. I. STEVENSON during 1887-8. *Cr. 8vo. 6s. net.*
A Colonial Edition is also published.
LETTERS FROM SAMOA. Edited and arranged by M. C. BALFOUR. With many Illustrations. *Second Ed. Cr. 8vo. 6s. net.*

Stoddart (Anna M.). See Oxford Biographies.

Stokes (F. G.), B.A. HOURS WITH RABELAIS. From the translation of SIR T. URQUHART and P. A. MOTTEUX. With a Portrait in Photogravure. *Cr. 8vo. 3s. 6d. net.*

Stone (S. J.). POEMS AND HYMNS. With a Memoir by F. G. ELLERTON, M.A. With Portrait. *Cr. 8vo. 6s.*

Storr (Vernon F.), M.A., Lecturer in the Philosophy of Religion in Cambridge University; Examining Chaplain to the Archbishop of Canterbury; formerly Fellow of University College, Oxford. DEVELOPMENT AND DIVINE PURPOSE *Cr. 8vo. 5s. net.*

Straker (F.). See Books on Business.

Streane (A. W.), D.D. See Churchman's Bible.

Stroud (H.), D.Sc., M.A. See Textbooks of Science.

Strutt (Joseph). THE SPORTS AND PASTIMES OF THE PEOPLE OF ENGLAND. Illustrated by many engravings. Revised by J. CHARLES COX, LL.D., F.S.A. *Quarto. 21s. net.*

Stuart (Capt. Donald). THE STRUGGLE FOR PERSIA. With a Map. *Cr. 8vo. 6s.*

Sturch (F.), Staff Instructor to the Surrey County Council. MANUAL TRAINING, DRAWING (WOODWORK). Its Principles and Application, with Solutions to Examination Questions, 1892-1905, Orthographic, Isometric and Oblique Projection. With 50 Plates and 140 Figures. *Foolscap. 5s. net.*

Suckling (Sir John). FRAGMENTA AUREA: a Collection of all the Incomparable Peeces, written by. And published by a friend to perpetuate his memory. Printed by his own copies.
Printed for HUMPHREY MOSELEY, and are to be sold at his shop, at the sign of the Princes Arms in St. Paul's Churchyard, 1646.

Suddards (F.). See C. Stephenson.

Surtees (R. S.). See I.P.L.

Swift (Jonathan). THE JOURNAL TO STELLA. Edited by G. A. AITKEN. *Cr. 8vo. 6s.*

Symes (J. E.), M.A. THE FRENCH REVOLUTION. *Second Edition. Cr. 8vo. 2s. 6d.*

Sympson (E. M.), M.A., M.D. See Ancient Cities.

Syrett (Netta). See Little Blue Books.

Tacitus. AGRICOLA. With Introduction Notes, Map, etc. By R. F. DAVIS, M.A., *Fcap. 8vo. 2s.*
GERMANIA. By the same Editor. *Fcap. 8vo. 2s.* See also Classical Translations.

Tallack (W.). HOWARD LETTERS AND MEMORIES. *Demy 8vo. 10s. 6d. net.*

Tauler (J.). See Library of Devotion.

Taunton (E. L.). A HISTORY OF THE JESUITS IN ENGLAND. Illustrated. *Demy 8vo. 21s. net.*

Taylor (A. E.). THE ELEMENTS OF METAPHYSICS. *Demy 8vo. 10s. 6d. net.*

Taylor (F. G.), M.A. See Commercial Series.

Taylor (I. A.). See Oxford Biographies.

Taylor (T. M.), M.A., Fellow of Gonville and Caius College, Cambridge. A CONSTITUTIONAL AND POLITICAL HISTORY OF ROME. *Cr. 8vo. 7s. 6d.*

Tennyson (Alfred, Lord). THE EARLY POEMS OF. Edited, with Notes and an Introduction, by J. CHURTON COLLINS, M.A. *Cr. 8vo. 6s.*
IN MEMORIAM, MAUD, AND THE PRINCESS. Edited by J. CHURTON COLLINS, M.A. *Cr. 8vo. 6s.* See also Little Library.

A

Terry (C. S.). See Oxford Biographies.
Terton (Alice). LIGHTS AND SHADOWS IN A HOSPITAL. *Cr. 8vo.* 3s. 6d.
Thackeray (W. M.). See Little Library.
Theobald (F. V.), M.A. INSECT LIFE. Illustrated. *Second Ed. Revised. Cr. 8vo.* 2s. 6d.
Thompson (A. H.). See Little Guides.
Tileston (Mary W.). DAILY STRENGTH FOR DAILY NEEDS. *Twelfth Edition. Medium* 16mo. 2s. 6d. *net.* Also an edition in superior binding, 6s.
Tompkins (H. W.), F.R.H.S. See Little Guides.
Towndrow (R. F.). A DAY BOOK OF MILTON. Edited by. *Fcap. 8vo.* 3s. 6d. *net.*
Townley (Lady Susan). MY CHINESE NOTE-BOOK With 16 Illustrations and 2 Maps. *Third Edition. Demy 8vo.* 10s. 6d. *net.*
A Colonial Edition is also published.
*****Toynbee (Paget),** M.A., D.Litt. DANTE IN ENGLISH LITERATURE. *Demy 8vo.* 12s. 6d. *net.*
See also Oxford Biographies.
Trench (Herbert). DEIRDRE WED and Other Poems. *Cr. 8vo.* 5s.
Trevelyan (G. M.), Fellow of Trinity College, Cambridge. ENGLAND UNDER THE STUARTS. With Maps and Plans. *Second Edition. Demy 8vo.* 10s. 6d. *net.*
Troutbeck (G. E.). See Little Guides.
Tyler (E. A.), B.A., F.C.S. See Junior School Books.
Tyrell-Gill (Frances). See Little Books on Art.
Vardon (Harry). THE COMPLETE GOLFER. Illustrated. *Seventh Edition. Demy 8vo.* 10s. 6d. *net.*
A Colonial Edition is also published.
Vaughan (Henry). See Little Library.
Voegelin (A.), M.A. See Junior Examination Series.
Waddell (Col. L. A.), LL.D., C.B. LHASA AND ITS MYSTERIES.' With a Record of the Expedition of 1903-1904. With 2000 Illustrations and Maps. *Demy 8vo.* 21s. *net.*
Also Third and Cheaper Edition. With 155 Illustrations and Maps. *Demy 8vo.* 7s. 6d. *net.*
Wade (G. W.), D.D. OLD TESTAMENT HISTORY. With Maps. *Third Edition Cr. 8vo.* 6s.
Wagner (Richard). See A. L. Cleather.
Wall (J. C.). DEVILS. Illustrated by the Author and from photographs. *Demy 8vo.* 4s. 6d. *net.* See also Antiquary's Books.
Walters (H. B.). See Little Books on Art.
Walton (F. W.). See Victor G. Plarr.
Walton (Izaak) and Cotton (Charles). See I.P.L., Standard Library, and Little Library.

Warmelo (D. S. Van). ON COMMANDO. With Portrait. *Cr. 8vo.* 3s. 6d.
A Colonial Edition is also published.
Warren-Vernon (Hon. William), M.A. READINGS ON THE INFERNO OF DANTE, chiefly based on the Commentary of BENVENUTO DA IMOLA. With an Introduction by the Rev. Dr. MOORE. In Two Volumes. *Second Edition. Cr. 8vo.* 15s. *net.*
Waterhouse (Mrs. Alfred). WITH THE SIMPLE-HEARTED: Little Homilies to Women in Country Places. *Second Edition. Small Pott 8vo.* 2s. *net.* See also Little Library.
Weatherhead (T. C.), M.A. EXAMINATION PAPERS IN HORACE. *Cr. 8vo.* 2s. See also Junior Examination Series.
Webb (W. T.). See Little Blue Books.
Webber (F. C.). See Textbooks of Technology.
Wells (Sidney H.). See Textbooks of Science.
Wells (J.), M.A., Fellow and Tutor of Wadham College. OXFORD AND OXFORD LIFE. *Third Edition. Cr. 8vo.* 3s. 6d.
A SHORT HISTORY OF ROME. *Sixth Edition.* With 3 Maps. *Cr. 8vo.* 3s. 6d.
See also Little Guides.
'Westminster Gazette' Office Boy (Francis Brown). THE DOINGS OF ARTHUR. *Cr. 4to.* 2s. 6d. *net.*
Wetmore (Helen C.). THE LAST OF THE GREAT SCOUTS ('Buffalo Bill'). Illustrated. *Second Edition. Demy 8vo.* 6s.
A Colonial Edition is also published.
Whibley (C.). See Half-crown Library.
Whibley (L.), M.A., Fellow of Pembroke College, Cambridge. GREEK OLIGARCHIES: THEIR ORGANISATION AND CHARACTER. *Cr. 8vo.* 6s.
Whitaker (G. H.), M.A. See Churchman's Bible.
White (Gilbert). THE NATURAL HISTORY OF SELBORNE. Edited by L. C. MIALL, F.R.S., assisted by W. WARDE FOWLER, M.A. *Cr. 8vo.* 6s. See also Standard Library.
Whitfield (E. E.). See Commercial Series.
Whitehead (A. W.). GASPARD DE COLIGNY. Illustrated. *Demy 8vo.* 12s. 6d. *net.*
Whiteley (R. Lloyd), F.I.C., Principal of the Municipal Science School, West Bromwich. AN ELEMENTARY TEXT-BOOK OF INORGANIC CHEMISTRY. *Cr. 8vo.* 2s. 6d.
Whitley (Miss). See S.Q.S.
Whitten (W.). See John Thomas Smith.
Whyte (A. G.), B.Sc. See Books on Business.
Wilberforce (Wilfrid). See Little Books on Art.
Wilde (Oscar). DE PROFUNDIS. *Sixth Edition. Cr. 8vo.* 5s. *net.*
A Colonial Edition is also published.

Wilkins (W. H.), B.A. See S.Q.S.
Wilkinson (J. Frome). See S.Q.S.
*****Williams (A.).** PETROL PETER: or Mirth for Motorists. Illustrated in Colour by A. W. MILLS. *Demy 4to. 3s. 6d. net.*
Williamson (M. G.). See Ancient Cities.
Williamson (W.). THE BRITISH GARDENER. Illustrated. *Demy 8vo. 10s. 6d.*
Williamson (W.), B.A. See Junior Examination Series, Junior School Books, and Beginner's Books.
Willson (Beckles). LORD STRATHCONA: the Story of his Life. Illustrated. *Demy 8vo. 7s. 6d.*
A Colonial Edition is also published.
Wilmot-Buxton (E. M.). MAKERS OF EUROPE. *Cr. 8vo. Fifth Ed. 3s. 6d.*
A Text-book of European History for Middle Forms.
THE ANCIENT WORLD. With Maps and Illustrations. *Cr. 8vo. 3s. 6d.*
See also Beginner's Books.
Wilson (Bishop.). See Library of Devotion.
Wilson (A. J.). See Books on Business.
Wilson (H. A.). See Books on Business.
Wilton (Richard), M.A. LYRA PASTORALIS: Songs of Nature, Church, and Home. *Pott 8vo. 2s. 6d.*
Winbolt (S. E.) M.A. EXERCISES IN LATIN ACCIDENCE. *Cr. 8vo. 1s. 6d.*
LATIN HEXAMETER VERSE: An Aid to Composition. *Cr. 8vo. 3s. 6d.* KEY, *5s. net.*
Windle (B. C. A.), D.Sc., F.R.S. See Antiquary's Books, Little Guides and Ancient Cities.
Winterbotham (Canon), M.A., B.Sc., LL.B. See Churchman's Library.
Wood (J. A. E.). See Textbooks of Technology.
Wood (J. Hickory). DAN LENO. Illustrated. *Third Edition. Cr. 8vo. 6s.*
A Colonial Edition is also published.
Wood (W. Birkbeck), M.A., late Scholar of Worcester College, Oxford, and **Edmonds (Major J. E.),** R.E., D.A.Q.-M.G. A HISTORY OF THE CIVIL WAR IN THE UNITED STATES. With an Introduction by H. SPENSER WILKINSON. With 24 Maps and Plans. *Demy 8vo. 12s. 6d. net.*

Wordsworth (Christopher). See Antiquary's Books.
*****Wordsworth (W.).** THE POEMS OF. With Introduction and Notes by NOWELL C. SMITH, Fellow of New College, Oxford. *In Four Volumes. Demy 8vo. 5s. net each.* See also Little Library.
Wordsworth (W.) and Coleridge (S. T.). See Little Library.
Wright (Arthur), M.A., Fellow of Queen's College, Cambridge. See Churchman's Library.
Wright (C. Gordon). See Dante.
Wright (J. C.). TO-DAY. *Fcap. 16mo. 1s. net.*
Wright (Sophie). GERMAN VOCABULARIES FOR REPETITION. *Fcap. 8vo. 1s. 6d.*
Wrong (George M.), Professor of History in the University of Toronto. THE EARL OF ELGIN. Illustrated. *Demy 8vo. 7s. 6d. net.*
A Colonial Edition is also published.
Wyatt (Kate) and Gloag (M.). A BOOK OF ENGLISH GARDENS. With 24 Illustrations in Colour. *Demy 8vo. 10s. 6d. net.*
Wylde (A. B.). MODERN ABYSSINIA. With a Map and a Portrait. *Demy 8vo. 15s. net.*
A Colonial Edition is also published.
Wyndham (George). THE POEMS OF WILLIAM SHAKESPEARE. With an Introduction and Notes. *Demy 8vo. Buckram, gilt top. 10s. 6d.*
Wyon (R.). See Half-crown Library.
Yeats (W. B.). AN ANTHOLOGY OF IRISH VERSE. *Revised and Enlarged Edition. Cr. 8vo. 3s. 6d.*
Young (Filson). THE COMPLETE MOTORIST. With 138 Illustrations. *Sixth Edition. Demy 8vo. 12s. 6d. net.*
A Colonial Edition is also published.
Young (T. M.). THE AMERICAN COTTON INDUSTRY: A Study of Work and Workers. *Cr. 8vo. Cloth, 2s. 6d.; paper boards, 1s. 6d.*
Zimmern (Antonia). WHAT DO WE KNOW CONCERNING ELECTRICITY? *Fcap. 8vo. 1s. 6d. net.*

Ancient Cities

General Editor, B. C. A. WINDLE, D.Sc., F.R.S.

Cr. 8vo. 4s. 6d. net.

CHESTER. By B. C. A. Windle, D.Sc. F.R.S. Illustrated by E. H. New.
SHREWSBURY. By T. Auden, M.A., F.S.A. Illustrated.
CANTERBURY. By J. C. Cox, LL.D., F.S.A. Illustrated.
EDINBURGH. By M. G. Williamson. Illustrated by Herbert Railton.
LINCOLN. By E. Mansel Sympson, M.A., M.D. Illustrated by E. H. New.
BRISTOL. By Alfred Harvey. Illustrated by E. H. New.

Antiquary's Books, The

General Editor, J. CHARLES COX, LL.D., F.S.A.

A series of volumes dealing with various branches of English Antiquities; comprehensive and popular, as well as accurate and scholarly.

Demy 8vo. 7s. 6d. net.

ENGLISH MONASTIC LIFE. By the Right Rev. Abbot Gasquet, O.S.B. Illustrated. *Third Edition.*

REMAINS OF THE PREHISTORIC AGE IN ENGLAND. By B. C. A. Windle, D.Sc., F.R.S. With numerous Illustrations and Plans.

OLD SERVICE BOOKS OF THE ENGLISH CHURCH. By Christopher Wordsworth, M.A., and Henry Littlehales. With Coloured and other Illustrations.

CELTIC ART. By J. Romilly Allen, F.S.A. With numerous Illustrations and Plans.

ARCHÆOLOGY AND FALSE ANTIQUITIES. By R. Munro, LL.D. Illustrated.

SHRINES OF BRITISH SAINTS. By J. C. Wall. With numerous Illustrations and Plans.

THE ROYAL FORESTS OF ENGLAND. By J. C. Cox, LL.D., F.S.A. Illustrated.

THE MANOR AND MANORIAL RECORDS. By Nathaniel J. Hone. Illustrated.

SEALS. By J. Harvey Bloom. Illustrated.

Beginner's Books, The

Edited by W. WILLIAMSON, B.A.

EASY FRENCH RHYMES. By Henri Blouet. Illustrated. *Fcap. 8vo. 1s.*

EASY STORIES FROM ENGLISH HISTORY. By E. M. Wilmot-Buxton, Author of 'Makers of Europe.' *Cr. 8vo. 1s.*

EASY EXERCISES IN ARITHMETIC. Arranged by W. S. Beard. *Fcap. 8vo.* Without Answers, 1s. With Answers, 1s. 3d.

EASY DICTATION AND SPELLING. By W. Williamson, B.A. *Fifth Edition. Fcap. 8vo. 1s.*

Business, Books on

Cr. 8vo. 2s. 6d. net.

A series of volumes dealing with all the most important aspects of commercial and financial activity. The volumes are intended to treat separately all the considerable industries and forms of business, and to explain accurately and clearly what they do and how they do it. Some are Illustrated. The first volumes are—

PORTS AND DOCKS. By Douglas Owen.

RAILWAYS. By E. R. McDermott.

THE STOCK EXCHANGE. By Chas. Duguid. *Second Edition.*

THE BUSINESS OF INSURANCE. By A. J. Wilson.

THE ELECTRICAL INDUSTRY: LIGHTING, TRACTION, AND POWER. By A. G. Whyte, B.Sc.

THE SHIPBUILDING INDUSTRY: Its History, Science, Practice, and Finance. By David Pollock, M.I.N.A.

THE MONEY MARKET. By F. Straker.

THE BUSINESS SIDE OF AGRICULTURE. By A. G. L. Rogers, M.A.

LAW IN BUSINESS. By H. A. Wilson.

THE BREWING INDUSTRY. By Julian L. Baker, F.I.C., F.C.S.

THE AUTOMOBILE INDUSTRY. By G. de H. Stone.

MINING AND MINING INVESTMENTS. By 'A. Moil.'

THE BUSINESS OF ADVERTISING. By Clarence G. Moran, Barrister-at-Law. Illustrated.

TRADE UNIONS. By G. Drage.

CIVIL ENGINEERING. By T. Claxton Fidler, M.Inst. C.E. Illustrated.

THE IRON TRADE. By J. Stephen Jeans. Illustrated.

MONOPOLIES, TRUSTS, AND KARTELLS. By F. W. Hirst.

THE COTTON INDUSTRY AND TRADE. By Prof. S. J. Chapman, Dean of the Faculty of Commerce in the University of Manchester. Illustrated.

Byzantine Texts
Edited by J. B. BURY, M.A., Litt.D.

A series of texts of Byzantine Historians, edited by English and foreign scholars.

ZACHARIAH OF MITYLENE. Translated by F. J. Hamilton, D.D., and E. W. Brooks. *Demy 8vo.* 12s. 6d. net.

EVAGRIUS. Edited by Léon Parmentier and M. Bidez. *Demy 8vo.* 10s. 6d. net.

THE HISTORY OF PSELLUS. Edited by C. Sathas. *Demy 8vo.* 15s. net.

ECTHESIS CHRONICA. Edited by Professor Lambros. *Demy 8vo.* 7s. 6d. net.

THE CHRONICLE OF MOREA. Edited by John Schmitt. *Demy 8vo.* 15s. net.

Churchman's Bible, The
General Editor, J. H. BURN, B.D., F.R.S.E.

A series of Expositions on the Books of the Bible, which will be of service to the general reader in the practical and devotional study of the Sacred Text.

Each Book is provided with a full and clear Introductory Section, in which is stated what is known or conjectured respecting the date and occasion of the composition of the Book, and any other particulars that may help to elucidate its meaning as a whole. The Exposition is divided into sections of a convenient length, corresponding as far as possible with the divisions of the Church Lectionary. The Translation of the Authorised Version is printed in full, such corrections as are deemed necessary being placed in footnotes.

THE EPISTLE OF ST. PAUL THE APOSTLE TO THE GALATIANS. Edited by A. W. Robinson, M.A. *Second Edition. Fcap. 8vo.* 1s. 6d. net.

ECCLESIASTES. Edited by A. W. Streane, D.D. *Fcap. 8vo.* 1s. 6d. net.

THE EPISTLE OF ST. PAUL THE APOSTLE TO THE PHILIPPIANS. Edited by C. R. D. Biggs, D.D. *Second Edition. Fcap 8vo.* 2s. 6d. net.

THE EPISTLE OF ST. JAMES. Edited by H. W. Fulford, M.A. *Fcap. 8vo.* 1s. 6d. net.

ISAIAH. Edited by W. E. Barnes, D.D. *Two Volumes. Fcap. 8vo.* 2s. net each. With Map.

THE EPISTLE OF ST. PAUL THE APOSTLE TO THE EPHESIANS. Edited by G. H. Whitaker, M.A. *Fcap. 8vo.* 1s. 6d. net.

Churchman's Library, The
General Editor, J. H. BURN, B.D., F.R.S.E.

THE BEGINNINGS OF ENGLISH CHRISTIANITY. By W. E. Collins, M.A. With Map. *Cr. 8vo.* 3s. 6d.

SOME NEW TESTAMENT PROBLEMS. By Arthur Wright, M.A. *Cr. 8vo.* 6s.

THE KINGDOM OF HEAVEN HERE AND HEREAFTER. By Canon Winterbotham, M.A., B.Sc., LL.B. *Cr. 8vo.* 3s. 6d.

THE WORKMANSHIP OF THE PRAYER BOOK: Its Literary and Liturgical Aspects. By J. Dowden, D.D. *Second Edition. Cr. 8vo.* 3s. 6d.

EVOLUTION. By F. B. Jevons, M.A., Litt.D *Cr. 8vo.* 3s. 6d.

THE OLD TESTAMENT AND THE NEW SCHOLARSHIP. By J. W. Peters, D.D. *Cr. 8vo.* 6s.

THE CHURCHMAN'S INTRODUCTION TO THE OLD TESTAMENT. By A. M. Mackay, B.A. *Cr. 8vo.* 3s. 6d.

THE CHURCH OF CHRIST. By E. T. Green, M.A. *Cr. 8vo.* 6s.

COMPARATIVE THEOLOGY. By J. A. MacCulloch. *Cr. 8vo.* 6s.

Classical Translations
Edited by H. F. FOX, M.A., Fellow and Tutor of Brasenose College, Oxford.
Crown 8vo.

A series of Translations from the Greek and Latin Classics, distinguished by literary excellence as well as by scholarly accuracy.

ÆSCHYLUS—Agamemnon, Choephoroe, Eumenides. Translated by Lewis Campbell, LL.D. 5s.

CICERO—De Oratore I. Translated by E. N. P. Moor, M.A. 3s. 6d.

CICERO—Select Orations (Pro Milone, Pro Mureno, Philippic II., in Catilinam). Translated by H. E. D. Blakiston, M.A. 5s.

CICERO—De Natura Deorum. Translated by F. Brooks, M.A. 3s. 6d.

[Continued.

CLASSICAL TRANSLATIONS—*continued*.

CICERO—De Officiis. Translated by G. B. Gardiner, M.A. 2s. 6d.
HORACE—The Odes and Epodes. Translated by A. D. Godley, M.A. 2s.
LUCIAN—Six Dialogues (Nigrinus, Icaro-Menippus, The Cock, The Ship, The Parasite, The Lover of Falsehood) Translated by S. T. Irwin, M.A. 3s. 6d.
SOPHOCLES—Electra and Ajax. Translated by E. D. A. Morshead, M.A. 2s. 6d.
TACITUS—Agricola and Germania. Translated by R. B. Townshend. 2s. 6d.
THE SATIRES OF JUVENAL. Translated by S. G. Owen. 2s. 6d.

Commercial Series

Edited by H. DE B. GIBBINS, Litt.D., M.A.

Crown 8vo.

A series intended to assist students and young men preparing for a commercial career, by supplying useful handbooks of a clear and practical character, dealing with those subjects which are absolutely essential in the business life.

COMMERCIAL EDUCATION IN THEORY AND PRACTICE. By E. E. Whitfield, M.A. 5s.
An introduction to Methuen's Commercial Series treating the question of Commercial Education fully from both the point of view of the teacher and of the parent.
BRITISH COMMERCE AND COLONIES FROM ELIZABETH TO VICTORIA. By H. de B. Gibbins, Litt.D., M.A. *Third Edition.* 2s.
COMMERCIAL EXAMINATION PAPERS. By H. de B. Gibbins, Litt.D., M.A. 1s. 6d.
THE ECONOMICS OF COMMERCE. By H. de B. Gibbins, Litt.D., M.A. *Second Edition.* 1s. 6d.
A GERMAN COMMERCIAL READER. By S. E. Bally. With Vocabulary. 2s.
A COMMERCIAL GEOGRAPHY OF THE BRITISH EMPIRE. By L. W. Lyde, M.A. *Fourth Edition.* 2s.
A COMMERCIAL GEOGRAPHY OF FOREIGN NATIONS. By F. C. Boon, B.A. 2s.
A PRIMER OF BUSINESS. By S. Jackson, M.A. *Third Edition.* 1s. 6d.
COMMERCIAL ARITHMETIC. By F. G. Taylor, M.A. *Fourth Edition.* 1s. 6d.
FRENCH COMMERCIAL CORRESPONDENCE. By S. E. Bally. With Vocabulary. *Third Edition.* 2s.
GERMAN COMMERCIAL CORRESPONDENCE. By S. E. Bally. With Vocabulary. *Second Edition.* 2s. 6d.
A FRENCH COMMERCIAL READER. By S. E. Bally. With Vocabulary. *Second Edition.* 2s.
PRECIS WRITING AND OFFICE CORRESPONDENCE. By E. E. Whitfield, M.A. *Second Edition.* 2s.
A GUIDE TO PROFESSIONS AND BUSINESS. By H. Jones. 1s. 6d.
THE PRINCIPLES OF BOOK-KEEPING BY DOUBLE ENTRY. By J. E. B. M'Allen, M.A. 2s.
COMMERCIAL LAW. By W. Douglas Edwards. *Second Edition.* 2s.

Connoisseur's Library, The

Wide Royal 8vo. 25s. net.

A sumptuous series of 20 books on art, written by experts for collectors, superbly illustrated in photogravure, collotype, and colour. The technical side of the art is duly treated. The first volumes are—

MEZZOTINTS. By Cyril Davenport. With 40 Plates in Photogravure.
PORCELAIN. By Edward Dillon. With 19 Plates in Colour, 20 in Collotype, and 5 in Photogravure.
MINIATURES. By Dudley Heath. With 9 Plates in Colour, 15 in Collotype, and 15 in Photogravure.
IVORIES. By A. Maskell. With 80 Plates in Collotype and Photogravure.
ENGLISH FURNITURE. By F. S. Robinson. With 160 Plates in Collotype and one in Photogravure. *Second Edition.*
EUROPEAN ENAMELS. By H. CUNYNGHAME, C.B. With many Plates in Collotype and a Frontispiece in Photogravure.

GENERAL LITERATURE

Devotion, The Library of

With Introductions and (where necessary) Notes.

Small Pott 8vo, cloth, 2s. ; leather, 2s. 6d. net.

These masterpieces of devotional literature are furnished with such Introductions and Notes as may be necessary to explain the standpoint of the author and the obvious difficulties of the text, without unnecessary intrusion between the author and the devout mind.

THE CONFESSIONS OF ST. AUGUSTINE. Edited by C. Bigg, D.D. *Fifth Edition.*
THE CHRISTIAN YEAR. Edited by Walter Lock, D.D. *Third Edition.*
THE IMITATION OF CHRIST. Edited by C. Bigg, D.D. *Fourth Edition.*
A BOOK OF DEVOTIONS. Edited by J. W. Stanbridge. B.D. *Second Edition.*
LYRA INNOCENTIUM. Edited by Walter Lock, D.D.
A SERIOUS CALL TO A DEVOUT AND HOLY LIFE. Edited by C. Bigg, D.D. *Second Edition.*
THE TEMPLE. Edited by E. C. S. Gibson, D.D. *Second Edition.*
A GUIDE TO ETERNITY. Edited by J. W. Stanbridge, B.D.
THE PSALMS OF DAVID. Edited by B. W. Randolph, D.D.
LYRA APOSTOLICA. By Cardinal Newman and others. Edited by Canon Scott Holland and Canon H. C. Beeching, M.A.
THE INNER WAY. By J. Tauler. Edited by A. W. Hutton, M.A.
THE THOUGHTS OF PASCAL. Edited by C. S. Jerram, M.A.

ON THE LOVE OF GOD. By St. Francis de Sales. Edited by W. J. Knox-Little, M.A.
A MANUAL OF CONSOLATION FROM THE SAINTS AND FATHERS. Edited by J. H. Burn, B.D.
THE SONG OF SONGS. Edited by B. Blaxland, M.A.
THE DEVOTIONS OF ST. ANSELM. Edited by C. C. J. Webb, M.A.
GRACE ABOUNDING. By John Bunyan. Edited by S. C. Freer, M.A.
BISHOP WILSON'S SACRA PRIVATA. Edited by A. E. Burn, B.D.
LYRA SACRA: A Book of Sacred Verse. Edited by H. C. Beeching, M.A., Canon of Westminster.
A DAY BOOK FROM THE SAINTS AND FATHERS. Edited by J. H. Burn, B.D.
HEAVENLY WISDOM. A Selection from the English Mystics. Edited by E. C. Gregory.
LIGHT, LIFE, and LOVE. A Selection from the German Mystics. Edited by W. R. Inge, M.A.
AN INTRODUCTION TO THE DEVOUT LIFE. By St. Francis de Sales. Translated and Edited by T. Barns, M.A.

Methuen's Standard Library

In Sixpenny Volumes.

THE STANDARD LIBRARY is a new series of volumes containing the great classics of the world, and particularly the finest works of English literature. All the great masters will be represented, either in complete works or in selections. It is the ambition of the publishers to place the best books of the Anglo-Saxon race within the reach of every reader, so that the series may represent something of the diversity and splendour of our English tongue. The characteristics of THE STANDARD LIBRARY are four :—1. SOUNDNESS OF TEXT. 2. CHEAPNESS. 3. CLEARNESS OF TYPE. 4. SIMPLICITY. The books are well printed on good paper at a price which on the whole is without parallel in the history of publishing. Each volume contains from 100 to 250 pages, and is issued in paper covers, Crown 8vo, at Sixpence net, or in cloth gilt at One Shilling net. In a few cases long books are issued as Double Volumes or as Treble Volumes.

The following books are ready with the exception of those marked with a †, which denotes that the book is nearly ready :—

THE MEDITATIONS OF MARCUS AURELIUS. The translation is by R. Graves.
THE NOVELS OF JANE AUSTEN. In 5 volumes. VOL. I.—Sense and Sensibility.
ESSAYS AND COUNSELS and THE NEW ATLANTIS. By Francis Bacon, Lord Verulam.

RELIGIO MEDICI and URN BURIAL. By Sir Thomas Browne. The text has been collated by A. R. Waller.
THE PILGRIM'S PROGRESS. By John Bunyan.
REFLECTIONS ON THE FRENCH REVOLUTION. By Edmund Burke.
THE ANALOGY OF RELIGION, NATURAL AND REVEALED. By Joseph Butler, D.D.

[Continued.

THE STANDARD LIBRARY—*continued.*

THE POEMS OF THOMAS CHATTERTON. In 2 volumes.
  Vol. I.—Miscellaneous Poems.
  †Vol. II.—The Rowley Poems.
†VITA NUOVA. By Dante. Translated into English by D. G. Rossetti.
TOM JONES. By Henry Fielding. Treble Vol.
CRANFORD. By Mrs. Gaskell.
THE HISTORY OF THE DECLINE AND FALL OF THE ROMAN EMPIRE. By Edward Gibbon. In 7 double volumes.
  Vol. v. is nearly ready.
  The Text and Notes have been revised by J. B. Bury, Litt.D., but the Appendices of the more expensive edition are not given.
†THE VICAR OF WAKEFIELD. By Oliver Goldsmith.
THE POEMS AND PLAYS OF OLIVER GOLDSMITH.
THE WORKS OF BEN JONSON.
†VOL. I.—The Case is Altered. Every Man in His Humour. Every Man out of His Humour.
  The text has been collated by H. C. Hart.
THE POEMS OF JOHN KEATS. Double volume.
  The Text has been collated by E. de Selincourt.
ON THE IMITATION OF CHRIST. By Thomas à Kempis.
  The translation is by C. Bigg, DD., Canon of Christ Church.
A SERIOUS CALL TO A DEVOUT AND HOLY LIFE. By William Law.
THE PLAYS OF CHRISTOPHER MARLOWE.
†Vol. I.—Tamburlane the Great. The Tragical History of Dr. Faustus.
THE PLAYS OF PHILIP MASSINGER.
†Vol. I.—The Duke of Milan.

THE POEMS OF JOHN MILTON. In 2 volumes.
  Vol. I.—Paradise Lost.
THE PROSE WORKS OF JOHN MILTON.
  VOL. I.—Eikonoklastes and The Tenure of Kings and Magistrates.
SELECT WORKS OF SIR THOMAS MORE.
  Vol. I.—Utopia and Poems.
THE REPUBLIC OF PLATO. Translated by Sydenham and Taylor. Double Volume. The translation has been revised by W. H. D. Rouse.
THE LITTLE FLOWERS OF ST. FRANCIS. Translated by W. Heywood.
THE WORKS OF WILLIAM SHAKESPEARE. In 10 volumes.
  VOL. I.—The Tempest; The Two Gentlemen of Verona; The Merry Wives of Windsor; Measure for Measure; The Comedy of Errors.
  VOL. II.—Much Ado About Nothing; Love's Labour's Lost; A Midsummer Night's Dream; The Merchant of Venice; As You Like It.
  VOL. III.—The Taming of the Shrew; All's Well that Ends Well; Twelfth Night; The Winter's Tale.
  Vol. IV.—The Life and Death of King John; The Tragedy of King Richard the Second; The First Part of King Henry IV.; The Second Part of King Henry IV.
  Vol. V.—The Life of King Henry V.; The First Part of King Henry VI.; The Second Part of King Henry VI.
THE LIFE OF NELSON. By Robert Southey.
THE NATURAL HISTORY AND ANTIQUITIES OF SELBORNE. By Gilbert White.

Half-Crown Library

Crown 8vo. 2s. 6d. net.

THE LIFE OF JOHN RUSKIN. By W. G. Collingwood, M.A. With Portraits. *Sixth Edition.*
ENGLISH LYRICS. By W. E. Henley. *Second Edition.*
THE GOLDEN POMP. A Procession of English Lyrics. Arranged by A. T. Quiller Couch. *Second Edition.*
CHITRAL: The Story of a Minor Siege. By Sir G. S. Robertson, K.C.S.I. *Third Edition.* Illustrated.

STRANGE SURVIVALS AND SUPERSTITIONS. By S. Baring-Gould. *Third Edition.*
YORKSHIRE ODDITIES AND STRANGE EVENTS. By S. Baring-Gould. *Fourth Edition.*
ENGLISH VILLAGES. By P. H. Ditchfield, M.A., F.S.A. Illustrated.
A BOOK OF ENGLISH PROSE. By W. E. Henley and C. Whibley.
THE LAND OF THE BLACK MOUNTAIN. Being a Description of Montenegro. By R. Wyon and G. Prance. With 40 Illustrations.

Illustrated Pocket Library of Plain and Coloured Books, The

Fcap 8vo. 3s. 6d. net each volume.

A series, in small form, of some of the famous illustrated books of fiction and general literature. These are faithfully reprinted from the first or best editions without introduction or notes. The Illustrations are chiefly in colour.

COLOURED BOOKS

OLD COLOURED BOOKS. By George Paston. With 16 Coloured Plates. *Fcap. 8vo. 2s. net.*
THE LIFE AND DEATH OF JOHN MYTTON, ESQ.
By Nimrod. With 18 Coloured Plates by Henry Alken and T. J. Rawlins. *Third Edition.*

[*Continued.*

General Literature 25

ILLUSTRATED POCKET LIBRARY OF PLAIN AND COLOURED BOOKS—*continued*.

THE LIFE OF A SPORTSMAN. By Nimrod. With 35 Coloured Plates by Henry Alken.

HANDLEY CROSS. By R. S. Surtees. With 17 Coloured Plates and 100 Woodcuts in the Text by John Leech. *Second Edition.*

MR. SPONGE'S SPORTING TOUR. By R. S. Surtees. With 13 Coloured Plates and 90 Woodcuts in the Text by John Leech.

JORROCKS' JAUNTS AND JOLLITIES. By R. S. Surtees. With 15 Coloured Plates by H. Alken. *Second Edition.*

This volume is reprinted from the extremely rare and costly edition of 1843, which contains Alken's very fine illustrations instead of the usual ones by Phiz.

ASK MAMMA. By R. S. Surtees. With 13 Coloured Plates and 70 Woodcuts in the Text by John Leech.

THE ANALYSIS OF THE HUNTING FIELD. By R. S. Surtees. With 7 Coloured Plates by Henry Alken, and 43 Illustrations on Wood.

THE TOUR OF DR. SYNTAX IN SEARCH OF THE PICTURESQUE. By William Combe. With 30 Coloured Plates by T. Rowlandson.

THE TOUR OF DOCTOR SYNTAX IN SEARCH OF CONSOLATION. By William Combe. With 24 Coloured Plates by T. Rowlandson.

THE THIRD TOUR OF DOCTOR SYNTAX IN SEARCH OF A WIFE. By William Combe. With 24 Coloured Plates by T. Rowlandson.

THE HISTORY OF JOHNNY QUAE GENUS: the Little Foundling of the late Dr. Syntax. By the Author of 'The Three Tours.' With 24 Coloured Plates by Rowlandson.

THE ENGLISH DANCE OF DEATH, from the Designs of T. Rowlandson, with Metrical Illustrations by the Author of 'Doctor Syntax.' *Two Volumes.*

This book contains 76 Coloured Plates.

THE DANCE OF LIFE: A Poem. By the Author of 'Doctor Syntax.' Illustrated with 26 Coloured Engravings by T. Rowlandson.

LIFE IN LONDON: or, the Day and Night Scenes of Jerry Hawthorn, Esq., and his Elegant Friend, Corinthian Tom. By Pierce Egan. With 36 Coloured Plates by I. R. and G. Cruikshank. With numerous Designs on Wood.

REAL LIFE IN LONDON: or, the Rambles and Adventures of Bob Tallyho, Esq., and his Cousin, The Hon. Tom Dashall. By an Amateur (Pierce Egan). With 31 Coloured Plates by Alken and Rowlandson, etc. *Two Volumes.*

THE LIFE OF AN ACTOR. By Pierce Egan. With 27 Coloured Plates by Theodore Lane, and several Designs on Wood.

THE VICAR OF WAKEFIELD. By Oliver Goldsmith. With 24 Coloured Plates by T. Rowlandson.

THE MILITARY ADVENTURES OF JOHNNY NEWCOME. By an Officer. With 15 Coloured Plates by T. Rowlandson.

THE NATIONAL SPORTS OF GREAT BRITAIN. With Descriptions and 51 Coloured Plates by Henry Alken.

This book is completely different from the large folio edition of 'National Sports' by the same artist, and none of the plates are similar.

THE ADVENTURES OF A POST CAPTAIN. By A Naval Officer. With 24 Coloured Plates by Mr. Williams.

GAMONIA: or, the Art of Preserving Game; and an Improved Method of making Plantations and Covers, explained and illustrated by Lawrence Rawstorne, Esq. With 15 Coloured Plates by T. Rawlins.

AN ACADEMY FOR GROWN HORSEMEN: Containing the completest Instructions for Walking, Trotting, Cantering, Galloping, Stumbling, and Tumbling. Illustrated with 27 Coloured Plates, and adorned with a Portrait of the Author. By Geoffrey Gambado, Esq.

REAL LIFE IN IRELAND, or, the Day and Night Scenes of Brian Boru, Esq., and his Elegant Friend, Sir Shawn O'Dogherty. By a Real Paddy. With 19 Coloured Plates by Heath, Marks, etc.

THE ADVENTURES OF JOHNNY NEWCOME IN THE NAVY. By Alfred Burton. With 16 Coloured Plates by T. Rowlandson.

THE OLD ENGLISH SQUIRE: A Poem. By John Careless, Esq. With 20 Coloured Plates after the style of T. Rowlandson.

*THE ENGLISH SPY. By Bernard Blackmantle. With 72 Coloured Plates by R. Cruikshank, and many Illustrations on wood. *Two Volumes.*

PLAIN BOOKS

THE GRAVE: A Poem. By Robert Blair. Illustrated by 12 Etchings executed by Louis Schiavonetti from the original Inventions of William Blake. With an Engraved Title Page and a Portrait of Blake by T. Phillips, R.A.

The illustrations are reproduced in photogravure.

ILLUSTRATIONS OF THE BOOK OF JOB. Invented and engraved by William Blake.

These famous Illustrations—21 in number—are reproduced in photogravure.

ÆSOP'S FABLES. With 380 Woodcuts by Thomas Bewick.

[*Continued.*

MESSRS. METHUEN'S CATALOGUE

ILLUSTRATED POCKET LIBRARY OF PLAIN AND COLOURED BOOKS—*continued.*

WINDSOR CASTLE. By W. Harrison Ainsworth. With 22 Plates and 87 Woodcuts in the Text by George Cruikshank.

THE TOWER OF LONDON. By W. Harrison Ainsworth. With 40 Plates and 58 Woodcuts in the Text by George Cruikshank.

FRANK FAIRLEGH. By F. E. Smedley. With 30 Plates by George Cruikshank.

HANDY ANDY. By Samuel Lover. With 24 Illustrations by the Author.

THE COMPLEAT ANGLER. By Izaak Walton and Charles Cotton. With 14 Plates and 77 Woodcuts in the Text.
This volume is reproduced from the beautiful edition of John Major of 1824.

THE PICKWICK PAPERS. By Charles Dickens. With the 43 Illustrations by Seymour and Phiz, the two Buss Plates, and the 32 Contemporary Onwhyn Plates.

Junior Examination Series

Edited by A. M. M. STEDMAN, M.A. *Fcap.* 8vo. 1s.

This series is intended to lead up to the School Examination Series, and is intended for the use of teachers and students, to supply material for the former and practice for the latter. The papers are carefully graduated, cover the whole of the subject usually taught, and are intended to form part of the ordinary class work. They may be used *vivâ voce* or as a written examination.

JUNIOR FRENCH EXAMINATION PAPERS. By F. Jacob, M.A.

JUNIOR LATIN EXAMINATION PAPERS. By C. G. Botting, B.A. *Fourth Edition.*

JUNIOR ENGLISH EXAMINATION PAPERS. By W. Williamson, B.A.

JUNIOR ARITHMETIC EXAMINATION PAPERS. By W. S. Beard. *Second Edition.*

JUNIOR ALGEBRA EXAMINATION PAPERS. By S. W. Finn, M.A.

JUNIOR GREEK EXAMINATION PAPERS. By T. C. Weatherhead, M.A.

JUNIOR GENERAL INFORMATION EXAMINATION PAPERS. By W. S. Beard.

A KEY TO THE ABOVE. *Crown* 8vo. 3s 6d. *net.*

JUNIOR GEOGRAPHY EXAMINATION PAPERS. By W. G. Baker, M.A.

JUNIOR GERMAN EXAMINATION PAPERS. By A. Voegelin, M.A.

Junior School-Books

Edited by O. D. INSKIP, LL.D., and W. WILLIAMSON, B.A.

A series of elementary books for pupils in lower forms, simply written by teachers of experience.

A CLASS-BOOK OF DICTATION PASSAGES. By W. Williamson, B.A. *Eleventh Edition. Cr.* 8vo. 1s. 6d.

THE GOSPEL ACCORDING TO ST. MATTHEW. Edited by E. Wilton South, M.A. With Three Maps. *Cr.* 8vo. 1s. 6d.

THE GOSPEL ACCORDING TO ST. MARK. Edited by A. E. Rubie, D.D. With Three Maps. *Cr.* 8vo. 1s. 6d.

A JUNIOR ENGLISH GRAMMAR. By W. Williamson, B.A. With numerous passages for parsing and analysis, and a chapter on Essay Writing. *Third Edition. Cr.* 8vo. 2s.

A JUNIOR CHEMISTRY. By E. A. Tyler, B.A., F.C.S. With 78 Illustrations. *Second Edition. Cr.* 8vo. 2s. 6d.

THE ACTS OF THE APOSTLES. Edited by A. E. Rubie, D.D. *Cr* 8vo. 2s.

A JUNIOR FRENCH GRAMMAR. By L. A. Sornet and M. J. Acatos. *Cr.* 8vo. 2s.

ELEMENTARY EXPERIMENTAL SCIENCE. PHYSICS by W. T. Clough, A.R.C.S. CHEMISTRY by A. E. Dunstan, B.Sc. With 2 Plates and 154 Diagrams. *Third Edition. Cr.* 8vo. 2s. 6d.

A JUNIOR GEOMETRY. By Noel S. Lydon. With 276 Diagrams. *Second Edition. Cr.* 8vo. 2s.

A JUNIOR MAGNETISM AND ELECTRICITY. By W. T. Clough. Illustrated. *Cr.* 8vo. 2s. 6d.

ELEMENTARY EXPERIMENTAL CHEMISTRY. By A. E. Dunstan, B.Sc. With 4 Plates and 109 Diagrams. *Cr.* 8vo. 2s.

A JUNIOR FRENCH PROSE COMPOSITION. By R. R. N. Baron, M.A. *Cr.* 8vo. 2s.

THE GOSPEL ACCORDING TO ST. LUKE. With an Introduction and Notes by William Williamson, B.A. With Three Maps. *Cr.* 8vo. 2s.

Leaders of Religion

Edited by H. C. BEECHING, M.A., Canon of Westminster. *With Portraits.* Cr. 8vo. 2s. net.

A series of short biographies of the most prominent leaders of religious life and thought of all ages and countries.

CARDINAL NEWMAN. By R. H. Hutton.
JOHN WESLEY. By J. H. Overton, M.A.
BISHOP WILBERFORCE. By G. W. Daniell, M.A.
CARDINAL MANNING. By A. W. Hutton, M.A.
CHARLES SIMEON. By H. C. G. Moule, D.D.
JOHN KEBLE. By Walter Lock, D.D.
THOMAS CHALMERS. By Mrs. Oliphant.
LANCELOT ANDREWES. By R. L. Ottley, D.D. *Second Edition.*
AUGUSTINE OF CANTERBURY. By E. L. Cutts, D.D.
WILLIAM LAUD. By W. H. Hutton, M.A. *Third Edition.*
JOHN KNOX. By F. MacCunn. *Second Edition.*
JOHN HOWE. By R. F. Horton, D.D.
BISHOP KEN. By F. A. Clarke, M.A.
GEORGE FOX, THE QUAKER. By T. Hodgkin, D.C.L. *Third Edition.*
JOHN DONNE. By Augustus Jessopp, D.D.
THOMAS CRANMER. By A. J. Mason, D.D.
BISHOP LATIMER. By R. M. Carlyle and A. J. Carlyle, M.A.
BISHOP BUTLER. By W. A. Spooner, M.A.

Little Blue Books, The

General Editor, E. V. LUCAS.

Illustrated. Demy 16mo. 2s. 6d.

A series of books for children. The aim of the editor is to get entertaining or exciting stories about normal children, the moral of which is implied rather than expressed.

1. THE CASTAWAYS OF MEADOWBANK. By Thomas Cobb.
2. THE BEECHNUT BOOK. By Jacob Abbott. Edited by E. V. Lucas.
3. THE AIR GUN. By T. Hilbert.
4. A SCHOOL YEAR. By Netta Syrett.
5. THE PEELES AT THE CAPITAL. By Roger Ashton.
6. THE TREASURE OF PRINCEGATE PRIORY. By T. Cobb.
7. MRS. BARBERRY'S GENERAL SHOP. By Roger Ashton.
8. A BOOK OF BAD CHILDREN. By W. T. Webb.
9. THE LOST BALL. By Thomas Cobb.

Little Books on Art

With many Illustrations. Demy 16mo. 2s. 6d. net.

A series of monographs in miniature, containing the complete outline of the subject under treatment and rejecting minute details. These books are produced with the greatest care. Each volume consists of about 200 pages, and contains from 30 to 40 illustrations, including a frontispiece in photogravure.

GREEK ART. H. B. Walters. *Second Edition.*
BOOKPLATES. E. Almack.
REYNOLDS. J. Sime. *Second Edition.*
ROMNEY. George Paston.
WATTS. R. E. D. Sketchley.
LEIGHTON. Alice Corkran.
VELASQUEZ. Wilfrid Wilberforce and A. R. Gilbert.
GREUZE AND BOUCHER. Eliza F. Pollard.
VANDYCK. M. G. Smallwood.
TURNER. Frances Tyrell-Gill.
DÜRER. Jessie Allen.
HOPPNER. H. P. K. Skipton.
HOLBEIN. Mrs. G. Fortescue.
BURNE-JONES. Fortunée de Lisle. *Second Edition.*
REMBRANDT. Mrs. E. A. Sharp.
COROT. Alice Pollard and Ethel Birnstingl.
RAPHAEL. A. R. Dryhurst.
MILLET. Netta Peacock.
ILLUMINATED MSS. J. W. Bradley.
CHRIST IN ART. Mrs. Henry Jenner.
JEWELLERY. Cyril Davenport.
CLAUDE. Edward Dillon.
THE ARTS OF JAPAN. Edward Dillon.

28 MESSRS. METHUEN'S CATALOGUE

Little Galleries, The
Demy 16mo. 2s. 6d. net.

A series of little books containing examples of the best work of the great painters. Each volume contains 20 plates in photogravure, together with a short outline of the life and work of the master to whom the book is devoted.

A LITTLE GALLERY OF REYNOLDS.
A LITTLE GALLERY OF ROMNEY.
A LITTLE GALLERY OF HOPPNER.
A LITTLE GALLERY OF MILLAIS.
A LITTLE GALLERY OF ENGLISH POETS.

Little Guides, The
Small Pott 8vo, cloth, 2s. 6d. net.; leather, 3s. 6d. net.

OXFORD AND ITS COLLEGES. By J. Wells, M.A. Illustrated by E. H. New. *Sixth Edition.*
CAMBRIDGE AND ITS COLLEGES. By A. Hamilton Thompson. Illustrated by E. H. New. *Second Edition.*
THE MALVERN COUNTRY. By B. C. A. Windle, D.Sc., F.R.S. Illustrated by E. H. New.
SHAKESPEARE'S COUNTRY. By B. C. A. Windle, D.Sc., F.R.S. Illustrated by E. H. New. *Second Edition.*
SUSSEX. By F. G. Brabant, M.A. Illustrated by E. H. New. *Second Edition.*
WESTMINSTER ABBEY. By G. E. Troutbeck. Illustrated by F. D. Bedford.
NORFOLK. By W. A. Dutt. Illustrated by B. C. Boulter.
CORNWALL. By A. L. Salmon. Illustrated by B. C. Boulter.
BRITTANY. By S. Baring-Gould. Illustrated by J. Wylie.
HERTFORDSHIRE. By H. W. Tompkins, F.R.H.S. Illustrated by E. H. New.
THE ENGLISH LAKES. By F. G. Brabant, M.A. Illustrated by E. H. New.
KENT. By G. Clinch. Illustrated by F. D. Bedford.
ROME. By C. G. Ellaby. Illustrated by B. C. Boulter.
THE ISLE OF WIGHT. By G. Clinch. Illustrated by F. D. Bedford.
SURREY. By F. A. H. Lambert. Illustrated by E. H. New.
BUCKINGHAMSHIRE. By E. S. Roscoe. Illustrated by F. D. Bedford.
SUFFOLK. By W. A. Dutt. Illustrated by J. Wylie.
DERBYSHIRE. By J. C. Cox, LL.D., F.S.A. Illustrated by J. C. Wall.
THE NORTH RIDING OF YORKSHIRE. By J E. Morris. Illustrated by R. J. S. Bertram.
HAMPSHIRE. By J. C. Cox. Illustrated by M. E. Purser.
SICILY. By F. H. Jackson. With many Illustrations by the Author.
DORSET. By Frank R. Heath. Illustrated.
CHESHIRE. By W. M. Gallichan. Illustrated by Elizabeth Hartley.
NORTHAMPTONSHIRE. By Wakeling Dry. Illustrated.
THE EAST RIDING OF YORKSHIRE. By J. E. Morris. Illustrated.
OXFORDSHIRE. By F. G. Brabant. Illustrated by E. H. New.
ST. PAUL'S CATHEDRAL. By George Clinch. Illustrated by Beatrice Alcock.

Little Library, The
With Introductions, Notes, and Photogravure Frontispieces.
Small Pott 8vo. Each Volume, cloth, 1s. 6d. net; leather, 2s. 6d. net.

A series of small books under the above title, containing some of the famous works in English and other literatures, in the domains of fiction, poetry, and belles lettres. The series also contains volumes of selections in prose and verse. The books are edited with the most scholarly care. Each one contains an introduction which gives (1) a short biography of the author; (2) a critical estimate of the book. Where they are necessary, short notes are added at the foot of the page.

Each volume has a photogravure frontispiece, and the books are produced with great care.

Anon. ENGLISH LYRICS, A LITTLE BOOK OF.
Austen (Jane). PRIDE AND PREJUDICE. Edited by E. V. LUCAS. *Two Volumes.*
NORTHANGER ABBEY. Edited by E. V. LUCAS.
Bacon (Francis). THE ESSAYS OF LORD BACON. Edited by EDWARD WRIGHT.

General Literature

Barham (R. H.). THE INGOLDSBY LEGENDS. Edited by J. B. Atlay. *Two Volumes.*

Barnett (Mrs. P. A.). A LITTLE BOOK OF ENGLISH PROSE.

Beckford (William). THE HISTORY OF THE CALIPH VATHEK. Edited by E. Denison Ross.

Blake (William). SELECTIONS FROM WILLIAM BLAKE. Edited by M. Perugini.

Borrow (George). LAVENGRO. Edited by F. Hindes Groome. *Two Volumes.*
THE ROMANY RYE. Edited by John Sampson.

Browning (Robert). SELECTIONS FROM THE EARLY POEMS OF ROBERT BROWNING. Edited by W. Hall Griffin, M.A.

Canning (George). SELECTIONS FROM THE ANTI-JACOBIN: with George Canning's additional Poems. Edited by Lloyd Sanders.

Cowley (Abraham). THE ESSAYS OF ABRAHAM COWLEY. Edited by H. C. Minchin.

Crabbe (George). SELECTIONS FROM GEORGE CRABBE. Edited by A. C. Deane.

Craik (Mrs.). JOHN HALIFAX, GENTLEMAN. Edited by Anne Matheson. *Two Volumes.*

Crashaw (Richard). THE ENGLISH POEMS OF RICHARD CRASHAW. Edited by Edward Hutton.

Dante (Alighieri). THE INFERNO OF DANTE. Translated by H. F. Cary. Edited by Paget Toynbee, M.A., D.Litt.
THE PURGATORIO OF DANTE. Translated by H. F. Cary. Edited by Paget Toynbee, M.A., D.Litt.
THE PARADISO OF DANTE. Translated by H. F. Cary. Edited by Paget Toynbee, M.A., D.Litt.

Darley (George). SELECTIONS FROM THE POEMS OF GEORGE DARLEY. Edited by R. A. Streatfeild.

Deane (A. C.). A LITTLE BOOK OF LIGHT VERSE.

Dickens (Charles). CHRISTMAS BOOKS. *Two Volumes.*

Ferrier (Susan). MARRIAGE. Edited by A. Goodrich-Freer and Lord Iddesleigh. *Two Volumes.*
THE INHERITANCE. *Two Volumes.*

Gaskell (Mrs.). CRANFORD. Edited by E. V. Lucas. *Second Edition.*

Hawthorne (Nathaniel). THE SCARLET LETTER. Edited by Percy Dearmer.

Henderson (T. F.). A LITTLE BOOK OF SCOTTISH VERSE.

Keats (John). POEMS. With an Introduction by L. Binyon, and Notes by J. Masefield.

Kinglake (A. W.). EOTHEN. With an Introduction and Notes. *Second Edition.*

Lamb (Charles). ELIA, AND THE LAST ESSAYS OF ELIA. Edited by E. V. Lucas.

Locker (F.). LONDON LYRICS. Edited by A. D. Godley, M.A. A reprint of the First Edition.

Longfellow (H. W.). SELECTIONS FROM LONGFELLOW. Edited by L. M. Faithfull.

Marvell (Andrew). THE POEMS OF ANDREW MARVELL. Edited by E. Wright.

Milton (John). THE MINOR POEMS OF JOHN MILTON. Edited by H. C. Beeching, M.A., Canon of Westminster.

Moir (D. M.). MANSIE WAUCH. Edited by T. F. Henderson.

Nichols (J. B. B.). A LITTLE BOOK OF ENGLISH SONNETS.

Rochefoucauld (La). THE MAXIMS OF LA ROCHEFOUCAULD. Translated by Dean Stanhope. Edited by G. H. Powell.

Smith (Horace and James). REJECTED ADDRESSES. Edited by A. D. Godley, M.A.

Sterne (Laurence). A SENTIMENTAL JOURNEY. Edited by H. W. Paul.

Tennyson (Alfred, Lord). THE EARLY POEMS OF ALFRED, LORD TENNYSON. Edited by J. Churton Collins, M.A.
IN MEMORIAM. Edited by H. C. Beeching, M.A.
THE PRINCESS. Edited by Elizabeth Wordsworth.
MAUD. Edited by Elizabeth Wordsworth.

Thackeray (W. M.). VANITY FAIR. Edited by S. Gwynn. *Three Volumes.*
PENDENNIS. Edited by S. Gwynn. *Three Volumes.*
ESMOND. Edited by S. Gwynn.
CHRISTMAS BOOKS. Edited by S. Gwynn.

Vaughan (Henry). THE POEMS OF HENRY VAUGHAN. Edited by Edward Hutton.

Walton (Izaak). THE COMPLEAT ANGLER. Edited by J. Buchan.

Waterhouse (Mrs. Alfred). A LITTLE BOOK OF LIFE AND DEATH. Edited by. *Eighth Edition.*

Wordsworth (W.). SELECTIONS FROM WORDSWORTH. Edited by Nowell C. Smith.

Wordsworth (W.) and Coleridge (S. T.). LYRICAL BALLADS. Edited by George Sampson.

Miniature Library

Reprints in miniature of a few interesting books which have qualities of humanity, devotion, or literary genius.

EUPHRANOR: A Dialogue on Youth. By Edward FitzGerald. From the edition published by W. Pickering in 1851. *Demy 32mo. Leather, 2s. net.*

POLONIUS: or Wise Saws and Modern Instances. By Edward FitzGerald. From the edition published by W. Pickering in 1852. *Demy 32mo. Leather, 2s. net.*

THE RUBÁIYÁT OF OMAR KHAYYÁM. By Edward FitzGerald. From the 1st edition of 1859, *Third Edition. Leather, 1s. net.*

THE LIFE OF EDWARD, LORD HERBERT OF CHERBURY. Written by himself. From the edition printed at Strawberry Hill in the year 1764. *Medium 32mo. Leather, 2s. net.*

THE VISIONS OF DOM FRANCISCO QUEVEDO VILLEGAS, Knight of the Order of St. James. Made English by R. L. From the edition printed for H. Herringman, 1668. *Leather. 2s. net.*

POEMS. By Dora Greenwell. From the edition of 1848. *Leather, 2s. net.*

Oxford Biographies

Fcap. 8vo. Each volume, cloth, 2s. 6d. net; leather, 3s. 6d. net.

These books are written by scholars of repute, who combine knowledge and literary skill with the power of popular presentation. They are illustrated from authentic material.

DANTE ALIGHIERI. By Paget Toynbee, M.A., D.Litt. With 12 Illustrations. *Second Edition.*
SAVONAROLA. By E. L. S. Horsburgh, M.A. With 12 Illustrations. *Second Edition.*
JOHN HOWARD. By E. C. S. Gibson, D.D., Bishop of Gloucester. With 12 Illustrations.
TENNYSON. By A. C. Benson, M.A. With 9 Illustrations.
WALTER RALEIGH. By I. A. Taylor. With 12 Illustrations.
ERASMUS. By E. F. H. Capey. With 12 Illustrations.
THE YOUNG PRETENDER. By C. S. Terry. With 12 Illustrations.

ROBERT BURNS. By T. F. Henderson. With 12 Illustrations.
CHATHAM. By A. S. M'Dowall. With 12 Illustrations.
ST. FRANCIS OF ASSISI. By Anna M. Stoddart. With 16 Illustrations.
CANNING. By W. Alison Phillips. With 12 Illustrations.
BEACONSFIELD. By Walter Sichel. With 12 Illustrations.
GOETHE. By H. G. Atkins. With 12 Illustrations.
FENELON. By Viscount St. Cyres. With 12 Illustrations.

School Examination Series

Edited by A. M. M. STEDMAN, M.A. Cr. 8vo. 2s. 6d.

FRENCH EXAMINATION PAPERS. By A. M. M. Stedman, M.A. *Thirteenth Edition.*
A KEY, issued to Tutors and Private Students only to be had on application to the Publishers. *Fifth Edition. Crown 8vo. 6s. net.*
LATIN EXAMINATION PAPERS. By A. M. M. Stedman, M.A. *Thirteenth Edition.*
KEY (*Fourth Edition*) issued as above. 6s. net.
GREEK EXAMINATION PAPERS. By A. M. M. Stedman, M.A. *Eighth Edition.*
KEY (*Third Edition*) issued as above. 6s. net.
GERMAN EXAMINATION PAPERS. By R. J. Morich. *Sixth Edition.*

KEY (*Third Edition*) issued as above. 6s. net.
HISTORY AND GEOGRAPHY EXAMINATION PAPERS. By C. H. Spence, M.A. *Second Edition.*
PHYSICS EXAMINATION PAPERS. By R. E. Steel, M.A., F.C.S.
GENERAL KNOWLEDGE EXAMINATION PAPERS. By A. M. M. Stedman, M.A. *Fifth Edition.*
KEY (*Third Edition*) issued as above. 7s. net.
EXAMINATION PAPERS IN ENGLISH HISTORY. By J. Tait Plowden-Wardlaw, B.A.

GENERAL LITERATURE

Science, Textbooks of

Edited by G. F. GOODCHILD, B.A., B.Sc., and G. R. MILLS, M.A.

PRACTICAL MECHANICS. By Sidney H. Wells. *Third Edition. Cr. 8vo.* 3s. 6d.
PRACTICAL PHYSICS. By H. Stroud, D.Sc., M.A. *Cr. 8vo.* 3s. 6d.
PRACTICAL CHEMISTRY. Part I. By W. French, M.A. *Cr. 8vo. Fourth Edition.* 1s. 6d. Part II. By W. French, M.A., and T. H. Boardman, M.A. *Cr. 8vo.* 1s. 6d.
TECHNICAL ARITHMETIC AND GEOMETRY. By C. T. Millis, M.I.M.E. *Cr. 8vo.* 3s. 6d.
EXAMPLES IN PHYSICS. By C. E. Jackson, B.A. *Cr. 8vo.* 2s. 6d.
*ELEMENTARY ORGANIC CHEMISTRY. By A. E. Dunstan, B.Sc. Illustrated. *Cr. 8vo.*

Social Questions of To-day

Edited by H. DE B. GIBBINS, Litt.D., M.A. *Crown 8vo.* 2s. 6d.

A series of volumes upon those topics of social, economic, and industrial interest that are foremost in the public mind.

TRADE UNIONISM—NEW AND OLD. By G. Howell. *Third Edition.*
THE COMMERCE OF NATIONS. By C. F. Bastable, M.A. *Third Edition.*
THE ALIEN INVASION. By W. H. Wilkins, B.A.
THE RURAL EXODUS. By P. Anderson Graham.
LAND NATIONALIZATION. By Harold Cox, B.A. *Second Edition.*
A SHORTER WORKING DAY. By H. de B. Gibbins and R. A. Hadfield.
BACK TO THE LAND. An Inquiry into Rural Depopulation. By H. E. Moore.
TRUSTS, POOLS, AND CORNERS. By J. Stephen Jeans.
THE FACTORY SYSTEM. By R. W. Cooke Taylor.
WOMEN'S WORK. By Lady Dilke, Miss Bulley, and Miss Whitley.
SOCIALISM AND MODERN THOUGHT. By M. Kauffmann.
THE PROBLEM OF THE UNEMPLOYED. By J. A. Hobson, M.A.
LIFE IN WEST LONDON. By Arthur Sherwell, M.A. *Third Edition.*
RAILWAY NATIONALIZATION. By Clement Edwards.
UNIVERSITY AND SOCIAL SETTLEMENTS. By W. Reason, M.A.

Technology, Textbooks of

Edited by G. F. GOODCHILD, B.A., B.Sc., and G. R. MILLS, M.A.
Fully Illustrated.

HOW TO MAKE A DRESS. By J. A. E. Wood. *Third Edition. Cr. 8vo.* 1s. 6d.
CARPENTRY AND JOINERY. By F. C. Webber. *Fourth Edition. Cr. 8vo.* 3s. 6d.
MILLINERY, THEORETICAL AND PRACTICAL. By Clare Hill. *Second Edition. Cr. 8vo.* 2s.
AN INTRODUCTION TO THE STUDY OF TEXTILE DESIGN. By Aldred F. Barker. *Demy 8vo.* 7s. 6d.
BUILDERS' QUANTITIES. By H. C. Grubb. *Cr. 8vo.* 4s. 6d.
RÉPOUSSÉ METAL WORK. By A. C. Horth. *Cr. 8vo.* 2s. 6d.

Theology, Handbooks of

Edited by R. L. OTTLEY, D.D., Professor of Pastoral Theology at Oxford, and Canon of Christ Church, Oxford.

The series is intended, in part, to furnish the clergy and teachers or students of Theology with trustworthy Textbooks, adequately representing the present position of the questions dealt with; in part, to make accessible to the reading public an accurate and concise statement of facts and principles in all questions bearing on Theology and Religion.

THE XXXIX. ARTICLES OF THE CHURCH OF ENGLAND. Edited by E. C. S. Gibson, D.D. *Fifth and Cheaper Edition in one Volume. Demy 8vo.* 12s. 6d.
AN INTRODUCTION TO THE HISTORY OF RELIGION. By F. B. Jevons, M.A., Litt.D. *Third Edition. Demy 8vo.* 10s. 6d.
THE DOCTRINE OF THE INCARNATION. By R. L. Ottley, D.D. *Second and Cheaper Edition. Demy 8vo.* 12s. 6d.
AN INTRODUCTION TO THE HISTORY OF THE CREEDS. By A. E. Burn, D.D. *Demy 8vo.* 10s. 6d.
THE PHILOSOPHY OF RELIGION IN ENGLAND AND AMERICA. By Alfred Caldecott, D.D. *Demy 8vo.* 10s. 6d.
A HISTORY OF EARLY CHRISTIAN DOCTRINE. By J. F. Bethune Baker, M.A. *Demy 8vo.* 10s. 6d.

MESSRS. METHUEN'S CATALOGUE

Westminster Commentaries, The
General Editor, WALTER LOCK, D.D., Warden of Keble College,
Dean Ireland's Professor of Exegesis in the University of Oxford.

The object of each commentary is primarily exegetical, to interpret the author's meaning to the present generation. The editors will not deal, except very subordinately, with questions of textual criticism or philology; but, taking the English text in the Revised Version as their basis, they will try to combine a hearty acceptance of critical principles with loyalty to the Catholic Faith.

THE BOOK OF GENESIS. Edited with Introduction and Notes by S R. Driver, D.D. *Fifth Edition Demy 8vo.* 10s. 6d.

THE BOOK OF JOB. Edited by E. C. S. Gibson, D.D. *Second Edition. Demy 8vo.* 6s.

THE ACTS OF THE APOSTLES. Edited by R. B. Rackham, M.A. *Demy 8vo. Second and Cheaper Edition.* 10s. 6d.

THE FIRST EPISTLE OF PAUL THE APOSTLE TO THE CORINTHIANS. Edited by H. L. Goudge, M.A. *Demy 8vo.* 6s.

THE EPISTLE OF ST. JAMES. Edited with Introduction and Notes by R. J. Knowling, M.A. *Demy 8vo.* 6s.

PART II.—FICTION

Albanesi (E. Maria). SUSANNAH AND ONE OTHER. *Fourth Edition. Cr. 8vo.* 6s.
THE BLUNDER OF AN INNOCENT. *Second Edition. Cr. 8vo.* 6s.
CAPRICIOUS CAROLINE. *Second Edition. Cr. 8vo.* 6s.
LOVE AND LOUISA. *Second Edition. Cr. 8vo.* 6s.
PETER, A PARASITE. *Cr. 8vo.* 6s.
THE BROWN EYES OF MARY. *Third Edition. Cr. 8vo.* 6s.
Anstey (F.). Author of 'Vice Versâ.' A BAYARD FROM BENGAL. Illustrated by BERNARD PARTRIDGE. *Third Edition. Cr. 8vo.* 3s. 6d.
Bacheller (Irving), Author of 'Eben Holden.' DARREL OF THE BLESSED ISLES. *Third Edition. Cr. 8vo.* 6s.
Bagot (Richard). A ROMAN MYSTERY. *Third Edition. Cr. 8vo.* 6s.
THE PASSPORT. *Fourth Ed. Cr. 8vo.* 6s.
Baring-Gould (S.). ARMINELL. *Fifth Edition. Cr. 8vo.* 6s.
URITH. *Fifth Edition. Cr. 8vo.* 6s.
IN THE ROAR OF THE SEA. *Seventh Edition. Cr. 8vo.* 6s.
CHEAP JACK ZITA. *Fourth Edition. Cr. 8vo.* 6s.
MARGERY OF QUETHER. *Third Edition. Cr. 8vo.* 6s.
THE QUEEN OF LOVE. *Fifth Edition. Cr. 8vo.* 6s.
JACQUETTA. *Third Edition. Cr. 8vo.* 6s.
KITTY ALONE. *Fifth Edition. Cr. 8vo.* 6s.
NOÉMI. Illustrated. *Fourth Edition. Cr. 8vo.* 6s.
THE BROOM-SQUIRE. Illustrated. *Fifth Edition. Cr. 8vo.* 6s.
DARTMOOR IDYLLS. *Cr. 8vo.* 6s.
THE PENNYCOMEQUICKS. *Third Edition. Cr. 8vo.* 6s.
GUAVAS THE TINNER. Illustrated. *Second Edition. Cr. 8vo.* 6s.
BLADYS. Illustrated. *Second Edition. Cr. 8vo.* 6s.
PABO THE PRIEST. *Cr. 8vo.* 6s.
WINEFRED. Illustrated. *Second Edition. Cr. 8vo.* 6s.
ROYAL GEORGIE. Illustrated. *Cr. 8vo.* 6s.
MISS QUILLET. Illustrated. *Cr. 8vo.* 6s.
CHRIS OF ALL SORTS. *Cr. 8vo.* 6s.
IN DEWISLAND. *Second Edition. Cr. 8vo.* 6s.
LITTLE TU'PENNY. *A New Edition.* 6d. See also Strand Novels and Books for Boys and Girls.
Barlow (Jane). THE LAND OF THE SHAMROCK. *Cr. 8vo.* 6s. See also Strand Novels.
Barr (Robert). IN THE MIDST OF ALARMS. *Third Edition. Cr. 8vo.* 6s.
THE MUTABLE MANY. *Third Edition. Cr. 8vo.* 6s.
THE COUNTESS TEKLA. *Third Edition. Cr. 8vo.* 6s.
THE LADY ELECTRA. *Second Edition. Cr. 8vo.* 6s.
THE TEMPESTUOUS PETTICOAT. Illustrated. *Third Edition. Cr. 8vo.* 6s. See also Strand Novels and S. Crane.
Begbie (Harold). THE ADVENTURES OF SIR JOHN SPARROW. *Cr. 8vo.* 6s.
Belloc (Hilaire). EMMANUEL BURDEN, MERCHANT. With 36 Illustrations by G. K. CHESTERTON. *Second Edition. Cr. 8vo.* 6s.

Fiction

Benson (E. F.) DODO. *Fourth Edition.* Cr. 8vo. 6s. See also Strand Novels.
Benson (Margaret). SUBJECT TO VANITY. *Cr. 8vo.* 3s. 6d.
Bourne (Harold C.). See V. Langbridge.
Burton (J. Bloundelle). THE YEAR ONE: A Page of the French Revolution. Illustrated. *Cr. 8vo.* 6s.
THE FATE OF VALSEC. *Cr. 8vo.* 6s.
A BRANDED NAME. *Cr. 8vo.* 6s. See also Strand Novels.
Capes (Bernard), Author of 'The Lake of Wine.' THE EXTRAORDINARY CONFESSIONS OF DIANA PLEASE. *Third Edition. Cr. 8vo.* 6s.
A JAY OF ITALY. *Fourth Ed. Cr. 8vo.* 6s.
LOAVES AND FISHES. *Second Edition. Cr. 8vo.* 6s.
Chesney (Weatherby). THE TRAGEDY OF THE GREAT EMERALD. *Cr. 8vo.* 6s.
THE MYSTERY OF A BUNGALOW. *Second Edition. Cr. 8vo.* 6s. See also Strand Novels.
Clifford (Hugh). A FREE LANCE OF TO-DAY. *Cr. 8vo.* 6s.
Clifford (Mrs. W. K.). See Strand Novels and Books for Boys and Girls.
Cobb (Thomas). A CHANGE OF FACE. *Cr. 8vo.* 6s.
Corelli (Marie). A ROMANCE OF TWO WORLDS. *Twenty-Sixth Edition. Cr. 8vo.* 6s.
VENDETTA. *Twenty-Third Edition. Cr. 8vo.* 6s.
THELMA. *Thirty-Fourth Edition. Cr. 8vo.* 6s.
ARDATH: THE STORY OF A DEAD SELF. *Sixteenth Edition. Cr. 8vo.* 6s.
THE SOUL OF LILITH. *Thirteenth Edition. Cr. 8vo.* 6s.
WORMWOOD. *Fourteenth Ed. Cr. 8vo.* 6s.
BARABBAS: A DREAM OF THE WORLD'S TRAGEDY. *Forty-first Edition. Cr. 8vo.* 6s.
THE SORROWS OF SATAN. *Fiftieth Edition. Cr. 8vo.* 6s.
THE MASTER CHRISTIAN. *167th Thousand. Cr. 8vo.* 6s.
TEMPORAL POWER: A STUDY IN SUPREMACY. *150th Thousand. Cr. 8vo.* 6s.
GOD'S GOOD MAN: A SIMPLE LOVE STORY. *137th Thousand. Cr. 8vo.* 6s.
THE MIGHTY ATOM. *A New Edition. Cr. 8vo.* 6s.
BOY. *A New Edition. Cr. 8vo.* 6s.
JANE. *A New Edition. Cr. 8vo.* 6s.
Crockett (S. R.), Author of 'The Raiders,' etc. LOCHINVAR. Illustrated. *Third Edition. Cr. 8vo.* 6s.
THE STANDARD BEARER. *Cr. 8vo.* 6s.
Croker (B. M.). THE OLD CANTONMENT. *Cr. 8vo.* 6s.
JOHANNA. *Second Edition. Cr. 8vo.* 6s.

THE HAPPY VALLEY. *Third Edition. Cr. 8vo.* 6s.
A NINE DAYS' WONDER. *Third Edition. Cr. 8vo.* 6s.
PEGGY OF THE BARTONS. *Sixth Edition. Cr. 8vo.* 6s.
ANGEL. *Fourth Edition. Cr. 8vo.* 6s.
A STATE SECRET. *Third Edition. Cr. 8vo.* 3s. 6d.
Dawson (Francis W.). THE SCAR. *Second Edition. Cr. 8vo.* 6s.
Dawson (A. J). DANIEL WHYTE. *Cr. 8vo.* 3s. 6d.
Doyle (A. Conan), Author of 'Sherlock Holmes,' 'The White Company,' etc. ROUND THE RED LAMP. *Ninth Edition. Cr. 8vo.* 6s.
Duncan (Sara Jeannette) (Mrs. Everard Cotes). THOSE DELIGHTFUL AMERICANS. Illustrated. *Third Edition. Cr. 8vo.* 6s. See also Strand Novels.
Findlater (J. H.). THE GREEN GRAVES OF BALGOWRIE. *Fifth Edition. Cr. 8vo.* 6s. See also Strand Novels.
Findlater (Mary). A NARROW WAY. *Third Edition. Cr. 8vo.* 6s.
THE ROSE OF JOY. *Third Edition. Cr. 8vo.* 6s. See also Strand Novels.
Fitzpatrick (K.) THE WEANS AT ROWALLAN. Illustrated. *Second Edition. Cr. 8vo.* 6s.
Fitzstephen (Gerald). MORE KIN THAN KIND. *Cr. 8vo.* 6s.
Fletcher (J. S.). LUCIAN THE DREAMER. *Cr. 8vo.* 6s.
Fraser (Mrs. Hugh), Author of 'The Stolen Emperor.' THE SLAKING OF THE SWORD. *Cr. 8vo.* 6s.
THE SHADOW OF THE LORD. *Cr. 8vo.* 6s.
Fuller-Maitland (Mrs.), Author of 'The Day Book of Bethia Hardacre.' BLANCHE ESMEAD. *Second Edition. Cr. 8vo.* 6s.
Gerard (Dorothea), Author of 'Lady Baby.' THE CONQUEST OF LONDON. *Second Edition. Cr. 8vo.* 6s.
HOLY MATRIMONY. *Second Edition. Cr. 8vo.* 6s.
MADE OF MONEY. *Cr. 8vo.* 6s.
THE BRIDGE OF LIFE. *Cr. 8vo.* 6s.
THE IMPROBABLE IDYL. *Third Edition. Cr. 8vo.* 6s. See also Strand Novels.
Gerard (Emily). THE HERONS' TOWER. *Cr. 8vo.* 6s.
Gissing (George), Author of 'Demos,' 'In the Year of Jubilee,' etc. THE TOWN TRAVELLER. *Second Ed. Cr. 8vo.* 6s.
THE CROWN OF LIFE. *Cr. 8vo.* 6s.
Gleig (Charles). BUNTER'S CRUISE. Illustrated. *Cr. 8vo.* 3s. 6d.
Harraden (Beatrice). IN VARYING MOODS. *Fourteenth Edition. Cr. 8vo.* 6s.

THE SCHOLAR'S DAUGHTER. *Fourth Edition. Cr. 8vo. 6s.*
HILDA STRAFFORD. *Cr. 8vo. 6s.*
Harrod (F.) (Frances Forbes Robertson). THE TAMING OF THE BRUTE. *Cr. 8vo. 6s.*
Herbertson (Agnes G.). PATIENCE DEAN. *Cr. 8vo. 6s.*
Hichens (Robert). THE PROPHET OF BERKELEY SQUARE. *Second Edition. Cr. 8vo. 6s.*
TONGUES OF CONSCIENCE. *Second Edition. Cr. 8vo. 6s.*
FELIX. *Fifth Edition. Cr. 8vo. 6s.*
THE WOMAN WITH THE FAN. *Sixth Edition. Cr. 8vo. 6s.*
BYEWAYS. *Cr. 8vo. 3s. 6d.*
THE GARDEN OF ALLAH. *Thirteenth Edition. Cr. 8vo. 6s.*
THE BLACK SPANIEL. *Cr. 8vo. 6s.*
Hobbes (John Oliver), Author of 'Robert Orange.' THE SERIOUS WOOING. *Cr. 8vo. 6s.*
Hope (Anthony). THE GOD IN THE CAR. *Tenth Edition. Cr. 8vo. 6s.*
A CHANGE OF AIR. *Sixth Edition. Cr. 8vo. 6s.*
A MAN OF MARK. *Fifth Edition. Cr. 8vo. 6s.*
THE CHRONICLES OF COUNT ANTONIO. *Sixth Edition. Cr. 8vo. 6s.*
PHROSO. Illustrated by H. R. MILLAR. *Sixth Edition. Cr. 8vo. 6s.*
SIMON DALE. Illustrated. *Seventh Edition. Cr. 8vo. 6s.*
THE KING'S MIRROR. *Fourth Edition. Cr. 8vo. 6s.*
QUISANTÉ. *Fourth Edition. Cr. 8vo. 6s.*
THE DOLLY DIALOGUES. *Cr. 8vo. 6s.*
A SERVANT OF THE PUBLIC. Illustrated. *Fourth Edition. Cr. 8vo. 6s.*
Hope (Graham), Author of 'A Cardinal and his Conscience,' etc., etc. THE LADY OF LYTE. *Second Ed. Cr. 8vo. 6s.*
Hough (Emerson). THE MISSISSIPPI BUBBLE. Illustrated. *Cr. 8vo. 6s.*
Housman (Clemence). THE LIFE OF SIR AGLOVALE DE GALIS. *Cr. 8vo. 6s.*
Hyne (C. J. Cutcliffe), Author of 'Captain Kettle.' MR. HORROCKS, PURSER. *Third Edition. Cr. 8vo. 6s.*
Jacobs (W. W.). MANY CARGOES. *Twenty-Eighth Edition. Cr. 8vo. 3s. 6d.*
SEA URCHINS. *Twelfth Edition. Cr. 8vo. 3s. 6d.*
A MASTER OF CRAFT. Illustrated. *Seventh Edition. Cr. 8vo. 3s. 6d.*
LIGHT FREIGHTS. Illustrated. *Fifth Edition. Cr. 8vo. 3s. 6d.*
James (Henry). THE SOFT SIDE. *Second Edition. Cr. 8vo. 6s.*
THE BETTER SORT. *Cr. 8vo. 6s.*
THE AMBASSADORS. *Second Edition. Cr. 8vo. 6s.*

THE GOLDEN BOWL. *Third Edition. Cr. 8vo. 6s.*
Janson (Gustaf). ABRAHAM'S SACRIFICE. *Cr. 8vo. 6s.*
Keays (H. A. Mitchell). HE THAT EATETH BREAD WITH ME. *Cr. 8vo. 6s.*
Langbridge (V.) and Bourne (C. Harold.). THE VALLEY OF INHERITANCE. *Cr. 8vo. 6s.*
Lawless (Hon. Emily). WITH ESSEX IN IRELAND. *Cr. 8vo. 6s.*
See also Strand Novels.
Lawson (Harry), Author of 'When the Billy Boils.' CHILDREN OF THE BUSH. *Cr. 8vo. 6s.*
Le Queux (W.). THE HUNCHBACK OF WESTMINSTER. *Third Edition. Cr. 8vo. 6s.*
THE CLOSED BOOK. *Third Edition. Cr. 8vo. 6s.*
THE VALLEY OF THE SHADOW. Illustrated. *Third Edition. Cr. 8vo. 6s.*
BEHIND THE THRONE. *Third Edition. Cr. 8vo. 6s.*
Levett-Yeats (S.). ORRAIN. *Second Edition. Cr. 8vo. 6s.*
Long (J. Luther), Co-Author of 'The Darling of the Gods.' MADAME BUTTERFLY. *Cr. 8vo. 3s. 6d.*
SIXTY JANE. *Cr. 8vo. 6s.*
Lewis (Cecil). THE MACHINATIONS OF THE MYO-OK. *Cr. 8vo. 6s.*
Lyall (Edna). DERRICK VAUGHAN, NOVELIST. *42nd Thousand. Cr. 8vo. 3s. 6d.*
M'Carthy (Justin H.), Author of 'If I were King.' THE LADY OF LOYALTY HOUSE. Illustrated. *Third Edition. Cr. 8vo. 6s.*
THE DRYAD. *Second Edition. Cr. 8vo. 6s.*
Macdonald (Ronald). THE SEA MAID. *Second Edition. Cr. 8vo. 6s.*
Macnaughtan (S.). THE FORTUNE OF CHRISTINA MACNAB. *Third Edition. Cr. 8vo. 6s.*
Malet (Lucas). COLONEL ENDERBY'S WIFE. *Fourth Edition. Cr. 8vo. 6s.*
A COUNSEL OF PERFECTION. *New Edition. Cr. 8vo. 6s.*
THE WAGES OF SIN. *Fourteenth Edition. Cr. 8vo. 6s.*
THE CARISSIMA. *Fourth Edition. Cr. 8vo. 6s.*
THE GATELESS BARRIER. *Fourth Edition. Cr. 8vo. 6s.*
THE HISTORY OF SIR RICHARD CALMADY. *Seventh Edition. Cr. 8vo. 6s.*
See also Books for Boys and Girls.
Mann (Mrs. M. E.). OLIVIA'S SUMMER. *Second Edition. Cr. 8vo. 6s.*
A LOST ESTATE. *A New Edition. Cr. 8vo. 6s.*
THE PARISH OF HILBY. *A New Edition. Cr. 8vo. 6s.*

FICTION

THE PARISH NURSE. *Fourth Edition.* Cr. 8vo. 6s.
GRAN'MA'S JANE. Cr. 8vo. 6s.
MRS. PETER HOWARD. Cr. 8vo. 6s.
A WINTER'S TALE. *A New Edition.* Cr. 8vo. 6s.
ONE ANOTHER'S BURDENS. *A New Edition.* Cr. 8vo. 6s.
ROSE AT HONEYPOT. *Third Ed.* Cr. 8vo. 6s. See also Books for Boys and Girls.
Marriott (Charles), Author of 'The Column.' GENEVRA. *Second Edition.* Cr. 8vo. 6s.
Marsh (Richard). THE TWICKENHAM PEERAGE. *Second Edition.* Cr. 8vo. 6s.
A DUEL. Cr. 8vo. 6s.
THE MARQUIS OF PUTNEY. *Second Edition.* Cr. 8vo. 6s.
See also Strand Novels.
Mason (A. E. W.), Author of 'The Four Feathers,' etc. CLEMENTINA. Illustrated. *Second Edition.* Cr. 8vo. 6s.
Mathers (Helen), Author of 'Comin' thro' the Rye.' HONEY. *Fourth Edition.* Cr. 8vo. 6s.
GRIFF OF GRIFFITHSCOURT. Cr. 8vo. 6s.
THE FERRYMAN. *Second Edition.* Cr. 8vo. 6s.
Maxwell (W. B.), Author of 'The Ragged Messenger.' VIVIEN. *Eighth Edition.* Cr. 8vo. 6s.
THE RAGGED MESSENGER. *Third Edition.* Cr. 8vo. 6s.
FABULOUS FANCIES. Cr. 8vo. 6s.
Meade (L. T.). DRIFT. *Second Edition.* Cr. 8vo. 6s.
RESURGAM. Cr. 8vo. 6s.
VICTORY. Cr. 8vo. 6s.
See also Books for Girls and Boys.
Meredith (Ellis). HEART OF MY HEART. Cr. 8vo. 6s.
'Miss Molly' (The Author of). THE GREAT RECONCILER. Cr. 8vo. 6s.
Mitford (Bertram). THE SIGN OF THE SPIDER. Illustrated. *Sixth Edition.* Cr. 8vo. 3s. 6d.
IN THE WHIRL OF THE RISING. *Third Edition.* Cr. 8vo. 6s.
THE RED DERELICT. *Second Edition.* Cr. 8vo. 6s.
Montresor (F. F.), Author of 'Into the Highways and Hedges.' THE ALIEN. *Third Edition.* Cr. 8vo. 6s.
Morrison (Arthur). TALES OF MEAN STREETS. *Sixth Edition.* Cr. 8vo. 6s.
A CHILD OF THE JAGO. *Fourth Edition.* Cr. 8vo. 6s.
TO LONDON TOWN. *Second Edition.* Cr. 8vo. 6s.
CUNNING MURRELL. Cr. 8vo. 6s.
THE HOLE IN THE WALL. *Fourth Edition.* Cr. 8vo. 6s.
DIVERS VANITIES. Cr. 8vo. 6s.

Nesbit (E.). (Mrs. E. Bland). THE HOUSE. Illustrated. *Fourth Edi* Cr. 8vo. 6s.
See also Strand Novels.
Norris (W. E.). THE CREDIT OF] COUNTY. Illustrated. *Second Edi* Cr. 8vo. 6s.
THE EMBARRASSING ORPHAN. 8vo. 6s.
NIGEL'S VOCATION. Cr. 8vo. 6s.
BARHAM OF BELTANA. *Second Edit* Cr. 8vo. 6s.
See also Strand Novels.
Ollivant (Alfred). OWD BOB, T GREY DOG OF KENMUIR. E Edition. Cr. 8vo. 6s.
Oppenheim (E. Phillips). MASTER MEN. *Third Edition.* Cr. 8vo. 6s.
Oxenham (John), Author of 'Barbe Grand Bayou.' A WEAVER OF WE *Second Edition.* Cr. 8vo. 6s.
THE GATE OF THE DESERT. F Edition. Cr. 8vo. 6s.
Pain (Barry). THREE FANTAS Cr. 8vo. 1s.
LINDLEY KAYS. *Third Edition.* 8vo. 6s.
Parker (Gilbert). PIERRE AND PEOPLE. *Sixth Edition.*
MRS. FALCHION. *Fifth Edition.* Cr. 6s.
THE TRANSLATION OF A SAVA *Second Edition.* Cr. 8vo. 6s.
THE TRAIL OF THE SWORD. I trated. *Ninth Edition.* Cr. 8vo. 6s.
WHEN VALMOND CAME TO PONTI The Story of a Lost Napoleon. / Edition. Cr. 8vo. 6s.
AN ADVENTURER OF THE NOR The Last Adventures of 'Pretty Pi *Third Edition.* Cr. 8vo. 6s.
THE SEATS OF THE MIGHTY.] trated. *Fourteenth Edition.* Cr. 8vo.
THE BATTLE OF THE STRONC Romance of Two Kingdoms. Ill *Fifth Edition.* Cr. 8vo. 6s.
THE POMP OF THE LAVILETT *Second Edition.* Cr. 8vo. 3s. 6d.
Pemberton (Max). THE FOOTST OF A THRONE. Illustrated. 7 Edition. Cr. 8vo. 6s.
I CROWN THEE KING. With Ill tions by Frank Dadd and A. F Cr. 8vo. 6s.
Phillpotts (Eden). LYING PROF Cr. 8vo. 6s.
CHILDREN OF THE MIST. *Fij tion.* Cr. 8vo. 6s.
THE HUMAN BOY. With a Fron *Fourth Edition.* Cr. 8vo. 6s.
SONS OF THE MORNING. Edition. Cr. 8vo. 6s.

THE RIVER. *Third Edition. Cr. 8vo. 6s.*
THE AMERICAN PRISONER. *Third Edition. Cr. 8vo. 6s.*
THE SECRET WOMAN. *Fourth Edition. Cr. 8vo. 6s.*
KNOCK AT A VENTURE. With a Frontispiece. *Third Edition. Cr. 8vo. 6s.*
THE PORTREEVE. *Fourth Edition. Cr. 8vo. 6s.*
See also Strand Novels.
Pickthall (Marmaduke). SAID THE FISHERMAN. *Fifth Edition. Cr. 8vo. 6s.*
BRENDLE. *Second Edition. Cr. 8vo. 6s.*
'Q,' Author of 'Dead Man's Rock.' THE WHITE WOLF. *Second Edition. Cr. 8vo. 6s.*
THE MAYOR OF TROY. *Fourth Edition. Cr. 8vo. 6s.*
Rhys (Grace). THE WOOING OF SHEILA. *Second Edition. Cr. 8vo. 6s.*
THE PRINCE OF LISNOVER. *Cr. 8vo. 6s.*
Rhys (Grace) and Another. THE DIVERTED VILLAGE. Illustrated by DOROTHY GWYN JEFFREYS. *Cr. 8vo. 6s.*
Ridge (W. Pett). LOST PROPERTY. *Second Edition. Cr. 8vo. 6s.*
ERB. *Second Edition. Cr. 8vo. 6s.*
A SON OF THE STATE. *Second Edition. Cr. 8vo. 3s. 6d.*
A BREAKER OF LAWS. *A New Edition. Cr. 8vo. 3s. 6d.*
MRS. GALER'S BUSINESS. Illustrated. *Second Edition. Cr. 8vo. 6s.*
SECRETARY TO BAYNE, M.P. *Cr. 8vo. 3s. 6d.*
Ritchie (Mrs. David G.). THE TRUTHFUL LIAR. *Cr. 8vo. 6s.*
Roberts (C. G. D.). THE HEART OF THE ANCIENT WOOD. *Cr. 8vo. 3s. 6d.*
Russell (W. Clark). MY DANISH SWEETHEART. Illustrated. *Fifth Edition. Cr. 8vo. 6s.*
HIS ISLAND PRINCESS. Illustrated. *Second Edition. Cr. 8vo. 6s.*
ABANDONED. *Cr. 8vo. 6s.*
See also Books for Boys and Girls.
Sergeant (Adeline). ANTHEA'S WAY. *Cr. 8vo. 6s.*
THE PROGRESS OF RACHAEL. *Cr. 8vo. 6s.*
THE MYSTERY OF THE MOAT. *Second Edition. Cr. 8vo. 6s.*
MRS. LYGON'S HUSBAND. *Cr. 8vo. 6s.*
THE COMING OF THE RANDOLPHS. *Cr. 8vo. 6s.*
See also Strand Novels.
Shannon. (W. F.) THE MESS DECK. *Cr. 8vo. 3s. 6d.*
See also Strand Novels.

Sonnischsen (Albert). DEEP-SEA VAGABONDS. *Cr. 8vo. 6s.*
Thompson (Vance). SPINNERS OF LIFE. *Cr. 8vo. 6s.*
Urquhart (M.), A TRAGEDY IN COMMONPLACE. *Second Ed. Cr. 8vo. 6s.*
Waineman (Paul). BY A FINNISH LAKE. *Cr. 8vo. 6s.*
THE SONG OF THE FOREST. *Cr. 8vo. 6s.* See also Strand Novels.
Waltz (E. C.). THE ANCIENT LANDMARK: A Kentucky Romance. *Cr. 8vo. 6s.*
Watson (H. B. Marriott). ALARUMS AND EXCURSIONS. *Cr. 8vo. 6s.*
CAPTAIN FORTUNE. *Third Edition. Cr. 8vo. 6s.*
TWISTED EGLANTINE. With 8 Illustrations by FRANK CRAIG. *Third Edition. Cr. 8vo. 6s.*
THE HIGH TOBY. With a Frontispiece. *Third Edition. Cr. 8vo. 6s.*
See also Strand Novels.
Wells (H. G.). THE SEA LADY. *Cr. 8vo. 6s.*
Weyman (Stanley), Author of 'A Gentleman of France.' UNDER THE RED ROBE. With Illustrations by R. C. WOODVILLE. *Twentieth Edition. Cr. 8vo. 6s.*
White (Stewart E.), Author of 'The Blazed Trail.' CONJUROR'S HOUSE. A Romance of the Free Trail. *Second Edition. Cr. 8vo. 6s.*
White (Percy). THE SYSTEM. *Third Edition. Cr. 8vo. 6s.*
THE PATIENT MAN. *Second Edition. Cr. 8vo. 6s.*
Williamson (Mrs. C. N.), Author of 'The Barnstormers.' THE ADVENTURE OF PRINCESS SYLVIA. *Second Edition. Cr. 8vo. 3s. 6d.*
THE WOMAN WHO DARED. *Cr. 8vo. 6s.*
THE SEA COULD TELL. *Second Edition. Cr. 8vo. 6s.*
THE CASTLE OF THE SHADOWS. *Third Edition. Cr. 8vo. 6s.*
PAPA. *Cr. 8vo. 6s.*
LADY BETTY ACROSS THE WATER. *Third Edition. Cr. 8vo. 6s.*
Williamson (C. N. and A. M.). THE LIGHTNING CONDUCTOR: Being the Romance of a Motor Car. Illustrated. *Fourteenth Edition. Cr. 8vo. 6s.*
THE PRINCESS PASSES. Illustrated. *Seventh Edition. Cr. 8vo. 6s.*
MY FRIEND THE CHAUFFEUR. With 16 Illustrations. *Seventh Edition. Cr. 8vo. 6s.*
Wyllarde (Dolf), Author of 'Uriah the Hittite.' THE PATHWAY OF THE PIONEER. *Fourth Edition. Cr. 8vo. 6s.*

Fiction

Methuen's Shilling Novels

Cr. 8vo. Cloth, 1s. net.

ENCOURAGED by the great and steady sale of their Sixpenny Novels, Messrs. Methuen have determined to issue a new series of fiction at a low price under the title of 'THE SHILLING NOVELS.' These books are well printed and well bound in *cloth*, and the excellence of their quality may be gauged from the names of those authors who contribute the early volumes of the series.

Messrs. Methuen would point out that the books are as good and as long as a six shilling novel, that they are bound in cloth and not in paper, and that their price is One Shilling *net*. They feel sure that the public will appreciate such good and cheap literature, and the books can be seen at all good booksellers.

The first volumes are—

Balfour (Andrew). VENGEANCE IS MINE.
TO ARMS.
Baring-Gould (S.). MRS. CURGENVEN OF CURGENVEN.
DOMITIA.
THE FROBISHERS.
Barlow (Jane), Author of 'Irish Idylls.' FROM THE EAST UNTO THE WEST.
A CREEL OF IRISH STORIES.
THE FOUNDING OF FORTUNES.
Barr (Robert). THE VICTORS.
Bartram (George). THIRTEEN EVENINGS.
Benson (E. F.), Author of 'Dodo.' THE CAPSINA.
Bowles (G. Stewart). A STRETCH OFF THE LAND.
Brooke (Emma). THE POET'S CHILD.
Bullock (Shan F.). THE BARRYS.
THE CHARMER.
THE SQUIREEN.
THE RED LEAGUERS.
Burton (J. Bloundelle). ACROSS THE SALT SEAS.
THE CLASH OF ARMS.
DENOUNCED.
FORTUNE'S MY FOE.
Capes (Bernard). AT A WINTER'S FIRE.
Chesney (Weatherby). THE BAPTIST RING.
THE BRANDED PRINCE.
THE FOUNDERED GALLEON.
JOHN TOPP.
Clifford (Mrs. W. K.). A FLASH OF SUMMER.
Collingwood (Harry). THE DOCTOR OF THE 'JULIET.'
Cornford (L. Cope). SONS OF ADVERSITY.
Crane (Stephen). WOUNDS IN THE RAIN.
Denny (C. E.). THE ROMANCE OF UPFOLD MANOR.
Dickson (Harris). THE BLACK WOLF'S BREED.
Dickinson (Evelyn). THE SIN OF ANGELS.

Duncan (Sara J.). *THE POOL IN THE DESERT.
A VOYAGE OF CONSOLATION.
Embree (C. F.). A HEART OF FLAME.
Fenn (G. Manville). AN ELECTRIC SPARK.
Findlater (Jane H.). A DAUGHTER OF STRIFE.
Findlater (Mary). OVER THE HILLS.
Forrest (R. E.). THE SWORD OF AZRAEL.
Francis (M. E.). MISS ERIN.
Gallon (Tom). RICKERBY'S FOLLY.
Gerard (Dorothea). THINGS THAT HAVE HAPPENED.
Gilchrist (R. Murray). WILLOWBRAKE.
Glanville (Ernest). THE DESPATCH RIDER.
THE LOST REGIMENT.
THE KLOOF BRIDE.
THE INCA'S TREASURE.
Gordon (Julien). MRS. CLYDE.
WORLD'S PEOPLE.
Goss (C. F.). THE REDEMPTION OF DAVID CORSON.
Gray (E. M'Queen). MY STEWARDSHIP.
Hales (A. G.). JAIR THE APOSTATE.
Hamilton (Lord Ernest). MARY HAMILTON.
Harrison
OF TH
Hooper (I.). THE SINGER OF MARLY.
Hough (Emerson). THE MISSISSIPPI BUBBLE.

Jepson (Edgar). KEEPERS OF THE PEOPLE.
Kelly (Florence Finch). WITH HOOPS OF STEEL.
Lawless (Hon. Emily). MAELCHO.
Linden (Annie). A WOMAN OF SENTIMENT.
Lorimer (Norma). JOSIAH'S WIFE.
Lush (Charles K.). THE AUTOCRATS.
Macdonell (Anne). THE STORY OF TERESA.
Macgrath (Harold). THE PUPPET CROWN.

Mackie (Pauline Bradford). THE VOICE IN THE DESERT.
Marsh (Richard). THE SEEN AND THE UNSEEN.
GARNERED.
A METAMORPHOSIS.
MARVELS AND MYSTERIES.
BOTH SIDES OF THE VEIL.
Mayall (J. W.). THE CYNIC AND THE SYREN.
Monkhouse (Allan). LOVE IN A LIFE.
Moore (Arthur). THE KNIGHT PUNCTILIOUS.
Nesbit (Mrs. Bland). THE LITERARY SENSE.
Norris (W. E.). AN OCTAVE.
Oliphant (Mrs.). THE LADY'S WALK.
SIR ROBERT'S FORTUNE.
THE TWO MARY'S.
Penny (Mrs. Frank). A MIXED MARRIAGE.
Phillpotts (Eden). THE STRIKING HOURS.
FANCY FREE.
Pryce (Richard). TIME AND THE WOMAN.
Randall (J.). AUNT BETHIA'S BUTTON.
Raymond (Walter). FORTUNE'S DARLING.
Rayner (Olive Pratt). ROSALBA.
Rhys (Grace). THE DIVERTED VILLAGE.

Rickert (Edith). OUT OF THE CYPRESS SWAMP.
Roberton (M. H.). A GALLANT QUAKER.
Saunders (Marshall). ROSE A CHARLITTE.
Sergeant (Adeline). ACCUSED AND ACCUSER.
BARBARA'S MONEY.
THE ENTHUSIAST.
A GREAT LADY.
THE LOVE THAT OVERCAME.
THE MASTER OF BEECHWOOD.
UNDER SUSPICION.
THE YELLOW DIAMOND.
Shannon (W. F.). JIM TWELVES.
Strain (E. H.). ELMSLIE'S DRAG NET.
Stringer (Arthur). THE SILVER POPPY.
Stuart (Esmè). CHRISTALLA.
Sutherland (Duchess of). ONE HOUR AND THE NEXT.
Swan (Annie). LOVE GROWN COLD.
Swift (Benjamin). SORDON.
Tanqueray (Mrs. B. M.). THE ROYAL QUAKER.
Trafford-Taunton (Mrs. E. W.). SILENT DOMINION.
Upward (Allen). ATHELSTANE FORD.
Waineman (Paul). A HEROINE FROM FINLAND.
Watson (H. B. Marriott). THE SKIRTS OF HAPPY CHANCE.
'Zack.' TALES OF DUNSTABLE WEIR.

Books for Boys and Girls

Illustrated. Crown 8vo. 3s. 6d.

THE GETTING WELL OF DOROTHY. By Mrs. W. K. Clifford. *Second Edition.*
THE ICELANDER'S SWORD. By S. Baring-Gould.
ONLY A GUARD-ROOM DOG. By Edith E. Cuthell.
THE DOCTOR OF THE JULIET. By Harry Collingwood.
LITTLE PETER. By Lucas Malet. *Second Edition.*
MASTER ROCKAFELLAR'S VOYAGE. By W. Clark Russell.
THE SECRET OF MADAME DE MONLUC. By the Author of "Mdlle. Mori."
SYD BELTON: Or, the Boy who would not go to Sea. By G. Manville Fenn.
THE RED GRANGE. By Mrs. Molesworth.
A GIRL OF THE PEOPLE. By L. T. Meade. *Second Edition.*
HEPSY GIPSY. By L. T. Meade. 2s. 6d.
THE HONOURABLE MISS. By L. T. Meade. *Second Edition.*
THERE WAS ONCE A PRINCE. By Mrs. M. E. Mann.
WHEN ARNOLD COMES HOME. By Mrs. M. E. Mann.

The Novels of Alexandre Dumas

Price 6d. Double Volumes, 1s.

THE THREE MUSKETEERS. With a long Introduction by Andrew Lang. Double volume.
THE PRINCE OF THIEVES. *Second Edition.*
ROBIN HOOD. A Sequel to the above.
THE CORSICAN BROTHERS.
GEORGES.
CROP-EARED JACQUOT; JANE; Etc.
TWENTY YEARS AFTER. Double volume.
AMAURY.
THE CASTLE OF EPPSTEIN.
THE SNOWBALL, and SULTANETTA.
CECILE; OR, THE WEDDING GOWN.
ACTÉ.

FICTION

THE BLACK TULIP.
THE VICOMTE DE BRAGELONNE.
   Part I. Louise de la Vallière. Double Volume.
   Part II. The Man in the Iron Mask. Double Volume.
THE CONVICT'S SON.
THE WOLF-LEADER.
NANON; OR, THE WOMEN' WAR. Double volume.
PAULINE; MURAT; AND PASCAL BRUNO.
THE ADVENTURES OF CAPTAIN PAMPHILE.
FERNANDE.
GABRIEL LAMBERT.
CATHERINE BLUM.
THE CHEVALIER D'HARMENTAL. Double volume.
SYLVANDIRE.
THE FENCING MASTER.
THE REMINISCENCES OF ANTONY.
CONSCIENCE.
PERE LA RUINE.
*HENRI OF NAVARRE. The second part of Queen Margot.
THE GREAT MASSACRE. The first part of Queen Margot.
THE WILD DUCK SHOOTER.

Illustrated Edition.
Demy 8vo. Cloth.
THE THREE MUSKETEERS. Illustrated in Colour by Frank Adams. 2s. 6d.

THE PRINCE OF THIEVES. Illustrated in Colour by Frank Adams. 2s.
ROBIN HOOD THE OUTLAW. Illustrated in Colour by Frank Adams. 2s.
THE CORSICAN BROTHERS. Illustrated in Colour by A. M. M'Lellan. 1s. 6d.
THE WOLF-LEADER. Illustrated in Colour by Frank Adams. 1s. 6d.
GEORGES. Illustrated in Colour by Munro Orr. 2s.
TWENTY YEARS AFTER. Illustrated in Colour by Frank Adams. 3s.
AMAURY. Illustrated in Colour by Gordon Browne. 2s.
THE SNOWBALL, and SULTANETTA. Illustrated in Colour by Frank Adams. 2s.
THE VICOMTE DE BRAGELONNE. Illustrated in Colour by Frank Adams.
   Part I. Louise de la Vallière. 3s.
   Part II. The Man in the Iron Mask. 3s.
CROP-EARED JACQUOT; JANE; Etc. Illustrated in Colour by Gordon Browne. 2s.
THE CASTLE OF EPPSTEIN. Illustrated in Colour by Stewart Orr. 1s. 6d.
ACTÉ. Illustrated in Colour by Gordon Browne. 1s. 6d.
CECILE; OR, THE WEDDING GOWN. Illustrated in Colour by D. Murray Smith. 1s. 6d.
THE ADVENTURES OF CAPTAIN PAMPHILE. Illustrated in Colour by Frank Adams. 1s. 6d.

Methuen's Sixpenny Books

Austen (Jane). PRIDE AND PREJUDICE.
Bagot (Richard). A ROMAN MYSTERY.
Balfour (Andrew). BY STROKE OF SWORD.
Baring-Gould (S.). FURZE BLOOM.
CHEAP JACK ZITA.
KITTY ALONE.
URITH.
THE BROOM SQUIRE.
IN THE ROAR OF THE SEA.
NOÉMI.
A BOOK OF FAIRY TALES. Illustrated.
LITTLE TU'PENNY.
THE FROBISHERS.
Barr (Robert). JENNIE BAXTER, JOURNALIST.
IN THE MIDST OF ALARMS.
THE COUNTESS TEKLA.
THE MUTABLE MANY.
Benson (E. F.). DODO.
Brontë (Charlotte). SHIRLEY.
Brownell (C. L.). THE HEART OF JAPAN.

Burton (J. Bloundelle). ACROSS THE SALT SEAS.
Caffyn (Mrs.), ('Iota'). ANNE MAULEVERER.
*Capes (Bernard). THE LAKE OF WINE.
Clifford (Mrs. W. K.). A FLASH OF SUMMER.
MRS. KEITH'S CRIME.
Connell (F. Norreys). THE NIGGER KNIGHTS.
Corbett (Julian). A BUSINESS IN GREAT WATERS.
Croker (Mrs. B. M.). PEGGY OF THE BARTONS.
A STATE SECRET.
ANGEL.
JOHANNA.
Dante (Alighieri). THE VISION OF DANTE (CARY).
Doyle (A. Conan). ROUND THE RED LAMP.
Duncan (Sara Jeannette). A VOYAGE OF CONSOLATION.
THOSE DELIGHTFUL AMERICANS.